Scholarship, Commerce, Religion

Scholarship, Commerce, Religion

THE LEARNED BOOK IN THE AGE OF CONFESSIONS, 1560–1630

IAN MACLEAN

HARVARD UNIVERSITY PRESS

Cambridge, Massachusetts, and London, England   2012

Copyright © 2012 by the President and Fellows of Harvard College
All rights reserved
Printed in the United States of America

Library of Congress Cataloging-in-Publication Data

Maclean, Ian, 1945–
  Scholarship, commerce, religion : the learned book in the age of confessions, 1560–1630 /
Ian Maclean.
    p. cm.
  Includes bibliographical references and index.
  ISBN 978-0-674-06208-5 (alk. paper)
  1. Scholarly publishing—Europe—History—16th century.   2. Scholarly publishing—
Europe—History—17th century.   3. Book industries and trade Europe—History—16th
century.   4. Book industries and trade—Europe—History—17th century.
5. Communication in learning and scholarship—Europe—History—16th century.
6. Communication in learning and scholarship—Europe—History—17th
century.   I. Title.
  Z291.3.M335 2012
  070.5094'09031—dc23   2011041320

For Pauline

Contents

Conventions of Transcription

In transcribing Latin and modern foreign languages, I have adopted the most common forms in each case, and not sought to make a diplomatic transcription. Names of Renaissance figures have been transcribed in the form in which they are most commonly found in bibliographies and library catalogues.

Illustrations

Acknowledgments

This book is a revised and expanded version of the lectures I gave at the University of Oxford in May 2010 as the Lyell Reader in Bibliography. I should like here to express my gratitude to the Lyell electors and to the continued support I have received from the Lyell Fund.

The images in this book are reproduced with kind permission of the following colleges, archives, and libraries: die Staats- und Universitäts-bibliothek, Bremen (2.2), die Herzog-August-Bibliothek, Wolfenbüttel (2.3, 2.8, 2.9), die Staatsbibliothek zu Berlin (3.7), die Universitätsbibliothek, Leipzig (7.5), het Prentenkabinet, Museum Plantin-Moretus, Antwerp (6.3, 6.5, 7.3), das Haus- Hof- und Staatsarchiv, Vienna (5.1, 5.4, 5.5), the Bodleian Library, Oxford (2.5, 2.7, 4.4, 6.1, 6.2), the Provost, Fellows and Scholars of the Queen's College, Oxford (2.4, 3.1, 4.5), the Governing Body of Christ Church, Oxford (2.6, 5.6, 7.2), the Warden and Fellows of Wadham College, Oxford (3.2), the Warden and Fellows of All Souls College, Oxford (3.3, 3,4, 3.5, 3.6, 4.1, 4.2, 4.6, 5.2, 5.3, 7.1, 7.4).

It gives me great pleasure to acknowledge some of the many individual debts I have incurred while working towards the publication of this book. The modern generation of librarians and historians have been extraordinarily generous with their time and their provision of information in the form of archival assistance, documents, paleographical and other textual difficulties, and forthcoming articles. I should specially like to thank Jim Adams, Paul Arblaster, Jean Balsamo, John Barnard, Jill Bepler, Robin Briggs, Colin Burrow, Warren Boutcher, Karen Bowen and Dirk Imhof, Isabelle de Conihout, Richard Cooper, Cristina Dondi, Thomas Elsmann, Ian Gadd, Jean-François Gilmont, Clive Griffin, Tony Grafton, Geneviève Guilleminot-Chrétien, Christian Hogrefe, Ulrich Kopp, Valentina Lepri, Jill Lewis, Martin McLaughlin, Neil Kenny, Noel Malcolm, Giles Mandelbrote, Theodor Mahlmann, Raphaële Mouren, Paul Nelles, Angela Nuovo, Vivian Nutton, Douglas Osler, Graham Rees and Maria Wakely, Antonio Ricci, Dennis Rhodes, Ron Truman, Alexandre Vanautgaerden, Martin West, Nick Wilding, and many more besides. I owe a special debt to the Librarians of various Oxford Colleges, most especially Norma Aubertin-Potter and Gaye Morgan (All Souls), Amanda Saville and Tessa Shaw (Queen's), Cristina Neagu (Christ Church), Tim Kirtley (Wadham), and Jeremy Hinchliff (Balliol). Tim Kirtley, Gaye Morgan, and Cristina Neagu undertook photography of documents in their respective libraries, which have been duly acknowledged. Leen van Broek helped prepare the bibliography. Fiona Godber cast a final critical eye over the whole text, and my wife Pauline not only did the same, but also put up with the long periods of mental distraction induced in me by the production of this text. It is to her that the book is dedicated with all my love.

Scholarship, Commerce, Religion

CHAPTER ONE

Setting the Scene

It may seem somewhat foolhardy to set out to chart on a European scale the impact of commercial practices on the learned book market over more than half a century of economic instability and religious turmoil. There are more focussed ways the subject might be approached, by restricting it to a shorter period of time, a given country, a single discipline or publisher. Indeed, there are many excellent monographs of this kind in existence, to which the lecture series on which this study is based owed a great deal. It is in no small measure because of them that I have felt able to undertake this broader survey, in which I hope to draw together the threads of many years of interest in the learned book and its markets, and offer a general understanding of its operation from which the particularity of any one case can be measured.[1] The Latin book trade is much more a feature of the continental than of the English book world in the late Renaissance, and has attracted more attention in European historical writing than in Anglo-American scholarship, which can sometimes give the impression that England was in the forefront of various developments in publishing: I do not believe this to be the case in the period I have chosen.[2]

The material I shall be dealing with is not easily susceptible of neat quantification or statistical analysis, although some general impressions can be formed about the size of the market and its modes of operation.[3] A sense of the learned book market can be more easily conveyed through case-studies, of which Chapter 2 is a sustained example. I have published elsewhere a collection of fourteen such studies, and shall be drawing, on occasion, on the fruits of this research.[4] The already published cases, and the ones I shall add here, will necessarily be drawn from the ranks of both the famous and the obscure, across the whole range of scholarly disciplines, in all the major continental publishing centres. I shall do my best not to turn this into a bewildering procession of names, book titles, and places.

It might be argued that to single out Latin books in a publisher's list is to ignore the whole field of publishing (including books in the vernacular) which sustained his commercial enterprise. The argument has some merit, in that it points to the common practice of diversifying output; in some of the cases I shall consider (notably Sigmund Feyerabend, Giovanni Battista Ciotti, and Johann Theobald Schönwetter), it is clearly true. But there are many publishers—Johannes Oporinus, Johannes Froben, Nicolaus Episcopius, Heinrich Petri and his heirs in Basel, the Wechel presses, Nicolas Bassée, Zacharias Palthen and his heirs in Frankfurt and Hanau, Jacob Stoer, Eustache Vignon and the Crespin presses in Geneva, Jérôme Drouart in Paris, Christophe Plantin and his heirs in Antwerp, to name but a few—who specialised in scholarly publication of various kinds, and whose enterprises are best understood in that context. In most cases, not all of their output took the form of learned monographs or editions; it included what now would be classed as textbooks.[5] Whether the latter subsidised the former will be one of the questions I shall ask in the course of this study.

There is one other preliminary remark I should like to make about the period on which I have chosen to concentrate and its relationship to earlier printing and publishing. In a review in the *Times Literary Supplement* which appeared a decade ago, Roderick Conway Morris claimed that "almost everything that was going to happen in book publishing—from pocket books, instant books and pirated books, to the concept of author's copyright, company mergers, and remainders—occurred during the early days of printing, the subsequent centuries offering but variations upon a theme."[6] This seems to me to be broadly true; that does not mean, however, that the relationship between scholarship, commerce, and their politico-economic context did not evolve. The claim has prompted me here to offer two initial contexts for the study which follows: the early years of the age of print, and the religious developments which culminated in a confessionalised Europe.

The Market before the Age of Confessions (1480–1560)

The argument for continuity from the scribal age to that of print has been strongly made by Rosamund McKitterick, who asserts that "contrary to the assumption that there was a total revolution in the dissemination of ideas as a consequence of the advent of printing, it needs to be stressed that the printers were able to exploit well-established modes for the dissemination of ideas, habits of book ownership, markets and patterns of distribution in the book trade."[7] In my view, this claim underestimates the radical change in the dissemination of ideas through the move from the commissioning of single manuscripts from an exemplar to the simultaneous production of multiple copies for which purchasers had to be found. It is certainly true that scribal culture was not extinguished by printing, but continued to play a part in the transmission of knowledge. By operating through commission (as a sort of "printing on demand"), it could easily be regulated by the universities where the largest scriptoria were situated, some of which forbade the selling of books to foreigners.[8] This may help explain the small initial uptake of the new technology in universities.[9] But if there was speculative production of manuscripts in the same way as there was speculative production of printed books, it must have been confined to very few scriptoria.[10] Printing brought benefits such as more secure dissemination of knowledge and the possibility of unlimited export to purchasers beyond the local or regional levels. The commercial application of the new technology changed the sequence text–scribe–reader to one which led from author or editor to printer and purchaser. It thus gave a new role to the person promoting copy, and created a market of unknown size, making all printing ventures acts of speculation. This provoked in turn a series of commercial crises in the book market, arising from false assumptions about uptake or market saturation, which in turn led to the development of syndicates to facilitate risk-sharing.[11] The resulting instability did not settle down until the 1520s. The impact of the new means of the transmission of knowledge generated a growing sense of the dangers of printing, not least in the Roman Church, which realised that it could lead to small or isolated minorities communicating doctrines and opinions to a broad public, contrary to the interests of the church or ruling elites.[12] Whence the guarded reception of printing in bulls of 1487 and 1501, and at the Lateran Council of 1513, and the institution and development of regimes of censorship by both ecclesiastical and secular authorities.[13]

The towns which by 1500 became major centres of the learned book trade shared a number of features, but, surprisingly, the presence of a local university was not one of these. The cities of Basel, Paris, Leipzig, and Cologne each harboured a university, but the following very active centres of printing did not: Lyon, Venice, Nuremberg, Strasbourg until 1556, Frankfurt, and Antwerp after 1564.[14] Nor was the existence of a fair a common factor, although most of these places entertained foreign merchants; but it is clear that cities with fairs at which books were offered as merchandise did eventually see the establishment and expansion of a resident printing trade with an international dimension. If one takes the gross figures of titles published for Leipzig, Frankfurt, and Strasbourg as indicative of local activity, the following comparison emerges:

1530–1535: Frankfurt 117; Leipzig 269; Strasbourg 355
1580–1585: Frankfurt 316; Leipzig 171; Strasbourg 98
1611–1615: Frankfurt 1390; Leipzig 1294; Strasbourg 289

Even though this is a very crude measurement, it indicates the rise of Frankfurt and its rivalry with Leipzig, and the relative decline of Strasbourg, which none the less remains a very important centre of printing for the international market.[15]

Nearly all early printing centres had easy access to paper mills, a vibrant intellectual life, a reservoir of artisanal talent, a supply of credit, a capacity to deal with money exchange and credit notes, and a sophisticated market organization, needed for efficient distribution (by 1500, a book could be obtained within a few months almost anywhere in Europe).[16] All these centres sat on trade routes, and operated internationally: the Alantsee brothers, for example, were Viennese publishers who used the printers and markets of Basel, Strasbourg, and Hagenau, and even extended their activity as far as Venice, which was by far the most productive centre of printing in the fifteenth and early sixteenth centuries.[17] Even where scholarly books were not produced in great numbers, such as at Augsburg, a town with extensive trading connections could become an important centre of distribution.[18] The European trade routes placed some countries at the periphery: these included England and Iberia, even though Lisbon and Barcelona were very important trade centres for different products.[19]

Printing could have become a trade secret regulated by a guild; that is what John of Speyer aspired to when he obtained a privilege giving him the sole right to exercise the new technology in Venice in 1469. But his attempt at securing a monopoly did not succeed, and printing became an "ars liberalis" both in Italy and elsewhere. So early printers and publishers inserted themselves into the existing guild structures of the various cities in which the new technology implanted itself. Initially, very few new specialised guilds or confraternities were established, and as Erasmus sarcastically pointed out, there was no clear apprenticeship structure: it was easier to become a printer than a baker.[20] The dominance of the towns I have mentioned went hand in hand with the dominance of countries. According to Andrew Pettegree's calculations, over 90 percent of the production of scholarly books of the sixteenth century can be attributed to France (19 percent), Italy (27 percent), Germany (40 percent), Switzerland (5.3 percent), and the Netherlands (7.7 percent). England, Iberia, Scandinavia, and eastern Europe constitute a periphery; only Spain among this latter group produced a significant number of learned books for the local market, but they failed to achieve much in the way of an international sale.[21]

Publishing was a trade that embodied the new conception of mercantilism. It brought together a number of separate proto-industrial processes (paper-making, printing, binding) and was characterised by "putting out"—that is, the separation of artisans into independent contributors to the completed end product.[22] Two models of marketing the product emerged: the Hansa model and the branch system, which I shall investigate in detail in Chapter 6 (pages 175–176). Profit in this world did not necessarily mean surplus profit or mercantile expansion. While it was possible to become rich and to accumulate goods, it is also true that many publishers harboured no more than the ambition to stay in business and to survive crises caused by the many external dangers (war, plague, economic downturns) and internal ones (saturated markets, unredeemed credit, problems of cash flow, persistent debt). To talk, therefore, in terms of supply-side economics, with its emphasis on increasing incentive to produce, or sophisticated business strategies involving capital formation, or even business plans which provide clear guidance as to priorities and economic choices, seems anachronistic. Equally, diversification as a way of spreading risk, or calculation of investment by discounting back to the present the future expected profits of the undertaking, are concepts which do not capture very well the nature of the enterprise, although a crude, unquantified awareness of both factors can be seen at work in the activities of publishers. But they did see the need to identify and attract purchasers for their speculatively produced multiple copies, and this led to changes in the presentation of scholarly and other works, such as modes of distribution, and the institution of the title page, which acted as an advertisement for the contents of a book. These and other factors constitute a "field" of early modern scholarly publication—a field in the

Bourdieusian sense (see below, pages 240–241)—that had a logic or rationality which was the outcome of the set of forces and pressures which shaped the activities of those who took part in the field: authors, publishers, booksellers, purchasers.

Two new elements had a massive influence on early printing: humanism and reformation. Much had been achieved by the first generations of humanists in the fifteenth centuries in recovering the world and literature of antiquity, and spreading the knowledge of new languages, notably Greek. Their activities in Italy were much aided by the presence of collections of important manuscripts of classical texts.[23] Printing was to be of inestimable value to their efforts. Scholars such as Erasmus praised the new technology as an "almost divine" invention, exposing the ignorance of the scholastic world and offering the possibility of the dissemination of accurate texts to a nascent republic of letters.[24] Such scholars went further than just supplying copy: they suggested books for publication, wrote prefaces to them, added celebratory verses about the new learning written by and to their colleagues and friends, and engaged in proofreading and editorial work on a vast scale. Of all these activities, the most important was perhaps the role of corrector, who was part of the team working in the printing shop, and whose presence guaranteed the scholarly integrity of the text.

Religious reformers went further than this, and saw the new technology as a providential act, instituted by God to ensure that the church would be cleansed of error and malpractice, and that the good news of the Bible would be communicated to the community of the faithful. A wide range of protestant writers welcomed the new technology unreservedly—Luther, Calvin, Miles Coverdale, John Foxe, Georg Sohn; but the Catholic and Imperial authorities, who had most to lose by the efficient dissemination of information, were equivocal about its blessings, and saw not only religious orthodoxy under threat, but good morals (if erotic literature were to be printed), political stability, and social cohesion (through the dissemination of libel and polemic).[25] The changed state of affairs and the way in which it was perceived heralded a new chapter in the involvement of theology and politics in the broad compass of scholarship.

The Confessionalisation of Europe

The development of religious confessions accounts for the greatest differences between the world of printers such as Aldus Manutius and the Kobergers, and that of the printer-publishers of the end of the century who are the subjects of these chapters. At various councils and meetings from the 1530s onward, Christian denominations produced their own versions of orthodoxy. The Lutherans did this first, in Augsburg in 1530, then again in 1540–1542 (the "confessio variata," which set out to accommodate the views of other reformed groups), and finally in 1577 (the gnesiolutheran "Formula of Concord"). The Roman Catholics (excluding the Gallican Church: a matter of some importance in respect of debates concerning papal authority, as we shall see) did this at the Council of Trent, between 1545 and 1563; elsewhere in Europe, other agreed confessions were formulated (the Gallican in 1559, the Belgic in 1561, the Helvetic in 1561–1562). The Synod of Dort (1618–1619) represents in one sense a culmination of the later declarations of doctrine, which were for the most part of Calvinist inspiration. The Church of England meanwhile had enacted its thirty-nine articles by 1571.[26] The consequence of these declarations was a hardening of attitudes which did not suit all of the scholars who were working in the decades before the Thirty Years' War.[27]

The institutional acts promulgated by churches as self-conscious units establishing their own discipline, dogmas, structure, and catechisms occurred during the historical phase often referred to as "confessionalisation." They were accompanied both by controversial theology, which proliferated from the second half of the sixteenth century onward, and by the publication of guides to ancient and modern heresies issued by the various denominations. I do not want to engage with the controversies over the term *confessionalisation,* but it is pertinent here simply to note some of the features on which all sides of the debate agree, namely that each confession needed to establish its own corpus and conception of pure doctrine, its own controls on rites and practice, its own propaganda and forms of censorship, its own educational system, and its own modus vivendi with the political and etatistic environment in which it operated.[28] More specifically, each confession had to establish the following elements to maintain the purity of its doctrine, rites, and practices: its accepted version of Holy Writ; its corpus of patristic literature; its teaching materials for the training of ministers; its instructional material (principally its catechism) for the laity; its version of Church history (which acts as its own genealogy); and its practice of censorship. The effect of these measures was greatly to expand the field of theological publication, and to make authors, publishers, even genres, no longer confessionally neutral: history, medicine (in the shape of Paracelsus and alchemy), elements of jurisprudence, and natural philosophy all became implicated in religion. Even humanist editions of the classics can have a confessional element, as Martin Mulsow has shown.[29] There may be some exceptions, but the infiltration of theological issues into the broad compass of scholarship and into its means of dissemination seems to me to be irrefutable.[30] I shall of course have more to say about both the commercial and the religious background to the trade in learned books; for the moment, I wish only to record the need, suggested by Conway Morris's claim about continuity, not only frequently to look back to the earlier period of book history which saw the rise of many of the practices about which I am going to talk, but also to bear in mind the very different scholarly atmosphere of the confessional age.

CHAPTER TWO

In Medias Res: A Literary Agent in Frankfurt, 1606–1615

What is a learned book? The conventional answer to this question would be in terms of scholarly fields and genres, and I shall address this in the next chapter: for now, I should like to quote a moral and cultural description produced by the French jurist Pierre Rebuffi in his work on the privileges of university scholars and booksellers, which first appeared in 1540:

> A book is the "temple of justice" according to Roman Law; or rather, it is the light of the heart, the mirror of the body, the repertory of virtues, the overthrow of vices, the crown of the prudent, the diadem of the wise, the honour of the learned, the clarification of the righteous, the companion on a journey (which is why scholars must carry books with them on journeys), a loyal member of the household, a companion in conversation, a colleague of a ruler, a vehicle full of wisdom, the right path to eloquence, a garden full of fruits, the source of intelligence, the basis of memory, the enemy of oblivion, and the friend of reminiscence.[1]

The book to which Rebuffi is alluding is one containing knowledge, exempt from commercial transactions. Mankind is not at liberty to treat knowledge as a commodity, and submit it to the rules of the mercantile world. As the proverb has it, "knowledge is a gift of God, and hence cannot be sold."[2] The production of this printed paragon of all the virtues, which, Rebuffi implies, has flowed from the pens of earnest scholars declaring themselves committed to the service of truth, was entrusted in Rebuffi's day to publishers who, according to the seventeenth-century critic Adrien Baillet, should embody the four virtues of "knowledge, fidelity, precision and impartiality."[3] He no doubt had in mind humanist figures of the stripe of Robert and Henri II Estienne, Sebastian Gryphius, Guillaume Roville (Rouville, Rouillé), Aldus and Paulus Manutius, Johannes Froben, and André Wechel, to name but a few.[4] But Rebuffi's contemporaries all knew that books, authors, and printers were not uniformly truthful, virtuous, and beneficial. Copy delivered to a printer could be inflected by political, religious, or other interests, and could be subject to inaccurate or partial production. And even if the highest academic and commercial ethics obtained, it was not certain that the book would reach the audience for which it was written, as war, plague, and human factors such as censorship and repression could prevent it from so doing, and if it did, it was not certain that it would avoid being egregiously read and misrepresented.

In this book I shall set out to examine the various elements mentioned here in turn—authors and their supporters, publishers, censors, sellers, purchasers—and attempt to show how they were affected by their self-imposed roles, by commercial considerations and the structure of the book market, by the ideology of scholarship as a liberal art, and by the confessional universe in which they operated. These issues will be investigated thematically in the subsequent chapters. Here, I have chosen to begin *in medias res* with an account (drawn from his surviving correspondence) of the decade in the early seventeenth century that Melchior Goldast von Haiminsfeld, a prolific author who might anachronistically be described as a literary agent, working on behalf of a wide group of scholars, spent in Frankfurt am Main.[5] Most of the scholars he represented were associated with the Reformed centres of Heidelberg and Zürich, and have been described as constituting a circle marked by "cultivated Calvinism [which] as the refuge of many sophisticated spirits, remained fundamentally erudite and non-dogmatic, critical and non-emotional."[6] Prominent members of this group included Janus Gruter, Marquard Freher, Georg Michael Lingelsheim, and the French diplomat Jacques Bongars. When writing to Freher, Goldast sends his best wishes to these and to less well-known figures, reinforcing the sense that they formed a tight-knit intellectual group, although they clearly also had strong links with all corners of the republic of letters of their day, including luminaries such as Joseph Scaliger, Isaac Casaubon, and Conrad Rittershausen of Altdorf, Goldast's old tutor.[7] At the end of this chapter, I shall return to the description of them as dispassionate and unbiased, to see how well it matches the evidence which I shall adduce here.

Frankfurt in the 1600s: Commerce, Scholarship, and Politics

Melchior Goldast von Haiminsfeld arrived in Frankfurt in 1606 and left in 1615 (he was to return later, in 1622).[8] These years mark the high point of production of Latin books in Germany, if judged by the declarations of publishers at the book fair; in 1613, the most prolific of these years, 1,134 titles were advertised in various genres, as compared with 575 only twenty years earlier in 1593.[9] This figure is only broadly indicative of the scale of the new publications: some were multi-volumed folios, some humbler single-gathering disputations; some, it is true, had been advertised before, or were reissues. Even so, the rise in numbers over two decades by a factor of nearly two is impressive. I shall argue in Chapter 7 that the market was already overextended in this period, prior to its dramatic decline in the 1630s, and that the warning signs of the coming collapse were already visible several decades earlier to some of the fair's most seasoned and shrewd denizens.

In the late sixteenth and early seventeenth centuries, the Imperial city of Frankfurt am Main, one of the major centres, if not the major centre, of learned publication, was riven with religious and social tensions. The patricians of the city were strict Lutherans.[10] The Council which they dominated played a role in the control of the fairs and in book production, asserting its right to inspect books before publication, to regulate book piracy, and to impose order on the printing industry.[11] As with many other such authorities in the early modern period, its ordinances in all three domains were not very effective, although the special court it set up to settle disputes between merchants during the fair itself was praised for its impartiality.[12] The Council enjoyed an uneasy relationship with the Imperial Book Commission, set up in the city in the latter half of the sixteenth century to represent the interests of the Holy Roman Empire and to enforce its laws concerning publication. The Commission was Catholic, and indeed (apparently without the knowledge of the Imperial Chancery) represented papal interests as well as those of the Empire. It was in a constant struggle with the City Council, but saw its power and status grow during the period of Goldast's residence, which coincided with the incumbency of the zealous Commissioner Valentin Leucht.[13] The richest of the local printer-publishers were neither Lutherans, nor Catholics, but members of the Reformed churches (mainly Calvinists) who had settled there as refugees from religious persecution in the southern Netherlands and France. They had no representation on the Council. A contemporary saying recorded wryly that "in Frankfurt, the Lutherans have the power, the Calvinists the money, and the Catholics the churches."[14]

It would be mistaken to believe that the two protestant sects had more sympathy with each other than with the Catholics.[15] The intolerant City Council, prompted by the Lutheran Consistory, went so far as to ban the practice of Reformed religion in the city for a period in 1596. The event that provoked this ban was the republication by the prestigious publishing house of Wechel of the Calvinist Bible edited by the Heidelberg scholars Immanuel Tremellius and Franciscus Junius (François du Jon).[16] Even after the repeal of this ban in 1601, feelings of hostility ran high. The Calvinist church was burnt down in 1608, and the Reformed population shrank to half its size by 1614.[17] One effect of this persecution was the migration of a number of important printers and publishers to neighbouring territories in sympathy with their beliefs, where they often obtained valuable concessions and tax exemptions from the ruler or the municipality. This process began in 1586, with the move of Christophorus Corvinus (Rab) to Herborn, to become the printer of the newly founded academy. From 1593 onward, neighbouring Hanau actively attracted printers and publishers, beginning with Wilhelm Antonius, followed by the prestigious Wechel firm, in 1596. Oberursel was host to reformed printers from 1596 to 1605 (when it reverted to Roman Catholicism), Lich from 1597 to 1604, Mannheim in the period 1608–1609, Offenbach in the period 1608–1612, and Oppenheim from 1610 to 1620, when Spanish troops wrested control of that city from the Palatinate.[18]

On the one hand, these moves had some cost implications in respect of transport and toll duties, and prevented the printers who migrated from maintaining their bookshops in Frankfurt, which only citizens could do, but on the other hand, the more favourable fiscal conditions they enjoyed allowed them to undercut those left behind in Frankfurt, as we shall see.[19] Lutheran as well as Calvinist publishers had recourse to printers outside Frankfurt to cut their costs and possibly to evade the censorship provisions of the city, and they saw a new publishing address as an advantage. The services of the printer Balthasar Hofmann of Darmstadt were employed in this way by Lutherans between 1605 and 1622.[20] Until 1613, there was no openly declared printing of Catholic materials in Frankfurt, although nearby Mainz harboured printers willing to satisfy the Catholic publishing needs.[21] Most publishers and printers remained exclusively loyal to one religious community, although there are a few cases of figures who either changed their allegiance or

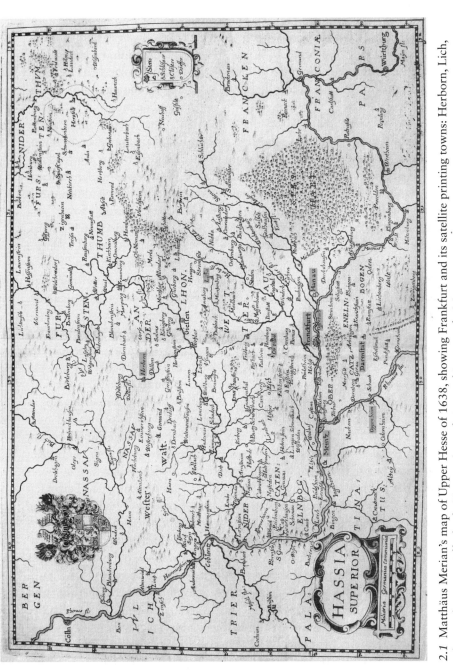

2.1 Matthäus Merian's map of Upper Hesse of 1638, showing Frankfurt and its satellite printing towns: Herborn, Lich, Oberursel, Mainz, Offenbach, Hanau, Oppenheim, and Darmstadt. Mea.

printed for various confessions.[22] It is clear that contemporaries were aware of these allegiances, as efforts were made by protestant publishers to imply that books were produced in neutral or even Catholic locations, if they aspired to a sale in other confessional areas. There is even the suggestion that printers were willing to lend their names for this and other clandestine purposes to books they had not in fact produced.[23]

As well as the multiplicity of Christian communities, there was a substantial Jewish presence in the city, amounting to a population of about 2,000, who engaged *inter alia* in money-lending (not least to the community of printers and publishers) and money-changing under the control of the City Council, over which, it was thought, they had too much influence.[24] Resentment against them boiled over during riots led by a grocer and baker called Vinzenz Fettmilch in the period 1612–1614. These began with the protest of various guilds to the Council over the establishment of a grain market and the export trade, but soon spread to encompass other grievances fueled by anti-Semitic and anti-patrician sentiment. This culminated in an attack on the Jewish Quarter in 1614, after which the Jewish population abandoned the city for several years. These protests involved some printers and publishers, who contributed to the list of grievances against the Council by accusing it of making extortionate financial demands through one of their officials, Dr. Kaspar Schacher, whose duty it was to enforce the Council's regulations concerning commerce and censorship.[25] They were supported also by a section of the remaining Calvinists in the city, who were accused by a contemporary Catholic polemicist of being behind the Fettmilch revolt. In contrast, the surrounding territories governed by rulers of the Reformed faith proved to be hospitable to the Jewish refugees. The revolt was brought to an end by Imperial military intervention, and Fettmilch and his fellow conspirators were executed two years later in 1616, the year in which the Jewish population returned to the city.[26]

During the time of Goldast's residence, Frankfurt was thus a city reflecting the tensions of a wider Europe. But only thirty years earlier, it had been described by the French-born Genevan humanist and publisher Henri II Estienne as a modern Athens, a paradise of learning and enlightenment, a city thronging with university professors and other scholars (some of whom walked halfway across Germany to be present at the book fair), who often stayed in the houses of the most prominent publishers, which buzzed with intellectual and literary activity.[27] I have already mentioned the group of Calvinist scholars based in Heidelberg, some of whom attended the Frankfurt fair quite regularly, and possibly other book fairs in the region (notably Strasbourg). They also relied on the fair as a place of postal exchange. Their letters were sent to booksellers and publishers, who forwarded them to their recipients elsewhere in Europe. They constitute the semi-private face of the republic of letters, whose public face consisted in its scholarly output of books and pamphlets.[28] It was only semi-private, as letters were frequently read by others through whose hands they passed on their way to their named recipients. Erasmus complained of this as early as 1524, and Goldast noted in a letter to Freher eighty years later that the eminent scholar Joseph Scaliger's letters were "falling into the worst hands."[29] At least one of Goldast's own correspondents, who clearly knew of this widespread practice, invited his host in the city, the octogenarian Prior of the Carmelite House, to open the letter and read it if Goldast should happen to be absent.[30]

The gazettes and broadsheets ("Messrelationen") circulating during the fair contained the latest political and military news; visiting publishers and scholars communicated these to their family and colleagues at home.[31] During Goldast's time in the city, international events had a considerable effect on its political and scholarly life. One of the most notable of these was the conflict between Venice and Pope Paul V, which led to the Interdict of 1606–1607, to which I shall return below. Another was the continuing tension between the Holy Roman Empire and the Papacy, on the one hand, and the Papacy and its claims over the loyalty of Catholics living in protestant lands, on the other, which was vigorously discussed in the years following the Interdict. The Jesuit Robert Bellarmine played a prominent role in the former debate, and attracted thereby opprobrium to himself and his order. Nor were the effects of these discussions confined to contemporary polemics: much of the investigation into the Empire's medieval past was motivated by these issues which exacerbated sectarian differences.[32] In the darker days of the 1600s, the city witnessed events such as a colloquy between Calvinists and a Catholic professor from Cologne which took place during the autumn fair of 1609.[33]

The city and its printing activities were governed by the rhythm of the eight-day-long, twice-yearly fair, in more than one way. Publishers from Frankfurt and abroad struggled to meet the March and September dates in order to present their latest publications to the market; the settlement dates for their accounts were six months in arrears, to coincide with the next fair; local printers took a fortnight's holiday after each eight-day fair to recover from that period of frenzied activity (a concession that may also reflect the fact that their counterparts under Catholic regimes did not have to work on holy days of obligation throughout the liturgical year).[34]

The Lutheran Council (who had the power to expel citizens convicted of adultery from the city, regulated the resident print shops, and even controlled where visitors could stay and how many guests could be invited to gatherings such as weddings) was active in the promotion of its international fair for obvious commercial reasons, and set out to welcome foreign merchants and provide them with good conditions for trade.[35] Armed escorts were provided for them as they entered the frontiers of the town's jurisdiction; officials met them with a welcoming glass of the local wine, rang the bells of the city's churches to mark the opening of the fair, provided them with free protection for themselves and their goods in the city, and regulated trade in a way which would benefit those coming from abroad. Books and all the other components of the printing trade—paper, punches, matrices, typeface—were prominent as commodities, but, as Henri II Estienne pointed out, cloth, silk, jewels, artefacts, arms, and horses were also sold, and in fact represented a greater volume of trade.[36] Exchange rates were imposed for major currencies (as at most other European fairs), local taxes were set at a low rate, and cheap warehousing was provided to facilitate the merchants' future visits to the city. The book depots had the effect of turning the city into a vast library; an astonishing range of printed material was available, some of it quite venerable, and scholars knew that they could ask scholars living in Frankfurt and other denizens of the fair to track down rare editions for them.[37] Certain publishers from other cities (Zürich, Heidelberg, and Antwerp) even chose to store a considerable proportion of their books all the year round in Frankfurt, while others either appointed a local bookseller as an agent, or employed someone themselves as a factor to remain there throughout the year.[38] Nearly all selling and buying went on between members of the book trade, although some scholars who attended the fairs bought for themselves or on commission for others. A trade price (the so-called "Frankfurter Tax") was set for books other than folios, based on the number of printed sheets in a book, net of transport and storage costs, although in practice variations in discounts offered to clients and in the quality of paper made this difficult to enforce. Many of the publishers and booksellers attending the fair relied on trade there for their survival. The Antwerp publisher Christophe Plantin, for instance, did about 40 percent of his business through the fair, where he could meet more than one hundred members of his trade, many of whom had traveled long distances to be there, as he himself had.[39] The international character of the fair meant that members of the book trade had to be polyglot: in the bookstalls and bookshops, French and German were spoken as well as Latin, the lingua franca of the learned trade.[40]

Despite all the money-changing arrangements, there was a constant problem of cash flow among the book merchants attending the fair. They often had recourse to credit notes, or settled bills by barter with other publishers, taking home with them an assortment of books which turned them willy-nilly into retail booksellers. The Book Commission required the Imperial privileges acquired by publishers to protect their new publications from piracy to be displayed on the book stalls. Together with these, broadsheet catalogues known as "nomenclaturae" were put up by the publishers to advertise not only their current products but their back-list as well. Unofficially from 1564, and officially (by author-ity of the City Council) from 1597, a catalogue listing all new books advertised at the fair was issued. It was arranged by genre, with Lutheran theology being given pride of place. The fair catalogues (which listed expanded or corrected editions with those which were altogether new) did not, of course, cover all the published material available at the fair. In Goldast's time, foreign publishers came from elsewhere in Germany, from Switzerland, from France, and from the Netherlands in consider-able numbers. Venice usually sent one representative to represent a consortium of publishers, as did England. There was patchy attendance from eastern Europe and parts of Italy other than Venice, and no Iberian presence at all, unless indirectly through the Plantin firm of Antwerp.

The conjunction of scholarship, with its associations of free exchange and liberality, and mercantilist-driven commerce in books was not al-ways a happy one. When Erasmus described Frankfurt as "a sink of hu-man vileness" and a "forum for the affairs of thieves, impostors, perjur-ers, usurers and pedlars," he was expressing a view which Goldast and his contemporaries echo quite frequently, as we shall see, and which influ-enced their behaviour as authors and agents in the field of publishing.[41]

Melchior Goldast von Haiminsfeld

The Calvinist Swiss scholar Melchior Goldast von Haiminsfeld came to Frankfurt in 1606. He was born in 1578 into an impoverished noble family, although his Jesuit enemies claimed that he had fabricated his ancestry, as they did in the more famous case of Joseph Scaliger.[42] After

CATALOGVS OMNIVM LIBRORVM
QVI IN OFFICINA IOANNIS BASSÆI ET M. LEONHARDI
BVRCKII FVTVRIS NVNDINIS AVTVMNALIBVS
Anno M. DC. XI. prostabunt venales & venundantur.

IVRIDICI LIBRI.

A Zeuedi Consilia. fol.
Berthazolii tractatus clausularum. 8.
Bruele de rennunciandi modo. 8
De militia politica. 8.
Bayardi additiones in Clarum. fol.
Clarus complet. fol.
Carpanus de poenis. 8.
Castillo de vsufructu. 4.
  Tractatus quotidianarum controuersiarum. 4.
Couppenerus de priuilegiis studiosorum. 8.
Euethardi synopsis locor. legal. 16.
Fichardi tractatus cautelar. fol.
Goedelman de Magis, Veneficis & Lamiis. 4.
Gournerus de diuersis Reg. Iuris. 8.
Mandosius de casibus annalibus. 8.
Mallei Maleficarum tomus tertius. 8.
Masucri practica forensis. 8.
Pedrochii Consilium. fol.
Peregrini Consilia. fol.
Ruckerus de commissar. 8.
Schepplitz promptuarium. 4.
  Idem in 8.
Surdus de Alimentis. fol.
  Idem 4.
Seraphin de priuilegiis suramerorum. Cum addition. Martini Beneckdorffii V.I.D.f.
Stracha de proxenetis & proxeneticis. 8.
Tractatus clausularum { Celsi Hugonis & Vitalis de Campanis. fol.
{ Cæs. Lampetri. &
De Iure patronatus { Rochi de Curte. 8.
  Prima pars.
  Secunda pars.
Thassatae compendiu in Errores notarior. 8.
Vranii Consilia. fol.
Vbaldus de Iure prothimiseos. 8.

Bücher im Rechten.

Daumbauderi practica { Ciuilis. & Criminalis. f.
Patrocinium pupillorum. fol.
Klammers Auszug etlicher Rechten. 8.
Nigrinus von Hexen. 4.
Policey Ordnung. 4.
Rorbachs Notariat Kunst. 8.
Sauers Formular. fol.
  Teutscher Proceß. fol.
  Iurament Formular. fol.
  Straff Buch. fol.
Vigelii Rechterbüchlein. 8.
Weyssens Notariat Kunst. 8.

THEOLOGICA CVM scholasticalis.

Andreas in Epistolam ad Corinthios. 8.
Buchanani Psalterium cum Hymnis. 8.
Euangelia & Epistolæ. 16.
Lutheri Catechismus. 8.
  Latino German. 8.
Moseis de rebus gestis. 8.
Psalterium Lat. 12
Prætorii Cantiones. 4.5.6.7. & octo Voc. 4.
Steyer Genealogia Christi. fol.
Tabulæ Lat. fol.

Theologische Bücher vnnd Schulgattung.

Brauns Donner Predigten. 8.
Amarum dulce. 8.
Euangelien vnd Episteln. 16.
Gigantis postilla. 8.
Gülden Kleinodt. 12.
Helbachs geistliche Schatzkammer. 8.
Hessische Fraagstück. 16.
Icones Euangeliorum. 4.
Jesus Sprach. 16
Leuchter in Salomonem. 4.
  In Hageum. 4.
  Alcoran. 4.
  Speculum de summo bono. 12.
Lutheri Catechismuß. 16.
  Testament. 8.
Milii Herzsfunck. 12
Namen Buch. 8.
Osianders Kirchen Historia. 9.10.11.12.13. 14.15. Centur. 8.
Psalter. 8.
Schotten gesangbuch. 12.
Titelbachs Gülden Klein odt. 8.
Taffelbletter.

MEDICI LIBRI.

Aldrouandus de Auibus. Vol. 2. fol.
Bauhini exectio foetus. 8.
  Animaduersiones. 4.
Massariae practica. 4.
Placentini anatomia. fol.
Rondeletius de vrinis. 12.
Ruland de morbo Vngarico. 8.
Syluatica de Compositione thetiæ. 8.
Sto: keri praxis morborum. 8.
Tharantae practica. 4.
Zinckius de Cnsibus. 11.

Bücher in der Artzeney.

Tabernæmontani Rathschlag wider die vergifftige Pestilentische Feber. 8.

VARII GENERIS LIBRI.

Plautus cum annotationibus Camerarii. 16.
Vrsini Colloquia Collecta ex Pontano, Viuio & Eratmo. 8.
Valesii de SS. Philosophia. 8.
Catonis disticha moralia. 8.

Allerhandt Sortten Bücher.

Alten Weisen Exempel. 8.

Æsopi Fabeln 8.
Chronicon der 4. Monarchien. 8.
Clauis Mart. 8.
Cato. Lat. & Germ. 8.
Gilhusii Grammatica. 8.
Modelbuch. 4.
Rollwag / Gartengesellschafft vnd Wegkürtzer. 8.
Werneri Fürstliche Tischreden. 8.
Wißbadisch Wissenbründlein 2. theil. 8.
Item 3. vnd 4. Theil.
Weinrechnung. 16.

SEQVVNTVR IAM LIbri pertinentes ad M. Leonhardum Burckium, qui in eadem Officina inueniuntur.

Theologica.

Macarii Homeliæ spirituales. 8

Theologische Teutsche Bücher.

Andreæ Osiandri Kirchen Historien Centuria 1.2.3.4. 8
Cent. 5. 8
Cent. 6. 8
Cent. 7. 8.
Psalmenbüchlein. 16.

Iuridica.

Bartholomæi Cæpollae consilia ciuilia & criminalia. fol.
Iacobi Ayrerii tractatus de Errore calculi. 8.
Michaelis Grassi receptat. sententiar. I. & II. pars. fol.
Nicolai Euerhardi Consilia. fol.
Petrus Rebuffus de Priuileg. vniuersitatum, studiosorum, Bibliopol. 8
Roderici Suaretz opera omnia. fol.
Sebastiani Medices de compensationibus. 8

Teutsche Bücher im Rechten.

Abraham Sawers Peinlicher Proceß. fol.
Fasciculus iudiciarii ordinis. fol.
Notariatspiegel. fol.
Iacobi Ayteri processus Belial contra Christum. fol.
Ioannis Eliæ Meichsners Formular / siue Thesaurus Aureus. fol.

Medica.

Petri Andr. Matthioli opera cum commentariis D. Casparis Bauhini. fol.

Teutsche Medicinische Bücher.

Johann Weyers Artzeneybuch. 8

Historica & Philosophica.

Georgii Dounani Logica. 8
Martini Crusii Chronica Sueuica. fol.

2.2 The broadsheet bookseller's catalogue ("nomenclatura") of Nicolas Bassée and Leonhard Burck printed for the 1611 Autumn Book Fair in Frankfurt. One of a number of "nomenclaturae" collected by Melchior Goldast during his time in Frankfurt.

Courtesy of Staats- und Universitätsbibliothek, Bremen.

local schooling, he received a legal education, first (for one year only) in Catholic Ingolstadt, thereafter (1595–1597) in Philippist Altdorf, where he took a master's degree but was too poor to proceed to the Licentiate or Doctorate, although he appears to lay claim to the former degree in a letter to Freher in 1605.[43] So, like many poor scholars of his day, he relied on rich patrons for material backing, and did their bidding. In 1599 he went to St. Gallen to work for and with the jurist and local historian Bartholomäus Schobinger, from whom he received financial support.[44] Neither he nor Schobinger was popular with the administrators of the library there. Not only did they borrow books and not return them; they even cut out pages from the volumes in their possession, and wrote comments on rare original manuscripts.[45] Schobinger and Goldast were later called to account for these acts by the Council in St. Gallen in 1604–1605. Their defence relied in part on the motive for their actions; their purpose was to celebrate and publicise the achievements of early German (as opposed to Roman) law and medieval vernacular literature as an expression of pride in the German past and German language.[46] This should alert us to the fact that at this date the vernacular, even the medieval vernacular, was not considered by a number of scholars of the German lands to be inferior to Latin, or more especially, to another vernacular, Italian, which had achieved a high status throughout Europe through its literary productions and its association with humanism.[47]

In 1600, Goldast moved to Geneva; it cannot have been a happy time, for he subsequently referred to the "inhumanity" of its scholarly community (with one exception).[48] While there, he became implicated in the publication of a lecture on religious toleration which the prominent humanist Justus Lipsius was alleged to have delivered in the Lutheran University of Jena while employed there in the early 1570s. Its title was *De duplici concordia*. The views it expressed were aggressively protestant, and the text has the author explicitly declaring himself to be a Lutheran. By 1600, Lipsius was teaching in Louvain and had returned to the Catholic fold. He was probably the best-selling scholarly author of his day, and any book allegedly written by him could be assured of a good sale. The manifest purpose of the forgery (if it was one, as Lipsius alleged it to be) was to discredit the Flemish scholar, who, as an apostate in the eyes of Calvinists, provoked revulsion and contempt.[49] From the surviving letters written to Goldast, it seems that scholars who abandoned what the Reformed community perceived as the true faith attracted deep opprobrium among their number. Another such figure was the renegade Gaspar Schoppe [Scioppius], a personal enemy of Goldast. Behind the distaste lay no doubt a fear that more defections would ensue under the pressure of the Counter-Reformation.[50]

Lipsius reacted vigorously, first by appealing to the City Council of Zürich, where the book was produced, to proceed against the printer, then by requesting the City Council in Frankfurt to have the book erased from the fair catalogue, and finally by making his own legitimate publisher, Jan I Moretus of the powerful Plantin firm of Antwerp, buy up all the copies he could at the fair and destroy them.[51] By that time, however, another bookseller had himself seized the opportunity to buy up a large part of the stock at a low price, and made a good profit from them. The episode shows how close to the surface confessional interests were in the republic of letters and how these could be exploited for financial gain. It is true that Goldast, who was suspected of being its author by those who thought that the Lipsius work was a forgery, maintained scholarly contacts with a number of Catholic figures, including the Augsburg historian Marcus Welser, and made common cause with them in recovering and publishing the medieval literary, legal, and historical monuments of German-speaking lands; but collaboration was not made easy by the confessionalised universe of knowledge. Welser's association with Jesuits, together with an unspecified act which Goldast was willing to disclose only *viva voce* to his friend Freher, led Goldast at a later date to describe him as a "vile man."[52]

Early Publications: Conditions of Life in Frankfurt

Goldast's patron, Bartholomäus Schobinger, died in 1604, the year in which the book of German medieval documents whose existence had been discovered some half-century before by Joachim von Watt (Vadianus), on which Goldast and Schobinger had been working, appeared. It was entitled *Paraenetica vetera* (Ancient Admonitions), and was accompanied by an essay by Goldast's old Altdorf tutor, the historian Conrad Rittershausen. The negotiations for its publication were conducted by Schobinger or his family, who entrusted the manuscript to the printer Johann Ludwig Brem. Brem's presses were located in Lindau, a small town on the shores of Lake Constance. They probably chose him because he was the most accessible printer to St. Gallen.[53] Brem himself did not have an intimate knowledge of the Latin market for books or of the Frankfurt book fair. Initially the more experienced Zürich scholar-publisher Johann Huldrich Wolf agreed to distribute the work, but this plan seems to have been abandoned.[54] The book was attractive enough as a proposition for the largest booksellers at the fair, the Willers of Augsburg, under the instigation of Marcus Welser, to offer to buy a hundred copies; but the inexperienced Brem tried to make him buy the whole edition of 1,500, and so risked losing the deal. In the end Welser suggested that two or three hundred should be sent speculatively to the fair. They were advertised there in the spring of 1605, not under the name of Brem but under that of the Willers.[55]

In the following year, another volume of documents, this time about the history of Swabia, was produced for Goldast and paid for by a printer-publisher called Conrad Neben, who had moved in 1604 from Lich to Offenbach. He joined forces with a resident Frankfurt bookseller and printer, Wolfgang Richter, to ensure the volume's sale both during the fair and throughout the year. Goldast later revealed that he received himself sixty free copies as payment for this work.[56] The title—*Suevicarum rerum scriptores aliquot*—recalls similar series of such collections of documents from all over Europe, published by various prestigious houses, including that of Wechel, whose confessional allegiance was the same as that of Goldast. It is somewhat puzzling that the volume did not appear with their imprint. It is possible that Neben knew of the success of their series, and offered better terms to Goldast as author-editor. The volume was advertised in the autumn fair catalogue of 1605. It appears that Goldast and his compatriot and friend Raphael Egly were forced to flee Switzerland against their wishes in that year.[57] Less than a year later, Goldast installed himself in Frankfurt and became the agent for a number of ex-tutors from Altdorf, Swiss colleagues from Zürich, and influential figures from Heidelberg, as well as other figures who approached him later in his stay because of the reputation he eventually acquired as an adroit negotiator in the publishing world.

Goldast began living in with the rector of the school, and then moved into the Carmelite monastery (which also housed the book stocks of various foreign publishers and was regulated by the City Council), having befriended the aged Prior Johannes Myntzenberger, who was later forced to expel him because of the rumours about him circulated by his Catholic adversaries; but during this time he was able to use its library.[58] Thereafter his straitened circumstances obliged him to become the guest of the bookseller Peter Kopf, for whom he acted as book-consultant and corrector (copy editor and proof reader), and through whom he arranged the publication of his own works and those of the scholars he represented; later still he found other lodgings with a certain

Herr Steinheimer.[59] His material circumstances were so bad that he appears even to have contemplated suicide at one point; he lost all desire to continue his scholarly work, and described himself as living among barbarians (a quite different image of Frankfurt from that of Estienne).[60] He was reduced to subsisting on bread and water for weeks at a time, and he contemplated selling off his valuable collection of books and manuscripts.[61] Threnodies about his poverty form a leitmotiv in his correspondence with Marquard Freher, to which I shall return. Goldast made it clear to his correspondents that he was desperately looking for patronage (or an advantageous marriage, regardless of the religious persuasion of the potential bride) which would relieve him of the drudgery which his impecunious situation forced upon him, and allow him to devote himself to scholarship, as he saw with envy the much-admired humanist Isaac Casaubon doing after his appointment as the librarian of Henri IV of France.[62] Casaubon's eagerly awaited partial edition of Polybius came out in 1610; it was rumoured that he had received the considerable sum 1,000 écus from his patron, to whom he had dedicated the work.[63]

Goldast eventually secured a similar, but much less prestigious, position in Bückeburg with the Count of Schaumburg in 1615, having also improved his material circumstances by marriage to Sophie Ottilie Jeckel, the daughter of a Frankfurt patrician, in 1612. Before that, to attract attention to his plight, Goldast sent out free copies of his books to potential patrons, and in some cases dedicated them to these figures. A letter from one of the scholars he represented, Marquard Freher, suggests that he did obtain some money in this way, but Goldast himself commented bitterly on the futility of such donations, claiming that even in this one case he was thirty-three guilders out of pocket after taking into account the cost of the book and its binding.[64] He even found it difficult to meet the costs of postage.[65] He survived by taking on such tasks as corrector; he also looked for profitable publishing ventures, such as that of collecting together and publishing the reviled Lipsius's letters after his death, together with a commentary on Suetonius written by him of which Goldast had procured a student's dictated copy.[66] Other payments came from written legal consultations, often based on evidence from the medieval documents he and his collaborators collected, exchanged, and published.[67] Most of the work he engaged in on behalf of foreign scholars was paid for not in money, but in books or favours, such as obtaining privileges for his own books in territories where they had influence, or providing subsidies paid to printers to enable them to publish their works. This was often referred to by his friends in terms of an exchange of mutual favours.[68] For his own enterprises he received a number of free copies which he distributed to colleagues and potential patrons. He resented bitterly the rumours that he was profiting from such remuneration.[69] He was required by his clients to ensure the successful passage of their texts through the censorship offices (both in Frankfurt, which seems to have charged for this service, and on occasions in Catholic Cologne), to check the accuracy of the printing, choose the format, the typeface, and the quality of the paper, even determine the wording of the title page: all of this at the same time as being discreet about his clients' secret negotiations with rival printers, getting them the best deal possible, and expediting the process of publication.[70] For his ex-tutor Conrad Rittershausen's printer in Amberg, Goldast even arranged the distribution in Frankfurt of the books published at Rittershausen's own expense, and their exchange with other works by *Tauschhandel*.[71] It is clear that at the end of his stay he had accumulated a substantial library (to replace the one he was forced by his flight from St. Gallen to leave behind him), and a substantial reference collection of publishers' catalogues.[72] These are now preserved in Bremen's Staats- und Universitätstbibliothek.[73] He was very busy during the fairs, having meetings with booksellers and other scholars, for whom he acted in various ways, and he kept in touch with the two other major book fairs, at Leipzig and Strasbourg, which he visited on occasions.[74] Throughout the year he sent missives to his contacts in the republic of letters, principally its "Christian" (i.e., Reformed) element.[75] In spite of all this peripheral activity, he managed in the decade of his Frankfurt residence to complete the editorial work on several thousand folio pages of both Latin and German manuscripts in the fields of history, law, politics, church history, theology, and humanism, and to facilitate the publication of works by a group of early to mid-sixteenth-century religious figures of moderate and relatively tolerant views in harmony with his and his friends' own theological outlook, including the Erasmians Andreas Dudith and Pier Paolo Vergerio.[76]

Problems arose from the scurrilous personal attacks in which he and his friends engaged and to which they were subjected in turn. This led him at one point to seek to prevent one such publication by Gaspar Schoppe which was due to be printed in Frankfurt. After Schoppe's defection to the Catholic camp in 1599, an attempt was made by an anonymous figure to destroy his reputation by the printing of his edition of the Latin phallic verse collection known as the *Priapeia* without his knowledge or consent in 1606.[77] In his personal and confessionally motivated attack on the eminent scholar Joseph Scaliger published in Mainz in 1607, Schoppe attacked Goldast also, accusing him of being behind the publication of the *Priapeia*. Scaliger and his friends attacked Schoppe in turn in a Menippean satire which was published in 1608, to which Schoppe composed an immediate reply. He initially arranged to publish this riposte with Johann Theobald Schönwetter, who also published some of Goldast's writings, but Goldast appealed successfully to both the publisher and the Frankfurt City Council to have it banned, although he was unable to prevent the work appearing from an undisclosed location in 1608 and again three years later in both Paris and Ingolstadt.[78]

A more subtle problem arose from his role as intermediary between the world of scholarship and the world of publishing. In his letters to Freher, full of complaints about his impoverished state, he also expresses the view that a nobleman and scholar such as himself should not engage in commercial activity. "I have always thought," he writes at one point, "that the calculating outlook of merchants ("mercantariam prudentiam") is unworthy of a nobleman of free spirit," quoting the Roman jurist Ulpian and Seneca in support of this view; as a consequence, he declares that he will not to stoop to asking for gifts or money, even though he relied on both to survive.[79] He writes somewhat caustically to Freher that he had obtained for him a payment for copy from a publisher, but himself did everything for him without charge.[80] Goldast subscribed to the aristocratic culture of the gift, in which there is no calculation, even if there is hope of reciprocity. This involved him in some seeming hypocrisy. Accepting a gift of a golden cup did not offend his sense of honour, but it could alleviate his material wants only if it was traded; the realities of mercantile exchange soon reasserted themselves.[81] Goldast's friends were aware of his sensitivity on the issue of calculated gifts, and found ways of giving him financial support which he would not spurn.[82] A particularly revealing letter is the one he wrote to a fellow antiquary, Georg Rehm of Nuremberg, on 9 September 1610. Rehm had imprudently described Goldast as the employee ("mercenarium typographicum") of the publisher Peter Kopf, on whom he depended for his accommodation, and implicitly as behaving in a low-born ("vilis") manner.[83] In his reply, Goldast indignantly rejects Georg Rehm's assumption that he is a "colleague" of the Wechel's corrector Gothofredus Jungermann (who, according to Goldast, looked upon him as his patron). He asserts his high status with publishers, who previously were in thrall to the local censors but now would not publish anything without seeking his advice, and reaffirms his noble status and his work as a well-paid legal consultant for the Palatinate. He also bemoans the fact that his Catholic adversaries, who conspired to have him exiled from Switzerland and expelled from the Carmelite Priory, had spread calumnies about him and about his nobility, and declares that he had himself to pay to clear his name through the publication of his *Replicatio* to the Jesuit Jacob Gretser.[84] Goldast was not alone among his friends to live by this anti-mercantile rhetoric; but unlike them, he was expected to secure good deals from publishers by engaging in hardheaded negotiations on his own and their behalf, and this compromised his noble pretensions. In all this, he did not hide his contempt for the profession, referring to them as "hoc genus hominum," expressing his distaste of their dishonesty and venality, and describing one of his own publishers (Johannes Berner) as "a man not of the best faith, and a shameless trickster."[85] It may not be too far-fetched to detect behind this expression of disgust the conscious or unconscious fear felt by Goldast the scholar that he shared some of the attitudes and practices of those whom he describes as his polar opposites.

Goldast and Marquard Freher

Goldast's correspondence with Marquard Freher, both sides of which survive, reveals much about many aspects of his stay in Frankfurt and the political and religious climate which reigned in the city. Marquard Freher was an influential member of the court and chancery at Heidelberg, a correspondent of Justus Lipsius, and a close associate with influential figures such as Joseph Justus Scaliger, Jacques Bongars, Janus Gruter, Goldast's old tutor Conrad Rittershausen, Georg Michael Lingelsheim, Jacques-Auguste de Thou, Friedrich Lindenbrog, and Marcus Welser, as well as the powerful publishing houses of the Wechel family, the de Brys, and Gotthard Vögelin.[86] Freher's acquaintance with Goldast dated back to the beginning of the century: in an adulatory letter dated 23 August 1600, Goldast asks to be numbered among his clients (in the Roman sense of the word); three years later, they had become firm friends and corresponded as equals.[87] They began to exchange documents and books, and met at the Frankfurt fair when Freher's busy life as a counsellor at the Palatinate Court in Heidelberg allowed it.[88] This heavy involvement in public life imposed some restraint on Freher's free expression of his opinions in letters (although we may surmise that he was less guarded when in Goldast's company), and made him a slow or tardy producer of copy, causing problems for his publishers.[89] His edition of Frankish texts, which Goldast eagerly awaited in order to include information from them in his own editions, was first spoken of in 1605 and did not appear until 1613, and the publication of the dual-language edition of the Donation of Constantine, which was intended for 1607, eventually appeared in 1610.[90]

The two scholars, both trained lawyers and humanists, were drawn together by their common scholarly and ideological goals as historians, Calvinists, and supporters of the Empire against the Papacy through the publication of medieval documents in what has been called Germany's "antiquarian revolution."[91] Theirs was a relationship of mutual support. Freher tried to secure for Goldast the patronage and material security he craved.[92] At the beginning of 1608, he wrote a triumphal letter to Goldast about the patronage in the form of monetary gifts from the Heidelberg court which he had secured for him, and chided him for despairing of receiving such support ("Gnadenpfennige"); but as we have seen, Goldast was out of pocket even in this case because of the costs he incurred in providing lavishly bound books used to attract these donations.[93] Freher also supplied preliminary verses for Goldast's publications when asked to do so,[94] but he did not involve Goldast in his negotiations outside Frankfurt with Heidelberg printers (who published documents in German for Freher after Goldast had failed to find him a printer, even in the cheaper centres of Herborn or Lich) and with prestigious publishers in Strasbourg and Hanau. He seems also to have remained in contact with Goldast's Jesuit adversaries, which led Goldast to write sarcastically about the limitations that Freher's public office placed on his demonstration of solidarity with his friends.[95] Freher frequently had to mollify the touchy Goldast, whom he accused at one point of finding fault even in those who were close to him.[96] Goldast was hoping for an active and sustained collaboration in the field of medieval archives, but was frustrated by Freher's failure to meet deadlines and to supply either documents to his friend or copy to the publishers with whom his friend was negotiating on his behalf; in one case the delay was a period of six years.[97] Goldast accused him of engaging in words rather than deeds, and of taking on too much at one time, with the result that the publishers he approached either suffered financially (as did the Wechel presses) or demanded that the complete copy be supplied before a judgement about publication could be made (as in the case of Trithemius's *Chronicon*, which appeared five years after this stipulation was made).[98] Eventually Goldast conceded that they were working toward different ends: his end, as a freelance scholar, was public, whereas Freher's was private, and not driven by a desire for prestige or preferment.[99] This divergence of aims is manifested in the title pages of their books: all of Goldast's publications cite his name, and many refer vaingloriously to his own library resources and editorial activity ("ex bibliotheca Haiminsfeldii Goldasti"; "studio (industria, recensione) Melchioris Goldasti"), whereas Freher allowed some of his to appear anonymously, or with a pseudonym.

Goldast protested that he hid nothing from Freher, but tellingly did not discuss with Freher his contentious edition of de Thou, of which more below, although Freher knew enough about it to obtain a privilege in the Palatinate for his friend's edition in October 1608.[100] But he was able to be of service to Freher in various ways: as a vehicle of information about mutual friends and any wider news circulating in the city, which Freher avidly sought, as a source of bibliographical information or rare books, as a copyist of manuscripts, as a recipient of monies, and principally, as a negotiator with a number of publishers.[101] These included several very entrepreneurial figures: Johannes Theobald Schönwetter and Konrad Meul, who paid for the printing of Goldast's *Rerum alamannicarum scriptores* in 1606, and printed also for Freher himself; Johann Berner, who started life as a type-founder, and although a Lutheran also supported the publications of Calvinists; the printers Nicolas Schramm, Wolfgang Richter, Johann Bringer, Conrad Neben, and Egenolff Emmelius, who both printed for others and tried their hand at publishing as well.[102] We may note here a difference in tone in the reference the two correspondents make to their publisher contacts: Freher described members of the trade as "probus et integer," "vir mirabilis," and "vir optimus," whereas Goldast can scarcely conceal his contempt for them.[103] Although Freher was complimentary about some of the printers and publishers he knew, he was no dupe of their practices, writing on one occasion about the offence he felt at their shady professional dealings ("tricae"), one of which was to hang on to the manuscripts submitted by authors against their wishes in case the publishers could eventually find a use for them.[104] The more severe Goldast, on the other hand, saw these "tricae" as symptoms of the divide which separated the noble and liberal ideals of scholarship from the base urges of the mercantile world.

Freher was very knowledgeable about the printing industry, in Frankfurt and elsewhere, and was keen to ensure that his books were printed elegantly, on the quality of paper, in the format, and with the typeface of his choosing: he even specified whether Arabic or Roman numerals should be used, and how the pages should be set out.[105] He used at least two Heidelberg printer-publishers (Gotthard Vögelin and Jean Mareschal), but also chose to extend his patronage to Frankfurt. Both he and Goldast used the de Bry brothers to publish their books in 1608; Freher also tried, with Goldast's help and influence in Frankfurt, to sort out a dispute between the de Brys and an esteemed colleague, Salomon Neugebauer, which threatened to end in litigation. The request reveals the sort of negotiations that Goldast was required to engage in on various fronts:

> You will soon be approached by the noble Lords Fioleji and their tutor, Dr. Salomon Neugebauer, a man known to me for many years, for whom I can vouch. As you will discover, there is some dispute between him and the de Brys, and the issue seems to be that they are not returning a manuscript to him, or that they cannot or will not publish it. Please ensure that he gets back what is his by asserting your and my authority, and that of the Mayor and your Prior [Johannes Myntzenberger of the Carmelite House], to stop the matter going before the courts.[106]

For some of his works, Freher appears to have paid the production costs himself (he offered also to stand surety for Goldast on one occasion); for others, he negotiated for payment either in money (per folio printed) or in the form of free copies (a hundred or more); and he reserved the right to ask those publishing his works for copies of other books on their list.[107] He allowed Goldast to negotiate on his behalf, and take any profit he could extract from the publishers above Freher's modest demands.[108]

The most intense period of their correspondence coincided with the crisis provoked by the Interdict pronounced on Venice by Paul V in 1606. Goldast's Zürich contact Caspar Waser, whom we shall meet again below, brought back documents about the Interdict from Venice, and arranged for their publication.[109] This prompted Freher to plan the publication of a number of anti-papal documents from the medieval period to convey the Reformed Party's convictions about the "Beast of Rome" and its solidarity with the Venetians, and try to secure them as allies.[110] On behalf of both, Goldast approached Johann Theobald Schönwetter, Konrad Meul, and Johannes Berner; all three employed the printers Wolfgang Richter and Johann Bringer, presumably on grounds of cost. The most potent of the documents in question was the Donation of Constantine, which the medieval Papacy had used to justify its supremacy over the Empire, and which had been famously exposed as a fraud by the philologist Lorenzo Valla in the fifteenth century. Publication of a full edition of both the Greek and Latin versions of the Donation was unfortunately delayed until 1610, by which time it had lost its topical force.[111] The other group of texts, on the excommunication by Pius II in 1460 of Sigismund Archduke of Austria, including the appeal against it by Sigismund's contemporary, the jurist Gregor von Heimburg, and his polemical exchange with the Bishop of Feltre on the limits of papal authority, did appear in 1607. Its path to publication reveals much about the market at the time.

The plan to publish texts to bolster the Venetians' case against the Papacy came from Freher, and was applauded by Goldast in a letter of 6 June 1606. Goldast recognised the urgency of getting the texts out for the spring fair of 1607; this urgency was stressed also by their correspondent in Venice, a Scotsman called Thomas Seghetus. Freher suggested that Berner be asked to publish them (he had just brought out Goldast's little book on Joan of Arc), but Goldast described the entrepreneur as unreliable, and instead approached Johann Theobald Schönwetter, who saw the chance of making money out of a very topical issue.[112] He agreed terms with him, initially for money, later for free copies (100 in the first instance, which became 150 later in the negotiations; Goldast asked for 20 of these to be given to him to distribute to his friends).[113] Freher specified elegant presentation, good-quality paper (at least for the free copies he would receive, many of which were to be sent to Venice already bound), the format (quarto), a decent-size point (called "Mittelschrift"), and the provision of notes (by Freher himself); Goldast added an index.[114] The work was submitted to the Frankfurt City Council's Censor, and approved in January 1607.[115] The publisher had serious concerns about the title, and was late in the printing of sheets (which Freher asked to inspect himself), being held up by Freher's failure to provide the notes that he had promised to supply to accompany the text.[116] While all this was going on, Freher was engaging in negotiations through Goldast over the publication of other medieval documents. The terms offered on this occasion were less generous, as the publisher recognised the topical nature of the Heimburg document, which he believed would guarantee a speedy sale. In the event, the work appeared at the spring fair of 1607. It was advertised in the fair catalogue with a provisional title which did not even refer to the Heimburg text; it was one of fifteen polemical documents about the Interdict.[117] The definitive title page of Freher's collection of texts (presumably printed either just before the fair or while it was proceeding) carried a dedication to the Doge and Senate of Venice.

Schönwetter did not do well out of this deal. As a result he declined to undertake the publication of Freher's third volume of German documents in January 1608, and complained to Goldast about the unsold stock of Heimburg.[118] Freher wrote on 20 February that he had found a solution to the latter problem, as he had identified another publisher, Egenolff Emmelius, who undertook to sell the remaining copies with a different title page carrying his own imprint.[119] Instead of highlighting the name of the excommunicated Sigismund, it gave prominence to Heimburg, and included extravagant laudatory epithets praising both the author and the work.

Freher suggested that he would add more material (a common ploy to boost the sales of reissued texts), but in the event, this did not happen.[120] All this may have been no more than a front for an act of self-financed publication. It is probable that Freher himself bought up the remaining stock from Schönwetter and transferred it to Emmelius. The strategy came too late to secure good sales. As early as the autumn catalogue of 1607, there was no longer a single polemical work referring to the Interdict; it had become old news. It is of note that Freher seems not to have used Goldast in discussions with publishers after this, and to have relied on his own contacts and powers of negotiation.[121]

The history of Heimburg's publication does not end here, for by 1610 Goldast had located and bought the manuscript of a much longer text than that published in 1607–1608. This appeared both in the third volume of Freher's *Germanicarum rerum scriptores* in 1611, and in Goldast's *Monarchia* published in the same year. I shall return in the next chapter to the commercial implications of producing repeated or expanded editions of the same work.

Goldast and Jacques-Auguste de Thou

I pass now to some of Goldast's other engagements with history, law, and theology. Many of his correspondents stressed the need for veracity and accuracy, but by 1600 the publication of documents or alleged documents about the whole Christian era could be, and often was, inflected by confessional bias and subject to misrepresentation.[122] That this was known at the time is indicated by the addition, in books about contemporary history, of epithets which stress the "unbiased" nature of the account at hand.[123] Readers of Anthony Grafton's *Forgers and Critics* will not be surprised by this; I shall cite here only one striking example, which illustrates that any work could be subtly subverted for

A PII PAPÆ II.

Excommunicatione iniusta

SIGISMVNDI ARCHI-
DVCIS AVSTRIÆ, COM.
TIROLIS, &c. ET GREGORII
de HEIMBVRG D. *96.4 Ju. (4)*

Appellationes & Contradictiones,

THEODORI LÆLII EPISCOPI FELTREN-
SIS, & dicti D. GREGORII HEIMBVRGENSIS
contrariis Disputationibus,
Nunc primum è M. S S. erutis, discussa & illustrata. *p.46. 6.*

CVM NOTIS,

Ad sereniss. Ducem & ampliss. Senatum VENETIARVM.

FRANCOFORTI,
Ex Officina Typographica Wolfgangi Richteri,
impensa CONRADI MEVLII.

M. DC. VII.

2.3 A 1607 title page so ill-designed that drove its publisher (Johann Theobald Schönwetter) to despair, and led to the book's turning out to be a commercial flop: the first edition of the anti-papal polemical texts by Gregor von Heimburg. *Courtesy of Herzog-August-Bibliothek, Wolfenbüttel.*

Jurisconsulti acutissimi, & Oratoris omnium, suo tempore, facundissimi,

GREGORII D

HEIMBVRG, D. QVON

DAM REVERENDISSIMI PRINCIPIS, &c. DI

THERI, Archiepiscopi Moguntini, &c. Consiliarii,
ac NORIMBERGENSIS Reipublicæ
Aduocati,

Scripta neruosa, Iuris institiæque plena:

QVIBVS, CVM ILLVSTRISSIMV

quondam Principem ac Dominum, Dn. SIGISMVNDVM,
Archiducem Austriæ, Comitem Tyrolis, &c. tum per-
sonam suam propriam,

*CONTRA PII PAPAE II. IMPIAS ET INIV-
stas Excommunicationis Bullas ; Itemq,*

THEODORI LÆLII, EPISCOPI FELTRENSIS,

modo dicti Papæ causam agentis, clandestina opprobria, &c.
solide defendit, simulque Papæ Primatum
Politicum eneruauit.

*Ex M. SS. nunc primum eruta, inq, vsum Studiosorum Iuris &
Historiarum, typis mandata.*

FRANCOFVRTI,
Impensis Egenolphi Emmelii Bibliopolæ.
M. DC. VIII.

2.4 The title page of the re-issue of the texts by Gregor von Heimburg in 1608.
Courtesy of the Queen's College, Oxford.

religious and political reasons.[124] The texts in question are the first and second parts of Jacques-Auguste de Thou's *Historiae sui temporis,* which a Parisian printer advertised at the Frankfurt fair in the autumn catalogues of 1604 and 1607 (in two formats: folio and 8vo). This frank account of recent history written in very elegant Latin by a distinguished Gallican magistrate with impeccable Catholic credentials was enthusiastically welcomed by opponents of the Papacy for its anti-Tridentine sentiments, and soon linked to the anti-papal literature inspired by the Venice interdict in the period 1606–1607. The Venetian cleric Paolo Sarpi (who arranged at this time through the bookseller Roberto Meietti to have polemical books about the Interdict smuggled into Venice) tried to persuade the entrepreneurial publisher Giovanni Battista Ciotti, whom we shall meet again (below, pages 198–200), to bring out an edition of de Thou's history there, while in Reformed circles in Frankfurt an "editio Germanica" was planned, which involved both Goldast and his employer Peter Kopf.[125] De Thou asked for this edition to be overseen by his friend Georg Michael Lingelsheim.[126] As a consequence of a hostile and complex diplomatic exchange between France and the papal authorities, de Thou's work was placed on the Roman Index on 14 November 1609, on the grounds of its praise of some scholars who were also heretics, its irenicism, and its explicit anti-papal Gallican views; but its support for the political independence of rulers from the Papacy was welcomed in various other Catholic quarters.[127]

This does not seem to have been the first contact between Goldast and de Thou; nor was it the last. Among Goldast's correspondence (between letters dated 15 and 16 May 1600) there is a undated document signed by de Thou, but without the name of an addressee, which makes seven points about the publication in Germany of medieval anti-papal documents, including the medieval scholastic William of Ockham's *De potestate pontificis,* which Goldast was to publish subsequently in his collection entitled *Monarchia* of 1611.[128] These points cover issues of presentation and accuracy, recommend the suppression of all the marginalia found in the earlier Parisian edition by Josse Bade of 1496, and suggest that the title page should avoid naming a place of publication or a printer with strong protestant associations in order not to expose the text to the accusation of having been tampered with.[129] If this was sent to Goldast as he contemplated the publication of Ockham's various tracts, he did not heed it, and indeed did not take any note of it in his dealings with de Thou's own text.

Goldast and Kopf realized that they could profit financially by under-cutting the Paris editions of de Thou's *Historiae* being advertised in Frankfurt (even the ones in smaller formats), and set about producing copy with the help of Quirinus Reuter, a Heidelberg scholar whom Goldast represented at Frankfurt. They located a cheap printer in Offenbach whom we have met already—Conrad Neben—who had the added advantage that he was not subject to the censorship controls in force in Frankfurt itself.[130] Goldast then did precisely what de Thou had counselled against in respect of Ockham: he (or Reuter) added explanatory marginalia which made the anti-papal content of the *Historiae* very explicit.[131] He also restored the passages about the Council of Trent which de Thou, under pressure from the French court, had excised from the Paris edition, but which he had imprudently sent to Lingelsheim, who must have shown them in turn to Reuter.[132] To these sins of commission, Reuter urged Goldast to add one of omission by suppressing de Thou's adverse comments about the late ruler of the Palatinate, Johann Casimir.[133] In the following month, Lingelsheim tried to dissuade Goldast and Kopf from publishing the vitiated edition, but they claimed that the printing had proceeded too far.[134] The original plan was to publish it with a false bibliographical address of Mannheim, with Nicholas Schramm as the declared (but fictitious) printer, in order to shield Kopf from Catholic pressure; this was abandoned when Freher informed Goldast that the ruler of the Palatinate did not approve of the stratagem.[135] The next idea seems to have been to publish it without a frontispiece, which would not have placated Lingelsheim, who could not have approved of the pirated Paris title page.[136] In the end, the second version, with a title page that mimicked that of the Paris in all details and an imprint naming Neben as the printer, appeared in Offenbach in 1609.

Not surprisingly, de Thou was furious. In the Paris edition in duodecimo of 1609, which failed to compete in price with the unauthorised edition of Goldast and Reuter, he added the following savage prefatory remark:

What the writer of these histories has wanted newly to be declared at the beginning of this work is his displeasure at the ambition of those miserable meddlers who seek to appear clever through the writings of others [. . .] by reason of the highly disobliging zeal of their idle printer, who at the last fair splattered the earlier books of my histories, which were published at Frankfurt, with inept and frivolous notes. These books were not copied in accordance with the last Paris edition, which should at least

IAC·AVG·
THVANI
HISTORI·
ARVM

sui temporis

PARS I.

PARISIIS.
ꝏ IↃ C IV.

ΑΛΗΘΕΙΑ   ΠΑΡΡΗΣΙΑ

2.5 The frontispiece of the Paris 1604 first edition of de Thou's *Histories.*
Courtesy of Bodleian Library, Oxford shelfmark 8° T 23 Art.

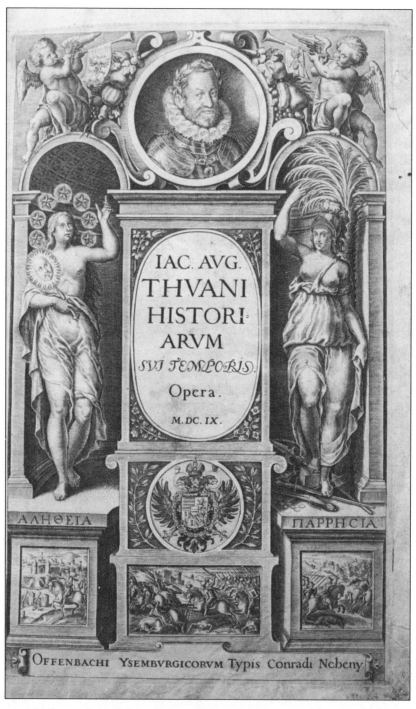

IAC. AVG.
THVANI
HISTORI=
ARVM
SVI TEMPORIS.
Opera.

M. DC. IX.

ΑΛΗΘΕΙΑ   ΠΑΡΡΗCΙΑ

OFFENBACHI YSEMBVRGICORVM Typis Conradi Nebeny

2.6 The frontispiece of the "German edition" of de Thou's *Histories* of 1609, showing the expense which the publisher and editors were willing to incur in order to suggest visually that the edition possessed due authority.
Courtesy of Christ Church, Oxford: shelfmark W f 8 13.

have been done. Truly, grave and honest men from all over Germany had urged the man in question to desist from his undertaking, and if he had heeded the promptings of either shame or impartiality, he would have had to obey them. But such was the stupidity of this mutton head, that he remained steadfastly deaf to these very wise counsels. Thus, since what has been done cannot be undone, the insult will appear sufficiently avenged, if the yokeldom of this trifler, exposed to mockery like the skin of Marsyas, frightens away and drives off other idiots of this sort.[137]

A later Frankfurt edition (of 1614), also financed by Kopf, sought partially to make amends for the tampering undertaken by Goldast by stressing de Thou's strict Catholic orthodoxy; but it is not to be supposed that this would have mollified the author, or indeed, his publisher.[138] It is likely that the "editio Germanica" robbed the Parisian publisher Jérôme Drouart of expected export sales by undercutting its price through the use of cheaper paper and an inexpensive local printer. The episode illustrates the advantages of being in Frankfurt, and the unscrupulousness of a venal publisher and a religiously biased editor when it came to ensuring a good sale and scoring some theological points. The genre of history thus continued to be an ideological battleground, as well as a source of profit for even cautious publishers such as the Wechel house, who initially recognised its appeal to "several classes of reader" but increasingly saw the benefit of publishing history with a clear polemical application to current events.[139]

Goldast, Quirinus Reuter, and Caspar Waser

I pass now to some of the other activities of Goldast on behalf of his cosectaries. Quirinus Reuter had clearly relished his collaboration with Goldast and Kopf in the publication of de Thou's histories, and came up with several other projects. The first of these involved the republication of various documents and exchanges of letters before or during the Council of Trent between Reformers and Catholics. The polemical significance of these publications lies in the attempt to redress the harm done to the Calvinist cause by the reprinting of authors such as the eloquent and humane opponent of Calvin, Jacopo Sadoleto, whose works had been published in Mainz in 1607, funded by Jonas Rhodius (or Rosa), a protestant Frankfurt bookseller who also published for the Reformed community in Heidelberg.[140] Sadoleto's letters appeared a year later in Cologne from the presses of the impeccably Catholic Maternus Cholinus. As a riposte, Reuter first conceived a plan to publish an edition of the *Orationes* and letters of Andreas Dudith, the irenic Lutheran bishop and latter-day Erasmian, which he mentioned to Goldast in October 1608.[141] He negotiated with Kopf as publisher, but tried to involve the Heidelberg printer Gotthard Vögelin, with whom he engaged in quite detailed negotiations. These included whether the printer would hold back any stock for himself, the possible press run (1,200), the format and line spacing, and the overall cost (8¾ florins for a bale: i.e., 5,000 sheets); but these arrangements do not seem to have suited Kopf.[142] Three months later, Reuter was alarmed to learn that there might be a new Imperial edict requiring all Reformed writings to be submitted to Catholic censure (i.e., the Book Commission), and that this might prevent Kopf from publishing Dudith's works in Frankfurt. This made him think of the same alternative printers mentioned in the case of de Thou: Nicolaus Schramm and Johannes Lancelottus.[143] Kopf was again approached through Goldast, but Reuter himself was in contact with Schramm, who said that he would undertake the task if Kopf encountered any difficulties.[144] As in the case of de Thou, Kopf elected to use the Offenbach printer Conrad Neben, which alarmed Reuter, who feared that lower standards of paper and typeface might be used, and insisted on seeing a sample of the printing. It also meant that the work was subjected, much against the wishes of Reuter, to the censorship of Offenbach's territorial ruler. The work eventually appeared in 1610 with an imprint naming "Arpold Philip Kopf" as publisher.[145] Reuter later complained that Kopf had failed to pay him as agreed in copies of the work, a ream of paper, and other books from his bookshop.[146]

As well as this, Reuter planned to reprint the exchange of letters (not included in the Cologne edition of 1608, or the *Opera* of 1607) between the bishop of Carpentras, Jacopo Sadoleto, and Calvin (these had previously appeared in Calvinist Neustadt an der Haart in 1608 from the presses of Nicolaus Schramm, at Reuter's instigation).[147] Reuter intended to supplement these with letters from two of their contemporaries, Johannes Sturm and Pietro Paolo Vegerio. Most of the letters eventually came out in a volume entitled *Discursus epistolares politico-theologici de statu Reipublicae Christianae degenerantis* in 1610, printed and prefaced by Emmelius, who acknowledged the help of Reuter, Goldast, and Rittershausen. Emmelius, like Kopf, failed to pay Reuter the agreed remuneration, and Goldast was instructed to see to its delivery.[148]

As I shall show in the next chapter, law was probably the most profitable sector of publishing; it is therefore not surprising that Quirinus Reuter should commission Goldast, himself a lawyer, to find a publisher

DISCVRSVS EPISTO-
LARES POLITICO-
THEOLOGICI

DE STATV REIPVBLICÆ
Christianæ degenerantis:

Tum

DE REFORMANDIS MORIBVS
& Abusibus Ecclesiæ,

Cum Christianissimi Galliarum Regis FRANCISCI I.
& Cardinalis Sadoleti Epistolis.

Omnia ex variis Bibliothecis collecta, & nunc primum coniun-
ctim edita, vt ex eorum lectione cunctis veritatis amantibus
liquido constare possit, quid fugere, quidve sequi in
hocce turbulento præsentium rerum
statu debeant.

FRANCOFVRTI
Apud Egenolphum Emmelium.
M.DC.X.

2.7 The collection of letters on the state of the Church in the early years of
the Reformation by Calvin, Melanchthon, Sturm, Sadoleto, and others, published in support of the Reformed cause in 1610 by Melchior Goldast, Conrad
Rittershausen, and Quirinus Reuter.
Courtesy of Bodleian Library, University of Oxford: shelfmark 4° M 33 (2) Th.

for four works by the Heidelberg jurist Nicolaus Cisnerus, including his work on history and philology. Some of these had previously been edited by the Jena professor Johannes Rosa, but had been printed inaccurately. Reuter had initially intended that Kopf would publish these, but then negotiated with Emmelius, who in late 1609 appears to have withdrawn from the deal they had struck. When the four works appeared in 1611, they simply named the bookseller—Jonas Rhodius—through whom they could be bought.[149]

Further involvement of Goldast with theology came through his association with the theologian and Zürich censor Caspar Waser.[150] Waser's connection with Goldast went back at least to 1600. He was a scholar of oriental languages, including Hebrew, Chaldean, and Syriac, whose ambition to have his book on ancient Jewish measures *(De mensuris)* and his commentary on Psalm 90 *(Analysis psalmi CX regii prophetae Davidis)* published was the subject of many of his letters to Goldast.[151] The commentary was not just a learned exercise; it announces on its title page that it is an attack on the use made of Melchidesdeck in Roman Catholic theology to validate its notion of priesthood. Waser could not use his friend Johann Huldrich Wolf, the local printer, because he did not know enough about Hebrew and would only have published these books if Waser met all the costs.[152] So he asked Goldast in 1609 to help him find a printer for both books, to act as corrector for them, and to negotiate payment in a number of free copies (at one point, he specifies 30–40 of the *Analysis;* at another 20–25).[153] He also offered some financial support to the publisher undertaking the publication of the latter work, as well as the purchase of a number of copies "at the proper (presumably discounted) price."[154] The *De mensuris* appeared in Heidelberg from the presses of Waser's long-time friend Gotthard Vögelin in 1610. The manuscript of the *Analysis* was given to the prestigious Frankfurt publisher Zacharias Palthen, who in the end did not print the *Analysis,* in spite of many entreaties, but clung on to the manuscript for more than a year before releasing it.[155] This was a practice about which many authors complained at this time.[156] Waser asked Goldast to recover the manuscript and give it to the rising scholar Johann Heinrich Alsted, so that his father-in-law, Christophorus Corvinus of Herborn, could publish it. This Goldast eventually did "in a virile and Swiss manner," as the grateful Waser put it.[157] However, it was not Corvinus who set his mark on the book, but the bookseller Antonius Hummius of Frankfurt (a friend of Nicolaus Schramm); the imprint states that the work was printed in Offenbach.[158]

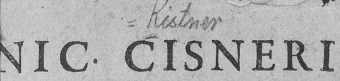

NIC· CISNERI

MOSBACHENSIS

Jurisconsulti celeberrimi Palatini
Consiliarij *Re 23*

DE

JURE ROMANO

Themata: & de

URE USUCAPIONUM

AD TITVLVM PANDECT.
seu digestorum

E USURPATIONIBUS
ET USUCAPIONIBUS

OMMENTARIVS ERVDITIS-
simus & Iuris Candidatis utilißimus.

FRANCOFVRTI,
In Bibliopolio JONÆ RHODII,
cIↃ IↃ C XI.

2.8 The title page of Quirinus Reuter's edition of one of the legal commentaries
by his colleague Nicolaus Cisnerus, which appeared in 1611.
Courtesy of Herzog-August-Bibliothek, Wolfenbüttel.

ANALYSIS
PSALMI CX.
REGII PROPHE-
TÆ DAVIDIS:

traditâ *698.2Th.(6)*

IN ALMA SCHOLA
Tigurinâ

à

CASPARO WASERO, TIG.

Refellitur hîc paucis argumentum Pontificiorum
de Typo Melchisedecki; quo Missæ sacrificium
exstruere nituntur.

OFFENBACHII,

Prostat apud Antonium Hum-
mium Francf.

M. DC. XII.

2.9 The title page of Caspar Waser's anti-Catholic commentary on Psalm 90, which appeared in 1612.
Courtesy of Herzog-August-Bibliothek, Wolfenbüttel.

From the surviving correspondence, it is clear that Waser badgered Goldast in a tiresome way to act on his behalf over the three years it took to get his book published; but he also kept Goldast informed of events as they occurred in his native Switzerland, and sent him snippets of international news.[159]

Two points need to be made about this. First, all the potential publishers served the Reformed community; their name on the imprint would have told any informed reader what the religious complexion of the book would be. We may compare this to the practice recommended for historical works by de Thou, namely that of avoiding any link with a non-Catholic city. Disguising the origin of books so as to ensure a Catholic sale was a very common practice, used, for example, by Lyon publishers who had books printed in Geneva to save money but put Lyon on the title page, and by speculative publishers such as Giovanni Battista Ciotti and Lazarus Zetzner, whose books intended for the Italian market carried the imprint Cologne rather than Frankfurt, where they were in fact printed.[160]

Second, it is worthy of note that Waser sent conflicting instructions to Goldast about the payment (in copies) he required. What is clear is that he could not himself afford to pay all the printing costs, although he offered to supply a modest subsidy to ensure that the printer would not be out of pocket. In the case of his book on Jewish measures, an entrepreneurial publisher who was also his friend—Gotthard Vögelin—was found; but the book cannot have sold very well, because at the time of the auction of the contents of Vögelin's warehouse in 1625, 526 remained, of a press run we can estimate at between 1,000 and 1,500.[161] In the end, the commentary on Psalm 90 appeared, without it being clear who financed the printing. It cannot have had poor sales, perhaps because of its polemical content, as a second edition appeared in 1623 or 1625.

The Publisher, the Scholar, and the Book

In order to provide a "thick description" of the world of scholarly publishing, I have looked in this chapter in detail at the fortunes of a group of scholars and publishers of the Reformed persuasion over a decade or so. I believe that it would be possible to map the same interactions and activities in a group of Lutherans, and that some of the features of Catholic publication also share characteristics with the two other major confessions. In the light of my account of Goldast and his associates, I shall now return to the issues I raised at the beginning of this chapter.

Do publishers live up to the ideal set out by Baillet as embodiments of "knowledge, fidelity, precision and disinterestedness"? They certainly protest, when seeking to obtain privileges to protect their publications, that they are faithful servants of the republic of letters, and only want a fair return for all the money, work, and effort they put into the production of books. But this is not how most authors and editors see them. It is true that one can find a few laudatory comments in Freher's missives, and in one of the letters sent to Goldast by Paulus Matthias Wehner, who describes Goldast's friend and supporter Johann Theobald Schönwetter (who had spent two years in prison for various misdemeanours) as "homo callidus et mirabilis" and Peter Kopf and Jonas Rhodius as members of a class of honourable ["honesti"] publishers—"honestus" being a word connoting the opposite of the "mercantile spirit" by which Goldast characterised publication.[162] Another of his correspondents, Johannes Henricus Suizerus from Zürich, believed that Goldast was acquainted both with persons willing to finance publications and with printer-publishers noted for their judgement, hard work, scrupulous care, and attention to detail.[163] But other assessments are very severe. These arise as the culmination of a set of experiences, or at the end of a particular trajectory, in the course of which the high regard that might have been felt for publishers gradually diminishes, and disillusion sets in. Quirinus Reuter writes bitterly that "we authors are used to acting as the servants of publishers: they get money from this, but what do we get?"[164] His sentiments are echoed by Janus Gruter, who refers to publishers as "low-born men who want everything to be done for no payment," and Conrad Rittershausen, who characterises the morals of publishers as "mercantile, that is to say, without any care for reputation or conscience," and accuses them of reserving all the profits of their enterprises for themselves.[165] The reference to conscience was reinforced in another attack on the venality of publishers by the Lutheran pastor Johann Friedrich Coelestin, who accused them of endangering their souls by conniving in the production of heretical writings.[166] In another context, his contemporary, the Tübingen professor Martin Crusius, who like Goldast compiled of a set of documents about Swabia in 1595, accuses the publisher's tail of wagging the scholarly dog: "it is lamentable," he wrote in his diary, "that we have to be subject to their whims."[167] They are also accused of "tricae," among them money-saving measures such as using low-quality paper, small typeface, and small formats. Throughout the letters sent to Goldast, there are expressions of impatience at the slowness with which publishers make decisions about the copy submitted to them,[168] their lack of urgency once printing is under way, their regrettable habit of not returning manuscripts in case they should ever be able to profit from them, their negligence in allowing poor copy to be produced (often because they produce copy too hastily), and their failure to pay the agreed remuneration in cash or kind once publication had occurred.[169] They stand accused, therefore, of lacking in fidelity and precision. As for disinterestedness, this also does not seem to be one of their virtues. Nearly all the publishers and printers we have met on this brief visit to Frankfurt are committed to one or another confessional group. In this, at least, they no longer resemble the humanist printer-publishers of the first age of printing. But it would only be fair to add that scholars expected them to carry stocks for very long periods of time. Freher, for example, was able to acquire a copy of Heroldus's anthology of Germanic law published by the Basel house of Petri from Sebastian Henricpetri half a century after its first publication.[170] As warehousing was frequently costly, and the value of stocks declined, one might justifiably say that this aspect of their business was a real and disinterested service to the republic of letters.

On the matter of the ethics of authors, or the moral virtues of books as set out by Pierre Rebuffi, however, the story is not a great deal more positive. Goldast's circle of scholars, described, as I noted above, as cultivated, erudite, non-dogmatic, critical, and non-emotional Calvinists, comes out of these letters in a rather different light. I have spoken of Goldast himself tampering with a text by commission to sharpen its confessional impact. His correspondents Reuter and Waser both urge omission on him to improve the image of Switzerland and its rulers in the documents he himself was preparing for publication. Goldast also forged a document for one of his legal clients.[171] They seem to me as a group to be deeply partisan. They were so alarmed and disgusted by the betrayal of those who abandoned their confession that they were willing to forge or resurrect compromising documents about them, and were as hostile to other protestants as they were to Catholics (Waser refers to the Mennonites and Socinians as detestable sects, and certain Marburg theologians as "leaden Lutherans").[172] If this story had been told about a group of Lutheran or Catholic scholars, I don't think that the result would have been very different, in spite of the fact that members of both of these camps produced books claiming to be "witnesses to truth."[173] Martin Mulsow is right to describe scholarly activity of this time as "a confused mixture of learned exchange, invective and irony, quests for manuscripts, strategies dictated by confessionality and tactics dictated by the search for publicity," and to stress the desire of scholars to achieve "authority, legitimacy and credibility" for their editions of medieval texts.[174] He is also correct in exposing the degree to which all their scholarly activities—even the production of humanist editions of texts of the ancient world—are coloured by their confessional allegiance.[175] Just as the noble Goldast combined a horror of the calculating spirit which ruled the business of publishing with an engagement with the base material facts of everyday life, both because of his own penury and the function he was required to fulfil for his fellow scholars in getting their works published, so also did those scholars, as well as their opponents in other confessional camps, combine their commitment to truth with a willingness to subvert this for other ends: polemical and politico-religious advantage, or the expression of territorial loyalty. In this way they were simultaneously partisan and neutral.[176]

The correspondence behind the published documents of the time reveals that authors were conscious of their omissions and commissions in respect of truth. Whether this flawed scholarly practice is perennial is not clear. Anthony Grafton has exposed even the great Erasmus as the forger of a patristic text, so it seems that the habit extends back at least to the early history of printing; but my own sense is that things had moved on since the 1520s.[177] Some sixty years after Rebuffi had written his paean of praise for books, they had become more like polemical objects or ideological weapons in the hands of the confessional scholarly communities which produced them than the temples of justice that he described in the quotation which opened this chapter. But as I shall argue in the Postscript to this study, these communities were at least aware of their shortcomings, and were not cynical about their aspirations to truth, fairness, and the ethics of their calling. To this extent, they did not betray their avocation.

CHAPTER THREE

Authors, Fields, and Genres

"If God would give me a publisher!" ("Deo typographum dante"): these words were written in his diary at the end of the sixteenth century by Martin Crusius, a distinguished university professor of Greek at Tübingen whom I mentioned in the closing remarks of the last chapter.[1] His predicament was shared by nearly all university teachers and independent scholars in the early modern period, and was common to all parts of Europe throughout the century. The Aristotelian and humanist Julius Caesar Scaliger struggled to find a publisher in Paris in the 1530s; the Italian polymath Girolamo Cardano noted in the account he published of his writings in 1557 that in 1536, as an out-of-work doctor living precariously off a small income from teaching in Milan, "the chance of getting published simply did not present itself"; and in Chapter 2 we encountered the Swiss scholar Caspar Waser and his problems with finding a printer in the first decade of the seventeenth century.[2]

Nowadays, the existence of Web pages and blogs may have removed the sense of exclusion which many writers in the past experienced in trying to get their works into print. As recently as this present decade, such a sense of exclusion could give rise to the feeling that publishers actively prevented some of the material submitted to them from seeing the light of day, not only for commercial but also for ideological reasons. In an interview he gave in Nijmegen in 1998, the Russian sociologist Aleksandr Zinoviev, a sharp critic of the "open society" of the West, even characterised the exclusion from commercial publication as a form of economic censorship, echoing the claims made by two sociologists in 1991.[3] This has caused some modern authors to look upon the world of publishing as a conspiracy, and as a consequence induced them to produce and distribute, at their own cost, works that had been rejected. It has even given rise to a number of publishing houses that will charge a full commercial rate to aspirant authors to an undertake publication, but do not take on the tasks of distributor and publicist.[4]

The Self-Payer and the Others

The phenomenon of self-financed publication in the early modern world is principally associated with literary figures, such as Lodovico Ariosto, but it occurred also in other areas for those who could afford it or were willing to take on the risk, as in cases of posthumous commemorative publication at their own expense by family members or colleagues of a scholar.[5] Because this provides the most certain route to appearing in print, I shall begin with this. The phrase "vanity publication" has been used of the writings of this class of author, but this is in many cases unfair. It is more common than might be assumed from the incidence of its parallel in modern publishing. Gustave Brunet's incomplete list of private presses of 1876 includes fourteen early modern authors and eighteen institutions (mostly monastic) who ran their own print shops.[6] Motives for self-publication are very varied. When Jacques Davy, Cardinal du Perron, grew weary in the second decade of the seventeenth century of the religious polemics in which he was engaged and wished to devote himself to his own writings, he retired to Bagnolet near Paris, where he established a printing press for which he acted himself as corrector, producing short print-runs for distribution to his friends.[7] The Venetian doctor Emilio Parisano decided to publicise his unorthodox views on embryology in a work entitled *De subtilitate*, which first appeared in folio in 1621, and which he went so far as to have protected by an expensive Imperial privilege.[8] Self-promotion can extend to promotion of a family or region, as in the case of the patrician Heinrich Rantzau from Holstein, who did both, or the fostering of humanist scholarship in a given town or region to celebrate its past or its archival resources, as Marcus Welser undertook to do with the publishing enterprise he funded in Augsburg.[9] Self-promotion could be defensive, and take the form of the repudiation of scurrilous personal attacks, as in the case of Goldast's *Replicatio* to his Jesuit adversary Jacob Gretser.[10]

Other motives for self-financing include the publication of a given scientific theory or set of observations, which inspired the wealthy Danish astronomer Tycho Brahe to install his own printing press on his island observatory in the 1590s, and Galileo Galilei to pay for a defence of his ideas about the compass.[11] There are cases of evangelical zeal, which may have prompted the Portuguese humanist Damião de Góis to produce his translation of a book of the Old Testament in Venice in 1535, or the German natural philosopher Johann Ingolstetter to contribute twice in the 1590s to the polemic provoked by the widely circulated story about a Silesian child in whose mouth a golden tooth had apparently grown, in order to expose it as the devil's work.[12] Some writers, for whom the encouragement of their friends and colleagues was not sufficiently persuasive, prayed for a sign from God, and on receiving it, resolved to publish their work, as did Edward, Lord Herbert of Cherbury, who brought out his *De veritate* at his own expense in Paris in 1624.[13] Others pinned their hopes on commercial profit, which spurred the Italian instrument maker Mutio Oddi to publish his treatise on an instrument of his design in *Dello Squadro*, which appeared in 1625.[14] Calvin's publishing career also began with an act of self-financed publication (of a commentary on Seneca's *De clementia*) in the hope of attracting scholarly preferment.[15] Producers of textbooks for local schools in which they taught, confident that they knew their market and could bring about the sale of a given press run, can also be found paying for their own works to be printed by a local press.[16] Another self-payer was Goldast's former tutor Conrad Rittershausen of Altdorf. His motives were the promotion of German humanist scholarship, the enhancing of his own reputation, and the castigation of the mores of his contemporaries through the publication of a shrewd observer of depraved human nature (the Gaulish historian Salvianus of Marseilles).[17] His is unlike some other cases, however, in that it represents an intermediate position. He certainly intended that a proportion of the books he produced at his own expense—a Greek and Latin edition of Malchus's *Life of Pythagoras* (1610) and his edition and commentary of Salvianus (1611)—would be distributed by his agent Melchior Goldast to his friends and colleagues; but he also attempted to recuperate his losses by having his works sold at the Frankfurt fair through the good offices of Goldast and the Amberg printer Johann Schönfeld, who suggested where to pitch the price.[18]

A final charming example of the self-payer is provided by the English divine John Andrewes, whose *Christ his Cross* of 1614 is preceded by prosopopeia in the form of a poem uttered by the book itself, revealing one of the great advantages of non-commercial publication, in the *et amicorum* tradition:

> My author did the impression buy
> And from the presse he did me take
> That none should sell me certainly
> But he himself which did me make
> Except it be his nearest friend
> Which may me sell, both give and lend.[19]

With the luxury of not having to seek for financial support, many self-payers were able to choose the printer or install their own press, determine the quality of paper, the format, the typeface, and the *mise en page,* set the standard for copy-editing and proof-correcting, specify the press run, and name the recipients to whom free copies would be sent. Such authors had the luxury of being free to dedicate their work to whomsoever they wished, and make their own arrangements for its promotion, advertisement, and distribution. In Rantzau's case, the author took personal control of the processes of publishing, chose his agent for sales, and distributed the copies he reserved for his own use with handwritten dedications and special bindings.[20]

All of these authors and many others elected to follow the route to self-financed publication; but some authors who never intended to pay for their own work to be produced ended up having to subsidise it in various ways. This happened to Cardinal Cesare Baronio, who had to take out a loan to support the printing of his ecclesiastical annals at the ailing Vatican Presses in 1593.[21] It occurred also in the case of the naturalists Ippolyto Salviano, who paid for the publication of his book on fishes in the 1550s, and Ulisse Aldrovandi, who eventually found himself in the financially damaging position of managing the publication and distribution of his *Ornithologia* in 1594.[22] The Hebraist Johannes Reuchlin had earlier found himself in the position of having to pay for the printing of his Hebrew grammar in 1506, and suffered from its poor sales. A half of a century later, this state of affairs, in respect of language primers at least, was remedied by the need of the various confessions to train theologians in the skills deemed necessary for the study of the Bible.[23]

Almost as fortunate as the self-payer was the living author or editor who was courted by a publisher, or who successfully stimulated a publisher to take an interest in him as a potential best-seller. The model for such figures was Erasmus, who was able boast in a letter in 1523 that "publishers know that there is scarcely any other name as saleable as mine."[24] He had achieved this happy state of affairs by carefully stage-managing his fame through a whole range of contacts in the book world, and by recruiting his friends to help with sales.[25] His example inspired others to attempt to tread the same path. Andrea Alciato, who chose to begin his publication career in 1515 in Strasbourg, in spite of his strong connections to respected Milanese and Roman publishers, went on to offer his works to Andreas Cratander and others in Basel. He was helped in this by the good offices of his pupil and friend Boniface Amerbach, the son of the famous printer, and ended up with Sebastian Gryphius and the Italian-dominated Compagnie des Libraires in Lyon, where he felt that the whiff of heresy was less strong than in Basel, and the chances of achieving good distribution in Italy better.[26] Girolamo Cardano was another figure who saw the advantages of self-advertisement. In 1538 he chose to append a privilege to a work of mathematics sponsored by a local merchant in which were listed thirty-four of his as yet unpublished writings, thereby alerting the wider community of scholars and publishers to their existence. This worked well for him. It was noticed by the talent scout of a famous publisher in Nuremberg, who eventually produced several of Cardano's writings, notably his mathematical *Ars magna* of 1545. For other works in this list, local Milanese humanists probably put him in contact with Sebastian Gryphius, the foremost scholarly publisher in Lyon, who brought out some of his philosophical and medical works, and later visits to Paris and Basel secured him further publishing outlets.[27]

These and a number of other authors from various disciplines—Joachim Camerarius, Juan Luis Vives, Pierantonio Matthioli, Girolamo Zanchi, Jean Bodin, Theophrastus Paracelsus, Carlo Sigonio, John Case, Cesare Baronio, Justus Lipsius, Matthäus Wesenbeck—constitute the trade books of their day.[28] They were the modern scholars patronised by early modern publishing houses, which were prepared to rank their publications according to the criteria of saleability and public benefit.[29] Not all these authors have survived the test of time equally well. It is pertinent to mention here also the unauthorised reproduction of lecture notes by disciples of popular living and recently deceased professors (a phenomenon most frequently encountered in the discipline of medicine). The former sometimes acquiesced in the practice, and sometimes protested violently against it. Vivian Nutton has suggested that it was a consequence of the reputation of the professor in question and the convenience of print: "once a market for their ideas had been created that could no longer be satisfied by manuscripts, then there was a steady flow of printed lectures, along with summaries and rearrangements of earlier material to fit new needs."[30] The most scrupulous publishers were always careful to approach authors and secure their permission to print their works, but others accepted student notes without the authority of the lecturer.[31]

At the other end of the spectrum from these privileged classes of author lie the legions of "mute inglorious Miltons," or in the terms of the early modern world, mute inglorious Erasmuses or Lipsiuses, whose unread manuscripts were neglected in their own time, and are now (if they survived at all) gathering dust in family archives or libraries. These authors were caught in a double bind even after their death. With very few exceptions, they would be included in the collective biographies of scholars which were becoming common at the end of our period only if they had been published in their lifetimes, and they would be republished after their death only if they had made their way into such collective volumes. Their fate was bemoaned as early as 1545 in his *Bibliotheca universalis* by Conrad Gessner—a man who believed that all such authors deserved publication on the Plinian principle that there is no book so bad that it does not contain something of value.[32]

In the middle ground are to be found the texts with which, together with self-financed publications I have mentioned, scholars of early modern intellectual life now have to deal, in all their diversity. It may be thought that all individual cases of successful publication are contingent on the circumstances which surrounded their printing, and that from them no general rules can be deduced. However, there are a number of common factors—not all of them sufficient or necessary conditions—which justify considering publication from the point of view of the scholarly author and editor. The author would have composed his work, and the editor would have selected one that he desired to edit, with an eye both to the field of scholarship to which he wished it to belong, to the patron who may also have been the possessor of an unpublished manuscript or historical document he intended to publish, and to the constituency of readers whom he imagined would read it, and he would have been aware to a greater or lesser degree of the material issues with which he would have to grapple to see his work into print. His approach to the field of scholarship might be conservative, involving the recovery or consolidation of knowledge, or it might be innovative, opening up new areas of investigation. His readers were not just his patrons, colleagues, or students, but an invisible and incommensurable body to whom the process of publication gave access to his writings. Moreover, the commercial aspects of getting into print had effects which involved compromise, or even collusion, with forces outside the world of scholarship. The author or editor had therefore to be flexible and versatile in his dealings with publishers. Even the great Erasmus had to take on a variety of tasks for them, writing prefaces, suggesting books for publication, proof-reading and undertaking other editorial work for the books of others, promoting his own works, and stifling the publication plans of rivals in the same field.[33]

An aspirant author or editor would have had to be prepared to seek help and support wherever he could find it. Conrad Rittershausen speaks in 1610 of four categories of such producers of texts: "authors, discoverers, retrievers (or revisers), and editors" ("auctores, inventores, recensitores, emendatores").[34] The modern designation "secondary author," being slightly broader than the last three categories mentioned by Rittershausen, is a useful term to evoke here. This figure or institution is the agent who is not the author of a document, but through whom it reaches print, and who may contribute to its appearance in a number of roles: as editor, illustrator, writer of prefatory material, translator, and so on.[35] The "secondary author" in the early modern period might be the editor or translator of a document, or a promoter of scholarship, or the owner of material intended for publication, or the publisher himself, or the patron or institution to whom a work is dedicated. We shall meet all of these figures below; but I shall start with the author himself, and the most obvious decision he had to make, that is, the choice of the language in which he was to write. Then, after a quantitative survey of the Latin book, which is the principal focus of this study, I shall survey the fields of scholarship in which authors elected to work, as they are distinguished by early modern bibliographers. These fields are occupied by authors who can be divided chronologically into four groups: those who wrote in antiquity, those who wrote before the advent of humanism, those born in the age of print who enjoyed publication or republication after their death, and those still living at the time of their publication. I shall sketch the different treatment these groups underwent, before turning to the support they received from their editors, patrons, and promoters, and the uptake of their texts by publishers. This will lead me finally to consider the genres in which authors wrote and their commercial implications. Not all of these factors constitute necessary conditions to achieve publication, but together they go quite a long way to answering the question why certain works were printed, and others not. Much

of the material I shall adduce will support the view I quoted in the introduction that there is nothing new in the world of book production. It will
also seem remarkably familiar to modern scholars in the age of research
assessment exercises, who, like their sixteenth-century counterparts, set
out to place their manuscripts with publishers, raise subsidies if required
to do so, negotiate contracts, and, in the vast majority of cases, contem-
plate ruefully the exiguous financial returns they have obtained.

Languages of Scholarship

I begin with the question of the languages of scholarship. Latin came in
diverse forms in the various faculties, including technically scholastic,
humanist, and purely instrumental (i.e., without concern for nicety of
expression, and consciously employing terms of art).[36] An international
sale entailed the use of Latin, but authors could, and increasingly did,
choose to write in their own vernacular. At the other end of the spectrum
of learned publications lie languages that one might call yet more recon-
dite than Latin. The sixteenth century saw the publication of two very
ambitious polyglot Bibles, both products of the humanist acquisition of
languages.[37] Of these, Hebrew and other Middle Eastern languages deserve separate study, and I shall not try here to chart their histories; but
Greek requires (slightly) less cursory treatment. Venice with its Aldine
press stood in the forefront of printing in that language: a few decades
later, Paris, Louvain, and Basel became important centres of Greek
printing, followed a little later still by Rome.[38] It seems to have been a
matter of national or municipal prestige to have the capacity to print in
a language emblematic of the new learning. The acquisition of Greek
manuscripts and their printing at Paris by a royal printer, together with
the founding of the Collège de France, was an important part of François I's cultural politics of the 1530s. A poem of 1591 celebrating Frankfurt printing singles out the Wechel presses for special praise on account
of their Greek publications. In Augsburg, the Catholic scholar Marcus
Welser was even willing to collaborate with protestant scholars such as
David Hoeschel, Joseph Justus Scaliger, and Janus Gruter in order to
bring Greek and Hebrew publication to his city.[39] But commercial success could not be counted among the attractions of publishing in Greek,
no matter what its prestige. Casaubon's heavily subsidised and eagerly
awaited edition of Polybius was not a commercial success.[40] Throughout
the century, books in Greek proved difficult to sell, and even prominent
publishers evinced unwillingness to take on the task.[41] The Wechel house's

refusal to publish the Greek letters of Joachim Camerarius in 1577 is an indication of how few highly competent Hellenists there were in the republic of letters.[42] Aldus Manutius himself was constrained at the end of his career to adopt a more cautious policy toward publishing in Greek, a language more venerated than mastered by many of those who had passed through the arts course to the higher disciplines of law and medicine. It was considered indispensable only in theology (especially in the confessional age) and humanist studies.[43]

The question of vernaculars, especially Italian, French, German, and Spanish, poses a different problem. There is no doubt that their status rose in the course of the sixteenth century, and that they brought a new class of reader into the sphere of scholarship, broadly defined.[44] The greatest volume of such publications belongs to the German language, and may be associated with three motives which bring about the proliferation of such works: pride in national identity, the downward spread of knowledge to new classes of reader, and the explosion of religious literature of various kinds.[45] Luther's remarkable linguistic achievement as a polemicist and translator was characterised by his followers as providential; but the enormous expansion in German-language publications is not wholly explicable by the "Luther effect," even though that accounted for half of all such publications in 1525 and three-quarters in 1530.[46] Ulrich von Hutten, who wrote his polemical anti-scholastic *Epistolae obscurorum virorum* for a university audience in 1512, felt impelled by 1521 to translate it into German for a broader public.[47] Humanist texts, ancient medicine, Roman law, medieval historical documents, and modern alchemy were all translated into German in the course of the century.[48] In France, the story is somewhat different, but the desire to wrest the monopoly of knowledge away from the universities is clearly indicated by the emergence of professional translators in Lyon and Paris in the late 1540s.[49] At about the same time, this movement was to find an ally in a turbulent academic, Pierre de la Ramée, who pursued an explicit programme of promoting social mobility by making knowledge accessible to all through the use of the vernacular.[50] Other measures such as the Edict of Villers-Cotterêts of 1539, which decreed that all French administrative documents should thereafter be composed in the French language, constituted decisive steps away from the hegemony of Latin.[51] A similar story can be told of other countries: England, for example, or Italy, where some of the most successful entrepreneurial publishers either specialised in Italian-language books including translations of medical and humanist texts, such as the Gioliti presses, or made books in Italian a substantial part of their list, as did the Venice-based Giovanni Battista Ciotti.[52]

For all this, Latin would not yield its place to the vernacular until after the period with which I am dealing, and remained the language of international communication.[53] Near-simultaneous publication in both Latin and the vernacular was not uncommon, to ensure access by the broadest audience. This is what religious writers of all persuasions, such as Philip Melanchthon (for the Lutherans), Peter Canisius (for the Catholics) and Otto Casmann (for the Reformed community), did, but the practice was also followed by authors in other disciplines.[54] The frontier between Latin and vernacular is not therefore that which divides learned from popular: there is an overlap in various disciplines.

The Latin Book

Not all Latin books in this period are works of scholarship; and not all works of scholarship are in Latin. But as a broad generalisation, it is safe to assume that this linguistic field will give a good indication of the numbers of scholarly works which should come under consideration in these chapters. In his very recent work entitled *The Book in the Renaissance*, Andrew Pettegree offered the following figures of printed outputs of scholarly works throughout Europe in the period 1450–1600:

France	35,000
Italy	39,600
Germany	37,600
Switzerland	8,470
The Low Countries	14,021
Subtotal	153,491
Percentage of total	92.48%
England	1,664
Spain	5,040
Scandinavia	793
Eastern Europe	4,980
Subtotal	12,477
Percentage of total	7.52%[55]

Five countries stand out as centres of production: Germany (40 percent), Italy (27 percent), France (20 percent), the Netherlands (7.7 percent), and Switzerland (5.4 percent). Iberia, England, Scandinavia, and eastern Europe account for less that 8 percent of the total between them. This measurement is necessarily crude (Switzerland, for example, was responsible for a high percentage of folio scholarly works, many multi-volumed), but broadly indicative of the prevalent state of affairs. Another such broad indication is afforded by the Latin bibliography produced by George Draut. It is likely that he was commissioned to produce this bibliography. Draut was a Lutheran pastor, although educated at the Universities of Marburg and Herborn, both marked by their philosophical eclecticism and irenic Philippism or crypto-Calvinism.[56] He was a habitué of the book trade, having been employed after graduation by two important Frankfurt printer-publishers, Nicolas Bassée and the Feyerabends, the former of whom was a pioneer in the field of bibliographical finding tools based on the Frankfurt book fair. Draut's two bibliographical compendia, the *Bibliotheca classica* of 1611 and the *Bibliotheca exotica* of 1610 (both revised and expanded in 1625), were compiled from a wider range of materials, including publishers' lists, Frankfurt fair catalogues from 1564 to 1624 (the principal source), and private libraries.

There is a certain amount of back-listing, but this is not complete. The Latin section of 1625 is divided into disciplinary fields, all of which are subdivided alphabetically by subject. There is some cross-referencing. This edition contains an estimated 33,000 entries in all. There are very approximately 11,000 theological books listed, 6,500 on law, 2,500 on medicine, 6,000 on history and geography, 4,000 on philosophy, 2,000 on poetry, and 1,000 on music. The disproportionate number for theology may be accounted for by the needs of the different confessions to supply for their own communities all the categories of books I listed above: Holy Writ; patristic literature; teaching materials for the training of ministers; instructional material for the laity; Church history; devotional literature. The comparison with Andrew Pettegree's estimate given above, which has to be scaled down for the shorter period covered by Draut (the relevant figure is about 66,400), leads me to think that we can take the works listed in the *Bibliotheca classica* to be a reasonable sample of the whole field in the period covered in this study. It does not, of course, tell us about the production of works of scholarship for local markets. I believe that both Paris and Italy (principally Venice) are under-represented in the work, although much of the scholarly output of these centres found its way to the market described by Draut through the process of reprinting or piracy. As a further check on the scale of the field of learned books, we can take the figures provided in Gustav Schwetschke's *Codex nundinarius bisecularis,* which lists

Ὅτε παρθύλος ἅπαν ἅπορον πόρμον. synthig.

BIBLIOTHECA CLASSICA,

Siue

Catalogus Officinalis.

IN QVO SINGVLI

SINGVLARVM FACVL-
TATVM AC PROFESSIONVM LI-
BRI, QVI IN QVAVIS FERE LINGVA EXTANT,

quique intra hominum propemodum memoriam in publicum prodierunt,
secundum artes & disciplinas, earumq; titulos & locos communes,
Autorumque cognomina singulis classibus & rubricis
subnexa, ordine alphabetico re-
censentur:

*Additisq; vbiuis loco, tempore ac forma impressionis, iusta
serie disponuntur.*

Vsque ad annum M. DC XXIV. inclusiuè.

*Accesserunt hincinde præter eas, quas ex Catalogis nundinarum collegimus, haud in-
fimæ notæ materiæ ac rubricæ, non tam ex peculiaribus Officinarum catalogis,
quam etiam alicunde congestæ, quæq; in prima editione non habentur.*

QVINETIAM NORIT EMPTOR,
Bibliothecæ Classicæ, quæ Anno 1611. in lucem prodiit (ne Bibliothecæ istius em-
ptio Emptori sit fraudi) SVPPLEMENTVM, ab Anno 1611. vsque ad Annum 1624 inclusiue, propediem separatim e-
ditum iri.

Accessit Authorum in toto opere dispersorum, iuxta ordinem Alphabeticum
obseruata cognominum ratione dispositio.

Omnia & singula, colligente ac disponente

M. GEORGIO DRAVDIO.

Anno M. DC. XXV.

Francofurti ad Mœnum, impensis Balthasaris Ostern.

3.1 The title page of the second edition of Georg Draut's monumental
Bibliotheca classica, which appeared in 1625.
Courtesy of the Queen's College, Oxford.

the declarations at the Frankfurt fair by year, language, and subject: between 1564 and 1630, his total for all Latin declarations is 40,238.[57] Schwetschke's figures have been strongly challenged as being too low overall, although I believe that his errors of calculation are more likely to fall in the area of vernacular books.[58] Not all of these 40,238 (or more) will count as learned books, but the brute figure is a striking reminder of the scale of the publishing phenomenon which is here being investigated.

Fields of Learning

The precise limits of the learned book in Latin are difficult to set. It goes without saying that not all books in scholars' libraries are scholarly, and their contents cannot be used as a secure criterion.[59] Liturgical books and catechisms, and a fortiori the very extensive devotional literature of the age (which found its way into many scholars' libraries), are not usually considered to belong to this category, but there is a penumbra of theological works, polemical in intent but scholarly in execution, which might have to be included. Not all school and university textbooks can be described as learned, although advanced grammars of various sorts, reference works such as those by Joannes Stobaeus, Dominicus Nanus Mirabellius, Ravisius Textor, Pedro Mexia, and Coelius Rhodiginus, do qualify.[60] So do such works as Scaliger's *Exercitationes,* John Case's various scholastic manuals, Clemens Timpler's *Physica et metaphysica,* the works of Bartholomäus Keckermann and Johann Heinrich Alsted, and the Conimbricenses editions of Aristotle. Not all university disputations and orations were necessarily part of the international learned world, although they were occasionally advertised at the book fairs. Music printed for performance is not a learned genre, but philosophical expositions of music theory, such as Heinrich Glareanus's influential *Dodecachordon* of 1547, clearly are.[61] Natural history and philosophy offers a more difficult set of cas-limites. Are vernacular herbals learned books? They certainly found their way into libraries of serious scholars and collectors of the period, and are usually multilingual; for this reason they could be included here. History written in the vernacular was sometimes described as being aimed at "less cultured and learned readers"; but much very serious historical writing was written only in the vernacular at this time.[62] As for polemical historical writings, its authors and editors might not have been motivated to publish it as an impartial service to the world of scholarship, but their production clearly did serve the republic of letters by supplying readily accessible and largely accurate documents.[63] All these cas-limites merely indicate that we are necessarily dealing with a loose definition of learning, and even of Latinity, insofar as some vernacular texts are conceived of as having an international audience.

One way to approach these fields would be to make the distinction, proposed by John B. Thompson in his *Books in the Digital Age* of 2005, between academic publishing (learned monographs and the like) and higher education publishing (manuals, grammars, and textbooks).[64] To some degree, this is also employed in the late Renaissance. Publishers knew when they were serving a market for textbooks in schools and universities, and when the works they were publishing formed part of the higher intellectual exchanges of the day. Normally only the second category were advertised at the book fairs.[65] There are many marginal cases. Ramus's plain text *Dialectica,* which was produced in prodigious numbers for school use after 1574 by the Wechel presses, was clearly a textbook; Beurhaus's 764-page edition and commentary of the *Dialectica* of 1596, which attempts to reconcile the Ramist approach to logic to that of its main rival in Germany by Philip Melanchthon, was clearly a work of scholarship in that it is a technical discussion of philosophical issues.[66] Between these two versions lie a number of works which could be attributed to either camp. As the liberal arts course (grammar, rhetoric, logic, ethics, mathematics, and natural philosophy) served as a propedeutic to the higher faculties, it provides the best examples of a continuous spectrum running from the unambitious textbook to the intricate inquiry into the principles of its various subject areas. Many of the works produced to serve it were innovative, especially in areas such as rhetoric, mathematics, political thought, and natural philosophy, this last being a broad field in which recent discoveries about the natural world and the cosmos played an important role.[67] In the contexts of the higher faculties of law and medicine, textbooks (which very often took the form of manuals and cheap plain-text editions of the Corpus Juris Civilis, or works by Galen and Hippocrates on the syllabus) are readily distinguishable both from works aimed at practitioners and from advanced commentaries for use in universities. Humanist editions of classical authors also fall into two very distinct categories, which by their formats reflect the different purchasing power of students and their teachers. The Plantin presses' editions in 24mo of classical authors were clearly targeted at purchasers with more modest means than those who might buy their ever more scholarly editions of texts annotated by the best contemporary humanists.[68] Authors who specified formats for their books often did so with one or the other of these readerships in mind; they often specified good-quality paper also, to ensure that no correlation was made between the tawdriness of the presentation and the tawdriness of the content, which could give rise to the sort of attack to which protestant books were subjected by Catholic authors (see below, page 230).[69]

Draut divided his *Bibliotheca classica* into the seven fields that the Book fair catalogues recognised as distinct: theology; law; medicine; history, geography, politics; philosophy (including several of the liberal arts); poetry (including humanism); music. These distinctions were recognised by nearly all scholars and bibliographers in the early modern period. They provide one way of mapping the field of learned books in terms of quantities and dominant subject areas and genres in each field over the course of the period under consideration.[70] A second way is to look at its four constituencies of authors: ancient, medieval, recently dead, and living; a third is to look at paths to publication, and the acts of collaboration these entailed (the self-payer did not need these, but living authors and the editors of dead authors clearly did). I shall look at these three not entirely separable ways in turn, concentrating on the salient points, without attempting a systematic survey of each, which is beyond the scope of this study.

Theology

The fact that theology dominated the numbers of titles declared at the book fairs should not surprise us. By 1625, writers were supplying for each of the major confessions the full array of works they needed to establish and maintain their identity. They ranged from approved versions of the Bible, of which there had been several very ambitious editions in the course of the sixteenth century, to commentaries on its books, the works of Church Fathers edited by a member of the relevant confession, ecclesiastical history, catechisms, church ordinances, pastoral literature, training manuals for ministers and clergy, not to speak of polemic.[71] Not all of these genres belong to the field of learning. Those that indisputably do, being part of the discipline of theology as traditionally understood, were not unaffected by the pressure to validate a given confession, as we have seen in the previous chapter. If we take the confessionalisation of the field of theology into account, we may have to revise our assumption that theology is in fact the area in which the greatest quantity of books appeared. If devotional literature is excluded from the field, and the remnant is divided by three to take account of the specific constituencies of works destined for the three main denominations, the resultant figure may not be very different from the quantities of books appearing in law and medicine.

From the earliest phase of the age of print, theological works were an important component of the field of publications. Great editions of the Church Fathers were produced by Erasmus and his contemporaries, and these were succeeded in the second half of the century by a further set of such editions, whose republication was made possible by a range of editor-promoters from the various confessions. These enjoyed financial support from political and religious institutions, for reasons of both national scholarly prestige (in the case of the royal printing house in Paris, where the *Bibliothecae sanctorum patrum,* edited by Margarin de la Bigne, began appearing in 1589, published by the royal-sponsored Compagnie du Navire) or confessional ideology.[72] With them were published a number of medieval theologians, including Aquinas (not surprisingly, given the confirmation of his status at the Council of Trent and his adoption by the Society of Jesus), Duns Scotus (a Franciscan counterblast to Thomism), and the fifteenth-century bishop of Avila, Alphonsus Tostatus, whose thirty-part folio edition of 1596, edited by Ranierus Bovisius and dedicated to Philip II of Spain, cost a considerable sum.[73] It seems that another edition had been planned by Charles V in 1547: this indicates the element of national prestige which might enter into the decision to publish a given author.[74] Other medieval theologians also clearly benefited from the need for new Counter-Reformation institutions and those founded by protestants to possess copies of them. Nicholas of Lyra's *Postillae* (much respected because of the author's knowledge of Hebrew) appeared in eight editions between 1471 and 1520, which must have saturated the market of the time. It was printed again in 1545 at Lyon, and at Venice in 1588. Hugo of Saint Victor, whose commentaries were still held in high regard for their methodology, had two incomplete editions in Paris, in 1506 and 1520. Thereafter his *Opera omnia* appears in Venice in 1588, and Mainz in 1617. There are likely to be other theologians who manifest the same pattern of publication.

The earliest generation of reformers tended to be published in the first instance by their local presses.[75] They were, as a group, very knowledgeable about book production and distribution, and although most did not profit from their publications, they helped make the fortunes of publishers who acted for them in Wittenberg, Strasbourg, Zürich, and

Geneva.[76] After 1560 the confessionalisation of Europe led to the emergence in various centres of printer-publishers with strong allegiances to one or another confession, which multiplied the number of places in which Calvin, or Luther, or their disciples were printed. The experience I have already described of Melchior Goldast at Frankfurt, which before 1560 was not a place in which major reformers were taken up by publishers, confirms this. The commitment of various printing centres to religious publication changed over the period. It declined, for example, in Geneva, as publishers turned to the lucrative market of unauthorised publication of classical texts and what one might term modern masters.[77] It rose, on the other hand, in Paris, when the generation of humanist printer-publishers began to disappear around the turn of the seventeenth century and members of religious orders became active as editors of patristic literature. Indeed, the Church Fathers were edited by scholars of all denominations from all over Europe in the period after 1560.[78] This is an area where motivation must be distinguished from effect. The desire to show that a given confession had the support of the early Church led sometimes to partial (i.e., biased) publication, but the effect was to create a pool of commentary and contextual erudition in which editors of all religious persuasions could, and did, fish.[79]

Law

I pass to the somewhat neglected case of law.[80] From the evidence of student numbers, the faculties of law in continental Europe were much larger than those of medicine (and their professors were better paid, and earned more from their other occupations as counsellors and practitioners), facts that would naturally lead one to suppose that there would be a concomitantly larger market for books.[81] This is indeed so, but medical and natural-historical books (especially those concerned with the new investigations into anatomy, botany, and cosmology) have been far more widely studied by modern historians of the book and of intellectual life. This may be explained in large measure both by the professional habits of early modern Europe and by the preoccupations of modern historians. On the one hand, early modern medical doctors and natural philosophers seem to have been disproportionately more active in producing books than their legal counterparts. On the other, the interest in accounts of new discoveries and their impact on intellectual life, and the belief that the origins of modern science can be found in early modern medicine and natural philosophy, has made these more attractive subjects than others to modern historians, for whom progress in science and the advent of enlightenment have been abiding preoccupations. A similar affinity with the past can be seen to be at work in other disciplines. The strong and abiding tradition in classical studies from the fifteenth century onward has created a bridge between the early humanists and their philological and literary successors, and history has had an equally perennial following. But law does not manifest the same continuity. There was a slow decline in the influence of both Roman law and canon law after 1600. The decline of the former was hastened by the recovery in various European contexts of customary law together with the development of a new conception of jurisprudence and natural law, with strong links to national and international politics and political thought. The decline of canon law can be attributed to its smaller zone of application in a confessionalised Europe.[82] A symptom of this decline is found in the activity of reprint specialists of the mid-seventeenth century, such as the Lyon publishing house of Huguetan and Ravaud, who engaged in lavish new editions of many deceased medical figures, but almost no jurists.[83] Even though ancient law did have a Renaissance—seen principally in the recovery by humanist lawyers of the Greek passages in the Corpus Juris Civilis, and the interest in pre-Tribonian jurists—this did not transform the discipline in the way that other disciplines, such as medicine and natural philosophy, were transformed.[84] Nor were customary law and Germanic law—areas much investigated in our period—included in the syllabuses of most law faculties in France, Spain, Italy, and the Empire.

This having been said, the publication figures show that more than twice as many law books as medical books were advertised at the book fairs up to 1620, and a cursory glance at Draut indicates that many of these publications were hefty folios. Martin Lowry has shown how profitable the early law book market in Venice was, and the comprehensive survey of sixteenth-century Lyon publication by Henri-Louis Baudrier indicates that the richest members of the Compagnie des Libraires specialised in the provision of the (hefty) standard texts both for university teachers and professional lawyers.[85] The consultations of practitioners occurred in the studies where, in order to impress their clients, they displayed their imposing reference books (called "libri da banco" by Armando Petrucci) as visible attestations of their learning and competence.[86] In this they were unlike their professional colleagues the physicians, whose consultations took place both in their houses and at the bedside of their patients. If they wanted to transport a manual of practical medicine with them, it had to be in a small format. By the 1500s, books of this size ("libri da bisaccia, libretti da mano") began to be produced for them and for their students.[87]

As well as standard texts and their glosses (initially seen in Lyon as two distinct domains and published by two different consortia: see below, page 111), entrepreneurial publishers saw to it that the monuments of medieval jurisprudence in various genres (criminal law, *consilia* and *decisiones*, specialist books on evidence and interpretation) remained in print. They actively pursued living authors for their writings, especially in the area of practical law, and set about printing them in their own market zones (or reprinting them if they had first been published elsewhere). The authors came from all over Europe: in one of the bibliographical surveys of law published in 1579, 45 of the living jurists in the Roman tradition came from France, 40 from Germany, 33 from Italy, and 13 from Iberia; indeed, law was one of the few areas in which Iberian scholars enjoyed a European reputation throughout the century.[88] To take but one example, the Spanish jurist Antonio Gomez, one can follow the path of his *Commentariorum variarumque resolutionum iuris civilis tomi tres* from Salamanca, where they were published in 1562–1563 and again in 1589, to Venice (editions in 1572, 1575, and 1586), Frankfurt (1572, 1584, 1596, 1597, 1602 [reissued 1607], 1616), Lyon (1585 and 1609), Antwerp (1603 and 1634), and Geneva (1615, 1622, and 1631). Of all the major scholarly printing centres, Venice, Frankfurt, Cologne, and Lyon were the most prolific producers (and pirates) of law books, although Florence (with an edition of its unique copy of the Pandects in 1553), Paris, Basel, and Antwerp also entered the field at various moments.[89] The strength of France and Germany in this field was recognised in Florence in 1547, where law books from those countries were alone exempted from the ban on book importing imposed to protect the interests of the newly appointed grand-ducal publisher-bookseller Lorenzo Torrentino.[90] It is pertinent to mention at this point the two most extensive legal miscellanies published in the course of the century. The eighteen-volume *Tractatus ex variis iuris interpretibus* was financed by the affluent Compagnie des Libraires of Lyon in 1549. It was designed to be a comprehensive reference book of standard works on civil and canon law, containing 458 separate works by over 200 prominent medieval and Renaissance authors from all over Europe, arranged by subject. It is printed in black letter, which was the traditional font for law books from Lyon but at that date was beginning to look somewhat old-fashioned. The miscellany was succeeded in 1584–1586 by the much expanded *Tractatus universi iuris,* which appeared "under the direction and auspices" of Pope Gregory XIII (the phrase may well indicate a financial subsidy). Its twenty-five volumes were published by the Venetian publisher and bookseller Francesco Ziletti.[91] It contains 754 titles by 362 authors, covering the same ground as the Lyon miscellany of 1549 and including jurists who rose to prominence after 1549 in the area of criminal law, such as Joost de Damhoudere. At the same time, it excluded authors whose name appeared on the Roman Indexes of 1559 and 1564, such as Johannes Oldendorp.[92] Both miscellanies achieved very wide diffusion, even in England, where pontifical canon law was no longer in force, and the innovative elements of civil law concerning evidence and criminal law had no local application. As well as in the Bodleian and the Cambridge University Library, copies are found in five Oxford and three Cambridge colleges.[93]

Judging by the records of the Holy Roman Empire's Chancery, it seems that publishers sought to protect their law books more than other disciplines. Certain publishers in Germany were very heavily specialised in law: the Feyerabend house, Nicolas Bassée, and Zacharias Palthen, who was himself a doctor of law.[94] When Johann Theobald Schönwetter set out on his career as a speculative publisher in 1599, his first four years of publishing fell overwhelmingly in the area of legal studies, and he even surprised one of his authors by the eagerness he displayed to publish more of his works.[95] Publishers of his kind used their position in Frankfurt to reprint without authorisation books first produced in Italy and France, as a number of court cases and complaints to the Imperial Chancery attest. The Lyon publisher Antoine de Harsy addressed a formal grievance in 1586 to the Frankfurt City Council, in which he bitterly claims that "nothing good [in law] comes out of Italy, France or elsewhere but that Bassée or another [Frankfurt printer] reprints it on bad [i.e., cheap] paper and then protects it with a local [i.e., Imperial] licence."[96] This led the Council to act in 1588 by issuing a general ordinance against such unauthorised (although not illegal) printing, which was, however, wholly ineffective.

It is not very surprising that living lawyers of international repute (then, but not now) such as Antonio Gomez, Jacopo Menochio, Prosper Farinacci, and Martin Azpilcueta were energetically competed for by publishers.[97] Thanks to the work of Donald Kelley on historical method rather than positive law, the names of their French contemporaries—Jacques Cujas, Charles Du Moulin, and Hugues Doneau—are better known to us, but they were as celebrated as their French counterparts

in their lifetime.[98] Moreover, the scorn for fifteenth-century philosophers expressed by the Italian humanist Gaudenzio Merula, which dis-
couraged any publisher from reissuing them in the 1540s, did not extend to jurists, nor indeed to physicians.[99] Publishers were aware of the
market for such authors, and sought to protect their investment in them
with privileges.[100] The following privilege sought from the king of
France in 1578 by Filippo Tinghi will, I suspect, figure names not
widely known to modern scholars of early modern intellectual life:

> Toutes les oeuvres de Albericus de Rosate, toutes les lectures et conseilz
> d'Alciat, toutes les oeuvres de Bartole, toutes les oeuvres de Balde, toutes
> les oeuvres de Petrus Paulus Parisius, Consilia Bertrandi, Consilia Cornei,
> toutes les oeuvres de Philipus Decius, toutes les oeuvres de Bartholomeus
> Socinus, toutes les oeuvres de Marianus Socinus, Consilia Barba[t]iae, le
> Cours civil avec les glosses, le Cours canon avec les glosses, Christophorus
> Portius super Instituta, les oeuvres de Ludovicus Romanus, les oeuvres de
> Jason Maynus, Consilia Ruyni, toutes les oeuvres de R[i]m[in]aldus,
> toutes les oeuvres de Turrecremata, toutes les oeuvres de Felin, toutes les
> oeuvres de Joannes Faber, les oeuvres de Dominicus de Sancto Geminiano,
> les oeuvres de Henricus Brichus, les oeuvres de Hippolytus de Marsiliis,
> les oeuvres de Joannes de Imola, les oeuvres de Lucus de Pena, les oeuvres
> de Mathaeus de Afflictis, les oeuvres de Rippa, toutes les oeuvres de Paulus
> de Castro, les oeuvres de Bartachinus, les oeuvres de Salicel, les oeuvres de
> Hostiensis, les oeuvres de Azo, les oeuvres de Zabarelle, le grand volume
> des Répetitions de divers autheurs, le grand volume des Grandz traictés
> de divers autheurs, les oeuvres de Cynus, la grande glosse ordinaire, Singu-
> larium omnium doctorum, toutes les oeuvres de Julius Clarus.

If one takes the most prolific period of writing of these figures as far as
this can be ascertained, this reveals that eighteen of these figures are
pre-sixteenth century, and that of those active in the later period, only
two (Alciato and Riminaldus) are indisputably humanist lawyers.[101]
The list includes both civilians and canonists. All were important as
authors of practical law or commentators on the canonical texts of the
law, and continued to exercise influence in the period we are considering. Their fortunes declined dramatically in the first decade of the
Thirty Years' War: when Peter Kopf went bankrupt in 1633, the majority of the books held in his warehouse were legal tomes.[102]

Medicine and Natural Philosophy

The question of language arises in the discipline of medicine more than
in others.[103] To one side of the medical corpus in Latin lies the revival

and republication of ancient Greek medicine in the original language, which might suggest that physicians, like theologians and humanists, were equipped to deal with such texts, but recent scholars such as Vivian Nutton and Frank Hieronymus have cast doubt on this, and have argued that Latin remained the preferred language of scholarly medical exchange. This does not mean, however, that physicians did not buy Greek editions for the purpose of a personal display of erudition.[104] On the other side, there is a wide and rich field of vernacular publication in various genres, most concerned with self-help or with surgery, an area traditionally associated with non-Latinate practitioners. In some cases these works were assimilated by the learned profession and enjoyed translation into Latin (not only surgical treatises and secrets literature, but also Theophrastus Paracelsus and his disciples in the field of chemical medicine).[105] Like law, medicine was published in a range of genres: plain texts for the use of students, lecture notes and other pedagogical materials, commentaries, monographs, *observationes, consilia,* letter collections, and other guides to practice written both by medieval and contemporary doctors, as well as extensive editions of the classic texts of ancient physicians.[106] New areas such as anatomy and botany developed very fast after the 1540s. As with law, Venice and Lyon dominated the early years of medical publication, but Paris and Basel soon became important rivals. By the middle of the century, German centres also began to engage in extensive publication in this area. Unlike law, the dominant format is not folio but octavo, for reasons I have indicated above (pages 64–65).[107]

The sixteenth century falls into three meaningful periods: first, the period before 1525, in which year the Aldine Galen in Greek was published. The second period runs from 1525 to 1565, during which Galen, Hippocrates, and other texts from antiquity were translated into Latin. In the same period, the main genres of the medical book market emerged and became stable; there were new trends in publication, including studies of new diseases, divination, astrology, and alchemy; and methods of diffusion and protection of books were regularised. In the third period from 1565, the most important scholarly apparatus of medicine— Latin translations of Galen and Hippocrates, post-Dioscoridean herbals, Brasavola's index to Galen, and other similar intellectual tools—were generally available. So also were better editions of the prominent Arab authors and systematisers; these continued to be read, in spite of widespread criticism of them. This rough division fits other events quite well. These include the emergence of Paracelsianism around 1565, through the efforts of Adam von Bodenstein and others, who saw to the publication in a decade of some eighty books of Paracelsus's writings, and the dominance of a number of entrepreneurial humanist printer-publishers specialising in medical literature.[108] The end of the third period is marked in 1625 by the publication of the ninth and last Giunti edition of Galen's complete works in Latin, which had first appeared in 1541–1542. Between 1590 and 1625, as a sign of the consolidation of the subject, at least three specialist bibliographies of medical writing were published, which owed much to the pioneering work of general bibliography undertaken by Conrad Gessner and his successors.[109]

By 1600 the learned medical book was international rather than local in character and widely distributed. Iberian (mainly Spanish) authors whose local editions were not available elsewhere in Europe were reprinted and distributed through Venice and other centres, and English and eastern European physicians were able to find publishers through their contacts with the Wechel presses in Frankfurt and Hanau. Even if there seems to be little direct evidence of the presence of northern medical authors in Italian libraries at this time because of the activities of the Inquisition, there is enough allusion to works by such authors for it to be possible to presuppose that the rule applied in other academic spheres under strict Catholic regimes—the citation of a banned author's ideas without naming him—applied here also.[110] The market was omnivorous, consuming ancient and medieval medicine with the same appetite as new discoveries, new theories, and new syntheses, and local productions as much as foreign ones. Medicine at this time was related to the publications in natural philosophy, geography, and mathematics in various ways, notably in their vulgarisation of empirical discoveries, their presentation in both the vernacular and Latin, and their use of diagrams and illustrations.[111]

History, Geography, and Politics

History and geography belong to a regime of publication rather different from that of the higher faculties and humanism. They were was not university disciplines, and history, in the age of confessions, was very often polemical in nature and ideologically charged, as we have seen. The study of the past of a nation or city and its physical geography often went together. As well as the general surveys of the ancient world by Ptolemy and Pomponius Mela, there were numerous studies of individual towns, provinces, and nations.[112] From early in the century, historical and regional studies had attracted those who through investigation of the past of their nations wanted to raise the status of France and Germany especially vis-à-vis Italy. It thus often served local loyalties ("baroque ancestor-worship," as one historian has put it), and was involved in discussions of both the temporal power of the Papacy and the religious purity of various national traditions, in England, France, and elsewhere.[113] It was presented in two distinct genres: one that offered documents, and gave their historical and archival context; the other written by humanists and others that dealt with contemporary or near-contemporary history. The new genre of political writing may be linked to these accounts of recent events; it arises also from the commentary tradition on ancient texts on the issue of government by Plato, Aristotle, and others. Such works appeared in both Latin and the vernacular, and could achieve best-seller status through notoriety (as did Niccolò Machiavelli) or good marketing (as in the case of John Case, Jean Bodin, Pierre Grégoire, Justus Lipsius, and Giovanni Botero).[114] Sixteenth-century historians of modern times often copied what was taken to be the practice of the ancient world in eschewing the use of justificatory data and footnotes.[115] The prime example of the latter are the *Historiae* of Jacques-Auguste de Thou, which we have met already. In the former camp fall the various works of Johann Carion, Philip Melanchthon, and Caspar Peucer.[116] Some of the most ambitious publications of this period were contributions to this field of knowledge, seen not only in the series of regional medieval documents ("rerum britannicarum [hungaricarum, suevicarum, germanicarum ...] scriptores") published by the Wechel presses and others, printed in folio, but also in the *Centuries* of Magdeburg (dealing with the period up to the fourteenth century) and its Catholic ripostes, notably the *Annals* of Baronio (covering the period up to 1194).[117] The *Centuries* were a marked commercial success for their publisher Johannes Oporinus. From the rush to obtain licences to print Baronio, it can be assumed that his *Annals* too were lucrative for publishers, even if not for the Vatican Presses where they started their life.[118]

Humanism and the Liberal Arts

Humanists filled various roles in early modern society, as orators, preachers, editors of learned works, producers of commonplace books, pedagogues, and correctors in publishing houses. We are concerned here with their activities as scholars, principally in the field of the recovery and presentation of literary and historical monuments (including early Church history). A great deal of the printing of humanist texts in the sixteenth century was not strictly scholarly: it was intended for school use (hence their designation as "libri scholastici"), and took the form very often of plain texts published in small formats. The pioneer of these editions was Aldus Manutius, with his italic publications of the early years of the century. Their appeal was such that they were immediately imitated.[119] Modern scholarship has concentrated on two issues relating to humanist publication: the production of *editiones principes* of classical authors, and textual criticism. The first editions involved Greek publication, and were often linked to projects to enhance national or municipal prestige. As we shall see, humanist textual criticism was one of the genres in which commerce played a part as well as learning through the process of accumulating commentary and annotations into new editions. One good effect of this was that the work of the earlier generations of humanists—Guillaume Budé, Angelo Poliziano, Beatus Rhenanus, and their colleagues—continued to be published. I shall examine one exemplary case of repeated publication—Eusebius—below (pages 84–91).[120] Nearly all these editions were preceded by a preface by the editor of the text: these have been collected, and can be consulted in the volume produced by Beriah Botfield in 1861.[121] They not only reveal the range of dedicatees from fellow humanists to dignitaries of Church and State, but also the expression of the pious ambitions of the editors as servants of the world of scholarship.

The second, related, issue concerns the rise of *ars critica* in its technical philological sense. A great deal of work was done in the course of the early modern period on the discovery of manuscripts in locations all across Europe, which led to the collocation of textual variants and the reading of difficult passages in manuscripts, and the arts of critical conjecture.[122] The works in this tradition were clearly an important component of the intellectual universe of their day.[123] In this regard the figure of Henri II Estienne stands out, being a lexicographer, a distinguished scholar in both Greek literature and the New Testament, and a publisher. He relied so much on his patron's material support in his ventures that he described himself on some title pages as "illustri viri Huldrichi Fuggeri typographus."

Another aspect of humanist scholarship which reaches beyond the textbook is the use of Greek or non-Latin ancient languages to elucidate texts in various faculties. The editions of the Greek Fathers were undertaken by distinguished humanists, as was the restitution of Greek passages to the Corpus Juris Civilis by Angelo Poliziano, Guillaume Budé, Andrea Alciato, and Jacques Cujas, and the edition of Galen's rediscovered treatises by the physician Giambattista da Monte and others.[124] In this sense also, the Jesuit Coimbra commentaries of the relevant works of Aristotle are examples of humanist publication destined as much for the scholar's library as for the Colleges of the Society of Jesus. The field of the liberal arts not only supplied students in universities with their manuals and plain texts, but also extended the limits of the scholarly world into new investigations of all aspects of nature, the cosmos, and the world of human institutions. In the former category, the publishing success of the century is Aristotle. This is a not surprising fact in view of his dominant position in university courses, but the scale of his diffusion—whether in Greek or Latin or both, and whether the whole works or individual works with commentaries—is awe-inspiring. Plato, in contrast, enjoys very few editions indeed.[125] Of classical authors, only Cicero approaches the success of the Stagyrite.[126] In other parts of the arts course, many of the works which succeeded best in terms of dissemination and repeated publication fall into the innovative, often controversial, areas linked to natural philosophy. Unlike the monuments of medieval practical law and medicine, their fortunes have been widely investigated and discussed, and I do not need to dwell on them here.[127]

Authors (Living and Dead), Editors, and Promoters

I now move from the fields of scholarship to the four categories of authors who wrote in them: the living, the recently dead, those from antiquity, and those from the middle ages. In the first category, the sixteenth century saw the emergence of professional authors (sometimes known as "poligrafi"): but those who lived from their pen did so largely in the various vernaculars.[128] The Ingolstadt professor of logic and theology Johannes Eck was an early exception in the world of scholarship: he invested in his own textbooks, and expected an eightfold return on the money he put in.[129] But even a writer such as Girolamo Cardano, who produced best-selling writings, was constrained to remain in employment as a professor of medicine despite his bragging about the potential profit from his various publications.[130] Erasmus certainly managed to live from his pen, and was very aware of the commercial value of his name, as I have indicated above (pages 50–51). After him, other profitable living authors emerged, and were nurtured by their publishers. Johannes

Oporinus of Basel, for example, named Joachim Camerarius, Joannes Rivius, and Juan Luis Vives in this category.[131] Another example of a much-published author is the botanist Pierantonio Matthioli, who recorded in the 1560s that 32,000 copies of his commentary on Dioscorides had been sold.[132] Later, Justus Lipsius clearly attained the status of best-seller. One sign of this was the immediate unauthorised reprinting of his works in Frankfurt after his publisher Plantin's death (and the automatic lapse of his privilege) by the shrewdest of book pirates, Johann Wechel.[133] A related indication of best-seller status is the application for privileges by publishers to protect their prized authors in the various chanceries of Europe.[134]

In Chapter 2, it became apparent how useful promoters (one kind of "secondary author") were to living authors (and those who had recently died) in helping them to make their way into print and reach a wider public.[135] For authors from the ancient and medieval worlds, they were a sine qua non. Both Erasmus and Conrad Gessner complained that in their day too many live authors were being published, and that important deceased writers were being neglected. They had in mind not only the unpublished classical texts which were the quarry of the humanist, but also the texts of late antiquity, including the patristics (both Greek and Latin fathers) restored to their original purity, as well as judiciously chosen products of the recent medieval past.[136] When Gabriel Naudé came to write his guide to establishing libraries in the 1620s, he made a particular point of recommending the acquisition of medieval authors in all disciplines.[137] Publishers also acted on their own behalf as promoters of works of dead authors, and employed scouts to locate unpublished materials from the ancient and medieval worlds in libraries and private collections.[138] I have already referred to the competition to publish late medieval legal practitioners. A catalogue of famous dead and living jurists first published in 1579 lists those who were not alive in various periods from 1150 to 1573; the majority of those printed by speculative sixteenth-century publishers fall in the period 1400–1500.[139] In medicine and natural philosophy, dead authors who were promoted and published include medieval mathematicians and authors of *practica* such as Arnau de Vilanova.[140]

The text of a dead author was rarely issued as a plain text, except in cases where they were on school or university curricula, and could be sold cheaply in bulk. Most dead authors had one or more editors who added introductions, or notes, or both. There were rich or well-placed humanists— another category of "secondary author"—active in locating and bringing together manuscripts worthy of publication, supporting those around them in their publishing ventures, or just encouraging fellow scholars to undertake the task of preparing copy.[141] Such a person in the earlier part of the century was the Augsburg jurist Konrad Peutinger, whose correspondence reveals his promotion of publication projects of texts from ancient texts to medieval chronicles.[142] A second figure of this kind was Theodor Zwinger, himself an author of prodigiously extensive projects such as the *Theatrum vitae humanae* (the first edition of which appeared in 1565), but the promoter as well of innovative anti-Aristotelian philosophy in his home town of Basel.[143] The Heidelberg circle, and Goldast himself, are further examples of promoters from the confessional age. A rather different example is afforded by Rembert Dodoens, who in republishing Antonio Benivieni, the writer of medical case histories who died in Florence in the early years of the century, was consciously providing himself with an intellectual genealogy, as Erasmus himself had done at the beginning of his career by celebrating his Dutch scholarly forebears in the figure of the dialectician Rudolph Agricola.[144] All these figures demonstrate the value of contacts in the trade, and their activities go some way to answering the question why some authors were published and others not.

The fourth group of dead authors I identified were those who had been born in the age of print, and whose works were produced after their death by disciples and admirers, notably in the higher disciplines of law and medicine. In the former of these disciplines, a good example of successful reprinting is provided by the substantial commentary on Justinian's *Institutes* written by the Wittenberg professor Johann Schneidewein (1519–1568), which appeared shortly after his death in Strasbourg, in 1571, edited by his pupil Matthäus Wesenbeck, a distinguished lawyer and later a best-seller in his own right. In 1592 a second commentator, Pieter Cornelis van Brederode, added his notes to those of Wesenbeck, as did a third (Denis Godefroy) in 1594. Between 1571 and 1626 Schneidewein's commentary was printed no less than eleven times in Strasbourg, eight times in Venice between 1603 and 1625 (hidden behind his Greek sobriquet Oinotomos, because Schneidewein was a prohibited author in the Roman Index), three times in Geneva, and twice in Lyon. In 1578, Schneidewein's heirs obtained an Imperial privilege for his works, which was renewed for a further ten years in 1587, but this did not prevent them from being widely produced by the speculative publishers of Venice, Geneva, and Lyon.[145] In medicine, there are similar examples. Paduan professors were given an especially high profile through this form of publication, even during their lifetime, both at home and abroad.[146] The most-published recently dead physicians include the Paduan professor Giambattista da Monte, whom no less than four colleagues from various parts of Europe promoted, Girolamo Cardano (from his manuscripts rather than his lecture notes), and, most notably, Theophrastus Paracelsus, who was translated into Latin by a trio of promoters and published for the Catholic market at the expense of Bishop Hosius of Cologne, and for the protestant market by the Basel publisher Conrad von Waldkirch.[147] When Paracelsus was succeeded by Paracelsianism, a new range of authors emerged: Jean Béguin, Oswald Croll, and Johannes Tanckius among them.[148] The interest in radical new philosophical approaches led in turn to the publication of original medieval thinkers such as Raymond Lull.[149]

These examples show that by the latter part of the sixteenth century, authors from earlier in the century as well as humanists such as Erasmus and Melanchthon had become in turn the subject of promotion in view of republication, in competition with many new authors striving to be published. The mixed fortunes of revered scholars from the earlier part of the century reveal both the contingent nature of their being found a publisher and the confessional struggles to which they might fall victim. Some recently deceased scholars who were very widely published in their day fell unaccountably out of sight (Josse Clichtove and Jacques Lefèvre d'Etaples are two of these).[150] Others were overlooked or shunned for more obvious reasons. The promulgation of the Roman and other indexes after the 1550s had a noted effect on the fortunes of Erasmus in Catholic lands. After the *Opera omnia* published by Froben in 1540, his unpopularity with Lutherans and strict Calvinists meant that he had to wait until 1703–1706 for a complete edition.[151] His very popular works such as the *Adages* continued to be published after his death in various forms: as an epitome, and in a complete version with a variety of additional commentaries and textual apparatus. After Erasmus's appearance on the Index, an expurgated edition appeared in Italy without the name of the author *(Adagia quaecumque ad hunc diem exierunt)*.

Catholic presses in Cologne also reprinted the full text and the epitome, but declined to suppress Erasmus's name. It is clear that up to 1617, at least, he preserved his status as best-selling author.[152] The Formula of Concord, which settled the disputes in the Lutheran Church in 1577, led to the more flexible figure of Philip Melanchthon becoming a casualty of Lutheran hardliners. His philosophical and humanist *Opera* appeared in 1540, in the wake of those of Erasmus; but his theological

ADAGIA
QVAECVMQVE
AD HANC DIEM
EXIERVNT,

PAVLLI MANNVCCII STVDIO, ATQVE INDVSTRIA,
Doctiſſimorum Theologorum conſilio, atque ope, (ex præſcripto Sacroſancti
Concilij Tridentini, GREGORIO XIII. Pont. Max. auſpice) ab omnibus
mendis vindicata, quæ pium, & veritatis Catholicæ ſtudioſum Lectorem
poterant offendere :

SVBLATIS FALSIS INTERPRETATIONIBVS,
& nonnullis, quæ nihil ad rem pertinebant, longis, inanibusq́, digreſſionibus.

Cum plurimis, ac locupletiſſimis Indicibus.

NVNC VERO IN HAC POSTREMA EDITIONE,
ab innumeris erroribus repurgata, & veræ lectioni reſtitutæ.

VENETIIS, MDLXXXV.
Ex Vnitorum Societate.

3.2 The title page of Paulus Manutius's expurgated edition of Erasmus's
Adages, which first appeared in 1575, omitting the name of the author-compiler,
as was required by the Roman Index of forbidden books.
Courtesy of Wadham College, Oxford.

Opera in four volumes, which appeared in 1562–1564 and were partially reprinted in the late 1570s, had to be reissued with new title pages in 1601, and seem even then to have had more success abroad than in Germany.[153] In other cases, even competition between publishers with a view to achieving a monopoly did not bring about a complete republication. This was the case of the French polymath Petrus Ramus, over whose works there was a fierce competition in the 1570s between Pietro Perna of Basel and André Wechel of Frankfurt but which did not lead to a collected works being produced by either publisher.[154] These successes and failures reveal the contingent nature of publishing in this period, and the importance of both active promoters and specific local conditions of publication in ensuring new editions of the works of deceased sixteenth-century scholars.

Steps to Publication: Patrons

I pass now to the authors and editors of documents in these various fields of scholarship, and their path to publication. For those who did not have the necessary means to pay for their books to be published, finance had to be found, even for the initial outlay—the creation of a fair copy of their work from which a compositor could work, and in many cases the cost of paper, which had to be met in advance.[155] Aspirant authors enlisted the unpaid help of their students and friends to fulfil a number of necessary functions, from copyists and correctors to intermediaries and postal agents.[156] Support could come from a patron, or a publisher who agreed to take on the commercial risk of printing himself, with or without a subsidy. The Antwerp publisher Christophe Plantin (whom we could classify as a "secondary author" in cases where he took on a publication) wrote to an aspiring author that he accepted about half of the proposals sent to him in this way, which is probably not an untypical number.[157] The need to attract a patron (another version of the "secondary author") could of course influence certain views an author expressed in a given work, but it is now generally agreed that such influence was not as corrosive to truth, sincerity, and the free expression of opinion as once was thought, since authors were careful to approach a patron likely to have some sympathy for their particular project. Patrons who were not themselves printers do not seem very often to have intervened in the processes of publication, where the agents were in nearly all cases either the publisher or the author or both.[158] Even so, these figures, if grandees, were often difficult to deal with. Permission to dedicate a book to them had in some cases to be secured in advance, and this did not always produce the desired financial support; in many cases the subsidy came, if at all, after the whole process of printing had been completed.[159] It was not always the payment that was most important to the author, but rather other favours which were in the gift of a patron, principally preferment of one kind or another. We have seen that university professors were not paid well enough wholly to finance their own publications; university printers did not offer subsidies (unless they received these from the local ruler), and restricted their activities in the main to short commissioned *pièces de circonstance* which they sold locally.[160] Clergy sometimes enjoyed the support of the local bishop or a pious layman, as did Francisco Suarez, Benito Arias Montano, and the editors of the Paris Chrysostom. Baronio's *Martyrologium Romanum* (but not his *Annals*) was also paid for by Church authorities.[161]

On some occasions the publisher himself sought a patron for a work on behalf of the author. It would appear, for example, that Johann Wechel persuaded Heinrich Rantzau to pay for the printing of the French jurist Barnabé Brisson's *De formulis* of 1593.[162] If the publisher did not specify a source of financial support on the title page, it is reasonable to infer that this was either found elsewhere or supplied speculatively by him. In such a case, one might expect a fairly large number of books to be dedicated by their authors to their publishers, but although this occurs, it is not widespread, presumably because of the conviction we have already encountered among many authors that publishers were venal and mean.[163] As a result, authors often felt free to choose other dedicatees. It is not unusual to find the author's home town council named in this role, no doubt in the expectation of financial support or favours of some kind. Colleagues and friends from the republic of letters were frequently chosen, often with reference to the gift culture which was said to characterise learned exchanges, to which I shall return in a later chapter. They sometimes reciprocated by supplying laudatory verses and epigrams to be included in the preliminaries of the book, for which they could be solicited in advance.[164]

Authors and Publishers: Selection and Remuneration

An author might have various reasons for choosing a given publisher, his prestige, his convenient proximity, or his location in a major printing centre being the most obvious of these. That there was benefit to be had from association with publishers of high standing was very clear. In 1595, for example, the Prince Bishop of Würzburg instructed his agent, the mathematician Adriaan van Roomen, who was a professor in the local university, to buy, during his visits to the Frankfurt fair, all the titles published by the prestigious Plantin house across the whole range of disciplines, and not just those with a strong Catholic interest, such as Baronio.[165] Authors other than self-payers and those with access to a printing house supported by their institution (such as the Vatican Presses) usually negotiated with a publisher or printer-publisher, and left the publisher to choose (if necessary) the workshop in which the work was to be produced, and the way the book would be advertised and distributed.[166] Various external considerations beyond those given above might affect the author's choice: confessional allegiance, avoidance of censorship in a given location, subsidy or other favours from a local magnate, specialist knowledge or equipment, the quality of the product in terms of its material presentation and accuracy.[167] This was why Catholic mathematicians such as van Roomen had recourse to a Genevan publisher (Pyrame de Candolle) who was willing to lay out a considerable sum to pay for the diagrams he required.[168] Publishers often expressed a dislike of working with authors at a distance, but authors did not show the same reluctance, unless problems occurred in the production of the book.[169] It seems that a number of Italian authors of the first half of the sixteenth century—Anio Paleario, Girolamo Cardano, and Andrea Alciato among them—actually preferred to be published abroad, presumably on the grounds that native publishers were not good at exporting and not eager to undertake it.[170] In many cases the agreement or contract reached with the publisher seems to have been relatively informal; but in some cases, as we have seen above in regard to Quirinus Reuter's contract for the publication of Andreas Dudith, it could be very detailed, and cover such issues as the format and quality of paper, obligatory purchase of part of the press run, advances from the author to cover the initial paper and labour costs, refundable contributions to printing costs, payment for illustrations, the provision of the protection of a privilege, and the issue of remuneration.[171] At least one publisher (Plantin) consulted authors on details of presentation by sending them a specimen of their work early in the printing process.[172] The date by which the printing was to be completed, and the means of distribution, seem rarely, if ever, to form part of the agreement, although they are issues to which authors were very sensitive, and gave rise, as we have seen, to a great deal of frustration.

Aldus Manutius set an early benchmark for prestige publication.[173] It was clear that by the 1530s, certain non-Italian publishers, notably in Basel, Paris, and Lyon, had acquired high status as the producers of learned books which were accurate and elegant (a much-praised feature of a book),[174] provided with textual apparatus, indexes, and errata sheets, and widely distributed. Around the middle years of the century, their number included Sebastian Gryphius of Lyon; Simon de Colines, Christian and André Wechel, and Robert Estienne of Paris; Joannes Froben, Johannes Oporinus, Heinrich Petri, Johannes Herwagen, and Nicolaus Episcopius of Basel; Christophe Plantin of Antwerp; Johannes Schott of Strasbourg; and Joannes Petreius of Nuremberg. By the end of the century, many more names had emerged.[175] Once an author had established himself with a publisher, both parties usually remained loyal to each other. But that did not mean that the publisher would take risks on the author's behalf. Sebastian Henricpetri, for example, published two of Martin Crusius's works, but refused to take on the next unless severe cuts in length were made. His father had declined to publish revised editions of Girolamo Cardano, and Christophe Plantin showed the same discrimination with respect to his authors.[176]

Authors often acted as their own copy editors and proof correctors. Indeed, the role of corrector (to which I shall return in the next chapter) was seen as highly respectable; it was filled by some of the most eminent scholars of the day. In such cases, it was not unusual for the author to stay in the house of his publisher. Such hospitality has added credence to the image of the humanist printer as an active agent in the republic of letters. Active engagement in the production of copy was denied to those who were published abroad, and so made the choice of publisher (one with a very good record for producing accurate texts) crucial. There are many indications in learned correspondence of how important the production of accurate copy was. What constitutes a "most faulty and neglected text," or one printed "turpiter et inepte," was not, however, necessarily one teeming with misprints. The reprinting of texts "cleansed of infinite errors" was often so near a facsimile that the attentive reader would do well to spot a dozen typos in a few hundred pages. The publisher who engaged in such reprinting often did little more than apply the list of errata present in the original edition to the text.

Authors might aspire to some form of remuneration beyond the prestige of being published, but there were no hard-and-fast rules about this, and whatever the material reward might be, it was in nearly all cases very modest; those who attempted to drive a hard bargain might well lose the contract altogether.[177] It is clear that even quite seasoned campaigners in publication, such as Caspar Waser, had no firm idea of what a reasonable return would be. It appears from Goldast's correspondence that manuscripts were put out to tender, and paid for by the printed sheet or in a number of free copies, at least in the German lands.[178] In other cases, a combination of free copies and some money (or payment on the author's behalf for a licence) was the result of the negotiation of the author with his publisher. The Heidelberg theologian Girolamo Zanchi, for instance, about whom we shall hear more below, received 600 florins for his *De tribus Elohim* from his Frankfurt publisher Georgius Corvinus (Rab), as well as 300 florins from his territorial ruler and patron, the Count Palatinate Frederick the Pious.[179] By far the most common arrangement seems to have been the provision of free copies, in varying numbers from 5 to 100 or more (Descartes, that nobleman disdainful of trade, struck a very hard bargain by demanding the very high figure of 200 free copies for his first publication: others were not as successful in their negotiations).[180] Bookseller-publishers might also offer payment by way of a selection of books from their stock.[181] There is some indication that the more prestigious the press, the fewer copies were on offer: Jan I Moretus of the Plantin presses generally proposed between 25 and 50, which is lower than the majority of the figures found in Goldast's correspondence.[182] When authors or promoters received free copies as remuneration, they sometimes negotiated either a period in which they would be free to sell their copies without competition from the publisher, or a market zone in which he agreed not to compete.[183]

Sometimes authors were paid in the form of a credit which could be redeemed against volumes from the publisher-bookseller's stock; there is evidence of this in the letters written to Goldast. In such cases, the "liberal" uncomputed view of exchange tends to apply: no very exact credit is established, and the author felt able to ask for books without any specific reciprocal benefit being mentioned, as in Freher's dogged pursuit of a copy of the Schönwetter publication about German privileges.[184] The highest recorded remuneration I have found was for a book of sermons published in 1600 by Georg Anwander, the promoter of the deceased theologian Moses Pflacher; he received 500 thaler, which one might compare with the 50 thaler paid to the very eminent jurist Huldrych Zasius for one of his books in 1529.[185] In rare cases, authors explicitly rejected remuneration of any kind: this was done by Andrea Alciato in the 1530s. The most plausible motive for this rejection (otherwise out of character in Alciato's case, given the obsession he had with the level of stipend he received from his various universities) was the desire to be in no way beholden to the publisher, and to retain thereby a rigid control over the mode (format, paper, point size, accuracy) and ancillary features (indexes) of the production.[186]

As a coda to this section, nothing could be more fitting than the letter Abraham Ortelius wrote to his nephew Emmanuel van Meteren on 17 November 1586, in which he gives a clear account of what it felt like to be an author seeking to find his way into print:

> It seems to me that, as far as I have been able to find out in our own days, authors seldom receive money for their books, for they are usually given to the printers, the authors receiving some copies if they are printed. They [the authors] also have some expectation from the dedication through the generosity of a Maecenas or patron, in which they are often and indeed, I believe, mostly disappointed. I have also been present when Plantin had one hundred daelders from an author who wanted to have his book printed. This was Adolphus Occo with his book of medallions. It may be that the printer gave him to understand that the work would not sell well. Then again, when books are costly, as when many pictures have to be made for them, this is commonly charged to the author. Sambucus paid for all the figures in his *Emblemata*. Plantin has recently accepted a little book that will bring him in 200 guilders. Although it seems to me that authors seldom receive money from the printers, as I have said, they do receive some copies. The greatest number I have heard of (and that was after prior agreement) was 100. When Plantin had printed my *Synonymia* he sent twenty-five [copies] to my house, for which I thanked him very much. What he will do with my *Thesaurus* (which he is now printing), time will show. Some authors, having seen that their work was beautifully printed, have presented him with a silver bowl. All this having been said, it may be that your opinion will be otherwise, and you will say with truth that none of this is appropriate to your case. For these have all written for their own sakes, and for the indulgence of their minds, and this for a variety of reasons, whether for honour, or the winning of friends or the payment by a patron, or to acquire fame (for which many fools are writing books today). This is not so for you, yours being a work commissioned by others, and is therefore worthy of payment.[187]

Authors and Publishers: Genres and Commerce

The widespread practice of piracy and unauthorised reprinting testifies to the constant pursuit of profit through ruthless exploitation of local markets and fairs; so do the strategies adopted in the first century or so of printing to generate repeated sales from narrow markets, in which authors and editors collaborated. Jean-François Gilmont points out that humanists expressed a preference for plain texts of the classics, but at the same time one of the major forms through which they promoted themselves was the commentary.[188] From the generation of Filippo Beroaldo, Pomponio Leto, Niccolò Perroti, and Giovanni Sulpizio (all active in the second half of the fifteenth century) onward, it advertised their learning, and the profit to the republic of letters that such learning afforded.[189] It could be pitched at various levels, from the very erudite to the "familiaris interpretatio" which Josse Bade adopted to temper the wind to his less learned northern readership of the 1490s. Commentaries could even appear in both of these guises in a single publication.[190] Other features added to texts to make them more attractive include indexes, introductory prefaces, scholia, chapter headings, and résumés. Textual apparatus was also a feature of both legal and medical works; in all cases, it could add to the saleability of a given edition.[191]

In an age that witnessed the progressive discovery of previous unknown manuscripts of classical and medieval texts, it is not surprising that editions were frequently revised. The publishers of scholarly books were thereby at the mercy of their suppliers, the scholars, who could provide copy of a given text or texts, and then send shortly thereafter an amended text or added material (often in the form of commentary or notes) arising from subsequent discoveries or related documents as these emerged into the public sphere.[192] It is, however, also the case that the European market for learned materials of all kinds was subject to rapid saturation, and the laudable pursuit of ever-improved editions flowed into commercial strategies designed to provoke new purchasing by those who already possessed what they probably thought of as an adequate working edition of a given text or texts. Live authors, and the agents or promoters of those who were deceased, had to connive in this commercial process, although they might have claimed that the overriding imperative of textual accuracy absolved them from the need to feel uneasy about this practice.[193] An early example, which gave rise to the following howl of agony in 1516, written by the publisher who suffered from it, is afforded by no less a figure than Erasmus, who exploited his position as best-selling author against the interests of his Parisian printer, Josse Bade:

> Such is your reputation among your fellow men that if you announce a revised edition of any of your works, even if you have added nothing new,

they will think the old worthless: and losses of this kind have been forced on me in respect of the *Copia,* the *Panegyricus,* the *Moria,* the *Enchiridion* (which I had undertaken for 500 copies) and the *Adagia,* of which I had bought 110.[194]

I shall be saying more about this practice from the publishers' point of view in the next chapter; here I shall look at the textual manipulations with which authors and editors were mainly concerned, and which could take a number of forms. A revealing example is that of two works by the fourth-century writer Eusebius: his *Ecclesiastical History,* which gave an account of the first four centuries of Christianity, and his *Chronicon,* which laid out the history of nineteen ancient civilizations in parallel columns, from the time of Abraham to that of Eusebius himself. Both were progressively brought up to date in the late medieval period in a series of supplements. The former work was first printed in the 1470s in the ancient translation by Rufinus. Copies of the *Chronicon* were speculatively created for distribution even in the manuscript period, notably by the Florentine stationer Vespasiano da Bisticci; it was first printed by Henri I Estienne and Josse Bade in Paris in 1512.[195] In this edition, the text was supplemented with the continuations up to 1449 by Jerome, Prosper Aquitanus, and Matthaeus Palmerius of Florence. The edition also contains a detailed index adapted from an earlier edition, which made the text accessible in new ways for purposes other than just serial reading.[196] Thereafter one finds a number of transformations designed to relaunch both the *Ecclesiastical History* and the *Chronicon* in the market, even from colleagues working in the same city, and selling in the same market zones. I shall set them out here schematically.

1. The Sammelband. Many bound volumes of the scribal age brought together different texts on the same broad theme, and it is therefore not surprising that the practice was continued in the age of print. To increase the marketing potential, one or more texts on the same topic were combined with the *Ecclesiastical History.* Geoffroy Boussard of Paris published Eusebius with Cassiodorus's *De Regimine Ecclesiae Primitivae* in 1497; Georg Husner in Strasbourg added the *Ecclesiastical History* of Bede in 1500 (there were subsequent editions in 1506, 1514, and 1521). In 1523, Johannes Froben's critical edition by Beatus Rhenanus (see below) added more Greek patristic material in translation. This was supplemented in 1541 in Paris not only by the translation of Theodoret's *Rerum ecclesiasticarum libri* by Joachim Camerarius that had appeared first in 1536 in Basel from the presses of Johannes Herwagen, but also by improved textual apparatus ("foeliciore indice et veriore"). In the case of the *Chronicon,* Heinrich Petri of Basel produced a different set of accompanying texts edited by Johannes Sichard, which was reprinted in 1535, 1549, and 1579. The idea of grouping texts on the same theme is found also in medicine (where there are collections on the *morbus gallicus* or Great Pox, on thermal baths, and on surgery), as well as composite volumes of letters written by physicians to their colleagues and patients.[197]

2. *The* Editio princeps *and Its Revisions.* Recent histories of scholarship tend to pay more attention to the *editio princeps* than the rest, but this was not necessarily always the case in the sixteenth century.[198] The publication of the Greek text of the *Ecclesiastical History* encapsulating the humanist enthusiasm for the return *ad fontes*—the palingenesis of the text—was undertaken by Robert Estienne in Paris in 1544 (it also is a *Sammelband*).

Unlike the case of Estienne's Dio Cassius's *Roman Histories* of 1548, which was printed from a single manuscript from the Royal Library and contained conjectural readings grouped at the end of the volume, the Eusebius is the product of textual collocation of a number of manuscripts by Estienne himself. The first Latin edition of the *Ecclesiastical History* to make strong claims about revisions from the Greek was that already mentioned of Geoffroy Boussard in 1497, which was reprinted in c. 1516 and in 1525. This text was pirated by the Giunti in Lyon in 1526, and (without a bibliographical address) again in Italy in 1533, where the simple claim of "editio emendata" in 1497 had been expanded to "one which has been brought out, revised with the greatest care, restored to its pristine integrity, which neglect over the centuries and the carelessness of printers had almost obliterated, and provided with an index of the principal points of note ('sententiae')."[199]

New versions may be accompanied by commentaries, editorial emendations, or other apparatus (such as the index to Estienne's edition of the *Chronicon,* and to that of the 1533 edition of the *History*).[200] The most important annotated edition was produced by Beatus Rhenanus, the friend of Erasmus, and printed by Froben in 1523. This achieved the reputation of being the best available text, and was reprinted in 1535 (with additions), 1539, and 1544 (with the Theodoret translation by Camerarius). In 1549, Wolfgang Musculus produced a revised translation, which was reprinted in 1554, 1557 (with additions), and 1562. Its status was in turn challenged by the edition commissioned by the heirs of

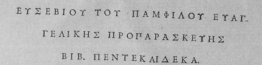

ΕΥΣΕΒΙΟΥ ΤΟΥ ΠΑΜΦΙΛΟΥ ΕΥΑΓ_

ΓΕΛΙΚΗΣ ΠΡΟΓΑΡΑΣΚΕΥΗΣ

ΒΙΒ. ΠΕΝΤΕΚΑΙΔΕΚΑ.

Euſebii Pamphili Euangelicæ præparationis   Lib. X V.

EX BIBLIOTHECA REGIA.

Βασιλ ̓ ἀγαθῷ κρατερῷ ̓αἰχμητῇ.

LVTETIAE.
Ex officina Rob. Stephani, Typographi Regii, Regiis typis.
M. D. XLIIII.

Cum priuilegio Regis.

3.3 The title page of the 1544 *editio princeps* of the Greek text of Eusebius's
Ecclesiastical History.
Courtesy of All Souls College, Oxford.

Froben from Johannes Jacobus Grynaeus of Basel, which incorporated translations by John Christopherson as well as those by Musculus and Camerarius. This appeared in 1570 and was reprinted in 1587, with the addition of the *Chronographia* of Abraham Bucholzer.

Another Basel press—the Henricpetri—republished this version in 1611.[201] A Latin version of the *Chronicon* meanwhile reappeared in 1604 in Bordeaux in a *Sammelband* edited by Arnauld de Pontac with much useful information about the Latin manuscripts. Two years later it was published in Greek at Leiden in Joseph Scaliger's *Thesaurus temporum,* the most ambitious of all early modern undertakings concerning world chronology, which includes a further six Latin and five Greek texts.[202]

These editions are the ancestors of the Variorum editions containing a critical discussion of all suggested textual emendations. They became popular in the Netherlands in the seventeenth century, but were already being produced in our period. An early example is afforded by Caesar's *Gallic Wars,* which appeared in Basel in 1591. Ovid, Horace, and Virgil were also published in this way. In law, where canonical texts surrounded by more than one encapsulating gloss is a medieval form of *mise en page* carried into the age of print, sixteenth-century commentators also attracted such multi-layered presentation: Johann Schneidewein's *In quatuor Institutionum imperialium libros* provides a good example of this.[203]

These "editiones auctiores" and "correctiores" have been blamed for the early collapse of the market in the fifteenth century.[204] We may ask whether they are signs of the successful accumulation of knowledge and its assimilation in view of an eventual palingenesis of an original text, or rather manifestations of the commercially inspired revisionism whose effects are still perceptible in historical and literary studies today. Some revised editions are clearly the result of genuine accumulation of knowledge, but others, especially those produced at the instigation of publishers, may not be so innocent. A similar question concerns the relation of the market to novelty in scholarship. It is noticeable, for example, that the favoured expositors of Paracelsus change over time (from the generation of Gerhard Dorn, Michael Toxites, and Adam von Bodenstein to that of Oswald Croll, Johannes Tanckius, and Jean Béguin). Whether this was driven by publishers responding to market demand for the up-to-the-minute presentation of an author is not clear.[205]

3. Translations into Vernaculars. A popular way of finding a new readership for such texts as Eusebius was translation. His *Ecclesiastical*

EVSEBII

PAMPHILI,
RVFFINI, SOCRATIS,
THEODORITI, SOZOMENI,
THEODORI, EVAGRII, ET
DOROTHEI

Ecclesiastica Historia,

Sex propè seculorum res gestas
complectens:

Latinè iam olim à doctissimis uiris partim scripta, partim è Græco à clarissimis viris, Vuolfgango Musculo, Ioachimo Camerario & Iohanne Christophersono Britanno, eleganter conuersa:

Et nunc ex fide Græcorum codicum, sic ut nouum opus uideri possit, per IoAN. IACOBVM GRYNAEVM locis obscuris innumeris illustrata, dubiis explicata, mutilis restituta:

CHRONOGRAPHIA insuper *Abrahami Bucholceri, ad Annum Epochæ Christianæ sexcentesimum: & lectionis sacræ historiæ luculenta* METHODO *exornata.*

Vnà cum INDICE rerum & uerborum locupletiss.

Cum gratia & priuilegio Cæsareæ Maiestatis.
BASILEAE.
Ex officina EVSEBII EPISCOPII, & NIC. FRA-
TRIS HÆREDVM. M. D. LXXXVII.

3.4 The title page of the *Sammelband* of 1587 containing Eusebius's
Ecclesiastical History, recording the aggregated contributions of five editors
and translators.
Courtesy of All Souls College, Oxford.

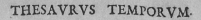

THESAVRVS TEMPORVM.

EVSEBII PAMPHILI

CAESAREAE PALAESTINAE

EPISCOPI

Chronicorum Canonum omnimodæ hiſtoriæ libri duo, interprete
Hieronymo, ex fide vetuſtiſſimorum Codicum caſtigati.
Item auctores omnes derelicta ab Euſebio, & Hieronymo continuantes.

EIVSDEM EVSEBII

Vtriuſque partis Chronicorum Canonum reliquiæ Græcæ, quæ colligi
potuerunt, antehac non editæ.
Opera ac ſtudio
IOSEPHI IVSTI SCALIGERI
IVLII CAESARIS A BVRDEN FILII.

EIVSDEM IOSEPHI SCALIGERI

Notæ & caſtigationes in Latinam Hieronymi interpretationem,
& Græca Euſebij.

EIVSDEM IOSEPHI SCALIGERI

*Iſagogicorum Chronologiæ Canonum libri tres, ad Euſebij Chronica, & doctrinam
de temporibus admodum neceſſarij.*

LVGDVNI BATAVORVM
Excudebat Thomas Basson
Sumptibus Commelinorvm.
cIↃ. Iↄ. c. vi.
CVM PRIVILEGIO CHRISTIANISSIMI REGIS.

3.5 The title page of the monumental edition of Eusebius's *Chronicon* by
Joseph Justus Scaliger, which appeared in 1606.
Courtesy of All Souls College, Oxford.

History underwent this process into German in 1530, into French in 1532, into Italian in 1547, and into English in 1577. Such editions (as well as the epitomes that I shall mention below) were perceived by publishers of the Latin text as threats to their profits, or to their monopoly of an author.[206] Translations were not just designed for those who did not know ancient languages. They were often owned by scholars, who used them explore the range of meanings which could be extracted from a given text in various disciplines, including theology (the multiple translations of the Psalms and the polyglot Bibles) and medicine (the manual known as the *Articella,* which contained several translations of the same texts by Galen and Hippocrates).[207]

4. *Opera omnia: The Development of the Author Axis.* The importance of the *Opera* genre is that it displaces the axis from the thematic content of works to the author, and to the overall coherence of his thought. Gessner's *Bibliotheca universalis* also made the author, not the field or genre, the organising principle of bibliography. The origin of this development may be found in the tradition of recording famous lives, which Gessner acknowledges as a model for his own approach. Among those he cites as his predecessors are Johannes Trithemius's *Liber de scriptoribus ecclesiasticis* of 1494, and the works on the lives of poets, jurists, and physicians by Lilio Gregorio Giraldi, Johann Fichard, and Symphorien Champier, respectively.[208] There are also writers who follow the ancient physician Galen in offering accounts of their own writings, beginning with Giovanni Vincenzo Biffi in the fifteenth century. Erasmus provides a well-known example of the genre, which he published as a guide to an edition of his complete works, perhaps inspired by the *Opera omnia* of Gianantonio Campano of 1495 and Angelo Poliziano of 1498, the first of the modern writers to have enjoyed such publication.[209] During our period, collections of famous lives in the various disciplines including references to the publications of the scholar in question are produced in some numbers. Paolo Giovio was a distinguished early writer in the genre, and a good later example is the collection of German bio-bibliographies by Melchior Adam, printed between 1615 and 1620.[210] By the end of the sixteenth century, complete works are grouped together in sales catalogues by booksellers. Giovanni Battista Ciotti's sales catalogue of books from northern Europe which appeared in 1602 contains at least a hundred such partial or complete works. They may also be multivolumed sets, designed for purchase either by individual volume or *en bloc.* I shall examine in Chapter 7 the commercial implications of this for publishers. The first complete works of Eusebius (in Latin transla-

tions) appeared in four folio volumes in 1542, from the presses of Heinrich Petri in Basel; this enjoyed repeated republication (1549, 1559, 1570, and 1579).[211]

The first edition of the complete works of Eusebius in their original language alone was the prestigious undertaking by the Royal Presses in Paris in 1628. There is no indication that this was a commercial success, but Gabriel Naudé suggests that the genre was particularly attractive to certain (in his view, not very discerning) collectors.[212]

5. *The Abridgement or Epitome.* The provision of access to major works through abridgements and translations is a sign of the widening of the literary public, and the activity of entrepreneurial publishers to create new market sectors.[213] A great deal of scholarly contempt was directed at epitomes. Aldus Manutius began this trend in 1513 by attacking Paul the Deacon's abridgement of Sextus Pompeius Festus in his note to the reader introducing that work.[214] By the end of the sixteenth century, they had come to be associated with the spread of Ramist modes of teaching throughout Europe.[215] It cannot, however, be denied that they constituted a financial success for their editors and publishers. In the same way, compendia, alphabetical organizations of scholarly materials, encyclopaedic works, and "loci communes" (organisation by topic) were genres which brought much commercial success to their publishers.[216] In the case of Eusebius, there was an early medieval epitome of the *Chronicon* by Haymo Bishop of Halberstadt, which was printed in 1531 in Cologne as one of the volumes comprising Haymo's complete works. Thereafter it appeared in Hagenau in the same year, in Schwäbisch Hall in 1550, and in Cologne in a very small format in 1573, 1600, and 1610, which suggests that a wider readership was targeted. A new epitome was published in Wittenberg in 1626.

In the above list of Eusebius editions, most publications are in folio, a format that was discovered to provide the best returns in the case of theological works.[217] The majority were financed by the publisher. The reprintings (and internecine Basel competition) show that this was a lucrative area.

Other Genres: Letters, Consilia, Decisiones, Observationes

This is not an exhaustive list of commercial strategies which authors espoused or in which they connived; some genres were particularly well suited to printing and reprinting, in that they offered scope for enlarged and improved editions. Notable here is the genre of collected letters,

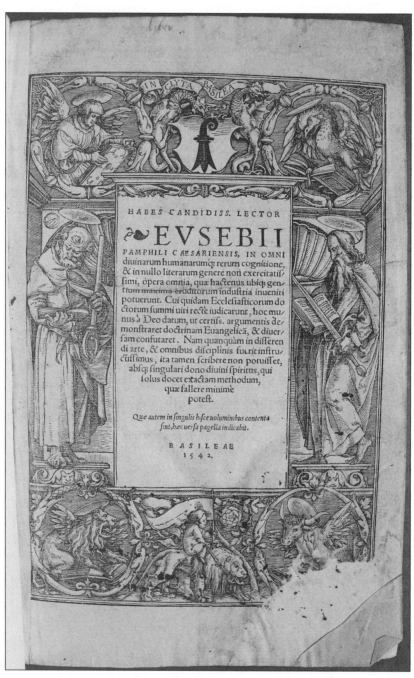

HABES CANDIDISS. LECTOR

EVSEBII

PAMPHILI CAESARIENSIS, IN OMNI
diuinarum humanarumcq; rerum cognitione,
& in nullo literarum genere non exercitatiſ
ſimi, ópera omnia, quæ hactenus ubicq; gen
tium maxima eruditorum induſtriâ inueniri
potuerunt. Cui quidam Eccleſiaſticorum do
ctorum ſummi uiri rectè iudicarunt, hoc mu
nus à Deo datum, ut certiſs. argumentis de
monſtraret doctrinam Euangelicã, & diuer
ſam confutaret. Nam quanquàm in differen
di arte, & omnibus diſciplinis fuerit inſtru
ctiſſimus, ita tamen ſcribere non potuiſſet,
abſcq; ſingulari dono diuini ſpiritûs, qui
ſolus docet exactam methodum,
quæ fallere minimè
poteſt.

Quæ autem in ſingulis hiſce uoluminibus contenta
ſint, hæc uerſa pagella indicabit.

BASILEAE
1542.

3.6 The title page of the first edition of the *Opera omnia* of Eusebius in Latin,
which appeared in 1542.
Courtesy of All Souls College, Oxford.

calqued on the ancient model of Cicero, which Petrarch had made popular in the early Renaissance; an early example in print is the collection of Angelo Poliziano's letters published by Aldus Manutius in 1498.[218] Josse Bade's publication of a selection of letters by humanists (the *Illustrium virorum epistolae*) in the following year in Lyon is another manifestation of humanist self-promotion. Letters were (quite reasonably) published serially in ever more complete editions as and when they were located. They were also published thematically by topic or geographical source, as were the letters of Justus Lipsius.[219] In the case of law and medicine, the collections of *consilia, decisiones,* and *observationes* also offered the possibility of repeated publication in slightly different permutations. The twenty-four books of Jacques Cujas's *Observationes,* for example, appeared in Lyon, Cologne, Paris, and Mainz in varying groupings between 1559 and 1618. Such works were referred to by jurists and physicians as guides to their forensic, notarial, and clinical practice, and publishers rightly perceived that their usefulness would make new editions readily saleable to these professions by subjecting them both to constant revision, and to accumulation. In the Giunti bookshop in Florence in 1604, there were no fewer than 130 volumes of legal *consilia* alone, many of them printed in prestigious formats, which practitioners of the law and university professors may well have felt the need to acquire.[220] In the case of celebrated jurists such as Cujas, the *Opera omnia*—with slight variations—could be subjected to repeated competitive publication, revealing the zoning of the book market, about which I shall more to say in Chapter 6. Between 1577 and 1615, versions of Cujas's works appeared in Paris three times (including an epitome), Cologne three times in various formats, Frankfurt and Hanau twice (from the Wechel presses), Geneva twice (one edition funded by a Lyon publisher), and Lyon once.

Getting Published (Eventually)

The fields we have surveyed here are very broad: humanism, the higher faculties, history, and natural history, all of which can claim to form part of the general field of scholarly publication. Why some authors managed to achieve publication and others not is not a question that can be answered by a neat set of necessary and sufficient conditions. Beyond the variables of location, subject matter, and genre, there lies a morass of contingencies for all except the self-payer. Those without the means to pay relied on not just the financial support of others, but also the mediation of secondary authors in the form of literary agents and promoters. As emerged from Chapter 2, the world of publishing was more collaborative than first appears. A surprising feature of it is the initiatives taken to republish medieval authors, especially in the fields of theology, law, and medicine; the importance of these initiatives and their scholarly justification was noted by Naudé at the end of our period, in his *Avis pour dresser une bibliotheque* of 1627.[221] The living authors' view of publishers could well be jaundiced, and reflect the perception that they were little more than venal in their motives, but happy outcomes did occur, even for those who had little experience of the market. The English alchemical and occult author Robert Fludd records that he would have had to pay for his works to be published in London in 1617, but through the good offices of an unnamed German he attracted the attention of Theodore de Bry in Oppenheim, who was not only was willing to pay him for his manuscript, but gave him a number of free copies in the bargain.[222] We should not forget, however, the struggles of Martin Crusius, or of the various figures represented at Frankfurt by Melchior Goldast. For them and their like, the chances of publication were greatly increased by the activity of an agent or promoter who acted as a go-between with a publisher, whose commercial outlook on such approaches will be the subject of the next chapter. The degree to which confessional allegiance played a part in the support given to an aspirant author is difficult to ascertain, but it would be unwise to dismiss it as a factor. Another point of importance to have emerged from this survey is the strong presence in the field of learned publication of several surprising groups: Roman law, medieval physicians, lawyers, and theologians, and the *recentiores* of the first two groups. There are some signs in the market that novelty influenced the choice of editors and texts, but there was also a strong conservatism, expressed through the conviction of Erasmus and Gessner that authors of the past should be printed before the new generation should be allowed to occupy the presses of their day. But whether this is a contributory reason behind Crusius's appeal to providence ("God give me a publisher!"), or whether his cry is a reaction to a powerful cabal of hardheaded businessmen is not clear. He managed eventually, through a colleague in Wittenberg, to get the publisher Samuel Selfisch of Wittenberg to agree to publish the work in question—a collection of sermons in Greek entitled *Corona anni*—in 1602–1603. He then tried out his Homer commentary on the same printer-publisher, who declined to publish it. It was also declined by Zacharias Palthen of Frankfurt, Josias

MARTINI CRVSII

GRÆCÆ ET LATINÆ LL.
atq̃ Oratoriæ Facultatis, in Academia Tybingensi olim
Professoris,

COMMENTATIONES,

IN I. LIB. ILIAD. HOMERI,
Grammaticæ, Rhetoricæ, Poëticæ,
Historicæ, Philosophicæ.

E Bibliothecâ Sereniß. ELECTORIS SAXONIÆ &c.
primum in lucem edita.

Insertus est suis locis Græcus Homeri textus, cum ver-
sione Argentinæ editâ, & jam pau-
lulum interpolatâ.

Accessit etiam Index omnium vocum, quotquot in
I. Iliad. semel sæpiusve reperiuntur, ex Indice
ASCANII PERSII Bononiensis,
Romæ edito, desumtus.

TYPIS GOTTHARDI VOEGELINI.

3.7 The title page of Martin Crusius's ill-starred commentary on the first book
of Homer's *Iliad*, which appeared in 1612.
Courtesy of Staatsbibliothek zu Berlin.

Rihel of Strasbourg, and Henning Grosse of Leipzig before it was eventually produced posthumously in 1612, after a delay of some years, by Gotthard Vögelin of Heidelberg through the agency of another friend, Oseas Hala, the Lutheran minister of Frankfurt and a literary agent in that city.[223]

It cannot have been a great success: two lots, totalling 1,057 copies, remained unsold from a press run of probably no more than 1,500, and were bought for a tiny sum at the sale of Vögelin's immense Frankfurt warehouse stock in 1625.[224] What is striking is that in Crusius's case, we are dealing not with risqué or eccentric views, but with the work of a highly respected scholar working on a text of central importance written in a language venerated as the very soul of humanism and Renaissance, who none the less found it very difficult to find his way into print.

CHAPTER FOUR

Labor, Impensa, Emolumentum: The Publisher of Learned Books

In one of G. K. Chesterton's Father Brown detective stories, an apparently insoluble crime (not, of course, beyond the wit of the formidable clerical sleuth) is committed by the postman. No one, as Father Brown points out as he unravels the mystery to the previously baffled policemen, takes any note of postmen as they enter and leave buildings. When I began to think about the lectures on which this book is based, I wondered whether the same was not true of the printer and publisher of a book who provide the invisible means of support to the author and the republic of letters, without whose input the text would not be recoverable. I suspected that many producers of scholarly books left no trace of themselves beyond their bibliographical address on the title page, which by the 1560s throughout Europe was at least as much a legal requirement as an act of self-advertisement. In one way at least, I was mistaken. To judge from the extensive collection of early modern portraits held by the Herzog-August-Bibliothek, Wolfenbüttel, portraits of printers and publishers exist in the same proportion as those of other early modern merchants of similar standing, and if one reads the paratexts of many of the learned books published about this time, they either contribute to this material, or are mentioned approvingly in it.

As producers of a commodity designed for an international market, publishers were prey to the same risks as their fellow merchants at this time: outbreaks of plague in the city, war interfering with travel and transport, general crises in the economy and in the money markets, legal and illegal competition, errors in commercial judgement about the saleability of their products, the policy on taxes adopted by their city

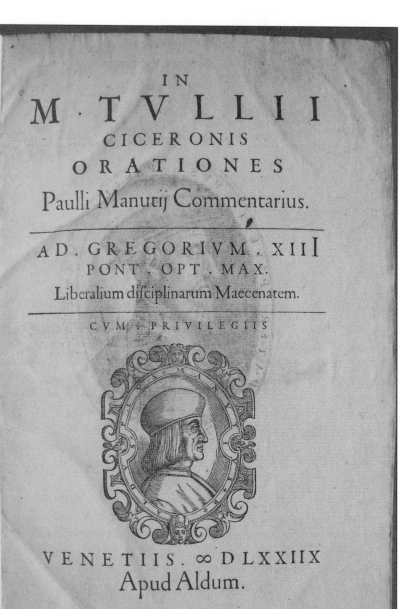

IN
M · T V L L I I
CICERONIS
ORATIONES
Paulli Manutij Commentarius.

AD. GREGORIVM. XIII
PONT. OPT. MAX.
Liberalium disciplinarum Maecenatem.

CVM · PRIVILEGIIS

VENETIIS. ∞ DLXXIIX
Apud Aldum.

4.1 The title page of Paulus Manutius's commentary on Cicero's *Speeches* of 1588, with the image of his father, Aldus, as the printer's mark.
Courtesy of All Souls College, Oxford.

4.2 The verso of the title page, with a portrait of Paulus Manutius himself. *Courtesy of All Souls College, Oxford.*

fathers which could give too great an advantage to merchants coming from elsewhere, political and religious interferences of one kind or another, the effect of confessional allegiances.[1] Such were the obstacles to profit or even solvency that the old quip about another trade could also be seen to apply to them. If one were to ask a seasoned wine merchant how to make a small fortune in the wine trade, the answer would be: start with a large fortune. In both cases, the merchant is obliged to carry an immense burden of illiquid (in one sense at least) assets. There are some remarkable cases of successful publishing houses lasting several generations or more, reinforced by intermarriage between publishing families, and the remarriage of widows to factors in the same house, but in nearly all cases their founders were already rich, and in most cases they engaged in a diversified portfolio of business, which sometimes included the spice trade, or jewellery, or linen, or wool: all much more rewarding mercantile activities than publishing.[2] A clear statement of the perennial commercial worries of less fortunate publishers is found in their submissions to the various chanceries in Europe that issued privileges, where they express these in a bald, if formulaic or rhetorically inflated, way. When seeking protection for the learned books they plan to publish, they stated their motive (to serve the republic of letters); they declared their interest (the "bitter labour" and "great expense" they had devoted to producing the text in question); and they expressed the hope that they would reap the due financial rewards from their labours and investment, and not be deprived of them by the "sinister arts" of unscrupulous competitors.[3]

Aspirant authors in our period seem not infrequently to have believed that publishers were rich.[4] They were encouraged in this belief by the premises in which the publishers worked. The most enterprising among them moved up the housing market as they expanded their business. Two examples that spring to mind are Nicolas Bassée and André Wechel. The latter's acquisition of a house in the richest part of Frankfurt in the 1570s provoked a sour comment at a meeting of the Lutheran Council about the upward social mobility of newly arrived Reformed merchants.[5] Wechel's sons-in law Jean Aubry and Claude de Marne had extensive premises built for them when they moved the presses to Hanau in 1597. These premises were requisitioned by the occupying army in 1634, and were sufficiently large to accommodate a captain, nine soldiers, and ten horses as well as Aubry's family and his workers.[6]

Apart from those who entered the trade with money already, most publishers, even those who had the benefit of preferential treatment by a municipality or local ruler, were undercapitalised, suffered from chronic problems of cash flow, and frequently relied on support in the form of injections of money and delayed or staggered debt repayments.[7] In at least one jurisdiction (France), it was possible for a bankrupt publisher to continue to produce books.[8] In Plantin's case, two-thirds of the books he published did not recover their costs in the first three years of their life, and 10 percent of his income went on servicing previous loans, often preventing him from printing new copy.[9] When borrowing, publishers often had to supply surety in the form of their stock (which they tended to overvalue, at its retail sale price), their equipment, their houses, and precious items such as gold or silver artefacts.[10] At Plantin's death, over three-quarters of his estate was in the illiquid form of books, which he used on occasions as surety for loans.[11] The rich publisher Sigmund Feyerabend even had to sell his house to free himself from debt, only six years after having been one the highest-taxed printers in Frankfurt.[12] One surprising feature of this world is the relative ease with which loans could be found. Thomas Platter's memoirs record that he was encouraged to take on debt from one creditor, who was not even looking for an early return, though it is not clear how typical this was.[13] Other loans were found from speculative investors such as Rumbold Mercator, or generous patrons of scholarship such as the Fuggers. Not all publishers looked outward to find support. The Wechels obtained money from one of their authors, and Christoph Plantin was forced at one point to borrow from his employees, commenting ruefully that a printing house was a labour-intensive bottomless pit which constantly threatened to devour both its master and those who worked for him.[14]

Printing and Publishing

The general term I shall use in this chapter—publisher—covers a quite broad spectrum of commercial activity. In Latin legal documents of the time, it was usually rendered as "typographus." At the one end of this spectrum we find the printers who never took initiatives themselves, but produced copy for others. Above them were master printers, who sometimes acted only for others, but on other occasions arranged finance, or themselves provided it, to allow printing to take place. The printer-publishers who took on few or no commissions were yet grander figures, who might or might not have had printing skills or even linguistic competence in various languages. Some printer-publishers were also retail booksellers, and engaged in all levels of printing, as did Christophe Plantin.[15] Some booksellers were publishers but not printers, as was, for example, Peter Kopf, but even he used the name "typographus" as well as "bibliopola" to describe himself in official documents.[16] The education that publishers of Latin and Greek received varied widely. Some possessed university degrees or even doctorates in the higher faculties (Christophorus Corvinus, Johannes Oporinus, Zacharias Palthen), while others seem to have learned their trade through private tuition, apprenticeship in the workshop or at the local grammar school (André Wechel, Henning Grosse).[17] Some were able to write elegant Latin, while others, who began their careers as artisans, had to have their prefaces in that language written for them.[18] The humanist printer-publisher is a rarer figure than is usually thought.

In the course of their career, publishers could pass from one to another of the categories described above. Even the richest could find themselves in financial trouble. Christophe Plantin, for example, seems to have begun his career as a printer by being employed by others, but then gradually built up a massive enterprise with more personnel and presses than anyone else in Europe. Yet at the end of his career he complained bitterly that he was reduced again to working for his colleagues, and seeing them benefit from the prestige which he had acquired for his name in the market.[19] Johannes Oporinus made the same complaint in the middle of his career.[20] At the other end of the scale we find Johann Wechel, who arrived in Frankfurt in 1581, borrowed some reflected onomastic glory from his more famous relation André Wechel and his successors, and eventually published some of the most exciting books of the age before his premature death in 1593. Nearly all his publications were either co-financed by him or paid for altogether by speculators.[21] In the middle of the field we can place Nicolas Bassée, a refugee from the Low Countries who settled in Frankfurt in the early 1560s, and who built up a considerable fortune in a short period of time by shrewd choice of copy, his taxation rating in the city of Frankfurt rising from 50 to 3,000 florins in that time.[22] Among the reputedly successful figures at the turn of the century who were bookseller-publishers, we find Peter Kopf (Bassée's son-in-law), Jonas Rhodius or Rosa, Johann Theobald Schönwetter, Lazarus Zetzner, initially of Strasbourg, and the Italian Giovanni Battista Ciotti. All of these five figures (or their heirs) were to fall on hard times or even go bankrupt because of the collapse of the international market in the 1620s, as we shall see.

Publishers of learned books either fulfilled this function alone (the Wechel presses, the French Royal presses, the Giunti) or combined it with other printing, whether liturgical books (Plantin), legal and ecclesiastical proclamations (Sébastien Cramoisy), or vernacular writings (Sigmund Feyerabend, Ciotti). Learned books, as I have already indicated, fell into two broad classes: textbooks for schools and universities, on the one hand, and more specialised humanist editions, historical, legal, theological, and medical works, on the other. Nearly all of the publishers I have mentioned or shall mention engaged in both classes of publication. Where they chose to locate their presses is a matter of some surprise. Many were based in cities without universities, and a surprising number of university cities were without printers who could compose in ancient languages. Even Basel, which had an institute of higher learning, was in the time of Erasmus and during much of its heyday as a centre of learned printing a city with a "rarely visited and cold academy" in comparison with that of Louvain.[23] Venice, Antwerp, Frankfurt, and Lyon had no university at all, and rising universities such as Bourges had no local printer. When one was enticed to take on this role during its golden age of legal studies in the 1530s, he chose to reside with his family in Paris (thereby setting a trend that persists to this day among French professors employed in the provinces).[24] In Italy the title of university printer was almost unknown.[25] While it was recognised that printing shops were a sign of the health of a country's scholarship as much as the institutions of higher learning, this does not seem to have weighed much in their location.[26] This was determined more than anything else by trade routes, local resources such as paper, the ready availability of artisanal skills relevant to publishing, and powerful local patrons. It would seem that small individual enterprises in a range of German towns found survival difficult unless the last condition was satisfied. For southern Germany, Helmut Gier records the collapse of such printing houses in Memmingen, Nördlingen, Regensburg, Passau, and Salzburg in the years between 1519 and 1568, the three exceptions in this area being Lauingen, which changed confessional allegiance; Dillingen, which was supported by the local bishop; and Augsburg, with a bi-confessional population, patrons such as Konrad Peutinger and Marcus Welser, and a strong sense of municipal identity.[27]

It is pertinent to set learned publication in the context of the material conditions of printing, and the operation of the workshop, which employed, beyond the team of compositors, pressmen, and general helpers, one or more correctors.[28] With the exception of the last figure or figures, a team of five journeymen would normally have been associated with each press. There were few economies of scale, although the operation of several presses (two seems to have been a frequently chosen number) could assist in the speed with which lengthy or complex texts were produced and hence able to be put on sale, and could determine whether production was continuous or concurrent with other printing tasks.[29] A reasonable estimate of the number of sheets which could be produced (i.e., composed) by a dedicated press in one week would be four or five; the number of pulls by pressmen in a day was computed as 1,300 in Geneva in the 1540s, representing about 650 gatherings or quires.[30] Both the masters of printing houses and city councils produced printing regulations, and had to deal with unrest and discontent among the journeymen.[31] The members of the printing shop might belong to local guilds or confraternities, as might their master, but not all masters went on to play a role in the guild or the city.[32] Guilds were arranged according to different principles in the various cities in which the newfangled technology became implanted.[33] In one case (Herborn), the journeymen were allowed to enrol in the local academy.[34] Not infrequently, the local city council was called upon to arbitrate in disputes between publishers and master printers and their work force. In most cases they seem to have heard the grievances from both sides, but not to have pronounced sentence unless they perceived a threat to their jurisdiction or to their own revenues, as was the case in Lyon in the 1580s.[35]

Accounting: Profit and Loss

A version of double-entry accounting was very widespread, after its introduction to the mercantile community by Luca Pacioli in the late fifteenth century. The standard elements in his terms were the *memoriale* (or ledger), the *giornale* (journal), and the *quaderno* (arranged by name of customer and supplier, usually on a double page opening, recording debt and credit on one side, facing sums incurred or earned by the publisher on the other). These were not balance sheets, but could easily be transformed into such.[36] There is little surviving evidence of profit-and-loss accounts. As most publishers attending the fairs dealt with other publishers on a wholesale basis, the accounts were usually settled in arrears on a six-monthly or yearly basis. It appears that they depended for their financial survival on being able to dispose of a large percentage of their new books at the first fair following publication, although payment for these would be delayed until the next fair.[37] It was not uncommon for a contract not included in the accounts to specify the details of repayment and the question of discounts and penalties. For this reason, cash flow is difficult to establish on the basis of these records.

It is possible, however, to infer from the Plantin-Moretus Archives that Plantin did not recoup his outgoings on two-thirds of the books published until three years after publication; and even then, much of the recovery would have been in the form of illiquid assets (i.e., books from other publishing houses).[38] Recovering debts from colleagues was a nightmarish procedure.[39]

Account books were quasi-legal documents, which could be requisitioned in court cases, and in some cases confiscated if evidence of tampering was detected.[40] They show a very surprising combination of precision and imprecision, of the recording of tiny debts and credits (as small as several florins) together with the use of approximation in regard to much larger ones. Not only are there quite frequent arithmetical errors (in my detailed analysis of the inventory of the stocks of a Lyon publisher, 13 percent of entries were miscalculated); there seems also to have been a widespread culture of adjusting figures, forgiving debts, engaging in mutual favours and acts of support that are not precisely quantified, and inventing discounts.[41] It is tempting to associate this arithmetical laxity with the liberal or noble culture of the gift that I discussed in relation to Goldast, and to which I shall return again, and there are some indications that this might be the case (the arrangements for sale or return, discussed below, and the symbiosis of publisher, author, and scholarly purchaser are some of these). But it was also in the interests of the whole publishing community to sustain trade ("faire vivre le commerce," as the French phrase has it), and the slight informality of arrangements and the acceptance of approximations that allowed trade to continue were, I believe, motivated by this as much as by a desire to adopt the values of the scholarly world.

One interesting insight into accounting is given by the surviving account book of the partnership between the Basel publishers Froben and Episcopius between 1557 and 1564, published by Wackernagel in 1881. The accounts are split into the costs of the two printing shops that the two men were operating, the costs of paper, the income from the Basel and Frankfurt fairs, the balances of outgoings and income of each partner, and debtors.[42] These accounts begin and end with prayers, biblical quotations, or other forms of divine invocation, which should remind us of the religious context in which mercantile activity took place. The most comprehensive collection of account books to have survived is that preserved in the Plantin-Moretus Museum in Antwerp. These have been very fully examined by Leon Voet, and I do not need to give a full description of them here.[43] They comprise the daily books from

S. 121.

Quoniam ego in flagella paratus fum et dolor meus in confpectu meo femper. quoniam iniquitatem meam annunciabo et cogitabo pro peccato meo. inimici autem mei vivunt et confirmati funt fuper me.

Martius
1564.   5

¶ NACHVOLGENDE POSTEN HATT NICOLAUS EPISCOPIUS UND SEIN SON NICOLAUS AUS-GEBEN UND BEZALT.

¶ CORRECTORES ET COMPOSITORES.

	lb.	sh.	dn.	
Vincentius Prallus hatt corrigiert 25 wochenn 4 tagk.	51	6	8	10
Philippus Neuwhaufer fampt der koft, lector.	25	12	8	
Samuel Uolhart fatzt 25 wochenn à 2 lb.	50	—	—	
Bartolomeus Varellus fatzt in Gregorio 20 wochenn a 2 lb.	40	—	—	15
Daniel Oftheymm fatzt 25 wochenn 4 tagk.	51	9	—	
Matthias vonn der Heckenn 25 wochenn 4 tagk minus ½ formm.	51	4	2	
Michelin Steub ein leerknab 4 wochenn 2 tagk.	8	14	6	
	278	7	—	20

¶ Truckhergfellenn. prefslonn. umbkhoftenn.

	lb.	sh.	dn.	
Hanfs Schauber truckt in Hieronymo, Gregorio à 30 sh. 25 w. 4 tag.	38	10	—	
Hanfs Wilhelmm des Schaubers gfpann.	38	10	—	25
Johan Dufoys in Gregorio et Hieronymo 25 wochenn 4 tagk.	38	10	—	
Benedict Rufsinn fynn gfpann.	38	10	—	
Prefsennlonn thütt 52 wochenn 1 tagk.	81	10	8	
Henckermall undt faftnachtkûchlin.	5	14	8	30
	241	5	4	

4.3 Details of the Froben-Episcopius accounts of 1563 transcribed by Rudolf Wackernagel. It begins with a quotation from a penitential Psalm (38 [37]:

	lb.	sh.	dn.
Item fur defect zů fetzenn undt truckenn.	—	6	8
Item vonn 6¹/₂ fert bůcher zů fierenn vomb Sefsell.	—	16	3
Item fur 3 fert bůcher zů fieren zumb Lufft.	—	9	—

5   ¶ Dyfs nachgfchrybenn zalt Nicolaus filius.

	lb.	sh.	dn.
Item wachtgelt vomb bůchhaufs, zoll, fchleyffgelt.	1	18	6
Item dem Theus Widerhornn vonn Mayntz fůracht vonn 31¹/₂ f. à 12 b. thůtt fl. 25. sh. 5. zalt imb zů Bafell 15 fl. 5 sh. undt zů Franckfort dye reft.	19	—	—
Item von 4 fafsenn in zů fchlagenn.	—	13	4
Item mher auff fůrlon gebenn von 4 fafsenn.	14	9	2
Item zoll zů Byefsenn vonn 16 fafsenn.	8	13	—
Item zů Franckfort zalt fur wynn, fafsruckenn, Kafparlin etc.	1	3	6
Item dem wyrt zů Franckfort gebenn fur fafs ruckenn undt auffraumen.	1	—	—
Item fur ein fefslin zů Franckfort zumb Bafler blunder	—	13	4
Item hab ich dem Oporino gebenn auff den Juftinum zů trucken 60 fl.	75	—	—
	124	2	9
	241	5	4
	278	7	—
	643	15	1

25 Thůtt fl. 515. sh. —. dn. 1.

Dyfe obgfchrybne fumma ift vonn Epifcopio ausgebenn undt bezalt wordenn. nach lautt fyneß regyfterß.

Papyr fo betzalt wardt.

17–19), followed by the costs of various print shop workers and incidental expenses incurred at the Frankfurt fair. Mea.

which fair copies were made, with income and outgoings distributed under different heads (equipment, materials, workers, retail sales, trade sales, running expenses). The rough versions of accounts (the carnets of the Frankfurt fair, and the journal) and the fair copies (the cahiers of the Frankfurt fair, the grand livre) often reveal discrepancies. Most of the accounts relating to Frankfurt are on a six-monthly basis, but other dealings were governed by different periodicities: paper, for example, was paid in three installments over a number of months.[44] Another complication was created by the practice of recording returned books as credits to the purchaser in a later account, which leads to an exaggeration of the volume of sales achieved. The dealings with foreign booksellers and publishers are usually recorded separately, and from these records something about the transmission of knowledge around Europe can be inferred. For a short period in the 1560s Plantin (under pressure from his business associates, the Bombergs) set out the accounts in such a way as to show the cost of individual acts of publishing, and hence of the relationship between the unit cost of a book and the price charged. Voet assumes that Plantin applied a multiplier to costs (two, or three), and speculates that the price of books was computed from the predicted retail price, but as he points out, the length of credit accorded to purchasers and the discounts they received made this calculation very impressionistic.[45] Plantin's accounts also cover printed books in stock (i.e., illiquid assets), and the rent charged to the partnership for the use of Plantin's matrices and presses.[46] After 1567, the year in which his association with the Bombergs came to an end, Plantin reverted to his previous habit of keeping account books for various purposes (retail sales, *quaderni,* materials, labour), but not costing the product. He continued to produce estimates of the cost of books when asked to do so by prospective authors, but seems to have done this by applying a unit-cost figure computed on the basis of sheets printed, format, and quality of paper, all derived from the experience of previous publications.[47]

It seems that nearly all publishers did not consider that they might at any time retire, or abandon the trade; so their notion of profit and loss seems to be based not on the accumulation of capital (although that did occur, and permitted certain of them to purchase personal dwellings and warehouses as well as raw materials and labour), but rather on the survival of their enterprise. In the rare cases one finds of publishers leaving the profession, this was done either in view of allowing children to succeed to the business (as Henri II Estienne did, or was forced to do) or because the person in question had had the role of publisher forced upon him or her by receiving a bequest in the form of books (Alexandre de Villeneuve of Lyon is an example of this).[48] For commercial publishers, their everyday existence was a struggle to keep or improve their place in the market, to deal with labour relations, and to acquire the necessary raw materials in spite of the problems of cash flow which bedevilled the industry. Their trade in the form of barter, about which I shall say more in the next chapter, obliged them to accept payment in kind and so become retail booksellers. Beyond that, their chronic problems of liquidity drew them into other functions, such as brewing beer (a rare case, in Basel), money-changing, providing postal services, and acting as dispensers of current news or providers of accommodation for visiting scholars and other contacts.[49] Even rich merchant printers relied on trade in other, more profitable, products, as I have indicated. In this sense they were all committed merchants before they were publishers. As I suggested in Chapter 1, their mercantile activity certainly involved calculations about risk and its reduction through diversification, but it is unlikely that they produced sophisticated business strategies with a view to accumulating capital, or made calculations about investment by discounting the future expected profits of the undertaking back to the present, except in an uncomputed way in which the factors such as investment or capital accumulation were grasped intuitively rather than precisely calculated. But even if in most cases they did not keep accounts which permitted them to know how well they were doing in respect of net profit, their decisions were none the less driven by a version of economic rationality. That is to say, they were based on the information they had, and the consistency of the criteria by which they processed it. Moreover, the contracts that they entered into were often detailed and comprehensive, and the issue of preserving good faith and a reputation as a creditworthy merchant was as important then as it is now.

We come now to the decisions that had to be taken, which involve the academic fields in which the house chose to print, the degree of risk, and the expectation of profit.[50] In many cases, houses engaging in learned publication specialised in one or two fields, and dabbled in many. The surviving fair and broadsheet catalogues ("nomenclaturae") of the major houses reveal how important the fields of theology and law were. Nearly all houses specialising in scholarly publication also engaged in some printing of medicine, history, the liberal arts, and humanism. Their catalogues did not usually list textbooks and manuals, although these too were a component of the production of most houses.

They established a portfolio of living and dead authors, and in most cases ensured that their texts remained in print and, where appropriate, were protected by privileges. It is not clear whether this represents a deliberate policy of diversification as a way of spreading commercial risk, or whether the portfolio is the result of an accumulation of those unsolicited proposals made to them which they accepted to publish, together with their portfolio of chosen authors. As we saw in the case of Melchior Goldast, publishers could be very slow in making decisions about submitted manuscripts (Cardano had described those in France in the 1550s as "egregious procrastinators"), presumably on the basis of their current state of liquidity.[51] If this is so, one might be inclined to describe their publishing policy as a combination of specialism and opportunism, which would account for the rather heterogeneous components in their catalogues at any one time.

It is claimed that the issue of risk caused the separation of printer-publishers into the three trades of printers, publishers, and booksellers in the middle of the century, but I know of no compelling evidence that risk was the factor which led to this redistribution of roles.[52] The bookseller-publishers who emerged as a group of commercial figures around 1580 (Ciotti, Zetzner, Kopf, Schönwetter, Rhodius or Rosa) were entrepreneurial merchants who entered the book trade either as apprentices or through marriage. As I stated above, the obscurity surrounding computation of profit even makes it difficult to assert with any confidence (except in the case of the Plantin-Bomberg association) how such figures came to compute prices for their books accurately enough to give them a profit or at least to continue their operations. These must have been set for the wholesale and retail markets, made consistent with the cost per sheet which was imposed on publishers by various fair authorities, and adjusted in the case of factors and branches.

Competition, Collaboration, and Co-existence

The early years of the age of print in Venice, its most productive centre, was marked by cutthroat competition. This never went away, especially not in cases where two printers were competing for a narrow market, as were Michael Forster and Johannes Schönfeld in Amberg, or where a profitable author or market zone was in question. Forms of sharp practice included the selling of books at a discount to undercut competitors in the same market zone, or even on occasions under-pricing the book of a competitor that had been acquired through barter.[53] But the benefits of collaboration and peaceful coexistence were apparent to most in the trade.[54] In Geneva in the time of Laurent de Normandie, it led to the creation of a cartel that existed to control all printing in the city and ensure good profits for its members against the interests of the rest.[55] Publishers entered into collaboration, whether formally or informally, for a variety of motives. The most common reason was the sharing of a project either because it was too large for one house to take on by itself, or to distribute risk across a number of publishing houses, which was a feature also of printing in times of crisis, such as the period of the religious wars in France.[56] As examples of project-sharing, one might cite the works of Alphonsus Tostatus, produced in Venice by various printers in 1596 under the direction of the publisher Melchior Sessa, and the Aquinas editions printed in Rome between 1569 and 1571 and in Lyon in 1591. A case of risk-sharing is the printing of the translation of Cardano's *De subtilitate* into French by different consortia in 1556, 1566, and 1578.[57] Both kinds of project fall under one of the three methods of financing an edition set out by Erasmus in a letter to letter to Polydore Virgil of 1524, referring to the practice of his friend Johannes Froben of Basel. Either he took on the project entirely at his own risk (usually only for small books); or he did so wholly at another's risk; or a partnership was set up.[58] This could exist before copy was chosen, or could be set up in view of a given project. His partner or partners might be colleagues, or authors, or they might come (as was frequently the case) from other sectors of the trade (such as papermaking, bookbinding, or bookselling); or they could also have nothing to do with the trade at all.[59] Early Italian associations, such as those of the Giunti family, were based on contracts of the kind drawn up between merchants in other fields.[60] They specified how copy was to be chosen, what the size of editions would be, how the books would be warehoused and who would have access to them, how the profits would be shared, and the ways commercial decisions would be reached (usually by majority vote).[61] By the middle of the century, such contracts were being drawn up in Augsburg, Paris (where they accounted for a high percentage of all publishing ventures), Basel, and Rome.[62] An instructive French example is the Grande Compagnie des Libraires of Lyon. It was initially founded in about 1519 in two parts: the Compagnie des Textes (these being the canonical texts of the law: the Corpus Juris Civilis et Canonici) and the Compagnie des Lectures (for commentaries on these texts).[63] Soon afterward, the two parts were merged. The Compagnie was managed in turn by members of the consortium, who organised competitive quotations for printing contracts, oversaw the warehouses in Paris, Antwerp, Frankfurt, Medina del Campo, Salamanca, Saragossa, and Lisbon, and regulated trade relations with Italy, and especially the Giunti family, some of whose number were members of the Lyon Compagnie. It was they who provided the model for an enterprise of this kind, run by a small group of protocapitalists organised in a cartel to spread risk and reduce competition. Shares in the company could be inherited, bought, and sold. Like the Giunti presses, the Lyon Compagnie was a very durable relationship, constantly renewed by the retirement of old members and the absorption of new members, who had often started out as rivals. The choice of copy and its presentation in prestigious formats was very similar to those of their Venetian counterparts, and operated through a more or less explicit zoning of the market, about which I shall say more in Chapter 6.[64]

Another kind of quasi-collaboration between printer-publishers was consciously managed co-existence or non-aggression pacts. This could take the form of a formal agreement not to sell in a given zone, such as that dated 1604 between the Giunti and Manolesco.[65] It could also be an agreement to desist from the printing of a given text to allow a colleague to market his edition on which work was well advanced.[66] It might take the further form of an informal sharing-out of an author's works or agreement to produce them in different formats. In Lyon, Sebastian Gryphius published certain texts by Andrea Alciato in octavo, at about the same time that the Grande Compagnie des Libraires was publishing them in folio; Zacharias Palthen and Wilhelm Antonius did the same with Otto Cassmann and Walter Donaldson, and Antonius had similar arrangements with the Wechel house and George Bishop of London.[67] Sometimes such agreements broke down. Moretus was on such close terms with the Hierats of Cologne that he knew their publishing plans three years in advance, but they fell out over Hierat's decision to publish a competing edition of Baronio in 1599.[68]

These agreements, whether in the form of collaboration or co-existence, could span the divide between confessions. Etienne Michel made common cause with a Lyon protestant publisher, Louis Cloquemin, as did Wechel and the Genevan printer Jacques Stoer with the Catholic Johann Gymnich in Cologne.[69] Jerôme Drouart of Paris clearly allowed the Wechel presses to produce a considerable number of his eagerly awaited edition of Casaubon's Polybius for the German market with their own title page and licence in 1610, allowing the German presses to make the false claim that they had printed the text. This may have been shrewd, as the Wechel copies were reissued in 1619, indicating a very disappointing initial sale.[70] For co-existence to occur in this way, the market had to be buoyant. It is noticeable, for example, that after the 1580s and the slump in Lyon's fortunes, joint ventures in that city became much less common.

Choosing Copy: Unsolicited Proposals, Specialities, and the Pursuit of Best-Sellers

We pass now from the economic conditions under which publishers worked to the production decisions they had to take. As Martin Lowry points out, the publisher had to sell quickly, and in quantity, to cover his costs and overheads. To do this, he had to decide what titles to select, how many copies to print, and where to place them on sale.[71] I begin here with the choice of copy. Publishers both pursued authors and editors having access to promising manuscripts they perceived as profitable, and reacted to promising approaches made to them. They appear to have been predisposed to accept work in a higher percentage of cases—according to Plantin, about half—than their modern counterparts.[72] Their publishing policy was therefore rarely completely planned: the nature of their trade made them opportunists for some of the time, opportunism being the zero degree of policy. But there was a rationale to the choices they made, which can be perceived most clearly when a succession in a publishing house occurs; heirs either remained loyal to the same range of authors and products, or they imposed their own priorities on the house, as Jan II Moretus did after the death of his father in 1609.[73] An important element of policy was the choice of fields in which to specialise, and the ways of achieving sales, whether through fairs or retail outlets. Some publishers, such as Gotthard Vögelin, were obliged by their territorial ruler to engage in both forms of distribution.[74]

While most publishers remained loyal to the authors most closely associated with their presses, sometimes publishers printed for both sides of a polemical debate, usually under pressure from their scholarly advisers.[75] In some cases, a change of policy could occur during the active lifetime of a publisher, as in the case of Jacob Stoer of Geneva, who began his publishing career in the 1570s and died in 1610. In the first decade of his career, he chose to publish historical works, often with a confessional slant, and in the second and third he increased his output of law and humanism (both scholarly tomes and textbooks). The final two decades were dominated by humanist publications (many of them reprintings of editions published by others) and the profitable sectors of theology (devotional literature and Bibles). He also acted opportunistically by reprinting profitable medical works such as Guillaume Rondelet's *Methodus curandorum morborum* (1600). In the final decade also, he concentrated on sales through the Frankfurt book fair. His career reveals that he perceived the Genevan market as too narrow to be viable after 1590, and that he sought to benefit from the wider selling zone afforded by the fair by establishing a warehouse in Frankfurt in 1603.[76]

Choosing Copy: Staples and Marginals

The second question to ask about the choice of copy concerns relative saleability. Did early modern publishers balance staples with marginals, and divide their lists according to the assessment of the commercial potential of various sectors? And how specialised or diversified did they set out to be? In his study of the Estiennes and Christophe Plantin, Robert Kingdon argues that profits from the sale of liturgical books allowed these publishers to print, or to have printed, worthy works of scholarship whose profitability was not assured, as a service to the republic of letters.[77] The financing of such works from the revenues earned by staples such as legal and administrative proclamations and schoolbooks is one hypothesis one could formulate to explain the choices made by publishers at this time.[78] But it seems to me more plausible to suppose that all learned books had to be seen potentially to be profitable (either of themselves, or with a subsidy) for a publisher to agree to produce them. This might be taken to be hardheaded or cynical if considered in the light of the prefaces and other paratextual material of books, in which reference is often made to service to the republic of letters and the need for scholarship to be freely available to all, but there is no doubting the real need that publishers had to achieve secure commercial returns. In Goldast's correspondence, and in the papers of the Plantin presses, the requirement of saleability is clearly set out.[79] Different assumptions were made about how to achieve this in the case of learned books. Christoph Froschauer assumed that a small sale of large folios in the limited field of theology was the correct route to profit, whereas André Wechel looked for "a wide range of potential readers" ("plurima genera lectorum").[80] There are not many well-attested cases of publication driven by sentiment or ideology. Perhaps Wechel's only foray into clandestine publication in Heidelberg with Jean Mareschal (works about the religious wars seen from a protestant perspective) and Gryphius's printing of his erstwhile corrector Claude Baduel are two of these.[81]

Reprinting and Reissuing

The most obvious practices in relation to market assessment concern reprinting, reissuing, unauthorised publication outside a protected zone, and piracy. Reprinting is a decision taken (or declined) in nearly all cases by the original publisher, and indicates the success of the first edition. A consequence of this is that the reprinting will continue until the market is saturated and the stock cannot be moved.[82] Many warehouses holding learned books show evidence of this (see below, Chapter 6). In that sense, the failure to sell off the latest edition (if all the previous ones had succeeded) with the consequent immobile stock might not have been seen by publishers in a tragic light, especially as it allowed them to continue to list what had been a best-seller, and, if necessary, protect it under an existing privilege.[83] If the first edition failed to sell out, however, it was often reissued with a "refreshed" title page (sometimes spuriously claiming that the text is a corrected version of the previous edition).[84] Another strategy open to publishers was to combine a title on a given topic with one or two others, in order to help its sales. Gryphius's heirs did this with Facio's *De rebus gestis ab Alphonso primo Neapolitarum rege commentariorum libri vi* in 1562, and Wilhelm Antonius with Alberico Gentili's *De legationibus* in 1596.[85] Sheets of such reissued texts were sometimes sold to other publishers, and appeared with quite different imprints.[86] As would be expected of so important a figure in the pedagogical and religious life in Germany in the midsixteenth century, the *Opera* of Philip Melanchthon, who died in 1560, were published between 1562–1564 in four folio volumes by his son-in-law Caspar Peucer. A partial new edition appeared in 1577, at the very moment of the publication of the Formula of Concord, which excluded many of his works from Lutheran orthodoxy. The reissued sheets of these two editions were advertised by an entrepreneurial publisher in 1601 with a new title page.[87] A more traveled example is that of the *Opera* of the Lutheran theologian Andreas Musculus, which first appeared in Erfurt in 1563, and was reissued in 1568 and 1573 in Erfurt, and in 1590 in Frankfurt an der Oder.[88]

Unauthorised reprinting ("Nachdruck") must be clearly distinguished from piracy ("Raubdruck"). The latter involves printing in a zone protected by a privilege; the former is merely sharp practice, designed to profit from an existing book by distraining on part of the first publisher's expected profits in a zone not protected by a privilege. Authors deplored the practice, as their original text could be, and often was, produced with errors that they were unable to correct. It was especially frowned on by publishers, as all the initial costs of page-setting and proof-correction were avoided by the pirate or printer of the unauthorised edition, who could undercut the original by using cheaper paper or a smaller typeface. The same fate was suffered by botanical illustrations.[89] There were cases brought before the Imperial Supreme Court (Reichskammergericht) in Speyer in 1533 and 1535, involving Strasbourg, Frankfurt, Basel, and Cologne printers; a later case brought by Peter Kopf of Frankfurt against Ernest Vögelin of Leipzig was begun in 1595 and dragged on for two years, before Vögelin's heirs settled out of court. It is no coincidence that Kopf and Vögelin were resident in cities with fairs. Fairs facilitated the work of the unauthorised reprinter, as they revealed to him successful publications from abroad that were not protected locally. In some cases the reprinter would add insult to injury by seeking on his own behalf a privilege in another zone, which would exclude the victim of such reprinting from selling there, and confer on the predator the right to buy up all other unauthorised reprints and so protect his investment.[90] This practice alarmed the Fair authorities, because it threatened to dissuade foreign publishers who had suffered in this way at the hands of unscrupulous local publishers from continuing to attend.[91] So it is not surprising that the Frankfurt Council issued an ordinance against it in 1588, directed at several of its native printers who made reprinting a profitable habit: Nicolas Bassée, Sigmund Feyerabend, and Johann Wechel.[92] Its ineffectual nature can be gauged from Wechel's reprinting of Lipsius within two years, on his learning of Plantin's death in 1589 and the consequential temporary lapse of his Imperial privilege.[93] One way to deter competitors from such actions was to publish works with illustrations which would be costly to reproduce, as Plantin's son-in-law Jan I Moretus chose to do.[94] In another sector of the market, Etienne Michel and Symphorien Beraud of Lyon were also very adept identifying potentially profitable works—many of them law books—which could be reprinted outside the area in which they were protected.[95] Reprinting occurred even in places linked by the same confession, such as Ingolstadt, Lyon, and Venice: Bellarmine's *Disputationes* were reprinted outside Ingolstadt—the zone in which they were protected by an Imperial privilege—in Lyon in 1587, and in Venice twelve years later.[96] Unscrupulous publishers justified their actions on the grounds that the editions they reprinted were legal as they were not protected by a privilege, were too expensively priced for the purchasing public, or had been produced in too few copies to meet demand.[97] In reaction to the 1588 ordinance, Feyerabend even went so far as to protest that an Imperial privilege granted to the Italian publisher Francesco Ziletti to protect one of his publications from Frankfurt's predators was "against the public interest of the nation."[98] The Imperial authorities issuing privileges recognised that "Nachdruck" was iniquitous, and that those who engaged in it were benefiting unfairly from the work of others; but they did not often accede to requests received from authors who sought to protect works that had been published abroad with a privilege.[99]

There were publishers who claimed to be very principled about reprinting by always seeking permission of the author or first publisher. The Oporinus, Plantin, and Wechel presses all make such declarations, but even among their number one can find examples of recourse to unscrupulous practices. Plantin was involved in a somewhat louche case of an edition of the Corpus Juris Civilis which Roville had asked him not to release in view of his own impending edition, but which Plantin went ahead with marketing through Jean Mareschal in Heidelberg in 1565.[100] Mareschal himself was involved in another case of shameless unauthorised printing in 1578, of the logical works of Zabarella. He boldly attributed to the first printer, the Venetian Roberto Meietti, the implausible view that he would not be offended by the reprinting because it was published in a market zone where his own books did not sell.[101] The fear of being subjected to this practice caused the price of books in some cases to be set artificially low by the original publisher, and may have influenced the often generous discount rates offered to colleagues at the book fairs.[102] These measures would have exacerbated the problems of cash flow and profit encountered by most publishers. This was not the only consequence of "Nachdruck" which acted in the favour of the purchaser. The breaking of a monopoly on a product exerted a downward pressure on prices, and the reprinting in a different zone helped in the transmission of knowledge; both effects had a positive effect on the republic of letters. Moreover, not all cases of reprinting were ruthless. It could also occur without the implications of sharp commercial practice, as in cases where a publisher passed on business to a colleague, or cases of new editions of out-of-print best-sellers such as More's *Utopia,* Guinther von Andernach's *Institutiones anatomicae,* or Manardo's *Epistolae medicinales*. In these examples, the reprinting of old titles was no more than a successful speculative act which did not harm the interests of fellow publishers.[103]

Production Decisions: The Choice of Printer

Choosing a printer had only to be done by publishers without a printing workshop at their disposal. We have seen from Kopf's behaviour in Frankfurt that publishers went to some lengths to find the cheapest printer. Kopf was also motivated in some cases by the desire on his part or that of his author to avoid having to submit a work to a given censor. In the second half of the sixteenth century, a wide range of Lyon publishers had recourse to printers in Geneva for various sorts of publications, to the great detriment of the printers in their own city, who brought the matter before the local council in 1588.[104] The entrepreneurial publisher Lazarus Zetzner also looked well beyond his native Strasbourg, having works printed in Cologne, Frankfurt, and possibly Neustadt an der Haart.[105] His Italian colleagues, such as Francesco de' Franceschi, also made use of printers in outlying cities—Bergamo, Pavia, Ferrara, Bologna, and Verona—to avoid the high costs of Venice.[106] These measures were responses to rising material and labour costs. According to Dietz, the cost of printing trebled in Frankfurt between the 1560s and the 1590s, and it is clear that in Lyon, the cartel operated by printers in the city, which led to ever higher charges, contributed to the recourse made by local publishers to cheaper Genevan houses.[107]

Paper, Illustrations, Format, Press Runs

As we have seen in Chapter 2, authors of scholarly works made their views known about their requirements in respect of the quality of paper, the typeface, and the format. Some even demanded that specimen pages be produced for them to approve, while others required the use of good-quality paper even for those works being produced in small formats.[108] It was not uncommon for the press run to be executed on different weights of paper for different markets and purposes (Heinrich Suizer specified cheaper paper for Switzerland; Freher demanded that the better quality be used for presentation copies).[109] The cost of paper could vary by a factor of three according to weight and consistency, and it could vary also from one locality to another.[110] Countries without their own industry for the right grades of paper (England and the Netherlands) were placed at a disadvantage, as they had to add the cost of transport to that of the product itself. The proportion of the cost of production represented by paper has been variously estimated between 33 percent and 65 percent. This is very unlike the much lower figure that pertains today.[111] Printers and publishers often demanded from those for whom they printed (even from impecunious professors) money in advance to pay for printing materials. As in the case of paper, the choice of format was in part determined by the field, the genre, and the targeted purchasers. The larger formats, often but not always produced in shorter press runs and at greater unit cost to the purchaser, were considered more prestigious.[112] Books produced for connoisseurs of "rarities"—the wealthier sector of the buying public—were also usually produced in the larger formats.[113]

To the prestige of size could be added other attractions such as illustrations. These were not a necessary adjunct to all scholarly publication, but certain fields—chorography, geography, ethnography, cartography, cosmology, zoology, physiology, botany, anatomy, mathematics, certain versions of history (such as collections of famous lives with portraits)—made use of them, in either pictorial or diagrammatic form.[114] Their association with printed texts was facilitated by the fact that in the early years, printers settled in towns and cities where the allied trades of visual arts, engraving, and wood-cutting were also practised; the Nuremberg Chronicle of 1493 is an early testament to such collaboration.[115] Although one, possibly ill-informed, author (Andrea Alciato) claimed that it would not cost his publisher much to add illustrations to his work, the general consensus seems to be that they were expensive, even if only in the form of diagrams. Adriaan van Roomen's Geneva publisher Pyrame de Candolle paid 300 écus to have his *In Archimedis circuli dimensionem expositio* furnished with diagrams in 1597.[116] From the beginning, illustrations were protected by privileges, and gave rise to bitter lawsuits, especially in the domain of botany.[117] They were not approved of by all: the anatomist Jacques Dubois deplored their use in the teaching of anatomy, and opposed the pictorial initiatives taken by his one-time pupil Andreas Vesalius.[118] Publishers sold such volumes both with the illustrations coloured in and with them uncoloured. They also used images extracted from texts to produce albums of illustrations which they sold separately. The phenomenon of illustration is a complex one which involves theories of representation and complex production processes. From the publishers' point of view, the decision whether or not to include images depended on the genre, the prestige of the project, the possibilities of subsidy (which they sought on occasion from authors themselves), and in the case of the Plantin presses, house style. All these issues have been investigated thoroughly in a number of excellent modern studies.[119]

The trend throughout the century was for smaller formats to be preferred, because they were more portable, cost less, required less paper, and tied up the presses for a shorter time.[120] Plantin claimed that his quartos sold better for these reasons than his folios, and experimented with a series of humanist and religious texts in 24mo.[121] Jacob Stoer in Geneva invested heavily in octavo publication as a way to achieve good profits.[122] Legal publications of live authors moved over the course of the century from folio or quarto to octavo in some, but not all, market sectors (Hanau and Tübingen). On the other hand, modern Italian authors such as Prospero Farinacci and Jacopo Menochio continued to enjoy publication in folio or quarto. Octavo was also the dominant format for medical books, although the larger formats were well represented, especially for works in which there were diagrams, dichotomies, and illustrations.[123] Some publishers opted for larger formats. This was done by Christoph Froschauer of Zürich with regard to theology, Peter Kopf with regard to the protochemical writings of Andreas Libau, Jean Mareschal with regard to the philosopher Jacopo Zabarella, Heinrich Petri with regard to Cardano's commentaries on Ptolemy and Hippocrates, and various Frankfurt publishers with regard to medical and historical books.[124] Plantin's son-in-law and heir, Moretus, also switched to a higher proportion of folio and quarto publications.[125] Even so, folios remained the least employed of all the formats. The figures for France for all production, which are probably indicative of the general state of affairs, show that about half of all books there were produced in octavo, 21 percent in quarto, and 13 percent in folio.[126] Press runs were determined by the efficient use of teams in the workshop. A commissioned work could have a press run of any length: in the Plantin archives, limited editions are recorded of between 25 and 100.[127] Even smaller figures may be found in cases where the author chose to take the path of scribal publication.[128] Commercially, it seems that for an octavo book, a figure between 1,000 and 1,500 (or a multiple thereof) was the norm. In the case of scholarly books, such a press run must have been predicated on achieving more than local sales, but was not so large that it made a return on an international sale over a reasonable period of time implausible.[129] It is not clear whether this scale of operation was simply accepted as financially viable for the usual team of five print room workers, or whether a given press run was computed by each publisher at the beginning of a commission or speculative undertaking.

Correction, Castigation, and the Provision of Textual Apparatus

Errors in published works were often blamed on printers by those republishing them: variations on the phrase "cleansed of the innumerable errors which abound [in this work] due to the carelessness of its printers" ("a mendis infinitis quibus typographorum incuria scatebant expurgatum") are found in many titles and prefaces of theological, legal, and humanist books.[130] In 1527 Erasmus anticipated that his complete works would have to be overseen by an editorial board to eliminate such errors.[131] Publishers as well as authors were very sensitive to this issue. Conrad Pellikan records in his *Chronik* that Johannes Froben preferred to repeat the day's work with all the costs rather than allow a single error to remain in a text he was printing.[132] This *horror erroris* was shared by humanists and jurists such as Angelo Poliziano and Andrea Alciato, but it was acknowledged by many that few texts could aspire to perfection. As the title page to Erasmus's edition of the *Lucubrationes* of Seneca of 1515 printed by Froben admits, "[the work] is purged if not of all, then at least of innumerable errors."[133] Earlier, Aldus had conceded this in his edition of Theocritus of 1496; a century later, Joseph Scaliger was to undermine the notion of a *textus receptus* by even saying as much of editions of the New Testament.[134] Some works were very poorly copy-edited, and grotesque errors ensued: one cited in Goldast's correspondence by Johannes Guilielmus Stuckius concerned the word "most perverse" ("pravissima"), which should have read "most serious" ("gravissima"), in the preface to the notorious *Oratio de duplici concordia* attributed to Justus Lipsius. The lynx-eyed Quirinus Reuter wrote to Goldast about an unspecified "howler" ("grande sphalma") on the title page of the *Dudithiana,* and another equally grave error, in which "in favour of the unmarried state" ["pro coelibatu"] was printed the place of "in favour of marriage" ["pro coniugio"].[135] His expostulations show also how exposed an author who was not present in the print shop could be to loss of reputation or even worse.[136] If religion as well as scholarship came into question, the principle of correctness, and the fear of mistakes, took on ever greater importance and repaid the financial outlay involved.[137]

Correctors (whom notaries as well as publishers employed) were held in high esteem. The post gave rise to instruction manuals even before the coming of print (the Carthusian Oswaldus de Corda's *Opus pacis* of 1417). So important was the role, that a book, called *Orthotypographia*, was produced in 1608 by Hieronymus Hornschuch to set down best practice: it was translated into German in 1634. From the early years of the century, publishers employed distinguished scholars—Erasmus, François Rabelais, Beatus Rhenanus, Theodor Zwinger, Friedrich Sylburg, John Foxe—as their copy editors and proof correctors, sometimes as payment or part-payment for printing their works (Giordano Bruno), sometimes for material benefits such as bed and board, sometimes for good wages.[138] They earned more than any other worker in the print shop.[139] Martin Lowry tells us that in the early years of printing, Venice correctors were well paid, and according to Erasmus, Froben "spent a fortune on correctors."[140] The same publisher also strongly defended the additional costs involved by claiming that "a man who buys a good book at a high price gets a bargain, while someone who buys a bad book cheaply makes a loss."[141] As well as employing correctors, publishers with the requisite skills undertook the role themselves, and encouraged their humanist friends and those of the author to do the same. Printers specializing in learned books retained as many as three, four, or even more correctors; Plantin set aside a room for them in which they could work together; his son-in law Jan I Moretus set down procedures for them to follow.[142] Printers might also have to pay a great deal for the specialist services of scholars in such fields as Hebrew. Plantin notes that such costs were not recoverable until after publication of the work in question; this was one of the reasons why publishers were keen to limit the amount of time allowed to correctors to fulfil their tasks.[143]

Correctors were accompanied much of the time by a "lector" who would read the author's copy aloud for the benefit of the compositor, whose text was scrutinised as it proceeded. In some print shops, as many as three successive proofs were produced and checked in this way.[144] Correctors were acutely aware of the processes by which a printed text came into being, which is why Anthony Grafton would wish to designate them as "print professionals." If errors were detected after the sheets had been pulled, these were dealt with in a number of ways, by including an errata sheet, or overstamping, or pasting over, or correcting by hand in ink on each copy. As scholars, correctors could not only adjust compositor's copy in this way, but also emend the text ("castigare"), sometimes by setting right errors and infelicities, sometimes even by altering its style and orthography, rather like a modern desk editor.[145] Over the course of the period we are considering, Anthony

Grafton has detected a shift in practice toward a greater respect for the transmitted text, and an increasing reluctance to take responsibility for anything other than emendations of manifest errors or omissions.[146] Correctors undertook a multiplicity of other tasks—writing out fair copies of an author's manuscript, composing blurbs for inclusion on title pages and in prefatory material, supplying the contents page and chapter headings, creating indexes, and penning the publisher's or printer's preliminary letter to the reader or a patron.[147] Given this skill set, it is not surprising that Conrad Pellikan, the forerunner of Gessner, passed from being a corrector to an indexer, and then to a library cataloguer.[148]

Privileges, Transport, and Storage

Publishers or those financing a publication had to decide whether to apply to one or more chanceries for the expensive legal protection of their book from piracy in given jurisdictions. I shall discuss this in the next chapter in conjunction with the question of censorship, with which it was closely connected in this period. Transport in bulk to fairs or to wholesale purchasers was made in various receptacles: barrels (containing about 6,000 printed sheets), chests of varying sizes, and bales, which were generally assumed to contain 5,000 sheets. Bound books were also taken to the fair. All these items were exposed to different risks at sea (water damage), and on land, where merchants' goods might be ambushed and held to ransom. If this occurred, the publisher had to pay a ransom not only for their release, but also for that of the carrier of the goods.[149] The risks and costs of transport were usually borne by the seller, and added to the cost of the books. This made a journey to the Frankfurt fair from London, or even Antwerp, expensive; it was also time-consuming, sometimes lasting as long as several months. Plantin's costs for transporting his books and himself to Frankfurt in 1566 amounted to 131 guilders, which represents an appreciable percentage of his turnover. The transport costs from Lyon to Medina del Campo have been computed at 10 percent of the price of the book.[150] Even the journey from Hanau, only a few kilometres away from Frankfurt, added so considerably to the cost of the books that the Wechel presses, which had moved there after 1596, were able to negotiate exemptions from local taxes from the territorial ruler as a condition of their staying in the city.[151] Booksellers from peripheral countries visiting the fair were prevailed upon to take books back with them for private clients. That is how Claude Dupuy of Paris had books delivered to his fellow bibliophile and collector Gian Vincenzo Pinelli in Padua, and how Pietro Perna had the stock he sold to Italian customers delivered from Basel to Italy.[152]

Publishers had depots in a number of cities or arrangements for storage with local booksellers: these could amount to a sizeable stock that could be used as surety when necessary. It is possible also that having such permanent storage depressed the expectation among book purchasers of bargains at the end of the fair to save on transport costs. Storage also added to risk and to costs, and could lead to the deterioration of books because of damp or the loss of pages through muddle and disorder in the warehouse. Newly advertised titles rather than existing stock commanded the best price at book fairs.[153] The risks involved in stock-holding were borne by publishers in both the Hansa and the branch models (in part because their prestige as publishers depended partly on being able to issue extensive catalogues and supply books that had been printed decades ago. The value of such back stock in most cases declined over time, except in the case of some books that were rare because of their age or notorious because of their pursuit by censors.[154] The low value of back stock made the storing of books doubly burdensome financially, in that they lost value and took up space in the warehouse which had to be paid for. This encouraged publishers to reissue books which had not sold well in the first instance at a higher price with a spurious claim that they constituted new editions.[155]

Advertisement: The First Gathering

I move finally to the first gathering of learned books, and its functions. This would be the last to be printed, and represents the publisher's and his author's mature reflections on the end product, in respect of its format, paper, general presentation, and potential readership. The time that elapsed between the inception of printing and the completed copy varied very considerably. Larger formats required longer production times. Polemics often obeyed the rhythm of the fair, and were produced within six months. For those authors who dealt with publishers at a distance, a wait of a whole year before production of their copy was not uncommon.[156] Authors grew impatient, and on complaining might then be treated to a plethora of excuses. When Guillaume Vaillant asked Christophe Plantin in 1571 why his edition of Virgil's *Bucolica* was unconscionably long in production, the publisher informed him of all the problems with which he had had to grapple. In the first place, he had been let down by the paper supplier, and had been forced to use stocks that were twice as expensive. The compositor to whom the task was entrusted at first did not understand the instructions he had been given and then inconsiderately died. Plantin could not divert any other compositors from their tasks because they were all setting the polyglot Bible at the time. He assured Vaillant that he had approached the Parisian publisher André Wechel through the respected humanist Denis Lambin to see whether he would accept the commission to print Vaillant's work at Plantin's expense, but the copy he sent to Paris was lost in transit, together with the clothes that Plantin was dispatching there to wear at his daughter's wedding.[157] Vaillant's reaction to this threnody is not recorded.

The preliminaries and paratext contained the pondered strategy for advertising the work in question, and giving it a specific inflection. It is not uncommon to find works produced with alternative first gatherings for different patrons or different markets. Flacius's edition of Melanchthon's preface to the Augsburg interim of 1549 had different first gatherings produced in Wittenberg and Magdeburg, for example; Alberico Gentili's works of 1605 had alternative dedications designed for the English and German market.[158] The title page acted as the threshold between the contents and the reader. It was the product of the age of printing and speculation as opposed to scribal culture and commission, and its layout and typeface were designed to attract the attention of the potential purchaser.[159] This could be more or less successful, as we have seen in the case of Freher's edition of Georg von Heimburg in Chapter 2. The inflationary claims made on title pages did not always please the author: Adriaan van Roomen (Adrianus Romanus) complained that he had been given the title of a professor of mathematics by his Genevan publishers (he was in fact a professor of medicine), and had been described as "excellentissimum," whereas he had asked for the book to carry only the words "authore Adriano Romano," which "the publishers think to be too lowly."[160]

It is pertinent to list here a few of the variables in learned publications which reflect the publisher's desire to attract purchasers. The author's national or municipal origin is usually given, often with an indication of institutional affiliation that may also indicate confessional allegiance. The national origin might act as a spur to purchasers of the same nation: this seems to be the case in the use of "Lusitanus" as an epithet, as I have argued elsewhere.[161] In the case of edited works, the promoter's or commentator's name sometimes appears more prominently than that

IN
ARCHIMEDIS
CIRCVLI DIMENSIONEM
Expositio & Analysis.

APOLOGIA PRO ARCHIMEDE,
ad Clariss. virum Iosephum Scaligerum.

EXERCITATIONES CYCLICAE
contra Iosephum Scaligerum, Orontium Finæum, & Raymarum
Vrsum, in decem Dialogos distinctæ.

AVTHORE ADRIANO ROMANO EQVITE
Aurato, Mathesewn Excellentissimo Professore in
Academia VVurceburgensi.

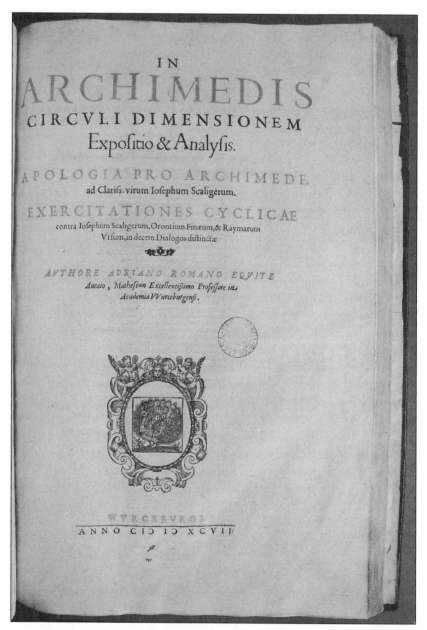

WVRCEBVRGI
ANNO CIↃ IↃ XCVII

4.4 The title page of Adriaan van Roomen's geometrical treatise of 1597, with the publisher's unwelcome eulogy of the author and his wrong association with a professorship of mathematics.
Courtesy of Bodleian Library, University of Oxford: shelfmark C 9 1 (2) Art.

of the text he is editing. Pierandrea Matthioli's edition of Dioscorides of 1565 provides an excellent example of this, but scholar-publishers such as Henri II Estienne or Paulus Manutius also employ larger typeface for themselves than for the author they are editing.[162]

This led the Italian bibliographer Sixtus Senensis to complain in his *Bibliotheca sancta* that "title-pages put forward without measure or shame inscriptions about the fame of their authors so that copies would be sold in greater numbers and more quickly".[163] In the case of some Genevan authors, authors' names are sometimes suppressed on the title page to make possible a Catholic sale: this was done, for example, for Théophile de Bèze's *De iure magistratuum,* published anonymously in 1576.[164] Other authors, such as Paolo Sarpi, employed pseudonyms to achieve wider sales.[165]

After the author and title, there is often a statement of the finding tools available in the volume (single or multiple indexes, table of contents). A great deal has been written recently about problems in the management of information in the early modern period; it is clear that such tools were thought of as valuable features to attract purchasers, and to be worth the additional cost involved in their production.[166] As well as indexes, the most prestigious publications also contained errata sheets. It is not uncommon to find the anticipated class or classes of purchaser mentioned also. Some books with discipline-specific titles are promoted as being of interest to a much wider range of scholars: the jurist Alberico Gentili's *De legationibus* of 1594 was advertised as being "highly necessary to scholars of every order"; the physician Girolamo Mercuriale's *De decoratione* of 1585 was recommended to "physicians, philosophers and students in every other discipline," and the title page of the philologist Benedetto Biancussio's *Indices tres observationum miscellaneorum* of 1597 was said to be "thoroughly useful to theologians, jurists, physicians, but indispensable for scholars of humane letters." The question of targeted readership takes us back to the question of genre: schoolbooks do not generally need to advertise the class of anticipated readers, but humanist and historical texts, works on the discoveries being made in the natural world, and those serving the higher disciplines might each aspire to different, often plural, readerships. A cursory glance at the libraries of professional men such as doctors reveals that they also were happy to acquire theological, natural-philosophical, and humanist books.[167]

The printer's mark or device is an important element on the title page. It represents a guarantee of quality, and was fiercely protected, as

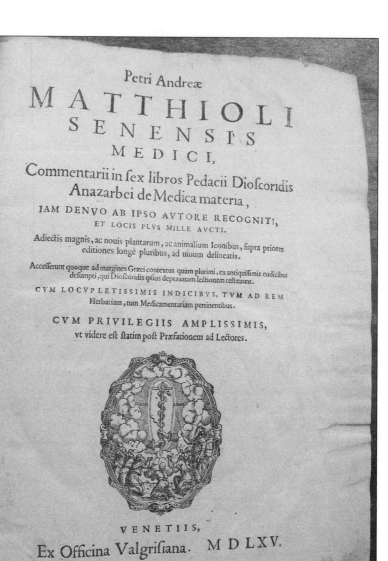

Petri Andreæ
MATTHIOLI
SENENSIS
MEDICI,

Commentarii in sex libros Pedacii Dioscoridis
Anazarbei de Medica materia,

IAM DENVO AB IPSO AVTORE RECOGNITI,
ET LOCIS PLVS MILLE AVCTI.

Adiectis magnis, ac nouis plantarum, ac animalium Iconibus, supra priores
editiones longè pluribus, ad uiuum delineatis.

Accesserunt quoque ad margines Græci contextus quàm plurimi, ex antiquissimis codicibus
desumpti, qui Dioscoridis ipsius deprauatam lectionem restituunt.

CVM LOCVPLETISSIMIS INDICIBVS, TVM AD REM
Herbariam, tum Medicamentariam pertinentibus.

CVM PRIVILEGIIS AMPLISSIMIS,
vt videre est statim post Præfationem ad Lectores.

VENETIIS,
Ex Officina Valgrisiana.   MDLXV.

4.5 The title page of Pierantonio Matthioli's commentary on Dioscorides of
1565, showing the greater visual importance accorded to the commentator than
to his subject.
Courtesy of the Queen's College, Oxford.

occurred in the lawsuit brought by the Giunti against their relative Filippo Tinghi in Lyon in 1578. The illicit use of the mark of another tradesman was defined as fraud ("crimen falsi"), as was the forgery of coinage, and could carry the death penalty.[168] I have already mentioned Plantin's regret at lending the prestige of his imprint and mark to the publishers for whom he acted as a hired printer at the end of his life. In Italy and France, printer's marks were also used as shop-signs.[169] In certain cases, they are ways of disclosing collaboration, or of dressing the title page with the right confessional hue, as in the case of Wechel's printing with the marks of his employers Ciotti and de' Franceschi, which took place in protestant Frankfurt but was declared as coming from Catholic Cologne.[170] In a similar way, Geneva could be declared openly as the place of publication, or disguised behind "Aureliae [or 'Coloniae'] Allobrogum" (although how many people were taken in by this transparent sobriquet is not clear), and Heidelberg could be hidden behind Lyon, as in the case of Jean Mareschal's self-description as "Lugdunensem" (see figure 5.5). Gotthard Vögelin sometimes omitted his place of publication, and, when publishing Martin Crusius's commentary on Homer, even suggests an Italian connection by contriving to include on the title page the name of a scholar of Bolognese origin who published a Homer concordance in Rome (see above, figure 3.7).[171] These cases indicate how important an international sale was to the publishers in question.

The bibliographical address could also declare the financier of the book ("impensis," "expensis," "aere," "sumptibus") separately from the printer, or could leave this ambiguous ("apud," "ex officina," "excudebat").[172] English imprints were commonly more informative than those on the continent at this time, as they habitually distinguished between printer, publisher or patron, and bookseller. This is done in Europe in cases where the book could be sold only through a citizen bookseller (as indicated by the phrases "venales habentur . . .," "prostat apud . . .," and "in bibliopolio . . ."). In the case of shared editions, it was sometimes the case that all the associated publishers were named, sometimes only one at a time, presumably to allow each to make arrangements for sale in his preferred zones of commercial activity. The last two elements on the title page are the optional statement of privilege and the date. The privilege could act as a sign that the book was acceptable in certain places: an Imperial privilege on a book printed in a protestant city, for example, was thought to improve the chances of sale and diffusion in Italy.[173] Isabelle Pantin has surmised that books were sometimes printed

Tho: Leigh.

VNIVERSA
GRAMMATICA
GRÆCA,

Ex diuersis auctoribus per ALEXANDRVM SCOT,
Scotum I. V. D. prius constructa: Nunc eiusdem
auctoris secunda cura facta politior,
& locis necessariis, non
paucis auctior.

Operi accesserunt indices duo, iis qui prius in editionibus
ANTESIGNANI *habebantur multo copiosiores:*
Rerum vnus, alter verborum, tyronibus
omnino necessarij.

Et in eorundem gratiam annectitur, PETRI ANTESIGNANI
libellus de praxi præceptorum Grammaticæ.
Auctorum nomina ex quibus quæq; partes sunt desumptæ
sexta continet pagella.

COLONIÆ ALLOBROGVM,
Excudebat GABRIEL CARTERIVS.

M. DC. XIII.
Cum priuilegio Regis.

4.6 The title page of Scot's Greek grammar of 1613, with the imprint of
"Coloniae Allobrogum" rather than Geneva, to make possible a Catholic sale.
Other editions of this work, presumably destined for the protestant market,
have this imprint obliterated and "Genevae" substituted.
Courtesy of All Souls College, Oxford.

with successive dates, to ensure that if reissued, the stock retained the appearance of being freshly published, held its price, and protected the publisher from being seen as an investor in unprofitable texts.[174]

The most important elements of the first gathering(s) (although not found in every publication) were the letter to the dedicatee and the address to the reader. Both could be written by the publisher rather than the author. In such cases, publishers with rudimentary Latin or no Latin at all called upon a scholar to compose the letter for them.[175] I have already spoken about the financial implications of this letter for authors: for publishers, the letters to patrons were stylised pieces with a predictable rhetoric.[176] The letter usually included reference to the lustre of patrons in comparison to the lowliness of the gift being offered to them (if they were of a great family), and their piety and scholarship were mentioned if appropriate. Much was made of the protection from unfair criticism ("calumnia") which the patron's name will afford the work. The possible benefits that might accrue from having access to clients of the patron in question were rarely spelled out. Very often the patron was connected to a given confession or circle in the republic of letters, and any benefits were given in kind rather than in money. Where there is no separate address to the reader, the aspiration to serve the common good of scholarship was usually expressed in the letter to the patron. It is common also for scholar friends of the author to supply liminary verses or epigrams, as a sort of lustrum, mimicking the formal support that members of universities would receive from their tutors, coevals, or students.

Change and Continuity

In many respects, publishers of learned books at the end of the sixteenth century faced the same challenges as had their illustrious predecessors: how to choose copy; how to manage the financial affairs of their printing house; what to do about competition; whether to collaborate or come to non-aggression pacts with others; how to deal with the material issues surrounding the production, advertisement, and distribution of books. When Michel Simonin wrote a piece asking "Can one speak of publishing policy in the sixteenth century?" he had these and other similar questions in his mind.[177] Succeeding generations of publishers grappled with such problems as chronic illiquidity, the development of international trade through the fairs, the growing requirement to hold large stocks in various places, and the tendency of the market to become saturated. They found ways of offsetting risk through trade associations, diversifying into other activities related to the republic of letters (postal services, money-changing, locating specific desiderata for others), and making commercially shrewd decisions about costs such as the paper and (where relevant) the printer. The widespread practice of piracy and unauthorized reprinting testifies to the constant pursuit of profit through ruthless exploitation of local markets and fairs, as does the practice of publishing *Sammelbände,* new editions, *Opera omnia,* and epitomes, which I mentioned in the last chapter. But the commitment of publishers to highly learned correctors ensured that the scholarly content of their books was largely safeguarded. That did not help them deal with the problem of confessionalisation, which could threaten distribution in Catholic countries and to some degree in Lutheran parts of Europe also, as could the name of the publisher himself. In this the world of books had moved on definitively from the age of Aldus and Froben.

Did the humanist printer-publisher mutate over the course of the century? Toward its end, there were certainly entrepreneurial publishers of learned materials who themselves were not even Latinate (Sigmund Feyerabend is a prominent example, but he still earned praise for his service to the republic of letters).[178] The proselytising zeal of Aldus Manutius for Greek, for the oral practice of which he appears to have planned an academy, seems no longer to be a feature of the generation around the turn of the seventeenth century.[179] The bookseller-publishers—Ciotti, Zetzner, Kopf, Schönwetter, Rhodius or Rosa—formed a new part of the publishing landscape of the end of the century. It would be harsh to assert that these figures were merchants before they were publishers and servants of the learned world, but there would, I believe, be some truth in the claim.

Continuity is found, however, in various publishing houses, and their prestige helped keep alive the image of the humanist printer-publisher. Henri II Estienne is one of these, Paulus Manutius another; both remained active until the last quarter of the century. Thereafter Christophe Plantin and his successors Jan I Moretus and Frans Raphelengius offer an example of the highest scholarly standards, as do André Wechel and his heirs.[180] André is an interesting case, as he had to entirely refashion himself after his nineteen years as a Parisian publisher, which ended in 1572 at the St. Bartholomew's Day massacre, when he fled to Frankfurt. Already during his Paris days, he chose to print on good-quality paper in Greek, Latin, and French, and cautiously extended the portfolio of his uncle Chrétien, which included Erasmus, high-level grammars and textbooks of rhetoric, modern humanists writing in new genres (Alciato's *Emblems*), humanist editions of the classics, innovative doctors (Jean Fernel), and even Albert Dürer. André added to this portfolio the controversial pedagogue Pierre de la Ramée (Ramus), the poets of the Pléiade, and some innovative jurists (Le Douaren and Baudouin), and he evinced his uncle's flair for images by publishing the anatomical drawings of Andreas Vesalius and the surgery of Ambroise Paré. Much of his Frankfurt list repeats that of his Parisian days: humanist texts, high-level textbooks, some French physicians, including Jean Fernel (whose niece he had married), and Ramus. He never attempted to recover his position in the French market, but instead found new authors among his contacts in the republic of letters from England, Germany, and eastern Europe. To his portfolio he added a series of publications of historical documents and some important scholarly protestant theology (a Bible edition).[181] After his death in 1581, his heirs continued in very much the same vein, as their printed catalogues of 1594, 1602. and 1618 show. The fortunes of his house show the virtues of steady accumulation of authors and high-class presentation in terms of accuracy and materials, but even the Wechel presses were not able to survive the crisis of in scholarly publication in the early years of the seventeenth century, as Chapter 7 will show.

CHAPTER FIVE

Controlling the Market:
Temporal and Ecclesiastical Authorities

This chapter is about the privileges granted by various authorities to applicants to protect their publications commercially, the approbations granted to license publications, the regulations imposed on print shops and booksellers insofar as these are relevant to the learned book market, and censorship in its various forms used to control the content of books. This last is usually seen as repressive, and its absence is usually taken to be a sign of a liberal and open society. The censorship operated by the Roman Church after the Council of Trent has tarred the Catholic parts of Europe who recognized its legitimacy with the brush of bigotry and illiberalism, and implicitly associated the rest of Europe with an incipient ideology of freedom of thought and scholarly and scientific openness. This is not a very surprising claim. More surprising is the proposition actually made by an early modern author that censorship can be seen to be liberating and can be gratefully acknowledged. The naturalist Ulisse Aldrovandi lived in papally controlled Bologna, and had to submit his work on birds to the censor Stefano Guarado Centensi in 1599 before its publication. He chose to dedicate the work to the censor, and in a witty prosopopoeia, gave his book ("liber") a poetic voice to thank the censor for setting it free ("liber"): "before, I wasn't free as a book, but as your work of censorship has refined me, Stefano, now I am a free book ("liber liber")."[1] This is an ingenious defence of pre-publication censorship in authoritarian societies: but we should not take the point made here too seriously, especially in view of the treatment meted out to Giordano Bruno and Galileo Galilei by the same censorship authorities slightly later. The liberty accorded to Aldrovandi's book is, after all, no more than release from suppression, not licence of expression.[2] Surprisingly, however, at least one modern scholar has made the same claim as Aldrovandi's liminary poem, by characterising censorship as a form of creative editorial work.[3]

After the advent of printing, political and religious controls began to be placed on books from the 1480s onward. By 1580, most European countries had settled into a given regime in respect both of censorship (whether pre-censorship or censorship after the fact) and of privileges or commercial protection. Legislation controlling publication in terms of both censorship and commerce goes back to the ancient world. The precedent for censorship is found in Justinian's *Codex* (9.36), in the laws on the tort ("iniuria") of defamation. This law defines defamation as a public act, and declares that not only the authors of scurrilous material ("libelli famosi"), but also those who possess it and distribute it, are equally punishable.[4] The equality of guilt and the connection between defamation and censorship were repeatedly reasserted in the early modern period.[5]

The privilege drawn up to establish a monopoly was known in Roman law as the "ius prohibendi" or "excludendi" (*Institutes* 2.1.5.14). In the medieval world it was applied to protect mining processes and the manufacturing of weapons.[6] In the early years of printing in Venice, it was given to one printer, John of Speyer, to protect his monopoly in the new technology.[7] This monopoly was never successfully asserted; if it had been, then the printing industry would have given rise to a guild structure with proper trade regulation, which it did not do, as Erasmus was sarcastically to point out.[8] It was therefore a free trade or art, and what controls were applied to it concerned not so much its production in workshops (although decrees were enacted in the various centres in which it flourished to regulate this) as its distribution. Attempts after John of Speyer to regulate the trade itself became less ambitious. A quarter of a century later, Aldus Manutius was given a more restrictive privilege for his Greek typeface, but in this case also the exclusion became unenforceable, and commercial protection devolved thereafter either onto individual acts of printing, or onto specific classes of printed matter or, if a general privilege, onto authors or printing houses.[9] Versions of privileges were promulgated in Würzburg in 1479, Milan in 1481, Naples in 1489, Spain and France in 1498, Portugal in 1501, Siena and Poland in 1505, Genoa in 1506, Scotland in 1507, the Holy Roman Empire and Sweden in 1510, Rimini in 1511, the Low Countries in

1512, Bavaria in 1516, Saxony in 1517, Florence and England in 1518, and Denmark in 1519.[10] From the beginning, it was possible to hold multiple privileges for different jurisdictions, which may have helped the process of standardisation. Some privileges were hereditable, some not, and in a few cases they came to be held by an institution such as a religious order.[11] Protection for books was delivered at different levels: Empire, Papacy, kingdoms, Imperial territories, and municipalities, which also enacted guild regulations to control the printing industry. All privileges are to be distinguished from licences, which were permissions to print ("imprimatur") granted in most cases by religious authorities and which had no commercial force. They come to be recorded on title pages with formulae such as "cum approbatione" or "cum consensu."

The rules for printing, publishing, selling, and distributing books expressed in early privileges were based on the mischief/remedy model; that is, they cover all the known strategies which had been tried to circumvent the legislation. As new ways round this, or new deleterious politico-religious circumstances, emerged, fresh acts of legislation added new clauses and new procedures to remedy the situation. In the process, the commercial protection of printing became inextricably linked to the controls imposed on it for political or religious purposes. These even impinged on printing shop practices, in that the quality of the books produced had political and religious implications in terms of both accuracy and local prestige, and acted as a spur to the employment of correctors in learned languages, and to the publication of Greek and Hebrew to enhance the standing of a given city or nation. Price fixing and controls on the importation of books are two other areas in which legislation had a direct effect on the transmission of knowledge.

The Imperial Chancery

All jurisdictions have their own history. The one about which I have most detailed information is that of the Holy Roman Empire, whose abundant records are preserved in Vienna.[12] I shall begin with an account of the operation of its Chancery, which regulated the book market in my chosen period, before engaging in a comparative study of publishing laws, licensing, and censorship.

The Imperial Chancery did not only, or even principally, deal with books: among its main functions was the conduct of diplomacy in the Empire. Like other chanceries, it harboured scholars, historians, and humanists, who were also found elsewhere in the court in various functions, including that of court preacher and personal physician to the Emperor.[13] The executive arm of the Emperor—the vice-chancellor—personally signed all the applications for privileges ("privilegia," "impressoria") in this period. These offered protection over the whole area over which the Empire claimed jurisdiction. In the sequence of those filling this office (together with their close assistants) under the Emperors Maximilian II, Rudolf II, and Matthias (1564–1619), there is a marked trend toward religious intransigence, on the one hand, and stagnation and breakdown, on the other.[14] Georg Sigismund Seld (d. 1565) was an irenic vice-chancellor with scholarly interests, who attended the Frankfurt book fair and met authors there.[15] He was succeeded by Johannes Baptista Weber (d. 1576), an opportunist apparently without *parti-pris* (who may have engaged in peculation). Thereafter came a sequence of ever stricter Roman Catholics in and around the office: Sigismund Vieheuser, Peter Obenburger, and Andreas Erstenberger, the last a convert from Lutheranism with a reputation for zealotry.[16]

The business of granting book licences in the Chancery began in the early years of the century, and was affected by a number of legal and administrative acts:

(1) The sequence of Imperial ordinances from 1521 to the end of the century against illicit printing practices and publications of a defamatory, erotic, or politically and religiously subversive nature.[17] These authorized the inspection of books before publication, a practice that had already been entrusted to bishops in the Roman Catholic Church. The Imperial Chancery did not as a matter of course engage in pre-censorship, but had the power to do so. Its task was greater than that faced by equivalent authorities elsewhere in Europe, given the large number of towns and cities within its jurisdiction in which there were legitimate printing presses (about 140 by the early seventeenth century).[18]

(2) The Peace of Augsburg of 1555 (§ 15–17, 23), which gave publishing rights to subscribers to the Augsburg Confession of 1530 (all Lutherans) as well as Roman Catholics, but not explicitly to other Reformed groups such as Calvinists or Zwinglians. Those who were signatories of the "variata" form of the Augsburg Confession of 1540, such as the Elector Palatine Frederick III, claimed publishing rights for their territories under the terms of this Peace document.[19]

(3) The establishment of a Book Commission at some time prior to 1569 in Frankfurt, and the first systematic attempts to control the market through a census of books taken at the Frankfurt fair of autumn

1579. This introduced the practice of inspecting bookstalls and shops, the requirement that a number of copies be provided for legal deposit ("Pflichtexemplare"), the right in collaboration with the City Council of Frankfurt of confiscation of books, and the requirement that those attending the fair should submit to the Commission a catalogue of their books. This catalogue was to include not just books newly offered for sale, but all the titles produced and offered for sale over the previous five years. Finally, the public display of Imperial privileges—whether general or specific—on the bookstall was made mandatory.[20] The city authorities required the stores of books kept at Frankfurt by foreign publishers to remain closed except during the fairs themselves.[21] In 1597 the number of Imperial commissioners was increased to two, marking the foundation of an effective Commission and revealing both a hardening of attitudes in Prague and the growing influence of the Roman Church over the Commission itself.[22] The Imperial Chancery gave no sign of being aware of the fact that Valentin Leucht, their Commissioner resident in the city, himself a priest, also represented papal interests. In 1601 Leucht, who was in conflict throughout his period as commissioner with the city fathers, secured the additional right to inspect bookshops in Frankfurt throughout the year: a recognition of the fact that the city housed vast stores of books of every confessional hue. Seven years later in 1608, a new mandate for the Book Commission was drawn up, which Leucht caused to be displayed in the Buchgasse (the street in which the books stalls were set up during the fair, and where several Frankfurt booksellers had their shops). This set the number of commissioners at three, prohibited clandestine (especially anti-Catholic) printing, which the Council in Frankfurt had acknowledged to be a growing problem, set out new controls over printers, booksellers, and warehouses, regulated the price of books, and made the collaboration of the Frankfurt Council with the Commission mandatory.[23] These measures were especially feared by the Reformed members of the publishing community in Frankfurt.[24] They were vigorously resisted by various territorial rulers, including the electors of the Palatinate and Saxony, who protested to the Emperor over their introduction and instructed their subjects who were publishers not to comply with them. They alleged that the imposition of a requirement to supply not only two copies of books bearing Imperial privileges for legal deposit to the Book Commission but also one copy of any new book put on sale at the fair or in the bookshops was motivated by the desire of the Jesuit order to obtain books free of charge for their educational institutions. Other protests were forthcoming from the Venetian publishers attending the fair and the cities of Leipzig and Frankfurt, where the authorities reasserted their independent right to regulate aspects of printing and publishing, with respect to both the organization and conduct of workshops and the contents of the books printed or advertised there in the Buchgasse and at the fairs. They eventually imposed their own censorship on certain religious books, and required the provision of "Pflichtexemplare" to the city, which exacerbated the financial problems of publishers.[25]

One symptom of the struggle between the interests of the Imperial Chancery and those of the city was the order of declarations in the printed Frankfurt book fair catalogues. In their first decades (1564–1597), the first section was theology, and Lutheran books were listed before Roman Catholic books and Reformed books (variously called "Zwinglian" and "Calvinist"). When the Frankfurt town council took over the publication of these catalogues in 1597, they maintained this order; but relentless pressure eventually led to the reversal of the precedence in favour of the Catholic Church in 1625, and the redesignation of their books as "Catholici," not "Pontifici."[26]

The Procedure

The Chancery issued privileges (the commercial protection of publications) to publishers both inside and outside the Empire, and received complaints and appeals about their violation.[27] According to Friedrich Lehne, their status as either a right or an Imperial grace and favour was not settled in this period.[28] I shall describe the procedure for deliverance of privileges here, as it shows the complex involvement of various interests and can act as a yardstick for those in operation elsewhere in Europe. The process began when a request was received from an applicant, who might be a printer, a publisher, an author, or even an institution such as a town council, and did not necessarily have to be an Imperial subject.[29] This was sometimes a beautiful calligraphic copy, sometimes even written on vellum. A prior privilege or a certified copy of it by a notary might be attached to it.[30] As privileges in the Empire were not hereditable, heirs to a publishing house had to reapply to secure protection for their existing books. The letter of application was addressed either to the Emperor, or to his vice-chancellor, or to the Chancery itself. The wording did not vary very greatly. It named the book(s) to be protected by privilege and the desired length of time the privilege should last (usually five, six, or ten years). It asserted the great cost and labour involved in its or their production, and the applicant's desire to serve the "bonum publicum" by the transmission of knowledge—a declaration which sometimes provoked the Chancery in the name of the Emperor to congratulate itself in turn on its public-spirited support of scholarship and religion.[31] It could apply to republication as well as new publication, although in most cases even republication was claimed to be an improved or enlarged version of the first edition.[32] Privileges specified either individual titles, or mixed lists of books, or as "privilegia generalia" they were sought to protect all past, present, and future publications in given fields ("genera"), or finally, as "privilegia universalia," blanket protection for all past, present, and future titles of a given house was applied for. An unusual case of a successful application for a general privilege was made by Pietro Perna, the Italian protestant refugee in Basel, who was the only major Basel printer not to be named in the prohibitions applied in the Roman Index of 1559 to publishers from that city.[33] He used a connection at court (the personal physician to the Emperor, Stephanus Laurens) to obtain protection for a medical book in 1561, and thereafter obtained a general privilege for all his non-theological books in 1568.[34] When a general privilege was granted to another non-Catholic, André Wechel, in 1574, it specified that both theological and historical books were excluded from protection.[35] The reason for the exclusion of history was, I suspect, the fear that Wechel might choose to publish tendentious accounts of religious and political events of the recent past. Universal privileges were very rare: three cases I am able to cite are those of the Jesuit scholar Martin del Rio, the physician Christophorus Guarinonius, and the humanist Marcus Welser of Augsburg.[36]

The applicant sought protection against piracy for the book conceived as an ideal object: that is, the book considered without regard to its precise material form in respect of title, typeface, format, and so on. This allowed texts reprinted with very minor changes not to count as piracy, to the indignation of the original author or publisher.[37] In the ordinance against piracy issued by the Frankfurt City Council in 1588, even summaries, epitomes, and scholia based on the text were to be treated as book piracy.[38] Although the privilege was a protection afforded to a work conceived of as an ideal object, it is not altogether cognate with copyright and literary property; what was in question was not the ownership of the intellectual work, but the right to reproduce it. Only in Venice (in 1544–1545) did publishers even need the agreement of authors for them to apply for a privilege to print one of their works.[39] Much later, other measures were taken to protect the commercial interests of authors. In his account of publishing which appeared in 1675, Ahasuerus Fritschius records the extension of authors' rights to include the enforcement of contracts for books which the publisher subsequently declines to print, their remuneration for books for which they have a contract even if not published, and their control over projected second editions, but even these do not address directly the issue of intellectual property, which was not codified until the eighteenth century.[40]

Sometimes the applicant sought support from figures connected with the Chancery or Imperial Court, such as the vice-chancellor himself, or the personal physician to the Emperor. Two of these were active in this way: the well-connected Johann Crato von Krafftheim, and Stephanus Laurens, who are both named in several impressoria documents.[41] Such figures, together with legal officials and the court preacher, represented scholarly interests as well as performing their professional duties.[42] In other cases, the application was accompanied by a letter of support from the relevant territorial ruler.[43] A particularly interesting case is that of the Calvinist theologian Girolamo Zanchi of Heidelberg, who applied on 24 October 1571 for a privilege to protect his work in defence of the doctrine of the Trinity, *De tribus elohim, aeterno patre, filio, et spiritu sancto.*

Zanchi's letter was at pains to stress that his book was impeccably orthodox (a word used here unusually in a supra-denominational sense). Presumably Zanchi's application received no answer, for on 19 March 1572, Zanchi's ruler and patron, the Count Palatinate Frederick the Pious, sent a supporting document pointing out that Zanchi's work constituted a powerful refutation of a heresy—Arianism—which was rejected by all the Christian Churches of the day. A curt note dated 8 April 1572 from the vice-chancellor was added to Zanchi's letter asserting the Chancery's right of pre-censorship: "let him show us the book."[44] Zanchi found the procedure offensive, but was very keen to have the privilege granted, as he believed that it would improve his chances of being sold and read in Italy. He had the book printed without privilege, and complied with the requirement to send a copy to the Chancery. At some time before 12 November 1572 (when Zanchi repeated the request), Zanchi's colleague Zacharias Ursinus sent letters to Crato at the Imperial Court to solicit his support for the privilege.[45] Crato's intervention led to the sought-for protection being issued on 4 November

Inuictissime et Clementissime Caesar

Non tam hortatu quam iussu Illustrissimi mei Principis Friderici Electoris Palatini scripsi libros aliquot de Trinitate: quibus pro mea uirili parte et orthodoxam sententiam, quam in nostris etiam Ecclesijs consentienter cum Veteri et Apostolica publice sonat tueor: et haereticam doctrinam atque sophismata quibus hodie multi Anti Christi Ecclesias turbare et Christum e suo solio ad ipsos quod attinet deycere conantur, refuto. Idque ut et Veritas ac gloria Dei promoueatur et ista Ariana ac Seruetiana sementis, quam Satan per sua organa etiam in agrum Dominicum iacere et spargere studet, discutiatur: aut iacta oriatur: et py in sana atque orthodoxa doctrina ubiq̃ confirmentur errantes uero in rectam uiam reuocentur. Hac de causa ut isti libri non solum a nostris, uerum etiam ab illis qui aliqua ex parte in alijs aliquot articulis a nobis dissentiunt sine ulla animi offensione legi possint nihil de ijs qua alioqui controuertuntur in ipsis disceptatur. Imo de industria ab huiuscemodi quaestionibus et uero etiam a nominibus illorum doctorum quorum uel sola mentio offendere potest abstineo. Ac rem ita se habere S.V. C.M. quam fallere nemo sine crimine aut etiam sine discrimine potest persuasum ut habeat humiliter supplico. Quantum autem intersit Ecclesiae utisse articulis de Deo sola uno

14

5.1 Girolamo Zanchi's letter to the emperor of 24 October 1571, supplicating for an imperial privilege.
Courtesy of Haus- Hof- und Staatsarchiv, Vienna.

et vt solus est trino, integer in domo Dei conseruetur.
S. V. C. M. pro sua singulari prudentia et pietate
facile iudicare potest. Restat igitur ut libri
imprimantur et euulgentur. Caeterum quia hoc
commode fieri non potest, nisi S. V. C. M. priuile,
gio muniantur. Idcirco humilis et supplex rogo,
ut pro sua Imperatoria clementia tale mihi di,
ploma gratificetur quo caueatur, ne quis intra
decennium hosce libros quibus titulus est De
Deo Patre Deo filio, Deo spiritu sancto
Vno eodemque Jehoua, sine meo consensu in toto S.
R. Imperio aut imprimere aut impressos uendere
audeat. Fecerit uero S. C. V. M. rem Deo gra,
tissimam, & Ecclesiae ipsius meo quidem iudicio
utilissimam. Ego porro huius beneficij in perpe,
tuum memor Deum (ut facio) ardentibus uotis
precabor ut S. V. C. M. tum suo semper regat spi,
ritu, tum nobis omnibus diu seruet incolumem
et suis cumulet benedictionibus. ✝ Heidelbergae
24 Octobris. 1571.

S. V. C. M.

✝ Humilis seruus

✝ Hieronimus Zanchius
Bergomas.

1572. Zanchi then added the privilege to the reissue of his work in 1573. When it was reprinted in 1589, he added two paragraphs of explanation, the first to explain to the reader what had happened, the second to make the point that the book had received an approbation from the theologians appointed by the Chancery, and was therefore deemed "orthodox" and acceptable to a Catholic readership.[46] The episode shows how important connections at court could be: the ruler of the Palatinate was ignored, but Crato was heeded.

The next thing to happen in the process was the initialling of the application by the vice-chancellor with an indication of the decision, which might exclude certain books from protection; then a lower official (usually an Imperial Counsellor or Hofrat) drew up the draft according to the form indicated by the vice-chancellor, including the precise list of books to be protected and the specific conditions (a legal formula). Before the Augsburg Peace, a "clausula religionis" was included in privileges granted to non-Catholics. However, it seems to have been omitted after 1555, only to be reintroduced (with slight variants) shortly after the beginning of Rudolf II's reign in 1576. This measure coincided with the tightening of controls at the book fair in 1579, and is a sign of the change of mood in the Chancery. It reads:

> Always provided that the aforementioned books contain nothing that is scandalous or damaging to the orthodox Catholic religion or to the constitutions of the Holy Roman Empire, either in its prefatory material, or in the text or anywhere else in any form, or is contrary to good morals.[47]

Before this, even Lutheran theological works could be protected with a privilege *qua* theology according to the provisions of the Peace of Augsburg; but when Caspar Peucer applied for a privilege for his father-in-law Philip Melanchthon's complete works, it was granted under the surprising general rubric "res literaria, militaris disciplina, et literaria monumenta."[48]

The clause following the "clausula religionis" specified the required number of "Pflichtexemplare" or copies for legal deposit (in this period, usually two or three, but later in the seventeenth century the number rose to seven).[49] The applicant was also required to pay for the not-inconsiderable cost of transport of these copies to the Chancery in Prague or Vienna. The draft was then read and corrected by a higher official, who deleted or added material according to his own views and corrected any errors made by the lower official. There are signs of differing attitudes to religion in the form of words used in some cases. In

Mihi vita Christus est, & mori lucrū

HIERONYMI ZANCHII,

DE TRIBVS ELO-
HIM, AETERNO PA-
TRE, FILIO, ET SPIRI-
TV SANCTO, VNO EODEM-
QVE IEHOVA,

LIBRI XIII.

IN DVAS DISTINCTI PARTES.

PARS PRIOR:

AD EDMVNDVM GRINDALLVM, AR-
CHIEPISCOPVM EBORACENSEM, AN-
GLIÆQVE PRIMATEM AM-
PLISSIMVM.

*In qua, tota orthodoxa de hoc magno mysterio doctrina, ex sacrarum
literarum fontibus, explicatur, & confir-
matur.*

CVM INDICE TRIPLICI.

Δὶς καὶ τρὶς τὰ καλά.

I. Corinth. 16. verf. 22.
Si quis non diligit Dominum Iesum Christum, sit anathema maranatha.

NEOSTADII PALATINORVM
Typis Matthæi Harnisij.
M. D. LXXXIX.

13.

*Liber Collegij oīum Aīarū fideliū defunctorū
de Oxon, ex dono Roberti Porter, Mri Artiū,
nuper Socij ejusdem Collegij An. D. 1598.*

5.2 Title page of Zanchi's *De tribus Elohim* of 1589.
Courtesy of All Souls College, Oxford.

AD LECTOREM.

ANNVS iam agitur decimus septimus, ex quo tempore opus hoc de tribus Elohim, primis quidem nundinis sine Priuilegio, sequentibus autem cum Priuilegio Cæsaris Maximiliani II. in lucem prodijt. Huius diuersitatis causa hæc fuit. Cùm author in aulam Cæsaris ad amicos scripsisset cum supplicatione ad ipsum Imperatorem pro Priuilegio huic libro impetrando: responsum fuit hoc fieri non posse, nisi opus ipsum in aulam mitteretur, & à viris ad hoc officium destinatis diligenter perlegeretur & examinaretur. Coactus itaque fuit author curare, vt opus ipsum sine Priuilegio imprimeretur, quò exemplaria aliquot in aulam mitti possent. Perlecto libro & approbato à Theologis Imperatoris, missum fuit Priuilegium, quo deinceps munitus liber, distractus fuit. Summa autem Priuilegij, ne singula, præsertim quæ ad mulctam pertinent, referamus, hæc fuit.

MAXIMILIANVS Secundus diuina fauente clementia Electus Romanorum Imperator semper Augustus, &c. Notum facimus tenore præsentium vniuersis. Quod edocti Hieronymum Zanchium pro suo de Republica Christiana bene merendi studio, de tribus Elohim æterno Patre, Filio & Spiritu sancto, vno eodemq; Iehoua, libros tredecim composuisse, quibus tam veteres quàm recentes errores aduersus sacrosanctam Trinitatem non sine grauiscandalo sparsi, piè & eruditè refutentur, humiliterq; requisiti, vt opus illud contra fraudes æmulorum labori alieno inhiantium nostra authoritate clementer munire dignaremur. Nos sanè persuasum habentes huiusmodi ipsius operam Ecclesiæ Dei non inutilem esse futuram, memoratis precibus ad communem Reipublicæ Christianæ vtilitatem spectantibus, deesse non potuimus, &c. Datum Viennæ 4. Nouembris, 1572.

Maximilianus,

Et infrà
Ad Mandatum sacræ Cæsateæ Maiestá-
tis proprium

Io. Baptista Weber D.

Obernburger.

Summam hanc ideo subijcere voluimus, vt omnes intelligant hoc libro non contineri doctrinam, quæ non ipsi etiam Romanæ Ecclesiæ probetur: quandò ea ab ipsis Cæsareæ Maiestatis Theologis post diligentem examinationem pia & orthodoxa esse iudicata fuit, & verò etiam testimonio, Priuilegioq; Cæsaris confirmata & obsignata. Hæc verò author in hac secunda editione recitari & præmitti voluit, vt ei sint responsionis loco aduersus omnes illos, qui ex Pontificatu doctrinam huius operis carpere ausi sunt, vel audere præsumserint. Ad singulorum enim maleuoloru, & imperitorum hominum calumnias atq; ineptias peculiari scripto respondere, rem omninò indignam esse arbitratur Seneca. Vale pie & Christiane Lector.

5.3 The verso of the title page of Zanchi's *De tribus Elohim* of 1589, showing the privilege and Zanchi's explanation for its absence in the first edition. *Courtesy of All Souls College, Oxford.*

5.4 The Imperial privilege granted on 12 July 1576 to Nicolas Bassée for a specified list of mainly law books. *Courtesy of Haus- Hof- und Staatsarchiv, Vienna.*

an application relating to a book about diabolical exorcism in 1609, the phrase by the applicant "pro communi Ecclesiae ac Reipublicae commodo" was changed into the apparently more irenic "in Christianorum usum" (only apparently, as exorcism was not accepted by the Calvinist churches, although it was by strict Lutherans).[50] On the other hand, publishers who were known to have produced anti-Catholic works could have their applications refused.[51] The precise wording of book titles was recorded, to prevent fraudulent application of the privilege to other, similar, titles. The penalty for infringement was set, usually in the form of a fine shared between the complainant and the Chancery (although it could also entail confiscation of equipment and imprisonment).[52] Eventually a fair copy with a seal and the Emperor's and vice-chancellor's signature was issued, at considerable expense to the applicant (20 crowns; 10 Reichsthaler), but from the beginning of the procedure in the early years of the sixteenth century, good connections could get the applicant off all or some of the cost.[53]

The Applicants

The largest group of applicants were printer-publishers and their successors, who supplicated to renew existing privileges which lapsed on the death of their holder, as did André Wechel's heirs Jean Aubry and Claude de Marne in 1582.[54] Some of these applicants were able to obtain general rather than special privileges, which covered all their future publications in given fields. One unwelcome consequence of this was the requirement to supply a great many "Pflichtexemplare" at considerable cost to the publisher.[55] Christoph Egenolff of Frankfurt obtained his first privilege for a specified list of books in 1536, and his heirs sent in a printed catalogue when they applied to renew it in 1558, shortly after his death.

Their submission claimed that in each case copy had been purchased by the deceased or his heirs, and uniquely printed by them at their own cost. The record of further renewals in 1577, 1595, and 1603 makes this one of the longest-held privileges for a specified list of books.[56] The "forma Egenolphi" is referred to in the Chancery as one of the standard forms of privilege.[57] A somewhat different case is that of Nicolas Bassée, the Flemish immigrant to Frankfurt who engaged in a great deal of unauthorized reprinting and was named in 1588 as one of those who provoked the Frankfurt City Council to enact their ordinance against piracy. When he chose to reprint a work he adjudged likely to sell well

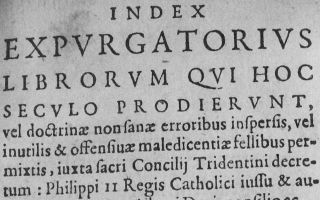

INDEX
EXPVRGATORIVS
LIBRORVM QVI HOC
SECVLO PRODIERVNT,
vel doctrinæ non fanæ erroribus infperfis, vel
inutilis & offenfiuæ maledicentiæ fellibus per-
mixtis, iuxta facri Concilij Tridentini decretum : Philippi II Regis Catholici iuffu & au-
ctoritate, atque Albani Ducis confilio ac
minifterio in Belgia concinnatus;
anno M D L X X I.

Nunc primùm in lucem editus, & præ-
fatione auctus ac regij diplomatis
interpretatione.

Apud Ioannem Marefchallum
Lugdunenfem
M D L X X X V I.

5.5 The title page of Franciscus Junius's edition of the *Index expurgatorius* of
1586, from the presses of Jean Mareschal of Heidelberg. Note the misleading
imprint "Lugdunensem" which Mareschal used on all his books (suggesting that
they had been produced in Catholic Lyon, and not in Heidelberg).
Courtesy of Christ Church, Oxford: shelfmark W k 8 7.

in his zone of distribution, he protected it with a privilege, thereby adding insult to the financial injury he had inflicted upon the original publisher.[58] He was thus not able to make the same pious claim as Egenolff of being the first publisher of the books on his list, but he none the less specifically asked for a privilege "in forma Egenolphi" when applying successfully for a general privilege in 1576. This was granted, and later was confirmed in 1583, 1593, 1603 (by his widow), and 1607 (by their heirs). As well as this general privilege, he and his successors also sought protection on occasions for individual books.[59] It was more unusual for booksellers to apply for privileges. One such case was that of the Augsburg house of Willer, who in 1597 bought up the rights to a long list of law books previously held by the Feyerabend house of Frankfurt.[60]

The number of author-applicants was small in relation to that of publishers. Authors who applied for privileges were usually either very well-connected at court or themselves quite rich. I have mentioned the case of Girolamo Zanchi: another such figure was Caspar Peucer of Leipzig, who successfully asserted his rights in both Saxony and Frankfurt, where his Imperial licence had jurisdiction. One might also mention the Ingolstadt law professor Francesco Zoanetti, whose case for a privilege was addressed to Vice-Chancellor Georg Sigismund Seld, with whom he was personally acquainted.[61] The heirs of writers might also seek protection for their father's writings: Godefrid Abraham Buchholzer did this in 1597.[62] There are a few more unusual applications to be found in the Archives: one from a bookbinder, in 1592, and another from an Augsburg merchant with the support of his city, in 1622. The latter is an example of an application written on vellum.[63] It would be possible to compile a list of special privileges sought in the period 1560–1620, as well as the numerous letters of grievance over infringements relating to specified publications whose outcome is rarely known. Such a list would reveal which books applicants predicted to be very profitable and to need protection from book pirates. This survey would show, I believe, that in the field of learned publications, the largest single subject area given protection was law. Catholic theology and Church history were also prominent categories.[64]

The procedure set out above was legally effective only in the Empire. For works which were seen to require protection in other jurisdictions, such as Vesalius's *Humani corporis fabrica* of 1543, or the Plantin polyglot Bible of 1568–1572, multiple privileges had to be obtained at considerable cost. Moreover, the Imperial procedure did not include every feature found elsewhere in Europe. The Chancery did not seek to fix the price of books (although this was in fact done at the Frankfurt book fair by the City Council); it did not specify the quality of paper or format to be used; its application of the right of prior inspection of texts was fitful; it did not issue explicit ordinances relating to the organisation and operation of printing houses, the quality of their productions, or the importation of books to given territories, cities, or towns; it made no mention of the enforcement of the Roman Index of prohibited books, or of any other local index.[65] It is pertinent, therefore, to chart the differences in the various parts of Europe where learned books were routinely produced.

Venice, Rome, Italy

The vibrant and sophisticated mercantile community of Venice ensured that from the earliest days of printing, book production and importation were encouraged and regulated. The Council of the City, which saw the advantages of competition and a broad base of practitioners of a given trade, resisted monopolistic arrangements (unlike other Italian cities).[66] Its supervision of printing, importation, and selling was undertaken in the knowledge that Venice constituted by far the biggest operation in Italy's book trade, and had very well-established contacts not only with the rest of Italy but also with northern Europe through the Fondaco dei Tedeschi and the trade route to Augsburg.[67] Book dealing was not limited to certain times of the year. There was, as it were, a permanent fair in the city, and wholesalers had their headquarters there, in which they kept large stocks of books. One of the main mechanisms of control was the privilege, which in Venice could be attributed to printers, editors, translators, and authors. It asserted the right to print and to protect literary property from foreign and local competition. After 1517, privileges were hereditable, could be held by printers outside Venice, were usually granted for a period of ten years, and were conditional on the quality (in terms of paper and accuracy) of the book, the rate of production and timing, and the anticipated effect on other printers. The book price was fixed at the time of the granting of the privilege, which could be renewed if justification was given.[68] As indicated above, from 1544–1545, publishers needed the agreement of authors for them to apply for a privilege.[69] Approbation of works to be published (i.e., pre-publication censorship) began in 1480. Privileges became a requirement in 1506. Among the specifically local concerns covered by the privilege were infractions arising from the activities of street hawkers, and the use of bogus imprints.[70] In 1569, legal deposit of two copies of any publication was instituted.[71] No single body had a clear competence to press and try cases under the privileges issued.[72] In order to extend protection to their own printers and defend the interests of the city, the Venetian authorities did not accept the validity of papal privileges. After the granting to Roman printers of a damaging monopoly to print the new liturgical books brought in by the Council of Trent, Venice reacted vigorously by issuing on 14 June 1596 a decree declaring all Roman privileges to be null and void in the Veneto.[73] At issue was the previous status of service books as "libri communi" which could not be protected by a privilege, and the anti-monopolistic policy pursued in Venice, where the authorities allowed any interested party to apply for privileges, to prevent too many exclusive rights falling into the hands of a small group of printers. When the Venetian Republic fell under papal interdict between 1606 and 1607, this refusal became an overtly political statement, in that privileges were issued for (or Roman prohibitions not enforced against) publications which were hostile to papal interests.[74] Initially, censorship was exercised through the bull *Inter multiplices* issued in 1487 by Innocent VIII, and entrusted first to the faculty of law of Padua, and thereafter to the Dominican order, who had fulfilled the role of Inquisitors in the medieval period. Early acts of censorship were directed against erotic images in literary works.[75] The first regulations adopted in Venice emanated in 1527 from the Council of Ten, the body charged with the security of the state. In 1545 the Reformatori dello Studio di Padua (Venetian patricians who were members of the governing body of the University), together with the Inquisition, were appointed as the official body for pre-publication censorship, and had to satisfy themselves that a book was acceptable on religious, moral, and political grounds. In 1596 a concordat defined the limits of ecclesiastical censorship and confirmed governmental control over book production.[76] But the secular arm was still strongly linked to the same Catholic interests that made aspects of the book trade difficult throughout Italy. At least two Venetian publishers—Roberto Meietti and Giovanni Battista Ciotti—engaged in the import of books from Germany that had been treated as suspect even before the publication of the 1564 Roman Index. Gaudenzio Merula of Milan had already advised the Basel printer Johannes Oporinus in a letter dated 11 July 1544 not to send theology to his Italian customers, as it landed them in trouble.[77] Venice's practice of relatively unfettered international import and export sat uneasily with the suppression of such books, and led these publishers not only to acts of subterfuge such as the substitution of title pages and smuggling, but also to the disguising of their wares in other ways.[78] In the catalogues they issued, the bibliographical addresses on books printed in offensively protestant cities by Frans Raphelengius at Leiden and by Hieronymus Commelinus at Heidelberg were not transcribed, reference being made only to the name of the publishers.[79]

I pass now to Rome, where the Papacy began issuing privileges in 1498, usually for periods of ten years. Two features were unique to papal privileges. They claimed validity throughout Western Christendom, although not, as one mid-sixteenth-century satirical text pointed out, in Germany, "because it is peopled by frightful Lutherans,"[80] and the penalties for infringement were not just monetary: they included excommunication. Two early papal bulls of 1487 *(Multiplices nostrae sollicitudinis curas)* and 1501 *(Inter multiplices)* were very cautious in their assessment of the new technology, and recognised that it could become a means of disseminating immorality, heresy, and dangerous sciences such as astrology, divination, and magic. These bulls, and the Fifth Lateran Council of 1513–1516, committed the Church to prior inspection of books or pre-publication censorship (the "approbatio"), for which no financial charge by the appointed ecclesiastical censors was allowed to be made.[81] Before the Council of Trent, it was not always clear to authors wishing to submit themselves to the judgement of the Church whom they should approach, as Erasmus pointed out to Wolfgang Capito in 1517.[82] In fact, the right of censure fell at that time to bishops under the provisions of the Fifth Lateran Council.[83] In 1542 the Congregation of the Roman Inquisition was instituted by Paul III, and it issued its first index of forbidden books in 1559; in 1543, the Master of the Sacred Palace (the pope's Dominican theologian) was also entrusted with the task of prohibition, which was thereafter extended to the newly created Congregation for the Index from 1571.[84] The multiplicity of regulatory bodies led to confusion and some conflict.[85]

The clearest manifestation of papal censorship was the Roman Index, which adopted the practice already adopted elsewhere in Europe in the wake of the Lutheran reformation. The first printed Index of Prohibited Books was published in 1544, not in Rome but by the Faculty of Theology of the University of Paris, followed by five more editions up to 1556. The Faculty of Theology of the University of Louvain published its own catalogues between 1546 and 1558. These academic initiatives were followed by lists compiled by local and national inquisitions, with Indexes issued at Venice in 1549 and 1554, in Portugal in 1547, 1551, and 1561, and in Spain in 1551 and 1559.[86] The first Roman Index, issued by Paul IV in 1559, listed more than 1,000 interdictions. The next Index, compiled by a commission established by the Council of Trent and published by order of Pius IV in 1564, became the basis of Catholic censorship policy for the entire modern period. Its successors came eventually to divide the field of prohibitions into authors under a blanket ban, authors of books requiring purgation, and works published anonymously or by several authors.[87] The Index published in 1596 by Clement VIII added more than 1,100 condemnations to those contained in the Tridentine Index. These Roman Indexes were intended to apply to all Catholic Christendom, but actually were accepted only in Portugal, Spain and the Spanish Low Countries, Bavaria, and Poland.[88] The Spanish and Portuguese Inquisitions also issued their own catalogues, which had authority in the Iberian Peninsula as well as in their American, African, and Asian colonies. These did not just contain prohibitions, but also issued instructions for the expurgation of certain passages in works which could only be distributed in their territories after these amendments had been carried out. The Roman Indexes, with rare exceptions, contained only prohibitions, the project to establish a list of expurgations not having been carried through. This left a void that was filled by the expurgatory indexes of Spain and Portugal, which were applied in other Catholic territories.[89] In some cases, surviving copies of expurgated texts carry the signature of the censor who carried out the expurgation, with the date on which it was completed.[90]

Prefacing the different editions of the Roman Index after 1564 were the papal documents and general rules proscribing in an absolute manner various categories of works and determining the modalities according to which control over the printed book must be exercised. The ten general rules contained in the Tridentine Index include in its prohibitions all books condemned prior to 1515 but not named in the inventory given; all books by protestants on religious subjects, with their works in other fields being permitted only after examination; all translations of Holy Writ unless examined; access of the laity to such translations except to persons holding a written licence issued by an inquisitor or bishop; all biblical lexica and concordances unless expurgated; finally, all erotic, occult, and divinatory writings.[91] It prescribed approbation or pre-censorship, reiterated that this should to be free of charge, and noted that this might lead to prohibition until expurgation had been performed on the text ("donec corrigatur").[92] It stated that possessing prohibited material was as grave an offence as its authorship and would entail the same penalties, and it required all bookshops to display the full list of books they held for sale. Excommunication as well as financial penalties were to be imposed on those who imported, or arranged the importation of, prohibited writings.[93] Book prices were to be fixed. As well as these defensive measures mainly directed against protestant books, there was a positive recommendation of accuracy through the use of good correctors. The Holy See was very keen to see that the learned books produced from Catholic presses could not be attacked for textual errors of any kind.[94]

Protection of the political and juridical rights and privileges of the Roman Church, the pope, and the hierarchy also find a notable echo in the Index. Thus, Gallican writings such as those of Jacques-Auguste de Thou and those advocating the right of civil authorities to intervene in ecclesiastical affairs swiftly gave rise to interdiction, as well as polemical works dealing with the political intervention of the Holy See, such as those published during its conflict with the Republic of Venice in 1606–1607, or concerning the oath of loyalty in England in the reign of James I and VI. Even compliant publishers fell foul of censorship. Christophe Plantin, for example, encountered some difficulty in obtaining a licence for his polyglot Bible, and had to destroy some of his own printings after the Roman Index of 1569 appeared.[95] In the 1559 Index, a large number of publishers based in Germany and Basel were put under blanket prohibition (the curious exception I have already noted was the Italian protestant exile Pietro Perna, who certainly was publishing alchemical and other materials which were, or would be, condemned by the Roman censors). A number of Catholic writers in Italy saw the danger of these condemnations, argued that they were wrong-headed given the general fallibility of mankind and the risk of losing polemical advantage against the protestants by ill-considered repressive measures, and urged upon the Papacy a different policy, but to no avail.[96]

I turn now to the expurgatory indexes, the first of which appeared at Louvain in 1550. The one which had the greatest currency was that issued by authority of Philip II of Spain in 1571.[97] Its distribution was subject to strict control.[98] It specified the inking-out of the names and even the portraits of authors (including Erasmus and more obvious targets such as Melanchthon), as well as any laudatory epithets attaching to their names.[99] In this, it continued a procedure which began before the Reformation, and was applied to other forms of transgressive material, such as the nude figures which appeared in an edition of Ovid's

Metamorphoses printed in Venice in 1497.[100] The obliteration of names and passages in any book of this period does not necessarily mean that it was a second-hand copy or one that had passed through the hands of a censor. Compliant booksellers such as the Giunti of Florence undertook to apply the strictures of the *Index expurgatorius* to all of the books they sold.[101] In Spain, readers themselves were expected to expurgate their own copies.[102] Special expurgated editions of popular works were prepared for the Catholic market, including such works as Erasmus's *Adages,* from which all references to the author as well as sensitive material about the church and its members were omitted (see above, figure 3.2). The inking-out of epithets such as "doctissimus" before the name of a protestant scholar appears trivial and ineffective to modern eyes and perhaps also to early modern readers, as did the suppression of acknowledgement in Catholic works of the fruits of protestant learning applied to biblical and other texts.[103] In an edition of the *Index expurgatorius* which appeared in Geneva in 1619, the Calvinist theologian Benedetto Turretini pointed out that he had no problem in accepting the scholarly credentials on matters of history and philology of such Catholic theologians as Thomas de Vio Caietanus, Santes Pagnini, Claude d'Espences, and Benito Arias Montano, and regretted the damage to the interests of truth and the republic of letters by the suppression of acknowledgement of protestant scholars.[104]

In a bizarre turn of events, however, the Index actually promoted rather than suppressed the books it censured. Protestant editions of this Index appeared in 1586, 1599, 1609, 1611, and 1619, and protestant librarians were keen to acquire it. As the Zürich librarian Johannes Jacobus Frisius explained, it allowed purchasers to avoid purchasing editions which had been "mutilated and despoiled" because of it, or as Turretini suggested, it facilitated the restoration of the obliterated passages.[105] It was also an instrument which some saw as revealing Catholic fraud and falsification.[106] Bodley's librarians actually used the Index as a way of selecting books for purchase in the 1620s.[107] The Index was much less well known by the latter part of the century, even to Catholics. When a Catholic visitor to the Bodleian Library later in the century declared to the Oxonian Thomas Barlow, later Bishop of Lincoln, that the *Index expurgatorius* was a protestant fiction created to discredit the Roman Church (perhaps on the basis of the existence of so many protestant editions of it), he was confounded by having Bodley's copy of the Madrid original of 1571 placed in his hands.[108] Earlier in the century, the Venetian scholar and theologian Paolo Sarpi described the Index

Folget die verzeichnuß der Bücher, so wir zum thail noch vnter der preß haben, vnd noch nit vor diser messen außgangen, new gemacht, vnd noch nit vor diser messen außgangen, new gemacht vorhanden.

IN IVRIDICA FACVLTATE.

Dn.Melchioris Kling Lectura super secundum antiquorum Decretalium.
Eiusdem Lectura super secundum sexti Decretalium.
Eiusdem tractatus de causa Matrimonialibus.
Eiusdem super quatuor libros Institutionum.
Item alia eiusdem, quae autor adhuc sub manibus habet.
Chunradi Lagi Traditio Iuris Methodica.
Ioannis Ferrarii Montani super usus feudorum Tractatus.
Eiusdem praeexercitamenta seu progymnasmata fori.
Eiusdem tractatus de Appellationibus.
Hieronymi Schurpffii Consiliorum Centuriae omnes.
Ioannis Oldendorphi Lexicon Iuris.
Eiusdem Axiomata seu loci communes Iuris.
Eiusdem Copia.
Eiusdem Topica legalia.
Eiusdem de duplici significatione uerborum tractatus.
Eiusdem Actionum Iuris classis quarta.
Thomae Linsi Enarrationes super quatuor lib.Institut.
Vaccedini Schellingij Actiones Iuris.
M.Antonino Ioannis super Tit.Codicis.
Guilielmi Hauitcento Processus Iuris.
Petrus Premus de Securitate, seu fide publica.
Consilia & Responsiones uariorum, per Doct. Iustinum Goblerum collecta.

IN MEDICINA.

Dioscorides cum Commentariis Valerij Cordi.

Macer de Materia Medica, cum Comment.Iani Cornarij.
Nicander Carmine redditus per Euricium Cordum.
De partu hominis libellus Euricij Rhodionis.
De Conseruanda bona ualetudine illud lib Scholae Salernitanae, cum scholijs Ioannis Curionis.
De Tuenda ualetudine libellus Eobani Hessi, cum comment. Ioannis Placotomi.
De Gubernanda ualetudine libellus Ioannis Kisdelij.
De Visu partium corporis humani Erotemata ex Galeno, per Ioannem Lonicerum.
De Compositione Medicamentorum Breuiarius Crocenburgius.
Hippocratis Aphorismi, cum comment. Ioannis Ferorij.
Naturalis historia de Plantis Adami Loniceri.

IN HVMANIORIBVS LITERIS.

Aphthonius cum comment. Reinhardi Hadamarij.
Arithmetica Adami Loniceri.
Arithmetica Lucae Lossij.
Benedictus Herbestus Orationem Ciceronis ad Quirites.
De institutione principum Rheidihardus Hadamarius.
De R.Metrica Iacobus Micyllus.
De re Metallica Encelius.
Dialectica Caspari Rheodolphi: Erasmi Sarcerij Lucae Lossij.
Eurici Cordi opera Poetica.
Eobani Hessi operum Pars.
Exemplorum in Grammaticam & Syntaxin Philippi Melanthonis declaratio & completio per Lucam Lossium.
Grammatica Graeca Ioannis Loniceri.
Grammatica Graeca Lucae Lossij.
Grammatica Latina Philippi Melanthonis aucta & recognita per Iacobum Micyllum.

In Grammaticam Philippi annotationes Lucae Lossij.
Grammatices Isagoge Petri Nigidij.
Grammatica Latina Chunradi Kremeri.
In Horatium Commentaria Hermanni Figuli.
Isocratis Latine redditus per Ioannem Lonicerum.
Linij orationes selectae cum scholijs Rheinhardi Hadamarij.
Luciani Samosatensis opera Latine reddita per Iacobum Micyllum.
Lucani opera cum comment.Iacobi Micylli.
De Mercuria Ioannes Lonicerus.
Physices & Ethices compendium per Io. annem Lonicerum.
Praecepta uitae & morum Erasmi Alberi & Christophori Auslei.
Ratio examinandorum ursium Iacobi Micylli.
Rhetorica Rheinhardi Hadamarij: Item Erasmi Sarcerij.
Stereometria Burchardi Mithobij.

Viri aliquot uirorum illustrium.

IN GERMANICIS.

Iustini Gobleri Tractatus,qui inscribitur der Rechten Spiegel.
Eiusdem Processus Iudiciarius.
Art Notariatus Germanicè.
Formulare omnis generis Instrumentorum,libellorum &c.
Gerichtbuch, von Gericht vnd Landtrechten.
Institutionum libri quatuor Germanicè per Iustinum Goblerum.
Gerichtsbock, Anweisung, Gerichtsks, Manuf.
Eiusdem de Iniurijs & diffamationibus libellus Germ.
Arzneibüchel Joannis Dryandri.
Arzneibüch Adami Loniceri.
Destillierbuch Gvalteri Ryffi.
Chirurgia Gvalteri Ryffi.
Schwangerer Frawen Rosengarten, Item Ryffii Medica omnia.
Hippiatria Germanicolatina cum figuris.

5.6 The printed supplication by the heirs of Christian Egenolff dated 20 November 1562 for a renewal of her husband's and their father's privilege.
Courtesy of Haus- Hof- und Staatsarchiv, Vienna.

as "the best secret means of causing religion to make men go mad."[109] He also noted that condemnations increased the attractiveness of books to purchasers in Catholic countries, as was the case of de Thou's *Historiae,* which Sarpi himself had sought to have published in Venice in the aftermath of the Interdict.[110] Of all the censorship measures taken, the various Indexes had the highest profile, the greatest dissemination, and the most diverse effects.

A general feature of the commercial protection of books in Italy was that to be effective, privileges had to be obtained for all the separate territories. Such protection applied to the printer's mark as well as his publications, whose importance in an Italian context I have already indicated.[111] Authorities were acutely aware of competition both from inside Italy and from towns in France and Germany; when Lorenzo Torrentino received his contract from Cosimo de' Medici in Florence in 1547, this danger was addressed through a ban on certain imports.[112] Elsewhere in Italy, censorship made German books difficult to obtain, even on subjects not connected with religion.[113] Local inquisitors were vigilant about their importation, and scrupulously examined goods passing through their territories. In 1581, there was a particularly good example of this in Como, through which most imports from Germany passed on their way to northern Italy. Pietro Perna's Basel exports were seized in that year by the local authorities, and a large number confiscated, including books by suspect authors on recent history and works by Raymond Lull and Paracelsus.[114] The same authorities were also sensitive to books published in northern European towns other than those clearly Catholic in orientation, such as Cologne and Mainz. But it would be wrong to claim too much for the efficiency of Inquisition and censors. As in the case of Spain, to which I shall refer below, it was possible to obtain copies of condemned books in disciplines such as medicine and philosophy. This is revealed by references to them in the writings of scholars in these fields resident in Italy.[115]

France, Germany, Switzerland

France offers a very complex picture. It is one of the few countries in which the privileges and immunities of printers, academics, and students under the law were set out in a legal tract, composed by Pierre Rebuffi in 1540. He associates the rights and duties of printers with those of the extant category of stationers or "libraires jurés" who were licensed under oath by the University of Paris, provided that they had applied for this licence. The provisions to which Rebuffi refers include such measures as the prohibition on the sale of imperfect copies by students and members of religious orders, the compulsion imposed on publishers to print a book if they had promised to do so, the requirement that merchants should sell the books they may have received as pledges or payments for debt, and the stricture applied to Jews to sell back to Christians the books they had bought from them. Other privileges included exemption from certain taxes and from civic duties such as the watch.[116]

Various other measures taken before 1540 are not mentioned by Rebuffi. These include the promotion of Greek studies, the use to be made of printer's marks to provide unique identification of a given publishing house, the presence of qualified correctors in the print shops, the requirement of legal deposit, and commercial privileges, which were issued from 1498 by the Royal Chancery, from 1505 by the Prévôt of Paris, and from 1507 by the Parlement de Paris.[117] They took a variety of forms (lettres patentes, lettres closes, arrêts, ordonnances du Prévôt de Paris), and cost very different sums, depending on which seal was used on them; in some cases, legal deposit was required. The university could also issue privileges, and had charge of the "libraires jurés," who alone were accorded the right to fix prices for local publications and to import untaxed books into Paris.[118] Major legislation concerning the operation and supervision of print shops was enacted in May 1571, on 12 October 1586, and on 1 June 1618.[119] In the various acts of legislation enacted in the period, the regulation of the printing industry, the commercial aspects of bookselling and book importation, the political problems caused by unauthorised publication and importation, the use of scholarly publication to enhance royal and national prestige, and the question of religious censorship appear alongside each other. The importance of scholarly publication to François I was made very clear by his appointment of an Imprimeur du Roi for Greek in 1538. It was enacted in the wake of his establishment in 1530 of the Parisian Collège Trilingue (later the Collège de France, where mathematics was to be taught as well as Hebrew, Latin, and Greek).[120]

The obscure relationship between various forms of legislation and a multiplicity of courts failed, however, to create the sort of centralised *ancien régime* control which the terms of enactment suggest, although the separation of religious and juridical powers did operate, at least in the capital, where the Parlement alone could enforce the banning of books. The theology faculty of the University of Paris was active in issuing condemnations, but it did not have the backing of an Inquisition, nor did it choose to invoke the authority of the Roman Index, which together with the other enactments of the Council of Trent was not recognised in France.

Outside Paris, Lyon was the major centre of publication.[121] There, the Sénéchaussée regulated the local printing industry, and arbitrated in disputes concerning merchant publishers and printers in the city. When, as a measure of protection for local printers, merchant publishers were forbidden in the latter years of the sixteenth century to issue, with the imprint of Lyon, books that were actually printed in Geneva, where printers were able to undercut the price of printing by Lyonnais workshops, the merchant publishers had recourse to the Parlement de Paris to obtain privileges, relying on the unresolved issue as to which of the two courts had jurisdiction in such matters.[122] The dispute had grave consequences for the printing industry in Lyon, which went into decline after 1588 as a result of the actions of publishers.[123]

In 1521 the faculty of theology in Paris was given the right to pass judgement on religious books, in the form of both approbations and condemnations. Its independence from Rome can be gauged from the fact that it issued an approbation to a protestant, Du Bartas, for his religious poem *La Sepmaine*, in 1578.[124] After various incidents in the 1530s involving the use of presses to spread protestant propaganda, the king intervened in the world of printing, setting in motion the process of state control over defamatory and heretical literature. A sequence of royal edicts and ordinances followed, including the comprehensive measures set out in the Edict of Villers-Cotterêts of 1539 and the Edict of Chateaubriand of 1551, culminating in the Edict of Moulins of 1566, which required that all books carry a royal privilege, and that printers should register their marks or devices and should declare their name and the location of their presses on title pages. Royal control was extended under Henri III as a mark of his resistance to papal demands that the new Tridentine service books should be printed by Italians for the French market. He set up two companies, the Compagnie des Usages to publish liturgical books, and the Compagnie du Navire to publish Church Fathers.[125] Although the Inquisition was not admitted on French soil, there are recorded cases of clerical censorship operating in printing centres.[126] From 1551 a blanket ban operated on books from Geneva, and other places associated with heresy, unless they had been inspected and passed, and the successful use of itinerant salesmen ("colporteurs") by the Genevan church to spread its evangelical message was recognized by a prohibition of this practice also.[127]

The faculty of theology of the University of Paris had the right to condemn books (this was done also subsequently for the Reformed community by the protestant academy in Sedan);[128] it issued catalogues of condemned books from the 1540s. It fell to the Parlement to carry out sentence against them (a position reaffirmed in 1583 and 1586). They did this by inflicting confiscation of equipment, fines, and corporal punishment on printers. In extreme cases this culminated in execution and burning, and in the ritual destruction of offending books by having them thrown down a staircase in the law courts, ripped up, and burnt on the same pyre as their authors or printers.[129] This display of power did not necessarily achieve the desired effect, as David Cressy has pointed out. Just as the Roman Index gave publicity and notoriety to the books it condemned, so also the Parlement drew attention to the books being destroyed by their actions and were unable to control what the spectators of any such event made of it.[130] It was also the case that the requirement that all books be licensed could be ignored by the French chancellor if it suited him for political purposes, as in the case of the polemical material directed at James I and VI in 1609, which was given what in the eighteenth century would be aptly described as a "permission tacite" to be published.[131] The Roman authorities looked on this state of affairs with a jaundiced eye. In 1609 the Legate Roberto Ubaldini sent a report from Paris to Cardinal Borghese (a member of the Congregation for the Index), noting the freedom of publication enjoyed by protestants and what was almost worse, Gallican critics of the Papacy, and deploring what he described as the regrettable "libertà di conscienza" which reigned in the capital.[132]

Papal authorities were scarcely more pleased with the state of affairs in various parts of Germany, especially those that engaged in policies of regulation independent from the Empire, whether territories or cities. As elsewhere, measures establishing religious censorship were found alongside those ensuring commercial protection. I have already dealt with the complex conditions in Frankfurt and the Imperial Chancery.[133] I shall now briefly review some other centres of German printing. In general, the Imperial ordinances from 1529 to 1570 concerning the censorship of defamatory books, and the repression of magic, atheism, heresy, sedition, and scurrilous and erotic literature (explicitly associated with French books) were respected throughout the German lands. Equally, as in France and elsewhere, clandestine printing was outlawed.[134] All sides of the religious divide engaged in censorship. In Augsburg, where Lutheran and Catholic communities coexisted, pre-censorship was practised up to the Peace of Augsburg of 1555; thereafter, the provisions permitting publication of Catholic and Lutheran theology were applied.[135] Where there were only Catholic authorities, the practice of censorship was not as unified as might be expected. In Ingolstadt and Munich, the Jesuits acted as censors, and the provisions of the Roman Index were enforced. In Dillingen, humanist texts for school use were bowdlerised of their erotic content in accordance with the rule set out in the Index of 1564. Erasmus, a prohibited author "donec corrigatur" according to the Roman Index, was not published in Bavaria after 1555.[136] But in Catholic Cologne, where the university held the reins of censorship, Erasmus continued to be published after that date, even more than in protestant Basel, indicating a range of responses to papal directives in various parts of Catholic Germany.[137] Mainz, like Cologne, was a major centre of printing in which works by Erasmus (including his Greek New Testament) had been printed before the Council of Trent. It might have been expected to show the same independence as Cologne, but Archbishop-Elector Daniel Brendel von Homburg was a keen supporter of both Trent and the Jesuit Order, whose college he founded and incorporated into the university in 1561. Under his rule the city became a major publishing centre of the Counter-Reformation in Germany.[138] Even after his death in 1582, the city remained staunchly Catholic in its printing, as one might expect from its proximity to and rivalry with the powerful protestant centres of Frankfurt and Heidelberg.

Lutheran territories and towns followed in the main the lead of Luther, who was in favour of pre- and post-censorship, and acted himself as censor from 1522 onward in Wittenberg.[139] In Tübingen, the Lutheran theology faculty was entrusted with the task of inspecting local bookshops.[140] Pre-censorship was instituted in Electoral Saxony in 1558 and entrusted to the University of Leipzig and the local Lutheran superintendent. In 1562 it devolved on the university alone, before being shared again in 1569, this time between the university and the City Council. A limited ordinance against defamatory literature was issued in 1571, followed by a general ordinance in 1594 controlling booksellers and printers. The later legislation passed stern judgement on the greed of publishers and the excessive desire of authors to be published, evinced the same preoccupation with the material quality and accuracy of books as in Venice and Rome, suppressed general privileges, banned clandestine printing, regulated dedications, and legislated against piracy.[141] It also specified the roles to be played by the University of Wittenberg, the City Council, and the University of Leipzig in the regulation of publication.[142] Attitudes hardened in the 1570s against moderate Lutherans, who came to be branded as crypto-Calvinists.[143] The application for a new privilege for Melanchthon's works, first published in 1562–1566, was refused in 1591, and the largest bookseller in the town tried to get his stocks of Calvinist books moved to Heidelberg before they suffered confiscation.[144] But the issuing of Saxon commercial privileges to both local and foreign publishers continued in spite of protests against their use by non-Saxons, and was reinforced in 1616.[145]

Among Reformed (or Calvinist) states and towns, a case worthy of mention is that of the Palatinate. This territory entrusted censorship to the University of Heidelberg, and issued privileges as did other states, but these are very rarely mentioned on the title pages or in the preliminaries of books.[146] I find this puzzling, as without public attestation of the privilege, it is difficult to see how it could be enforced.[147] Perhaps the distribution of books was so well controlled in that area that it was felt otiose to declare the protection offered by the territory. One feature of Palatinate privileges which Melchior Goldast found unfair was the practice of charging the same for a privilege protecting a single book as for one protecting eight, ten, or twelve.[148]

On the commercial side, we find a number of struggles across jurisdictions to enforce the provisions of Imperial and Saxon privileges. The case of Peucer's pursuit of his rights over the *Chronicon Carionis* is enlightening in this regard. Peucer, who already held a fifteen-year general licence from Saxony, solicited a general licence from the Imperial Chancery on 18 April 1566 for all his and Melanchthon's works produced at his own expense, whether already printed or not yet written or published. It was first advertised on the title page of the 1566 continuation of Johann Carion's *Chronicon*, which he began in the 1530s. This was a history of ecclesiastical events, beginning in the ancient world and culminating eventually in a specifically protestant account of the post-Reformation era. It was a spectacularly successful publication in commercial terms. Carion had entrusted its continuation to Melanchthon, who revised and added to the first two parts, which were published in 1558 and 1560, respectively. Peucer contributed an entirely new supplement at about the same time.

In the same year as the new, Imperially protected, edition of Carion with Melanchthon's and Peucer's additions appeared, a pirated version was published without Peucer's consent by the powerful Frankfurt publisher Sigmund Feyerabend in consort with Simon Hüter, in which was interpolated some material of a politically sensitive sort about the Elector of

Brandenburg which had not been authorised by Peucer. We are now familiar with tamperings of this nature from the Goldast-de Thou case which I set out in Chapter 2. Once apprised of the act of piracy, Peucer took vigorous action. He appealed to the Elector of Saxony, who on the authority of the Saxon licence was able to order the confiscation of all copies of the pirated edition on offer at the Leipzig New Year Fair of 1568, together with the impounding of all of Feyerabend's and Hüter's stock (an immense quantity of books) stored in Leipzig, and a fine of 10 marks and 100 guilders. Next Peucer had the ban on sales extended to Frankfurt through the Imperial licence. This was a more difficult legal battle to fight, as Feyerabend was a very powerful local merchant and the Frankfurt city fathers (fellow Lutherans and colleagues as merchants) were probably loath to act against him, but were obliged at least to investigate the matter. They received from Feyerabend a long document in his defence, making the following points: that no precise details of the privilege were given in Peucer's edition; that the offending book was produced before the effective date of the privilege, but printed with a postdated title page; and that the *Chronicon Carionis* was in the public domain. This was his most plausible line of defence, as the work had no protection in Basel or Geneva, where it was certainly treated as though in the public domain by printers, one of whom, Petrus Sanctandreanus, did not scruple to publish it under a Lyon and Heidelberg imprint as well. Feyerabend finally claimed that all those involved in the modification to the text concerning Brandenburg and hence responsible legally for the consequences of including it in the *Chronicon* had died, and were therefore beyond legal prosecution. Feyerabend's submission ends with a desperate plea for the release of his books in Leipzig and the restitution of the Frankfurt copies of the *Chronicon*. There can be no doubt as to the commercial damage suffered by him and by his partner Hüter, who was bankrupted by the affair. There are a number of other cases of this kind one might cite (Egenolff, Schönwetter) to show how various authorities were enjoined to pursue cases of piracy and unauthorised reprinting, and how the publishers in question tried to evade this pursuit.[149]

A compendious résumé of German legislation on the rights, duties, and practices of printers, publishers, and booksellers is given in Ahasuerus Fritschius's treatise on the subject entitled *Tractatus de typographis, bibliopolis, chartariis et bibliopegis, in quo de eorum statutis et immutatibus, abusibus item et controversiis, censura librorum, inspectione Typographiarum et Bibliopoliorum, ordinatione Taxae etc. succincte agitur.*

Pro usu Rep[ublicae] Literariae, which appeared in 1675. It ranges very widely, referring to all the Imperial ordinances from 1529 onward, and citing Rebuffi and a French edict guaranteeing the importation rights of "libraires jurés" in Paris. This gives indications of the growing rights of authors and the importance of booksellers, but remains otherwise remarkably consistent with previous positions concerning the production, marketing, protection, and censorship of books, suggesting that a satisfactory general regulatory structure was in place by the end of the period which is of interest here.[150]

A few words should be said about two Swiss towns, Geneva and Basel. By 1539 the Consistory in Geneva had undertaken to censor all books; from 1542 onward, as did Luther in Wittenberg, Calvin took an active part in censoring books in Geneva. He instituted pre-publication censorship; in this he was followed in due course by the Petit Conseil.[151] Censorship gave rise to some unease, however. Later in the century, the Company of Pastors wanted to prevent the Talmud, then being printed by the Froben presses in Basel, from being distributed in the city, and asked Calvin's successor, Théodore de Bèze, to justify its repression.[152] Calvin himself had a very low opinion of the many printers who had sought refuge in the city, seeing them as dissolute and quarrelsome; but he was alarmed also by the poor reputation of Geneva books.[153] As a reaction, the Petit Conseil passed a measure in 1556 to bring some order to the industry, to regulate the printing of Holy Writ, and to require printers to employ "learned and diligent correctors."[154] In 1560 a more comprehensive ordinance was enacted, whose aim was to raise the status of printing in the city. It addressed the conduct both of printing shops and of those employed in them, and all commercial aspects of publication. The privilege system was set on a new footing, and certain rights were conferred on living authors in respect of the first printing of their works. It did, however, retain in the same anti-monopolistic spirit as was to be found in Venice at the time, a category of "common books," such as catechisms, prayers, and psalms, for which privileges could not be obtained.[155] As Jean-François Gilmont has shown, however, a cartel of powerful publishers was able to dominate trade in the city, causing resentment in the printing community.[156] The practice of legal deposit was also confirmed at around this time, a measure to improve the quality of paper used by printers was put in place, and eleven years later, book prices were also fixed.[157]

Basel was an early centre of entrepreneurial printing of scholarship intended for an international market. In the early decades of the century in Basel, Erasmus had acted there as advisor on censorship. He was in favour of prior inspection, but opposed the burning of heretical books.[158] Decrees on censorship and commercial controls of printing were passed by the City Council in 1524 and 1531, with the now-familiar clauses forbidding clandestine printing, piracy, and legal deposit (this last not being compulsory, the beneficiary being the university library).[159] During this early period, it was also possible for Basel printers to seek approbations from the theology faculty of the Catholic University of Louvain, in the hope that this would increase the chance of a good sale in Catholic markets.[160] Attitudes had, however, hardened by 1558, when a new ordinance was issued, which prescribed pre-censorship by the rector of the university, brought correctors under the university oath (rather as in Paris), and made legal deposit obligatory, as well as payment to the pre-censor (in contrast to the Roman Church).[161] Religion is not explicitly mentioned in this document, but printers such as Oporinus regretted the loss of "printing freedom" ("Druckerfreiheit") that the ordinance introduced, as it prevented him, in spite of support from the influential Reformer Heinrich Bullinger, from publishing Thomas Cranmer, and later from printing Girolamo Zanchi, when the Strasbourg authorities prevailed on the Council of Thirteen, whose duty it was to see that the Ordinances of 1558 were enforced, to ban the printing.[162] These prohibitions were, however, relatively mild in comparison with Oporinus's punishment (imprisonment) for printing the Koran.[163]

Iberia, the Netherlands, England

As one would expect, Spain (and the whole of Iberia after 1580) offers an example of very strict censorship and control, especially following the measures taken in 1558–1559 designed to close the country to influence from the protestant north.[164] These measures also took effect in the parts of the Netherlands under Spanish control. The law of 7 September 1558 controlled the importation of Spanish works and of books printed in England, France, and Germany, and even regulated the circulation of books within the country. The Councils of the Crown showed a particular sensitivity to books about America.[165] Publishers were required to obtain a licence from the Consejo Real (which had taken over this function from the Inquisition in 1554) and to print it in the preliminaries of the book, together with the author's name, the place and date of printing, and the price.[166] The law also authorised the inspection of bookstores and private libraries by church authorities and local judicia-ries. The pre-publication censorship procedure for new works produced in Spain was also exceptionally exacting. A fair copy of the work in question had to be submitted by the author to the censor, who would inspect it and pass it on to the printer with emendations if necessary; this "original copy" was then copy-edited, before being returned to the censor, and after him to a member of the Consejo Real, for it to be con-ferred with the "original." Every repressive measure taken elsewhere in Europe was replicated in Spain (including book-burning, as occurred also in France and England: the Spanish were very fond of public *autos da fe*).[167] What, however, is remarkable, as R. W. Truman has shown through his discovery of a report written by Ponce de Leon in 1629, is that in fourteen different respects, these controls were never carried through efficiently, largely because there was no single administrative body charged with enforcing their implementation.[168]

In the Spanish Netherlands, the Emperor Charles V had outlawed the possession of heretical books as early as 1530, and instigated the first catalogues of forbidden books, produced by the University of Louvain from 1546 onward.[169] When Christopher Plantin arrived in Antwerp around 1550, he was obviously aware of this state of affairs, and set about securing powerful patrons, through whom he might seek appro-bations and privileges for his ventures, one such figure being the Cardi-nal de Granvelle.[170] His greatest challenge was the publication of the polyglot Bible in 1570–1571. This was not only because it represented a massive commercial risk, but also because he undertook to print the Hebrew and Greek texts alongside the Vulgate—recently affirmed at the Council of Trent as the authoritative text, in spite of its differences with the "veritas graeca" of Erasmus's New Testament and the Hebrew Bible as transmitted by Jewish scholars and edited by Arias Montano. Both of these texts touched very sensitive Catholic nerves, and obtaining appro-bation for the polyglot turned out to be a very long and arduous busi-ness.[171] When it eventually appeared, it was protected by privileges from Spain and its subordinate territories, the Privy Council in Brussels, Bra-bant, the Imperial Chancery, the king of France, Venice, and the pope.[172] Plantin's son-in-law and successor, Jan I Moretus, was to show an equal interest in the protection of his profitable publications, such as those by the Church historian Cesare Baronio, over whom he had on occasions to pursue grievances in Frankfurt against piracy by a German colleague. He also benefited from the privileges held by best-selling authors such as the humanist Justus Lipsius and the botanist Carolus Clusius in their own names.[173] He was very energetic in pursuing rivals who infringed his privileges, although on some occasions the authorities to whom he appealed allowed even pirated editions to be completed if to prohibit them would cause financial hardship to the defendant.[174]

A final word should be devoted to England, which was not a very active contributor to the learned book market at this time.[175] As in the case of France and Germany, the religious strife in the country drove the agenda of control. Henry VIII introduced restrictions on printing and bookselling (including the importation of bound books in 1534: an act which has apparently never been repealed).[176] Edward VI removed many of these restrictions. They were reintroduced under Mary, who also oversaw the establishment of the Stationer's Company as a licensing body.[177] The surviving records of this Company (which are not complete) are a rich source of book history.[178] They reveal the commercial practices which led John Wolfe first to flout its control, and then to outflank it by printing Italian texts, and the fierce competition for privileges and monopolies, the breach of which could lead to imprisonment.[179] Recent work by Graham Rees, Maria Wakely, and John Barnard is enlightening in this respect.[180] By the end of the century, the licensing of books in London (which was by far the most prolific English centre of printing) was entrusted to the Court of High Commission, the Star Chamber, the archbishop of Canterbury, and the bishop of London. In the universities, it fell to the vice-chancellor, who at this time was in holy orders. These provisions were seen as liberal when compared to other regimes: when Thomas Moffett was made to suppress his anti-Galenic tract in Basel, he reacted bitterly by praising "English freedoms."[181] Two other points relating to freedom may here be noted. It seems that a licence was necessary to import Catholic books (one was issued to Ascanius de Renialme in 1585), and unlike the continental case, there was a debate about the printing of law books.[182] One side of this debate felt that the common law was the preserve of the legal profession, and should not be divulged to a lay public; the other was in favour of disclosure. Among the issues involved here are guild control, the relationship of the subject to the crown under the law, the issue of secrecy, and that of the permanence given to the law by its appearing in the fixed form of print.[183] Once printed, it was feared that the law would become common in a different sense, and less subject to the control of its practitioners.[184]

Censorship and Self-Censorship

Authorities at every level between town and Empire grappled with the control of all aspects of the book trade. They set out to regulate the behaviour of print shop workers, their working practices, the quality of the product in terms of paper and accuracy, the modes of selling, and the import and export of books. As censors, they instituted the prior inspection of texts, and oversaw the condemnation and pursuit of those that were banned. It was rare that these acts of regulation were uniformly effective; even in the most regulated society, Spain, the gap between rules and their successful enforcement is very wide. When failures were perceived or new threats to good political, religious, or commercial order emerged, new legislation was passed to deal with such mischiefs. Over the course of the sixteenth century, a positive result of all this for scholarship and learning was the increasing insistence on accuracy of copy; on the negative side, we may note the new barriers to the free circulation of information that were erected. In spite of this, even in Iberia and Italy, the existence of most material unpalatable to local authorities could be heard about and even obtained. Local inquisitors and censors on trade routes such as Como were very knowledgeable about material aspects of printing such as typefaces and bibliographical ornaments, and were aware also of the ruses employed to smuggle forbidden books into their territories; but even they were unable to prevent frontiers remaining very porous.[185] To attribute attempted repression of scholarly, political, and religious material only to the Catholic Church would be a mistake, however. Lutheran Germany and Calvinist Geneva entertained censorship regimes which were exercised both before and after publication, and even the penalty of excommunication, which was an explicit threat in papal privileges, was meted out to protestant printers who stepped over the line of their own orthodoxy.[186]

This survey illustrates the degree to which the regulation of printing had become homogenised throughout Europe by the early seventeenth century. Knowledge of the likely imposition of commercial regulation and censorship led publishers, booksellers, and authors to act themselves as censors. In the case of publishers, the motive might be the shoddiness of the product which would threaten the reputation for accuracy and quality of a given house (such cases involving André Wechel and the Plantin presses have already been referred to); or it might be the special preparation of editions with different content for different markets, as in the base of the Bomberg Bible, which was issued for a Christian public with a Psalm commentary which was omitted from the edition intended for a Jewish readership.[187] Theodor Bibliander's edition with Oporinus of the Koran, which was printed "with a thick coating of anti-Islamic texts," is another example of attempted reassurance of the Christian religious authorities of all persuasions.[188] Benito Arias Montano, made responsible by Philip II of Spain for the Catholic orthodoxy of the polyglot Bible, censored his own contributions accordingly.[189] Other examples of authors or editors acting as censors of their own work are afforded by Jacques-Auguste de Thou, who under pressure from the French court removed some elements of his *Historiae*, and René Descartes, who recast his *Traité du monde* after hearing of the condemnation of Galileo in 1633.[190] There are also examples of booksellers acting as censors. We have seen how certain Italian bookshops acted as agents of the Papacy by guaranteeing to make the amendments required by the Index to the texts they offered for sale. I have also mentioned the initiative taken by Jan I Moretus at the Frankfurt book fair in 1600 to buy in and destroy as many copies as possible of the *De duplici concordia*, allegedly written by his author Justus Lipsius, as a way of protecting his reputation. The phenomenon of self-correction by all these denizens of the book trade is probably much more common than these few examples suggest.

CHAPTER SIX

Sellers and Purchasers: Markets, Distribution, and Collection-Building

Early modern publishers, by their own account, had a hard time of it, having to deal with unsold copies of expensively produced editions, small returns for a number of years on the outlay on production, the depreciating value of stocks, the high charges for storage, the costs of transport and danger of loss of stock in transit, the commission to be paid on money-changing, the failure of clients to pay their bills: all of this leading to chronic problems of cash flow, which threatened the continued running of their businesses.

In the early years of the century, the Koberger firm of Nuremberg had already bewailed the absence of purchasers with ready money at the fairs they attended.[1] This problem bedevilled the Plantin presses, one of the largest publishers in Europe in the latter years of the century, who invested heavily in visits to Frankfurt, and declared an average of over twenty books at each book fair between 1580 and 1620. My own point of departure in this chapter lies in the Archives of the Plantin-Moretus Museum, where their struggles to keep afloat are recorded. In the spring of 1571, the envoy of Christophe Plantin, Jan I Moretus, had just married the daughter of his employer for whom he had been working for a number of years, and he was sent to act on the firm's behalf to the Frankfurt fair, which he had visited before, but perhaps not with the same burden of commercial responsibility.[2] He kept a daily notebook (a "carnet"), which he later transposed into a fair copy ("cahier"). Where both of these survive, it can be seen that the fair copy does not coincide exactly with the carnet, and disguises the rough-and-ready negotiations which underlie the sanitised figures found in the cahiers.[3]

The carnets reveal much about the real transactions of the fair. There is a lot of imprecision in the sums of money stated, and approximation in the computing of accounts; one finds settlement of debt in the form of books rather than cash, or a mixture of the two, and not infrequent use of letters of credit. Nowhere is there mention of the religious affiliation of those with whom Moretus dealt. His various trading partners—some Catholics, some protestants of various persuasions—were there as trading partners, nothing more. They came from France, Geneva, Germany, and Italy. As yet, there was no representative from England. In nearly every case, they were publishers or booksellers; very little was sold to individual purchasers at the fair, although certain German librarians and university professors were required to attend.[4] One particular entry caught my attention:

> Over the last few fairs I have not settled my account with Pietro Longhi, and I find that I owe him about 28 or 30 florins in books. Please note: he has played a trick on me at the last fair, in that I gave him 40 écus in cash for a copy of the works of Tostatus, which he said I would soon receive, as the bale was on its way and would be in Antwerp on my return from Frankfurt. He even gave me a note of the books which were packed with the same Works in the same bale; the bill for this is copied into the Cahier I wrote for the last fair. But up to now I have received nothing, and have written to Venice more than fifteen times to have news of the said bale. Longhi has never sent a single word in reply. So I want him to give me back the 40 écus, to which he should add a good rate of interest for all the loss and shame that I have had in having promised [to deliver the said works], seeing that I did not think for a moment that I would find myself so completed gulled in this way.[5]

Several points might be made about this entry:

(1) Pietro Longo or Longhi was an Italian bookseller and (briefly) a speculative publisher of legal works; he was a frequent visitor from the 1560s to the Frankfurt fair, was closely connected to various prominent protestant publishers such as Pietro Perna (in whose house he learnt German) and André Wechel, and was a key figure in the transfer of books of all kinds (including banned protestant theology) from northern Europe to Venice. He was arrested by the Inquisition in Venice in late 1587 and executed there in early 1588, probably for his heretical beliefs rather than his illicit importations.[6]

(2) The edition of Alphonsus Tostatus is something of a mystery. I have mentioned above (page 62) the folio edition in 30 volumes of 1596, produced in Venice at horrendous expense; the only previous edition was also a multi-volume set, published between 1507 and 1530. It is somewhat surprising that an edition of this venerable age could command the price suggested by Moretus's note; most books declined quite sharply in value over time. This would suggest that rare books commanded a considerable premium. But it is also possible that Longhi had caught wind of the project to publish Tostatus, and rashly promised to deliver the as-yet unpublished text.[7] It is not rare to find projects of editions being spoken of many years before their execution.

(3) Moretus refers to the shame he feels toward a client whom he has let down. As I shall show below, publishers were not only drawn into bookselling as a result of the methods of exchange prevalent at the fair; they were also buying agents, either speculatively by attempting to predict the requirements of customers, or directly, being commissioned to procure given books.

(4) The key issue here is one of trust in commercial transactions. Moretus did not draw up a contract with Longhi; he therefore has to add here that he wants to impose interest payments on him. His only weapon against Longhi is the latter's fear of loss of reputation, which would affect his transactions at the fair. The other notable feature of this paragraph is the fact that Moretus admits to a debt to Longhi of 28 *or* 30 florins in the form of books. I shall come back to this imprecision later on, and what it might reveal about the mentality which dominated the profession of publisher.

The Plantin firm kept accounts of debts for more than a decade before writing them off. In some cases, the non-payment was due to the deferral of settlement to the next fair: the Scottish publisher Andro Hart seems to have attended the fair only once, incurring a debt of 8 florins which he never reappeared to settle. It remained in the Plantin books from 1593 to 1615.[8] We may compare Moretus's handling of Longhi's debt to that meted out to Etienne Michel of Lyon about twenty years later. He had chosen to bid a considerable sum (over 23,000 francs) for the stock of his deceased partner Symphorien Beraud, knowing that he would have to recover debts from all over southern Europe, and realize sales on the stock held in Lyon and Medina del Campo, while at the same time continuing to act as a entrepreneurial publisher and attend book fairs. His creditors initially trusted him, then employed a bounty hunter to pursue him, and finally enlisted the support of one of the richest Spanish merchants, Simon Ruiz of Medina, through whose agency he was eventually arrested. The enforced valuation of the stock he had purchased from Beraud's estate revealed its value to be less than a quarter of his debt. What is perhaps most puzzling about this story is the optimistic attitude of Michel, who was a seasoned campaigner in publishing, which led him to bid so high a figure for Beraud's stock.[9]

Marketing Practices: The Hansa Model and the Branch Model

It is traditional to divide the sales process in the continental book trade into three forms: the fair; the factor (under which figure is subsumed disposal of stock through booksellers established in a single location); and the itinerant seller of books (who sold more than just popular vernacular materials or religious propaganda).[10] These categories are not mutually exclusive; nor do they exactly reflect the distinction between international, local, and regional trade, but there is an analogy to be made.[11] I am dealing here only with learned books (and I have excluded schoolbooks, legal and administrative proclamations, and liturgical texts, which can be taken to be staples for the monopolists who operated in these fields). The questions that arise are the following: Was the market for such books necessarily international, or at least transregional, and could publishers survive only if they had access to this wider market? Was it a unified market, or did it operate in different ways in different places? For example, why did Paris, a major producer of prestigious books in this period, not follow the same pattern as Lyon, or Antwerp, or Basel, or Cologne, or Mainz, or Frankfurt, except during the period 1600–1620? Did Italian publishing need northern European outlets? Was the market equally open to all the confessional interests operating in world of Latin books? Or to put it a different way, how far did the marketing, sales, and distribution of these books affect the transmission of knowledge at this time? I shall first examine the two models of sales and distribution: the Hansa model and the branch system, the former predominantly northern European, the latter Italian, although there is clearly much interpenetration of the models, whose common features I shall briefly outline; I shall then look at the distinctive features of these models, the zoning of the market; second-hand selling and purchasing, and finally aids to collection-building at the end of my period.

Two models of marketing practice among book producers and sellers emerged in the early modern period. The Hansa model is one by which merchants traveled with their goods to fairs and other outlets, sold to other wholesale merchants, kept factors and warehouses in fair cities, sited their headquarters in a centre on a prominent trade route with good local artisanal resources, and licensed itinerant salesmen ("Buch-führer") to sell their goods. An early example of this is afforded by the firm of Koberger, who were based in Nuremberg, but had strong trade connections with Basel, Frankfurt, Augsburg, Lyon, Paris, and Venice. Those who embraced this model of trade relied on being able to dispose of a high percentage of their new books at the first fair following their publication.[12] The branch system, calqued on Italian banks and the practice of wool and silk merchants, grew up in Italy where there was not the same number of important fairs, where the population distribution was different, and where the urban centres were already acclimatised to the presence of shops, some of which were branches of far-distant manufacturing enterprises. The Italian trade in books was dominated from the beginning by Venice. Barter between wholesalers of books was common, and largely conducted *a risma,* that is, by the ream; where there was not the possibility of barter, books were sold *a precio* or for a unit price. Sales to retail booksellers were either made outright with discounts, or on commission. This latter procedure is to be distinguished from sale or return (what in Roman law is referred to as *contractus aestimatorius*), and usually stipulates a given period for sales to be effected; it leaves the wholesaler with the financial risk. As a result of the drawbacks to this system, wholesalers began to establish branches in major cities identified by their printer's marks used as shop signs. They had more control over these branches, they received returns more rapidly from them, and they could use them to make informed judgements about the potential for local sales. Publishers who were adept at this organization were the Giunti, the Manutius house, and two expatriate family houses in Lyon, the de Gabiano and Portonari. Their arrangements with their local managers were often complex and turbulent.[13] The two systems—Hansa and branch—are of course not mutually exclusive; some northern and some Italian firms—Froben, the Giunti—resorted to both methods, as did most of the members of the Compagnie des Libraries de Lyon.[14] Publishers who did not travel to the fairs might also use a colleague as a selling agent there: this was done by Sebastian Gryphius of Lyon, who employed Andreas Cratander of Basel at the Frankfurt fair in this role.[15] In cases where publishers acted also as booksellers, they were able both to dispose of stock through the Hansa system and conduct trade in it by exchanges with other booksellers: this is what Simon Millanges did in Bordeaux. His network of outlets extended throughout the centre and south of France, and included publishers in Lyon, Cahors, and Poitiers through whom he acquired stock for sale in Bordeaux.[16] Such arrangements could cross confessional divides, as in the case of the dealings between Jacob Stoer of Geneva and Jan I Moretus in Antwerp.[17]

Stocks

The two models shared the common requirement that very large stocks had to be held in warehouses or distributed by the publisher to retail outlets.[18] By convention, the value of stocks declines with their age; in the case of learned books, this decline was exacerbated also by the tendency of publishers to issue new "improved" editions of standard works. Very soon, such stocks became partially unsaleable or very difficult to sell. By 1602 the Plantin firm was dividing its Frankfurt warehouse and shop stocks into two categories: "minus vendibiles" or "non vendibiles," and "vendibiliores."[19] When one of the Lyon Giunti family wanted to realize the illiquid capital she held in the form of books in 1577, she had to offer them to a selling agent both on sale and return and at a 12 percent discount.[20] The size of stocks routinely held by publishers of learned books was impressively large. The Beraud inventory (only a small proportion of all the stock held by the Grande Compagnie des Libraires of Lyon) records in 1591 a stock of three million printed sheets extending back over seventy years; at his death, Sigmund Feyerabend held at least 16,000 books in his store; Gotthard Vögelin's Frankfurt warehouse stock, sold off by the ream to Clemens Schleich of the Wechel presses in 1625, was immense and very varied. Booksellers also held very large stocks.[21] When, having received a considerable gift by legacy in 1612, the University of Rostock wanted to set itself up with a library on the model of Leiden, which had already published its catalogue in 1595, it was able simply to buy most of the desired books from the local bookseller Johann Hallervord.[22] Even in provincial Italian fairs such as Lanciano, or in northern Spanish cities such as Burgos, the holdings of firms such as the Giunti were very considerable, as were the inventories of their shops (making such inventories became a requirement of the Council of Trent and other jurisdictions.[23] Other examples of vast stocks are afforded by Etienne Toulouze and Simon Millanges of Bordeaux, and Cornelis Claez of Amsterdam.[24] The commercial ratio-

CATALOGVS
LIBRORVM
· Qui in
IVNCTARVM
BIBLIOTHECA
PHILIPPI HÆREDVM
Florentiæ proſtant.

FLORENTIAE
MDCIV.

6.1 The title page of the 1604 catalogue of the Giunti bookshop in Florence.
Courtesy of Bodleian Library, University of Oxford: shelfmark 8° Σ 27.

nale behind these stocks must have been that the publisher should be in a position to satisfy the needs of his customers, to maintain his credibility in the field of learning, and to engage in barter. The Giunti shop in Florence issued a catalogue in 1604 which lists 15,000 or so titles, many of them (one may presume) in more than one copy.

These include no less than 160 law books with the title *Consilia* and a further 75 *Decisiones;* Bodley's Library in Oxford had been actively collecting works with these titles from the beginning of the century, but by 1620 had only acquired 44 of the former and 33 of the latter genre.[25] Such stocks as the Giunti's were predicated on high volumes of sales, as were the multiple copies of new editions transported (in the case of the Hansa model) by publishers to the Frankfurt fairs. Oporinus, for example, took 60 bales (i.e., 300,000 printed sheets) to the fair of 1557; his warehouse contained ten times this number at his death in 1563.[26] By his purchase of the Vögelin stock in 1625, Schleich found himself with a formidable number of learned books on his hands: this reveals the inbuilt tendency not so much to bankruptcy in the trade as to chronic oversupply of stock. Schleich clearly thought that he could benefit from such an acquisition, but as the market conditions worsened toward the end of the 1620s, it must have been a millstone round his neck. His partner Daniel Aubry blamed the failure of their commercial enterprise on the effects of the Thirty Years' War (principally the billeting of troops), but their vast illiquid assets could not have helped their financial situation.[27] Another figure who was similarly acquisitive, Peter Kopf, the employer of Goldast, went bankrupt in 1633, probably from a similar act of overreaching himself and a similar drying up of sales.[28]

Sale or Return

The system of sale or return, or goods on approval, and the use of catalogues, was common also to both systems. It has been argued that the credit trade acted as a stimulus to further purchasing (on credit) by the recipient, as the risk remained with the publisher or wholesaler.[29] Sale or return is a marked feature of the branch system, and although it was probably governed by contract (the return the books within a specified number of years, in perfect condition), its clauses were seldom exactly respected.[30] When Beraud's executors in Lyon (where the branch system was practiced by the members of the Grande Compagnie with Italian connections) tried, initially through his surviving partner Etienne Michel, to recover either books on approval or money in lieu from a long list of Italian provincial booksellers, they encountered very great difficulties.[31] Books were also returned in bulk by booksellers who made purchases at the Frankfurt fair, such as Georg Willer, sometimes with a comment revealing his clients' adverse reactions (of a historian of the German wars whom Oporinus had published, he wrote that his "intricate and obscure style" had put off purchasers).[32] Plantin accepted the commission of transporting the numismatic books by the self-payer Hubert Goltzius to the Frankfurt fair in 1558 on the basis of sale and return; the firm also occasionally sent books on approval to some of its clients.[33] Perhaps the most surprising case is provided by Pietro Perna, who in 1559 sent some books to Boniface Amerbach with the comment, "I hope that they interest you: you may keep them if you like, or even buy them."[34] A similar comment is made by Giovanni Baptista Ciotti in 160, just before he sent his foreign-books catalogue to the Duke of Urbino, in which he asked the Duke's desiderata to be marked up. The catalogue contains no prices, and no money is mentioned. Presumably Ciotti was hoping either for a gratuity of approximately the right size, or perhaps payment in kind through some specific favours for himself or a member of his family.[35] I shall return below to the mentality this reveals.

Publishers' and Booksellers' Catalogues and Lists

Both publishers at the fairs and booksellers in the branch system (whose catalogues are considered separately below) produced catalogues. These are first attested in the fifteenth century, and by the end of the sixteenth had become quite sophisticated as means of advertisement.[36] Such catalogues were distributed both as broadsheets and in the form of pamphlets. The broadsheets *(nomenclaturae)* could be used as advertisements on stalls in fairs; the pamphlet form (usually octavo, but found also in quarto) was more often sent to potential clients.[37] Both varied considerably in content and layout, but the majority listed more than just the most recently published volumes. Some of these catalogues distinguish in-house publications, and books that have either been bought in or exchanged (as does the Oporinus catalogue of 1552).[38] Most were arranged not alphabetically but by genre, no doubt to assist the potential purchaser. It is extremely rare to find any reference either to the year of publication or the price: the former omission allows for the reissuing of unsuccessful books, and the latter avoids the embarrassment of stating

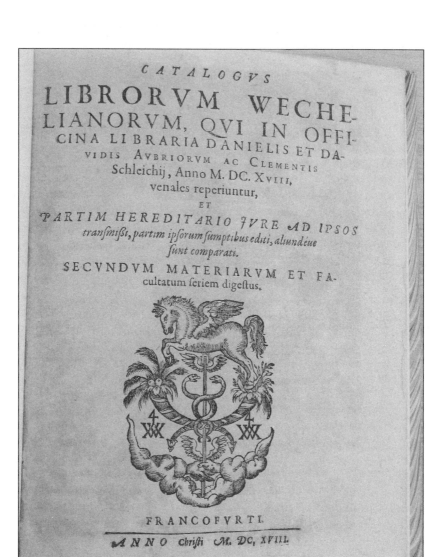

6.2 The title page of the Wechel presses' catalogue of 1618.
Courtesy of Bodleian Library, University of Oxford: Broxb. 106.

variable discounts, which certainly were a feature of negotiations at the fairs.[39] The first catalogue to include all the elements we would now expect—author, title, imprint, date, number of pages, price—was that issued by the Wittenberg bookseller Samuel Selfisch in 1608.[40]

Many catalogues included a fairly complete back list including books inherited from previous owners of the presses; sometimes they recorded the results of barter as well as speculative bookselling. Books no longer available that were printed by the house in question might also be included, and marked with an asterisk. Here one can surmise that a strong statement is being made about the prestige of the house in question as measured by its past achievements, and perhaps also a warning that any privilege associated with the work would be asserted in future.[41] Some catalogues followed the order of categories (and languages) laid down in the book fair catalogues, that is, the precedence of subjects in universities: Latin theology, law, medicine, history, the liberal arts, followed by extra-curricular subjects, vernacular books, and those in languages other than German. Most others gave prominence to the specialties of the press in question: such was the case for Nicolas Bassée, Johann Gymnich of Cologne, and Zacharias Palthen of Frankfurt, all of whom concentrate on legal publications.[42] A well-documented set of examples of such lists is provided by the Wechel presses, which I have already mentioned. As well as the manuscript catalogue submitted by André Wechel to the Imperial Book Commission in 1579, the printed lists of 1594, 1602, and 1618 survive.

The number of entries increased from 190 to 523 in this time. More or less all the titles listed in the catalogue of 1594 were available in 1618, as well as some Wechel publications dating from the 1560s which were not declared in 1594. The order of entries changed in 1618 to conform to that of the book fair; in earlier catalogues the innovative textbooks of Greek grammar, logic, and rhetoric, the prestigious editions of the classics, the collection of historical documents begun in 1575, and the writings of Ramus were given pride of place. The 1594 catalogue is a *nomenclatura* (for a similar example, see above, figure 2.2). Such a broadsheet might be accompanied by sample pages from the first gathering, as an additional advertisement.[43]

From Barter ("Tauschhandel") to Gift

Both in the branch system and in the Hansa system, barter (known in German as "Tauschhandel") was common.[44] Its principles were set down in Roman Law (C 4. 64 *De rerum permutatione*).[45] In its strictest form, it was made printed sheet for printed sheet. Johannes Eck, the theology professor of Ingolstadt, is an early example of a commercially shrewd author who defended the unpopular proposition that it was legitimate to put out capital for interest, and looked for an eightfold profit on the books he published. He arranged in 1518 an exchange with the Viennese publisher Lucas Alantsee of sixteen of Eck's *Adversus philosophos* (304 sheets) against ten of the same author's *Diarium* [or *Disputatio Viennae habita*] (300 sheets) which had been printed by Johann Miller in Augsburg.[46] There was a less precise measure of exchange "per modum cambii," whereby a wholesale batch of books was exchanged for others; in the early years of the sixteenth century, Anton Koberger dispatched an agent to Venice with 300 copies of the biblical *Glossa* for exchange in this way.[47] Sometimes the books for exchange were given a value and marked up as a credit in the accounts. This is how Christopher Plantin had dealings with his Lyon colleague Guillaume Roville.[48] Sometimes the books for exchange were the result of previous bartering with other publishers (as in the case of Plantin and Thomas Guarin of Basel), and were not the product of the publisher's own presses, and might even include prohibited books in Catholic Antwerp, or even just returned stock.[49] There are many examples of this in the Plantin archives. It was one way in which the English book trade, which did not have much in the way of native wares to barter, was able to engage in continental trade. One Plantin-Moretus cahier records on the same page an exchange in 1612/1613 between John Norton and John Bill and the Plantin presses, and a cash transaction with Jacques Chouet of Geneva which it is pertinent here to discuss in detail.

The Chouet entry has nothing on the facing page, indicating that there was no exchange of books: two subsequent additional notes confirm this, with the comments "paid in part September 1612 [i.e., the autumn fair]: agreed a price of 38 fl. for the Corpus [Iuris] Civilis [i.e., a 33 percent discount from the figure of 52 fl. given in the list above]" and [in another hand] "Lent [Fair] 1613 paid the remainder".[50] Together with a number of humanist editions and law books, the books bought by the Plantin presses include two high-profile prohibited works by protestants: Flacius Illyricus's *Catalogus testium veritatis* and Calvin's *Institutiones religionis Christianae,* confirming the house's willingness to put commerce before ideology. Above this entry, there is an exchange of titles with John Norton of London, leaving a credit of 9 florins for the Plantin press to carry forward. Only two works (by Isaac Casaubon

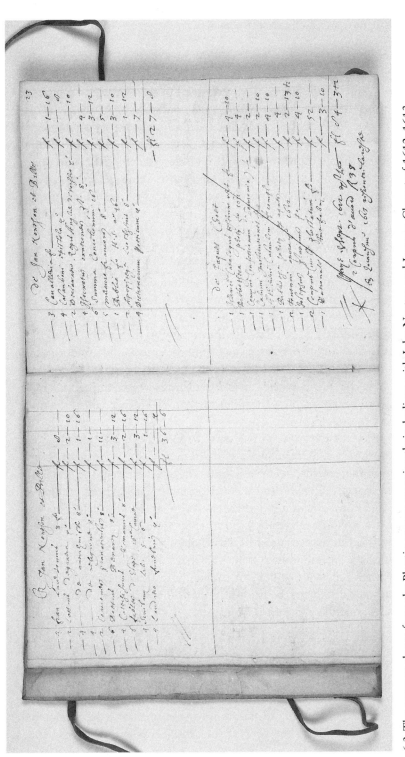

6.3 The account sheets from the Plantin presses covering their dealings with John Norton and Jacques Chouet of 1612–1613. *Courtesy of Prentenkabinet, Museum Plantin-Moretus, Antwerp.*

and James I and VI) are from Norton's own presses. Three titles were printed in Geneva, and possibly acquired in a previous act of barter: the *Summa conciliorum* (Hevidius, various dates), Isocrates's *Epistolae* (Crespin, 1609), and *Dictionarium poeticum* (Stoer, 1609). There is one copy of the presumably rare prohibited *Biblia* printed by Robert Estienne in Paris in 1546 (probably sought after for its record of textual variants in the margins), five of a French newssheet (Richer's *Mercure françois* of 1611), and two copies of Lycosthenes's *Apophthegmata*, presumably in the edition printed at Cologne by Lazarus Zetzner in 1611. The three copies of a folio *Cavalleria* is the Danzig edition of 1610 of Alessandro Massario Malatesta's *Compendio dell'heroica arte di Cavalleria*, which is a slim volume, and explains the very low price for a book of that format.[51] It seems likely that Norton stored these books at Frankfurt, rather than bringing them with him from England. This page from a set of accounts reveals a number of features of exchanges: they could be just books, or just money, or a mixture; they involved discounts agreed relatively informally by the parties; the books exchanged do not all always come from one source, and are not necessarily recent printings. It is worthy of note that exchanges between publishers constitute the vast majority of transactions at the fair; individual purchasers account for no more than 10–15 percent of the total sales.[52]

The effect of the negotiations was twofold. First, books themselves became currency, as debts were settled by provision of printed sheets. This was convenient, because at international markets the economy was imperfectly monetarised through its multiplicity of currencies. In all transactions concerning money-changing, a loss was made, as happened to Christopher Plantin, who in 1586 agreed sales to the value of 200 florins, but as a result of money changing only received in the end 178 florins.[53] The holding of immense stocks now becomes more explicable: these represent capital for exchange, and act as a sort of bank account or currency in the form of printed sheets. The second effect of "Tauschhandel" is more radical. Because exchanges were taking place across the board, publishers returned home with a large number of titles not printed by them, all in relatively small numbers. In their catalogues they often record separately books that they themselves have published, books they have bought from other publishers, and books they have exchanged.[54] This transformed them willy-nilly into retailers. It also made them agents of the transmission of knowledge who acted rather as if they were the bees of the republic of letters, transporting scholarly pollen from flower to flower. While it seems that care was taken by some Catholic publishers after 1564 to avoid returning home with heretical books or books by condemned authors, this was not always done, and one can detect even in the Plantin house the presence of protestant theology; in their case, however, it was always possible to send those books on to the protestant wing of the family, Raphelengius, in Leiden.[55] When "Tauschhandel" ceased to be a general practice (after the Thirty Years' War), one of the consequences for countries that were still on the periphery of the book market, such as England, was that their less prominent or less well-connected scholars received less publicity. Whereas English divines such as Whitaker, Sutcliffe, and Perkins were well known before 1620 because of their exposure to the market through exchange, their successors in the 1670s did not achieve the same degree of fame.[56]

A possible contributory factor in the collapse of the Frankfurt book market around 1630 was the decline in "Tauschhandel." The Plantin presses had already reduced their use of this means of transaction to about 12 percent of their turnover some twenty years earlier, whereas it had been much higher in the middle years of the sixteenth century.[57] It is also claimed that the Dutch booksellers who became active in the Frankfurt market after 1600 refused to engage in "Tauschhandel," which effectively limited the possibilities of exchange at the fair. Non-engagement with market practices of this kind would also have had a negative effect on the ease of scholarly transmission that was fostered by the process of barter.[58] It is difficult to determine the reasons behind such a refusal. It may reveal that the Dutch publishing houses did not wish to import books printed elsewhere because they saw no demand for them, given how well-stocked the bookshops around them were, or because they themselves intended to supply printed copy of the same works. In the first case, two related factors cannot be ruled out: the first, that publishers such as the Elzeviers had correctly identified a saturated market in which further production of anything other than staples was commercially unviable; the second, that the trade in second-hand books was becoming more efficient. This would fit well with the particular mercantile conditions of the Low Countries, which saw the rise of the book auction at the beginning of the seventeenth century.[59] It may also be linked to the preferences of the growing Dutch banking industry.[60]

Barter is at the basis of a quite different form of exchange, in which no explicit account is made of the value of the items exchanged, but both sides of the exchange are represented as gifts. A great deal has been written about the gift culture of early modern Europe. Its extreme forms are found in the cases where books are distributed as free gifts. Noel Malcolm has kindly provided me with an example of 1654, in which an English author invited all his friends and acquaintances simply to ask for a copy of his book.[61] As in the case of the famous slogan "et amicorum" found on bindings and book plates, and inscribed on title pages, gifts of books can be used to establish reciprocal networks of allegiances and deliberately uncomputed indebtedness. This is, of course, reminiscent of the aristocratic anti-mercantile culture we have met already in the case of Goldast. It exemplifies what has been called in other contexts an "ethos of mutual obligation," which is a feature of the republic of letters in its various guises at this time.[62] It might remind us also of other practices we have encountered: the imprecision of the accounts of publishers, which facilitated exchanges; their almost casual supply of books to colleagues on sale or return; and the open-endedness of the republic of letters, in which the gift of knowledge is both specific to its immediate recipient and also an offering to other, unseen and unknown, beneficiaries.[63] My favourite case of incommensurable exchange is that between the bibliophile Lutheran Duke August of Braunschweig-Lüneburg, the co-founder of the famous library at Wolfenbüttel, and the pious Catholic Duke Wilhelm V of Bavaria, through the mediation of August's agent in Augsburg, Philipp Hainhofer. August wanted books; Wilhelm wanted relics, and knew that those residing in the churches of northern Lutheran territories, where they were now no longer objects of veneration, might be released against other favours. In the period 1613 to 1617, August arranged the transfer from his territories of the following: one-half of the arm of a saint, the knife used in Christ's circumcision, three skulls, and the whole body of a saintly virgin (which seems to have pleased Duke Wilhelm the most), against an unspecified number of books, of which the majority were probably from presses in Spain and Italy and unobtainable through the book fairs.[64]

The Fair: Rhythm, Catalogues, Novelty

I have already said something about the Frankfurt fair, that place "like a Noah's Ark full of clean and unclean animals," as the Catholic writer Richard Verstegan called it in 1618. Thomas Coryate, an English visitor in 1611, described it as the greatest concentration of learned books he had ever seen.[65] It was the earliest fair to attract foreign as well as German booksellers in numbers. By the middle of the sixteenth century, it was one of three fairs in Germany which attracted booksellers, the other two being Strasbourg and Leipzig. Strasbourg did not issue composite catalogues, and so much less is known about the books made available for on sale there. Leipzig issued catalogues from 1594 onward, and it is generally supposed that Leipzig overtook Frankfurt as the preeminent fair for the book trade in the first decade of the seventeenth century, but this is true only of the vernacular production in the period we are considering.[66] It is, however, the case that much of the trade with northern and eastern Europe was mainly conducted out of the Saxon city. Other important fairs were held at Medina del Campo and Lyon, where the fair took place twice and four times a year, respectively, and the same freedoms pertained as in Frankfurt with regard to import and export tolls, usury, money-changing, and legal regulation. In Italy, only Lanciano, Recanati, Foligno, and Naples attracted booksellers in any numbers. There were fairs in Venice, but as the saying had it, there was an all-year fair there which made the specific times of the specific fairs less significant.[67] Whether an unspoken pact made it possible for merchants to attend a number of fairs in sequence is not altogether clear: during the months in which travel was possible, such a sequence does seem to occur in two market zones (Frankfurt, Strasbourg, Leipzig, and Basel: Medina del Campo and Lyon).[68]

The volume of trade in books and paper of the Frankfurt fair by the end of the century was considerable, although it initially represented only about one-twelfth of all the mercantile activity at the fair.[69] In the spring of 1579, for example, Plantin shipped six barrels of books containing 67 titles and 5,212 copies to Frankfurt; he was able to sell or otherwise dispose of two-thirds of these by the end of the fair.[70] Among his and his successors' most important clients were the Willers of Augsburg, whose sphere of activity as booksellers ranged over a wide swathe of southern Germany, and who regularly bought about a tenth of Plantin's books on offer.[71] Other surviving accounts support the presumption that the level of trade was high. I have already mentioned Oporinus's sixty bales of books transported to the fair in 1557; the resident Frankfurt figure of Sigmund Feyerabend did 2,627 guilders of business in 1566.[72] The international nature of the visitors can be gauged from Schwetschke's records. In 1569, for example, the fair was visited by three Venetian publishers, four from Lyon, and several Genevans. By 1609 there were still very few Venetians (although the one who came represented a consortium of printers), but there were twenty-two publishers from Paris, and six from Lyon.[73] The price of books was regulated at the fair by the City Council; but it was exceedingly difficult to police, as transport and other costs could be added, and books sold to important clients or agents at variable rates of discount.[74] This helps explain the absence of any prices from published catalogues and *nomenclaturae*.

Several further points about the fair catalogues need to be made here. It is likely that they were compiled in the first few days of the fair, and it is not difficult to demonstrate that they were not very reliable guides to the books on offer.[75] Not all of these were recorded; the *nomenclaturae* on the stalls indicated other potential purchases available through the warehouses maintained at Frankfurt by the major foreign publishers. After about 1570 the fair catalogues concentrated on new declarations, as the wording on their title pages indicate; they also listed in an appendix the books which were due to be available at future fairs, some of which might have been advertised before their production had been completed by the distribution of the mock-up of the first gathering.[76] Such declarations were clearly intended as a preemptive strike against pirating and unauthorised printing. The twice-yearly rhythm of the fair determined the settlement dates between publishers, and had a clear effect on learned disputes. It dominated any polemical exchange, whether religious or scientific; witness the Calvin–Pighius exchanges, those between Heinz Buscher and Johannes Piscator, those concerning Georg am Wald and alchemy, and those concerning the affair of the golden tooth in 1595–1597.[77] It caused certain publications to lack proper apparatus, as in the case of Casaubon's Polybius of 1617, or to be finished in a scrappy way, as happened to Corvinus's publication of Georg Sohn's works in 1591.[78]

Distribution by Retail Sales, Colportage, and Individual Scholars

Publishers could of course dispose of multiple copies outside the fairs: Julianne Simpson's recent study of the sales of the Plantin polyglot affords one good example of this.[79] The branch system, and the supply of books to retail booksellers in given zones, also had the consequence that multiples of most books were provided as stock. From the beginnings of the book market, the setting up of branches, either by individual publishers or consortia, was practised: by 1515, for example, Basel had outlets in both Lyon and Paris.[80] One might quote as later examples of this practice the Plantin branch in Paris run by Plantin's son-in-law Gilles Beys (until Plantin was forced through financial hardship to sell it to Michel Sonnius in 1577) and the Leiden operation run by Frans Raphelengius, who as a protestant could act as a useful imprint for certain books, and an agent for others that the Catholic outlet in Antwerp could not be seen to handle.[81] Plantin and his successors were very active as distributors of their books to the retail trade in northern France and the southern Netherlands.[81] André Wechel set up outlets in Prague and Vienna which were run by his eventual sons-in-law and heirs Claude de Marne and Jean Aubry.[82] As Angela Nuovo has shown, this is the dominant means of distribution in Italy. When Vincenzo Valgrisi was interrogated by the Inquisition on suspicion of heresy in 1559, he admitted to having bookshops in Bologna, Macerata, Padua, Foligno, Recanati, Lanciano, and Frankfurt, although it is likely that in the latter four cases, these were temporary stalls operating only during the fairs. The Giunti and Giolito families also had multiple outlets.[83] In Frankfurt, the resident booksellers Nikolas Roth, Johann Stein, and Johann Spiess stocked books on behalf of publishers in Augsburg, Nuremberg, and Strasbourg, which they could sell outside the periods of the fair.[84] The Willer bookshop in Augsburg was so well stocked that it was preferred to the Frankfurt book fair itself as a source of books by some southern German booksellers.[85]

It might be argued that the credit extended to the retail business by publishing houses was a stimulus to the acquisition of further stock by such outlets, and promoted a more efficient transmission of learned books. For cities where only citizens could sell books between fairs, publishers from elsewhere found agents among their number. The first great Frankfurt bookseller who devoted himself entirely to the retail trade was Paul Brachfeldt, who prided himself on the extent of his holdings, and advertised his services in the fair catalogue of spring 1597, offering to send books to scholars to save them from unnecessary journeys.[86] We have already met in various contexts another such enterprising bookseller, Peter Kopf, who got into trouble in Leipzig in the 1590s by trying to sell books there outside the fair dates.[87] Publishers could also have direct arrangements with local booksellers, as did the Plantin presses. Indeed, after 1609 the balance of their trade shifted from the Frankfurt fairs to this local distribution.[88] The Low Countries had a number of well-stocked outlets, which had the lowest level of interference from the confessional pressures which were felt in much of Europe, and stocked theology of all persuasions. Two might here be mentioned: that in Emden, whose stock was catalogued in 1567, and the Amsterdam shop of Cornelis Claesz, whose extensive catalogue of 1604 was said to list only a fraction of his total stock.[89]

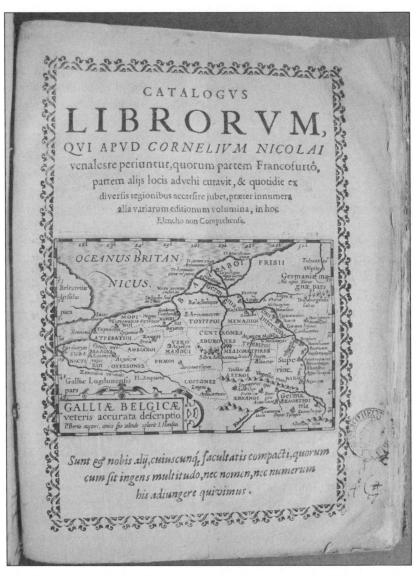

6.4 The title page of Cornelis Claesz's bookshop catalogue of 1604.
Courtesy of Bodleian Library, University of Oxford: shelfmark 4° C 57 (1) Art.

Such bookshops were often regulated with respect to the price they could charge for books: the Elzevier in Amsterdam were allowed to charge only a small mark-up on the price set by the fair authorities in Frankfurt, as was Hans Gruppenbach in Tübingen.[90] I have already mentioned the Giunti bookshop in Florence, with its 15,000 titles. In the same year as that catalogue was issued (1604), the heirs of Guillaume Roville also produced one in Lyon, listing about a third the number of entries.[91] Both of these contain legal, medical, and natural-philosophical books which figured in the Roman Index, but no protestant theology. The Giunti interestingly also claimed in the preface to their catalogue to be no more than "semidocti," thus disavowing any responsibility for the Latin titles in the bookshop. They portray themselves as not full members of the world of learning, but merely its servants in locating, acquiring, and stocking desiderata for scholars.[92] This is not the impression given in northern Europe by Cornelis Claez of Amsterdam or Paul Brachfeldt of Frankfurt in the same decade; neither was modest about his own expertise. The difference may well be a reflection of the presence or absence of the Inquisition. The instruction issued by this body in the period 1597–1603 to Italian religious houses, requiring them to supply complete inventories of their libraries, may have prompted Italian bookshops to comply with the much earlier Tridentine order to make lists of their stock available to local ecclesiastical authorities, and that in turn may have encouraged bookshops abroad to do the same.[93]

Below the level of distribution of the bookshop lies the less easily mapped area of "colportage" and initiatives taken by publishers and scholars on each other's behalf. The contemporary term "Buchführer" covers both bookshop owners and itinerant salesmen, who were active throughout Europe. Those attending the book fairs could also be distributors at this less formal level.[94] Publishers such as Plantin and Simon Goulart were often sent to the book fairs with specific commissions; and we have seen that Pietro Perna was happy to send out books to prospective clients on approval, based on their assumed interests.[95] Goulart made purchases on behalf of Sebastian Schobinger in this way in 1618, and Claude Dupuy and Gian Vincenzo Pinelli also acted as speculative agents for each other in the distant markets of Paris and Venice, using the good offices of printers attending the fair to ensure that the books were delivered.[96] The catalogues of books from outside Italy produced by Ciotti and Meietti constitute also a rather exalted form of *colportage*. In both cases, this was associated with personal risk: Ciotti suffered imprisonment for importing German books in 1599, and Meietti was excommunicated during the Venice Interdict of 1606–1607 partly on the grounds of his involvement with northern Europe.[97]

Bookshops and Sociability

A feature of bookshops, as of publishers' houses in Paris, Frankfurt, and Antwerp, was their use as places of sociability. The wares on offer were able to be read by visitors, making the shop a sort of public library. Angela Nuovo has recorded the meetings of churchmen, nobles, scholars, and academicians in Rome, where in a relaxed and unhierarchical environment, free discussion was able to take place.[98] From Georg Willer's account of reader reaction to one of Oporinus's publications, we may deduce that the same occurred in Augsburg, and Henri II Estienne's essay on the Frankfurt fair says that it was the case there also.[99] It is difficult to measure the effect of this sort of social space on the development of the republic of letters, but one may assume that it was not negligible. One feature of bookshops which has already been noted led to their use as libraries, namely the exceptionally high stocks carried by booksellers, and their pride in their holdings. I have already mentioned Brachfeldt in Frankfurt; Claesz in Amsterdam; the Giunti in Florence; Millanges and Etienne Toulouze in Bordeaux. In Paris and Lyon, the situation may have been somewhat different, especially after the events of 1572, which saw the persecution and in some cases assassination of prominent protestant booksellers and publishers. It seems unlikely that thereafter bookshops continued to act as meeting places; and it may be no coincidence that the emergence of scholarly assemblies in private libraries and studies dates from around this period. The one surviving near-contemporary image of a bookselling is that by Abraham Bosse dating from 1630, showing bookshops in the Galerie du Palais in Paris as meeting places for fops.[100]

The Second-Hand Market: Book Auctions

One might expect, given the evidence of long survival of books and market saturation from the early part of the sixteenth century, that an efficient second-hand market would have developed and that the effect of such books on the market for new publications would attract comment from publishers, which it does not. One must distinguish here between rare books, which were often known about only through being seen in scholars' libraries, and books of not recent date, the details of which were known through such instruments as *nomenclaturae* and which were often presumed to be available through the publishers listing them, even though published as much as fifty years earlier. Rare books, such as the work on Anglo-Saxon laws seen by Lingelsheim in Freher's library in the 1600s, often were unobtainable and had to be borrowed from their owners.[101] Goldast let Freher know the titles of the rare books he was able to acquire, such as a 1506 work on Saxon law published in Cracow, or a 1477 work on feudal law published in Venice.[102] He does not say how he acquired these, but it is to be presumed that they were on sale somewhere among the vast book stocks available for purchase in Frankfurt. In Paris it may have been relatively easy to find one's way to such books if one was a member of the scholarly community, as one or two guides to libraries had appeared (notably that by Robert Constantin), as well as the invaluable Gessner and its continuations.[103] Perhaps such instruments allowed Jacques-Auguste de Thou to know about the edition by the Parisian printer Josse Bade of William of Ockham of 1496 (see above, page 33). In Johann Crato von Krafftheim's letters, and in the set of medical letters entitled *Cista medica* that appeared in 1626, there are other indications of data about rare books being exchanged, and by the final part of the century, specialist bibliographies began to appear, which are discussed below.[104] It is not clear, however, at what point books became collectable because of their age. "Livre viel" is not a complimentary term in the inventory of the holdings of Symphorien Beraud (it betokens poor saleability); a generation later, black letter or gothic printing was said by Naudé to put off modern scholars.[105] When bookshops in Italy were sold up, their contents were liquidated by the ream.[106] But there are hints elsewhere that antiquarian collecting and the pursuit of rarities extended beyond the market for manuscripts.[107]

An indication that a work on sale is second-hand was that it was offered already bound, as nearly all new books were sold unbound at this time.[108] Angela Nuovo records such stocks in Italian bookshops, and in the inventory of the late Sigmund Feyerabend's stock, there are 600 bound folio works of law, which may well have been second-hand.[109] In university towns such as Oxford and Cambridge, there are inventories of the libraries of deceased fellows, and a few clues as to the manner of disposal of the libraries of such scholars.[110] In some universities, the private libraries of professors were sold or auctioned in the institution itself after their death.[111] Other collections came to be heard of through less official means, and bids made for them. The itinerant bibliophile Giovanni Bonifacio got wind of the disposal of the library of two pastors in Lörrach near Basel, and sent the executors a note on which he recorded his desiderata, and the sums he was prepared to pay.[112] Earlier, a Spaniard with the name Casidoro de Reyna bought up the library of the deceased Johannes Oporinus in 1568, and shipped it to Frankfurt, where he managed to sell it off after some initial difficulties.[113] Angela Nuovo and Kevin Stevens have written about the disposal of Pinelli's library and that of the jurist Omobone Redenaschi in the first decade of the seventeenth century in Italy, but such cases are not very often recorded.[114] Gabriel Naudé recommends second-hand purchasing to aspirant book collectors in the 1620s.[115] It seems quite common for whole libraries to be sought and acquired in this period: the municipal authorities of Augsburg did this, as did the Elector palatinate (from Ulrich Fugger); Naudé makes a point of recommending it as a strategy of acquisition.[116] The Earl of Arundel set out to do the same with part of Willibald Pirckheimer's library in the 1630s, but his ploy of trying to reduce the price by referring to old editions as unappealing did not work.[117] As for auctions, these do not seem to antedate the last decade of the sixteenth century, and they were initially a uniquely Dutch phenomenon.[118]

Market Zones

The evidence from library holdings shows that publishers of identical or similar texts operated successfully in certain relatively well-defined zones. Zoning occurs in both the Hansa and the branch models; the branch model, however, was marked by an earlier grasp of wide distribution as the means of achieving an international sale, as is shown by Martin Lowry's study of the Strozzi network.[119] Lazzaro de' Sourdi managed to distribute books to Salamanca, Lyon, Pavia, Bologna, Rimini, Ancona, Naples, Ferrara, Rome, Lisbon, and the fair cities of Lanciano and Recanati; this and similar cases—the Giolito, Sessa, and Zenaro houses—are detailed by Angela Nuovo.[120] Printing for a more limited zone was clearly a profitable strategy too. An example which shows this is afforded by Guinther von Andernach's *Institutiones anatomicae*, which first appeared in Paris in 1536, and thereafter in Venice in 1538, Basel in 1539, Wittenberg in 1585, and Padua in 1590. The textbook that replaced it, written by Caspar Bauhin, enjoyed a similar peregrination through international publishing houses or presses serving university cities. It began in Bern in 1604, it passed successively to Basel in 1609, Wittenberg in 1611, Basel again in 1615, and finally Frankfurt in 1616. Another book itinerary which reveals the zoning of the market is that of the popular law anthology entitled *Communes opiniones doctorum* produced by Franciscus Vivius of L'Aquila. First published in Perugia in 1565 in octavo, it was reprinted twice in Venice in 1566, in both Lyon and Venice (an enlarged edition with other works, both with the same printer's mark) in 1567, in Frankfurt in 1568–1569 (also with other works), and in folio in L'Aquila (probably a commemorative edition) in 1582. This last edition did not sell, and was reissued in Rome in 1588, and in L'Aquila in 1589. A final edition appeared in Frankfurt in 1611.

The zoning of the market can also be seen from the dedication written by the philosopher Giulio Pace, then living in Frankfurt in the house of Johann Wechel, to the works of his ex-tutor the Paduan logician Jacopo Zabarella, a living author whose work was a commercial success for Roberto Meietti in Italy, and whom Jean Mareschal of Heidelberg (passing himself off as a Lyonnais, so as not to alienate potential purchasers from Catholic countries) had commissioned Wechel to reprint.[121] In his dedication, Pace states that Jean Mareschal faced two problems: locating one of the scarce copies of the printed edition to be found north of the Alps, and assessing the reaction of Meietti to the plan for a new edition. In the second case, he declares to Zabarella:

> There is no need to fear that the publisher Meietti would complain about the appearance of this edition, which has been brought out not for financial gain but for the public good; his character and probity are known to me; he is more likely to see himself as having been helped by Mareschal in the task of disseminating your excellent doctrine, for he will be able to sell his copies in Italy and neighbouring places. Nor will there be any harm to him through the fact that copies of another edition are on sale in German lands, which few copies of his own edition reach.[122]

Somewhat later, an edition of this kind was described as "editio Germanica," as in the case of de Thou's *Historiae sui temporis* of 1609 discussed in Chapter 2, or in André Du Laurens's *Opera anatomica* of 1595 reprinted from the Lyon edition of 1593 by Wilhelm Antonius of Hanau for the Frankfurt bookseller Peter Fischer.

Pace's letter's claim—that Italian books did not penetrate the northern European market well—may suggest that an international sale was not necessary for the survival of printers such as Meietti, but a counter-indication is the establishment of the Societas Veneta—the exporting consortium—a representative of which traveled regularly to the Frankfurt fair in the 1590s and 1600s.[123] Venice may have achieved a certain market share through such efforts as these: Rome, it appears, did not. I have already mentioned the different fortunes of the editions of Cesare Baronio's *Annals* by the Vatican and the Plantin presses. Other testimony, such as that of the Würzburg professor Adriaan van Roomen, highlights the relative ease of transferring books from the north to Venice, and the difficulty of doing so to Rome in the same period (the 1590s). In the end, van Roomen had to rely on the services of a colleague to achieve this.[124] Others also had to rely on colleagues to secure books from sources such as Bologna or Spain in the same way.[125] This evidence of the difficulty of transmission is paralleled by signs that the reverse also applies, that is, that northern editions of legal and medical works failed to find their way into Italian libraries; but it would be wrong to infer from this that such books were not known about, or not obtainable, given a certain amount of persever- ance and some obliging contacts.[126] An indication of the poor pene- tration of books from northern presses around 1600 is to be found in the inventories of Italian religious houses that the Roman Inquisition required them to supply in the period 1597–1603.[127]

I have already discussed the practice of unauthorised reprinting. Here I am more interested in the ways in which different publishers achieved sales in different parts of Europe. Two fault lines appear in the map of European zones: that determined by trade, and that determined by con- fessionalisation. The most striking instance of the first is that which sepa- rates the Paris trade from the rest of Europe. The religious wars affected the printing and exportation of books, notably in the periods 1562–1569 and 1572–1589, as did the turmoil suffered in the second half of the cen- tury by conflict on the eastern border of France, which interfered with the passage of merchandise. The effects of the St. Bartholomew's massacre of August 1572 were especially severe in respect of protestant printers in Paris and Lyon. Some publishers fled these cities, and for some time af- ter that date Jacques Du Puis was the only Parisian still to put in an appearance at the Frankfurt fair. These downturns had deleterious local effects on trade as well: this can be inferred from the greater number of shared editions, and the closing down of Paris branches by foreign pub- lishers such as Plantin.[128] The absence of a local fair at which books were sold in numbers did not help imports. But other evidence—this time concerning export—suggests that a contributory factor was the ability of Parisian publishers of learned books to sell enough in the capital and at small French fairs for them not to have to seek outlets in foreign markets.[129] Near-simultaneous Paris and Lyon imprints of the same work suggest that the markets worked successfully in parallel.[130] It is striking that in the case of medicine, innovative Parisian authors such as Martin Akakia and Jacques Dubois were reprinted in, not exported, to Italy in the 1550s, through the initiative of Vincent Vaugris, who became the naturalised Italian Valgrisi. In the 1560s, several works by the Montpellier doctor Guillaume Rondelet were reprinted in Venice and Padua, as well as enjoying printing in Antwerp, Paris, and Lyon.[131] Very few Parisian books in relative terms in the period 1570–1620 were advertised at the Frankfurt fair.[132] It seems also that Bodley and his agents obtained their Parisian imprints from different commercial circuits than the dominant German ones.[133] All this makes Paris an exception to the general trade practices of the late Renaissance.

Other indications of zoning come from the practice of unauthorised reprinting for a local market as opposed to the fairs. Basel was both the target of such reprinting outside its normal distribution networks, and an agent of such activity. Sebastian Gryphius thought in 1552 that he could profit from his contacts in France, Italy, and Spain to reprint successfully Rafaele Maffei Volaterrano's *Commentariorum urbanorum libri* that had previously appeared in Basel editions on 1530 and 1544. Michael Isingrin for his part chose in 1551 to reprint the *Epitome omnium Galeni operum* which had previously appeared in Venice in 1548. In the 1550s, the Paris publisher Guillaume Cavellat reprinted two scientific books by Hartmann Beyer and Erasmus Reinhild that had previously been produced in Wittenberg, and one by Johann Scheubel that had appeared in Basel.[134] Later, printers in Cologne targeted their colleagues the Plantin presses in a similar way.[135] There are humbler examples of such localised reprinting, as, for example, in Erfurt in the 1580s.[136]

Of French provincial centres, only Bordeaux and Lyon seem to have aspired to more than local sales, the former through the entrepreneurial Simon Millanges, who engaged in the printing of humanist texts but rarely advertised his titles at the book fairs.[137] Lyon, on the other hand, was frequently represented there. Its publishers were major exporters of law books in the sixteenth century, sharing the lucrative market with Venice by collaboration, that is, by pacts of non-competition with regard to certain modern authors, or, in the case of the multi-volume texts of Roman and canon law, by sticking to market zones, or engaging different editors to produce substantially different editions. From the evidence of surviving libraries of the appropriate period, it would seem that Lyon fared much better than Venice in various zones, in particular in Iberia, where there were substantial warehouses of Lyon books at Medina del Campo and Salamanca, in northern Europe, and in those parts of Italy under Spanish rule, such as Naples.[138]

The second fault-line, that due to confessionalisation, is also quite easily charted. The most important divide here is that which separates Italy and Iberia from northern Europe. Spain and Portugal did not participate directly in the international market, and importing was made difficult after 1559. But after that date in Italy, there were determined attempts to import books from northern Europe. Giovanni Battista Ciotti and Roberto Meietti both produced printed catalogues in 1602 uniquely devoted to such books, which include a great deal of learned publication, and one or two prohibited scholars in the fields of humanism, law, and medicine, but no protestant theology.[139] At the same time, two of Justus Lipsius's correspondents in Italy, Andrea Chiocci and Sebastiano Macei, complained of the inactivity of Italian publishers and booksellers in this regard.[140] Plantin's exports to Italy in 1566 were tiny in respect of Germany, France, and England. Angela Nuovo has pointed out that none of the major learned publishers of the north had branches in Italy, but it is difficult to see how this could have occurred except in the case of the Catholic Plantin, who noted the very high transport costs of books to the south of the Alps, and seemed disinclined to develop his trade there except through the Frankfurt fairs.[141] Wechel, on the other hand, thought that his Italian sales were good (certainly better than in France or Spain), suggesting that the transfer of non-theological material was not too problematic in his time.[142] Those who wanted to find Italian outlets had to use safer Catholic cities, such as Cologne, on the imprint of books, or disguise their origin, as do the Geneva printers of humanist material, and the "Lugdunensis" Jean Mareschal (see above, page 129).[143] Venice achieved good sales in Augsburg, and during the time of the operation of the Societas Veneta (an exporting association which used the good offices of publisher-booksellers, such as Ciotti, who knew the northern market well), it achieved good sales also in the north; but these were eclipsed by the entrepreneurial publishers of Basel and Frankfurt.[144] Rome hardly figures in the Frankfurt sales catalogues at all. It is not clear how far the Italian trade suffered from the dearth of exporting; but Angela Nuovo and Ennio Sandal have charted the

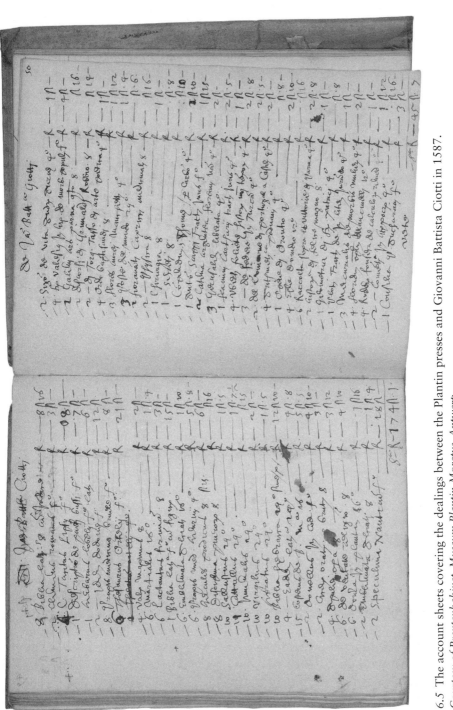

6.5 The account sheets covering the dealings between the Plantin presses and Giovanni Battista Ciotti in 1587. *Courtesy of Prentenkabinet, Museum Plantin-Moretus, Antwerp.*

downturn in trade after the 1580s, which may indicate that, like the Swiss and German publishers, it needed an international market to survive.[145] It is also not clear whether Italian paper and books were more expensive than those in the north. Ciotti's practice of using printers such as Johann Wechel suggests that it was, but this may also reflect either their willingness to use cheaper paper or his ambition to achieve a German as well as Italian sale. His "Tauschhandel" with Plantin in 1587 reveals that his purchases cost 174 florins (which were offset against the 45 florins-worth of books Plantin acquired), and that in return for mainly humanist texts and editions, he supplied mainly Italian vernacular literature, not Latin books.[146]

Peripheries: England and the Frankfurt Fair

It is instructive to look at the English printer-publishers whose engagement with the continental book trade reveals their initial ignorance of its operation, and their gradual coming to terms with its practices.[147] The generation of English humanists of the early sixteenth century all understood that publication on the continent was necessary for them to make an international impact, and apart from one or two isolated ventures, they did not attempt to find local publishers for their works.[148] In terms of trade, links with Frankfurt were strengthened during the residence in London of the Huguenot bookseller Robert Cambier between 1569 and 1580. The first phase of the involvement of English publishers in the fair is marked by the London printer John Wolfe's incursion into the Frankfurt book market. This began in 1581 and lasted until he ceased printing on his own behalf in 1591. The London, Oxford, and Cambridge markets for scholarly books in Latin appear to have been quite small. Wolfe needed the sales in Frankfurt to remain in business, and was shrewd enough to have some very saleable authors attractive for their notoriety in the shape of Niccolò Machivelli and Pietro Aretino. There is no evidence that Wolfe engaged in "Tauschhandel," but perhaps he did not need to, as he could count on a sale of authors who had been subject to prohibition in various parts of Europe. The second phase of engagement with the market involved the Oxford University printer Joseph Barnes, who published a number of English authors of Latin works from the late 1580s onward. Given the small uptake to be expected at home, Barnes was almost certainly counting on sales on the continent of two Oxford authors, John Case and Alberico Gentili, but he fell foul of aggressive competition. He knew that he had protection for his publications in England, but could not control the continental, especially the German, trade, who were able to reprint speculatively all of the works issuing from his presses, notably those of John Case, in which they perceived a potential profit. Case was an assiduous commentator on the elements of the Aristotelian corpus that were taught throughout Europe as part of the arts course. Barnes began publishing his works and sending them to the Frankfurt fair, probably because the Oxford market was too narrow to support a reasonable print run. Barnes does not seem, however, to have been aware of the practice of "Tauschhandel" which oiled the wheels of the publishing industry by dispensing with the need for settling in ready money. Barnes's failure to profit from his dealings with the fair may thus have arisen in part at least from his view of it as a place of sale but not of exchange. He may not have realized that hardheaded and unscrupulous local publishers kept an eye out for likely best-sellers to university markets that were not protected by law in Germany. As a result, all of Case's principal works, from the *Summa veteris interpretum in universam dialecticam Aristotelis* of 1584 onward, suffered unauthorised reprinting by Frankfurt or Hanau printers. Barnes's trade was severely compromised by this, but he did not always give up the fight. In 1592 he himself reprinted Case's *Summa veterum interpretum* after Johann Wechel of Frankfurt had produced it in 1589, and did so again in 1598 after Nicolas Bassée of Frankfurt produced a new edition of 1593. This did not, however, deter his German rivals. Wilhelm Antonius reprinted Case's *Thesaurus oeconomiae* in 1598, after Barnes had produced its first edition in 1597. It is worthy of note that the Antonius edition, and not that of Barnes, figured in the printed catalogue of the Bodleian Library in 1605, suggesting that Barnes was subject to the competition of Frankfurt even on his home ground.

The third phase in the activities of English printers in Frankfurt can be dated from the mid-1590s and continued until the decline of that market around 1630. It was inaugurated by the London stationers George Bishop and John Norton. The latter was joined later by his factor and successor John Bill, whose involvement with the fair lasted intermittently from 1612 to his death in 1630.[149] From 1600 onward, Bishop and Norton were selling their books for themselves and other London publishers through the stall or shop of the Frankfurt bookseller Peter Kopf, and "apud Wilhelmum Anton[ium]." There are clear signs of the commercial acumen which was lacking in the case of Barnes: these publishers engaged in barter, although the books they supplied were not in the main English printings. Among the few native products which did well in this category were William Gilbert's *De magnete* of 1600 and the various works of King James I and VI. Surviving documents in the Plantin-Moretus Archives in Antwerp show that Norton bought books from Plantin from 1594 onward, and that Plantin bought books on a small scale from Norton, presumably when they were both present at the Frankfurt fair.[150] The Plantin connection seems to have been a very important stepping-stone to English involvement with the fair. England itself was important enough a market for him to have an agent (who was possibly also a relation), called Ascanius de Renialme, based permanently in London.[151] In January 1616, the Stationers' Company set up their "Latin Stock," which accumulated continental publications up to 1628. John Bill, who sold his own stock of continental books to the Company in 1621, printed his own version of the Frankfurt book catalogue for distribution in London from 1617 onward. The Stationers' Company took over from him when the two stocks were merged in 1621, and continued until 1627, when the project came to an end.[152]

Collection-Building and Bibliography

It seems probable (although it is difficult to establish this except from anecdotal evidence) that one of the major reasons for the creation of an international market for learned books was the need to satisfy the demands of the widespread community of collectors of such books, whether private or institutional. From the Plantin records, it has been surmised that the average press run for any book was between 1,000 and 1,500, and the break-even figure for sales over two or three years was about 600 (breaking even here meaning a figure sufficient to allow the publisher to remain solvent).[153] The size of the scholarly purchasing community rich enough to buy books in Europe has, to my knowledge, never been quantified, but it would seem that this community was large enough to support a sale of this order. However, the fact that the same texts in all the major faculties (philosophy, theology, law, medicine), not to speak of humanism and history, were repeatedly published in new editions put some strain on purchasers in the market. Girolamo Cardano, for one, declared that he had impoverished himself buying books, and the same appears to have been true of Melchior Goldast (see above, pages 22–23).[154] As well as the scholar-purchasers, we must consider also the bibliophiles, the buyers on behalf of academic and religious institutions, and perhaps also the speculators in books. How did they find out about past editions? How good was their knowledge of the current market? And what could they know about forthcoming publications? These are questions which relate not only to the sellers of books, but to the transmission of knowledge, which is one of the major concerns of this study. They can be given only indicative and cursory treatment here.

The most straightforward issue is that concerning information about forthcoming publications. One of the most efficient ways of learning about these was through the exchange of letters between scholars, and their interaction with publishers. I have mentioned the case of Casaubon's edition of Polybius, which was known to be imminent for several years before its appearance in 1610. Even confessional rivals got wind of each other's publishing plans in this way, as the Goldast correspondence reveals.[155] Fair catalogues had a section containing the titles of books due to be available at the next fair. Publishers attending the fairs, such as the Plantin presses, were often aware of their colleagues' publishing plans for several years in advance. This led sometimes to pleas between colleagues to desist with a given edition in order to allow the same text that was already on the point of completion to be marketed.[156] Simultaneous editions continued to occur in cases where such information either was not available or was ignored (two examples are the *Opera* of Arnau, in 1585 and 1586, and the textbooks of Bartholomäus Keckermann, in 1613 and 1614).[157]

Acquisitions of new and older editions from the stocks of publishers and booksellers were made by private individuals and institutions. Bibliophilia—the desire to collect books as material objects and not just for the knowledge they contained—motivated some purchasers, to the scorn of those aspiring to promote the idea of a scholarly library, such as Gabriel Naudé.[158] Bibliophilia was a feature of the scribal age, not just among the elite. Tiziana Pezenti described the doctor Giovanni Marcanova, whose library in 1467 numbered 521 books, as a medical bibliophile.[159] In the first part of the sixteenth century, perhaps the most assiduous and discriminating collector of books was Fernando Colón, whose massive library amounted to over 15,000 volumes acquired from all over Europe.[160] Purchasing books as investments for possible resale also seems to have been practised in the sixteenth century: Jeremias Martius's catalogue of his books of 1572 may well reflect such a strategy.[161] It may be the case that Ulrich Fugger's purchasing of books was also in part motivated by the possibility of resale.[162] There were

also institutional and religious motives for collection-building. The idea
of assembling libraries was one of the early preoccupations of Luther.
In his open letter to the mayors of city councils written in 1524, he set
down recommendations for Christian schools which were to be furnished with certain books taken from religious houses which had agreed
to undergo reform, and prescribed the role of librarian in respect of
making inventories, organizing the books into classes, determining who
had access to them, and establishing rules for borrowing.[163] These libraries often acquired materials beyond the Christian: the example of
Hanover shows both that cities were willing to fund and house these
collections, and that they came to possess learned humanist materials in spite of Luther's doubts about them.[164] In the confessional age
which followed this initiative, all denominations sponsored institutions that acquired libraries, many of which either already possessed
large scholarly collections across the disciplinary spectrum or set about
acquiring one.

Three problems had to be addressed by those involved in setting up
such libraries: how to find out what was available, whether to apply a
principle of selection on scholarly principles or on ideological grounds,
and how to organise the books they acquired. An early and very important example of a municipal library with scholarly pretensions and a
strategy of organization is that of Zürich. In the 1530s, the humanist
Conrad Pellikan, who had cut his teeth as a corrector and complier of
indexes for the printer Christoph Froschauer, was instrumental in making its municipal collection accessible by a triple index (alphabetical by
author, shelf-lists, and by subject groupings under commonplaces).[165]
His initiative paved the way for the greatest and most ambitious catalogue of books, Gessner's *Bibliotheca universalis,* which appeared first
in 1545. It listed 5,000 authors (both published and unpublished) and
30,000 titles (by 1578, its revised edition was to contain three times this
number).[166] Three years later it came out in the form of Pandects which
were organised by subject.[167] Where the *Bibliotheca* is programmatically
non-selective, the Pandects are selective. They distribute topics by university disciplines (theology, law, the arts course: only medicine, Gessner's own speciality, is omitted, although he subsequently managed to
publish several subdivisions of this in different works) and the humanist
fields of history and poetry. Many sections of the Pandects were dedicated to leading publishers, whose back lists were included. In the
1540s, Gessner himself had compiled a list in the form of an octavo
booklet for the local publisher Christoph Froschauer to accompany

him to the Frankfurt fair, and his enquiries of Parisian and Basel printers may have sparked the renewed vogue for published catalogues which proliferated around this time.[168] The subsequent editions of Gessner's work greatly increased the number of entries, and made it possible through assiduous gap-filling for scholars to discover the existence of prior editions of both medieval and ancient writers. When Conrad Rittershausen wanted to work on the medieval writer Salvianus, he was presumably able to know about previous editions by using bibliographies such as those of Gessner and his continuators.[169] In this way bibliography clearly contributed to the development of critical studies. Rittershausen and others also knew about the contents of the greatest libraries of the time, whether public or private. In Fischart's satirical *Catalogus Catalogorum perpetuo durabilis* of 1593, a number of such libraries are listed, including those of the Palatinate, the dukes of Bavaria in Munich, the Imperial Library in Vienna, the Fuggers, and Heinrich Rantzau.[170]

Gessner's initiative set the agenda for later bibliographies, and stimulated their production, as it had for publishers' catalogues. These and the book fair catalogues were to be used extensively by collection-builders of all kinds in the coming decades. I have already discussed the fair catalogues, introduced in 1564 on the initiative of the Augsburg bookseller Georg Willer. These soon established themselves, even in Catholic Italy, as a means of finding out about the latest publications.[171] The culmination of these catalogues is found in the union versions: that produced in 1592 by the publisher and bookseller Nicolas Bassée, covering the years 1564 to 1591, followed by Henning Grosse's catalogue of the Leipzig declarations from 1593 to 1600, and Joannes Clessius's catalogue covering the period 1500 to 1602, financed by the Frankfurt bookseller Peter Kopf, whom we have already met.[172] These efforts were, however, eclipsed by the most comprehensive work of all, in terms of accumulation, in the sophistication of its subject classification, and in ease of reference: Georg Draut's *Bibliotheca classica,* which appeared first in 1610–1611, and subsequently in 1625, about which I have already spoken. There is strong evidence that Draut was used as a finding list.[173] In it, the Renaissance aspiration to encyclopedism (a closed if incomplete corpus of knowledge) is still evident.

In Draut's bibliography, reference can be found to many other *Bibliothecae,* by discipline, religious order, library, town, and country.[174] These fall into two distinct classes. The first are those, like Gessner and Draut, which aspire to be comprehensive and unselective; the second are selective. Some of these contain references to unpublished works they have heard about, such as Bartolomaeus Eustachius's much-vaunted but unpublished anatomical pictures, which Georg Schenck von Grafenberg mentions in 1609, giving the source of his information (they were eventually published in 1714).[175] The selective bibliographies were mainly Catholic, such as those by Sixtus Senensis and the Jesuit Antonio Possevino, and were as much concerned to preserve the piety of the reader as to promote his knowledge of a given field of learning.[176] There were also more technical guides to authors which prescribe an order of reading of their works.[177] Somewhat later, union catalogues of libraries in given places are produced: Jacopo Filippo Tomasini's *Bibliotheca patavina* of 1639 for Padua is the first of these, followed by Louis Jacob's *Traité des plus belles bibliothèques* of 1644, which deals in turn with most major European cities.[178]

The shrewdest guide to collection-building is Gabriel Naudé's *Advis pour dresser une bibliotheque* of 1627. Here the encyclopaedic aspiration of the previous century gave way to an acknowledgement that the field of knowledge was open-ended, and that one of the duties of a librarian was to recover lost scholarly or scientific monuments and to make available to the public in the most convenient form the books assembled in a given library. Naudé scorns those who are obsessed as collectors with rarity and beauty, and lays great stress on the "service et utilité que l'on peut recevoir."[179] Like Gessner, Naudé lays stress on the author axis, and justifies the pursuit of the Nachlass of innovative authors in the hope that their unpublished materials would contain their most audacious thought.[180] He does not seek to develop a perfect taxonomy of books, but is content to use existing categories well known to potential readers. His enterprise is specifically non-sectarian. It is the duty of librarians to be dispassionate about the materials over which they preside, at the same time as exercising good judgement ("juger sainement et sans passions de toutes choses").[181] For that reason, he advocates the collection of not only heretical books, but also unfashionable medieval medicine and science, and heterodox moderns such as Bernardo Telesio, Francesco Patrizi, Theophrastus Paracelsus, William Gilbert, and Petrus Severinus. He also believed that it was important to chart the history of disciplines, in order the better to understand their present state, and to keep alive the memory of past schools of thought through which present error might be eliminated, empirical knowledge preserved, and polemical exchanges settled. Such an approach naturally leads to a breaking down of strict disciplinary boundaries and the development of new disciplines. Naudé is clear that his work was produced for an unknown constituency of readers, even if they are not yet so unspecified as to constitute a "public."[182]

The acquisition of books by private individuals needed the bibliographical tools I have just discussed. It was also much aided by the exchanges of information in the nascent republic of letters. I have already alluded to the fact that Claude Dupuy and Gian Vincenzo Pinelli also acted as speculative agents for each other in the distant markets of Paris and Venice. Pinelli was an avid collector of books and manuscripts, and used any catalogues he could obtain to check on gaps in his library and desiderata. His collection included the catalogues of books donated to public institutions in Venice by Cardinal Bessarion and others, the library lists of his contemporary bibliophiles, and the catalogues of natural philosophers, physicians, and mathematicians around him.[183] Venice was a city with a long history of book acquisition in both new and older subjects: humanism, history and geography, botany and anatomy, natural history, and the traditional higher disciplines. Pinelli built on that culture, and benefited from the latest news about books in Paris sent to him by Dupuy. This was how he heard about the imminent publication of the botanical work of Jacques Dalechamps and the Paris edition of the Corpus Juris Civilis, and obtained advice about the best edition of Pliny.[184] He also learned about Frankfurt declarations from his connections with the fair. There are likely to be many such examples of exchange of information about new publications in the surviving correspondence of members of the republic of letters at this time, which crossed even the most difficult frontiers and ensured the transmission of scholarship.[185]

The Market and the Transmission of Knowledge

The questions that I asked at the beginning of this chapter can now be addressed. Is the market for learned books necessarily international or at least transregional, and can publishers only survive if they have access to this wider market? The evidence from England suggests very strongly that this is the case. The only clear counter-example I can think of is Paris, which seems (at least during its periods of political and religious stability) to have sufficient outlets for its wares not to have to engage very fully with the European markets. It is true that a large number of Parisian publishers were attending the fairs in the early years of the seventeenth century, but they each made very few declarations, and there is not much evidence from the modern location of books that they made significant sales in Germany and further east. In the case of England, it seems that the purchase of books printed in Paris was undertaken separately from those imported from the Frankfurt fair. Spain may also be self-sufficient (by necessity) as a market, but I have found little data on the prosperity of Spanish publishers, nor on the scale of their operations after 1559.[186] The case of Italy is more difficult. The existence of a consortium at the end of the sixteenth century shows both the need to spread costs and the desire to find a market for Italian books. At the same time, the importation of books from the north was hampered by the activities of the Inquisition. Both the booksellers and publishers who attempted to do this ran into difficulties with the authorities, and neither seems to have made their fortune by undertaking this risky task. From this, I believe it possible to affirm that the market is not unified, but operates in different ways in different places.

How far did the marketing, sales, and distribution of these books affect the transmission of knowledge at this time, and the ability of those who wished to do so to build up comprehensive collections of scholarly materials? Books were more easily accessible in some parts of the European world than others, but it seems that a determined purchaser could learn about new works of scholarship through fair catalogues and more informal contacts in the republic of letters, and in many cases acquire those that they wanted. Publishers spread such knowledge throughout Europe through their support of new authors, but also as an unintended consequence of their trade practices. In seeking to protect a work with a privilege, they advertised the fact that they thought it to be potentially profitable, which in turn acted as an unwitting encouragement to those who specialised in unauthorised reprinting. Barter at the fairs ensured the transfer of goods from one market zone to another, and back stocks not only acted as reservoirs of exchangeable books but also ensured the survival of scholarship over decades and even half centuries.

A different consideration is the delay suffered by the parts of Europe less favoured by efficient trade routes in the delivery of new scholarly books. One estimate suggests that there was an average lapse of five to seven years in the case of the delivery of northern European and Italian books to clients in Spain. But given the inefficiency of the systems in place to prevent the ingress of prohibited material, this seems to me to be an excessive claim.[187] Scholars of Italian thought have made much of the impoverishment of Italian intellectual life through the operation of censorship and of the various indexes. This may be true to some extent, but Paul Grendler and others have shown that smuggling was rife, and that new publications from Frankfurt were relatively easy to obtain.[188] I doubt, therefore, whether it was the deprivation of northern European books which caused the alleged decline in intellectual vigour in Spain and Italy (as the frontiers, even into Spain, were very porous). It would seem more likely that the active repression of thinking outside the limits set by the Catholic Church and the threat of interrogation by the Inquisition deterred scholars more than their being deprived (which they were in many cases not) of books by innovative thinkers from beyond the Alps.

The speed of correspondence between scholars from Paris to Venice, and from Frankfurt throughout the book-buying world, was not slow, as we have seen from the examples of Du Puy, Pinelli, and Goldast; nor was delivery time of books to clients.[189] But some destinations were more difficult to reach, Rome being one of these, according to Adriaan von Roomen.[190] It is true that the physician Leonhard Schmaus complained about the time it took to obtain books in Salzburg in 1519; but by the 1530s this problem seems to have been largely overcome.[191] The Augsburg doctor Achilles Pirmin Gasser, then living in Lindau, which was as far from trade routes as was Salzburg, recorded the date he received all the books he bought and their cost on the title page. From this it transpires that he obtained his copies mostly within a year of publication, not only from Germany but from France and the southern Netherlands as well.[192] It is therefore difficult to attribute deprivation of intellectual stimulus to the early modern scholarly world either to location or to repressive measures.[193]

The question of information about new publications and books already published poses rather different problems of transmission. By the early years of the seventeenth century, publishers, booksellers, and bibliographers had learned how to communicate efficiently what they had to offer the world of scholarship. This was the culmination of a process that had begun with Gessner in the 1540s. Scholars and librarians became accustomed to seek out catalogues of various kinds in which to look for desiderata, and were sufficiently in touch with the scholarly world to know what might be found in the most famous public libraries of Europe. The second-hand market clearly operated before the advent of auctions, albeit somewhat mysteriously.

There is a further noteworthy dimension to the relationship between the authors, publishers, sellers, and readers of books. At given moments and places in the sixteenth century, humanist publishers, authors, and purchasers all belonged to the same community and subscribed to the same ideals of learning, which linked them to a gift culture and a moral purpose. In this way, the purchasing communities were not clients but colleagues of the authors and publishers. This community consisted of both humanists and professional groups such as lawyers and doctors; the latter groups were more obviously served in their social and political functions by publishers than the former. The scholarly ideals of all three groups (authors, publishers, readers) meant that any improvement in textual or historical accuracy overrode the economic convenience of accepting a nearly perfect edition through the happy coincidence of the interests of scholarship and commerce. But at the same time as authors demanded that their better texts, histories, and grammars be published in the name of truth, they were conniving in a culture of built-in obsolescence *avant la lettre*. From this came also the infiltration of the culture of the gift into the mercantile world of the printing industry, which led in turn to the sense of betrayal in Goldast and his colleagues, who looked upon the likes of Schönwetter and Kopf as mere merchants, and no doubt looked back on the generations of Aldus, Froben, and Estienne with nostalgia. Critics of late humanism, like Montaigne and Fischart, come to describe the sense of betrayal as potentially hypocritical on the part of scholars and the practice of republication commercially unsustainable on the part of publishers. A point had to come when the economic system represented by the cult of scholarly improvement and perfection could no longer sustain the cycle of renewal. That is the subject of the next chapter.

CHAPTER SEVEN

The Rise and Fall of the Learned Book Market, 1560–1630

I begin, as I began in the last chapter, with the Plantin publishing house in Antwerp; this time more than forty years later, in 1614, a year when things were apparently flourishing at the Frankfurt book fair, if one judges by the number of declarations of new Latin books. The year before a record number had been declared (1,134), a figure which would never be achieved again. We might therefore expect the letter written by the press's representative at the fair, Jan II Moretus, to his brother Balthasar in Antwerp on 26 April 1614, to be at least guardedly enthusiastic and optimistic. But we are all used to hearing tradesmen and merchants complaining about the difficulties of the market, just as we are used to hearing farmers complaining about the vagaries of the weather, so it will come as no surprise, therefore, that Jan begins with a threnody:

> Dearest brother, Here I am at the fair, and what do I find? the market is withering away, and purchasers are overcautious. Those attending want few of our folio Breviaries, because of the cheaper editions coming from Venice and Van Keerberghen (an Antwerp printer). As in time these will become known about and sought after, so will the works of Lipsius, the individual parts of which many [purchasers] have had in the past and now don't want the complete works but just the title page; and although no copies of the Lyon edition are on offer here, they must be lying around elsewhere, or were on sale here at the previous fair; Georg Willer and others don't want any of our edition among other things. We must conquer by perseverance.
>   I have had a meeting with Antonius Hierat about the number of copies of Cesare Baronio's *Annals* he would have: there are 600 com-

plete works surviving hitherto, and if volumes 9, 10, 11 and 12 are re-printed, then he will easily complete up to 100 copies.[1]

Various points are of interest here:

(1) The Plantin firm had changed their sales policy in 1609 (see below, page 219), which suggests that they had already seen systemic problems in the operation of the Frankfurt fair.

(2) Van Keerberghen was associated with the Plantin presses as well as being a rival in the production of liturgical books.[2] This may remind us that as well as coexistence and collaboration, competition was never far beneath the surface.

(3) The entrepreneurial Lyon publisher Horace Cardon, who had inherited the Roville presses, preempted the Plantin presses by producing a folio edition of Justus Lipsius's complete works outside the area in which they were protected by the Plantin presses' privilege, and offered it for sale at the autumn fair of 1613.[3] As it happens, another speculative publisher, Zacharias Schürer of Wittenberg, had provided yet more unwelcome competition by advertising a new edition of Lipsius's very popular work, the *De constantia,* at the same fair. I wrote in Chapter 3 about the practice of getting purchasers to buy slightly different editions or collections as a means of dealing with a narrow market. Cardon had done this successfully by an act of quasi-piracy, and Moretus felt very unhappy about it. His own attempt to recover the position by adding a title page to one of the seven quarto volumes of Lipsius's works published between 1601 and 1611 and deeming the whole to be an *Opera omnia* failed miserably.

    Purchasers had already acquired the other volumes, and they only wanted the title page itself (which bore the wholly menda-cious words "recently extended and amended": "postremum aucta et recognita"). It was particularly galling to Moretus that one of the Plantin presses' best clients, the Willer firm of Augs-burg, bought none of his cobbled-together edition.[4]

(4) Baronio's *Annals* were a multi-volume best-seller for the Plantin presses. They gave rise in 1599 to struggles over the printing rights of the *Epitome* published at Mainz by the Cologne publishers Antonius Heirat and Johann Gymnich. Moretus tried unsuccessfully to solve the problem first by appealing to

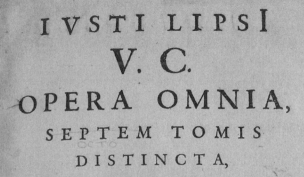

IVSTI LIPSI
V. C.
OPERA OMNIA,
SEPTEM TOMIS
DISTINCTA,

Poſtremùm aucta & recognita.

ANTVERPIÆ,
EX OFFICINA PLANTINIANA,
Apud Viduam & Filios Ioannis Moreti.
cIɔ. Iɔc. XIV.
*Cum Priuilegiis Cæſareo & duorum Regum,
& Principum Belgarum.*

7.1 The title page provided by the Plantin presses for Justus Lipsius's so-called *Opera omnia* of 1611, to enable those who had bought prior editions separately to class them as his complete works.
Courtesy of All Souls College, Oxford.

Baronio's secretary Joannes Baptista Hansenius, then to the Book Commissioner Valentin Leucht, and finally to the Frankfurt City Council. He next thought of trying to sell all the remaining copies of the various volumes to another bookseller. These he offered in 1606 to Michael Sonnius of Paris (who clearly did not take up the offer) for the enormous sum of 4,050 florins. Here we find him negotiating with Antonius Hierat of Cologne the disposal of the stock kept at Frankfurt.[5]

Later in the same letter he goes on to say:

For the large quantity of books I have brought here I foresee lower sales than expected, and I don't want to get into equal selling and buying. Let them [i.e., my fellow book merchants] wait for the next market, rather than expect to scorn my books by an unequal exchange [i.e., by buying few of mine and having me buy more of theirs], and in the case of most [of theirs] we have made sufficient provision at home, so that I don't think it is necessary to buy a multitude of books when there is [a multitude already] acquired.[6]

It is indeed a feature of most of the dealings of the Plantin firm that they disposed of more books in exchanges than they acquired, leaving a sum in ready money payable at the next fair, but how important this was for the continuing existence of the firm is not clear. Three days later, Moretus wrote another letter, in which he complains about the slowness of the fair and the poor sales of Breviaries. He reports that when the news got around about the latest edition of the works of Lipsius, the appetite of purchasers was not stimulated by it. He writes that he is sending to Antwerp ten copies of the Frankfurt edition of the fair catalogue, from which he complains that some of their press's (Catholic) books have been left out.[7] This is not the only sign of confessional friction between publishers. In 1608, Jan I Moretus had complained to the Imperial Book Commissioner Valentin Leucht that Johann Theobald Schönwetter had printed a Latin Vulgate Bible which had infringed his rights, and, to add insult to injury, had managed to sell 200 copies of his edition to an Antwerp bookseller on Moretus's doorstep.[8]

Less than a week later, a third note mentions difficulties in respect of the preaching manual of the deceased Louvain professor Thomas Stapleton (1535–1598) entitled *Promptuarium morale*, whose first edition appeared in Antwerp in 1591–1592. This had soon been pirated in Lyon, Paris, and Venice. Moretus had financed a new edition jointly with Hermann Mylius of Cologne in 1610, which was printed in Mainz.

PROMPTVARIVM
MORALE
SVPER EVANGELIA
DOMINICALIA
TOTIVS ANNI:

⎰Inſtructionem Concionatorum⸗

AD ⎱Reformationem Peccatorum⸗

⎰Conſolationem Piorum⸗.

Ex Sacris Scripturis, 3 S. Patribus , & optimis
quibuſg̃. Authorib ſtudioſè collectum:

Authore THOMA STAPLETONO, ANGLO;
S. Theol. Doctore, & Regio Profeſſore Louanii.

Editio altera , ab ipſo Authore aucta & recognita.

PARS HYEMALIS.

Rom. 1.

Euangelium virtus Dei eſt, in ſalutem omni credenti.

MOGVNTIÆ,

Apud Balthaſarum Lippium, Sumptibus Ioannis Moreti, & Hermanni Mylii.

M. DC. X.

Cum Gratia & Priuilegio.

7.2 The title page of the collaborative edition of Thomas Stapleton's
Prompuarium morale of 1610.
Courtesy of Christ Church, Oxford: shelfmark Hyp G 25a.

He noted that at the normal price ("pretium solitum") the book was scarcely selling, so he was negotiating with Mylius to cut the price in order to stimulate sales, from which it might reasonably be inferred that the market had already been saturated by that date.[9] All in all, no good commercial news was conveyed in these letters.

Nor were these the earliest suggestions of difficulties. In spring 1598, Jan's father had written of the shortage of purchasers with ready money at the fair, and mentioned that some of the exhibitors had already packed up their stalls, choosing to delay their declarations until a later fair. This should alert us to the fact that the apparent increase in declarations, which I shall establish in a moment, may be exaggerated by the practice of duplicate entries in succeeding fair catalogues (many also appear with appendices of later declarations, which are also repeated in the next catalogue). A year later, in 1599, Moretus complained that the Augsburg booksellers Willer were buying much less than before, and referred to the legal and financial problems that the Feyerabend firm of Frankfurt were suffering, and the cheap disposal of their stock. The Feyerabends also sold their privilege for a long list of legal books at this time.[10]

A different indication of difficulties is found from 1602 in the inventories drawn up of the warehouse and shop of the Plantin firm in Frankfurt, which divide the stock into "not saleable" (or "less saleable") and "more saleable," according to principles which do not immediately seem clear, even if the commercial message of the division is.[11]

The presence of Lipsius's *De cruce* is an obscure case in point. It appears in both categories of the books to be found in the one of the stores of the Plantin presses: 100 copies in octavo are "minus vendibiles," yet 6 in quarto and 10 in octavo, even though "viels" (i.e., from a superseded edition), are "vendibiliores" (other copies are listed on other pages). The *De cruce* (a historical account relating to the form of the cross on which Jesus was crucified) was first published in 1593 in octavo; its second, improved, edition came out in 1595, its third (also improved) in 1597, and its last (the final one to be improved) in 1599. This, together with an edition in 1594, was in quarto.[12] What this shows is not only that new editions left remainders which had to be written off, but that some of these were still marketed, presumably at a discount.

There are other remainders from now-superfluous editions in the 1602 inventories: Godescalius Stewechius's notes on Apuleius, for example, published in 1586, were made redundant after the new edition by Petrus Colvius in 1588, which was superseded in turn by Bonaventura Vulcanius's edition in 1600, all from the same presses. The "[libri]

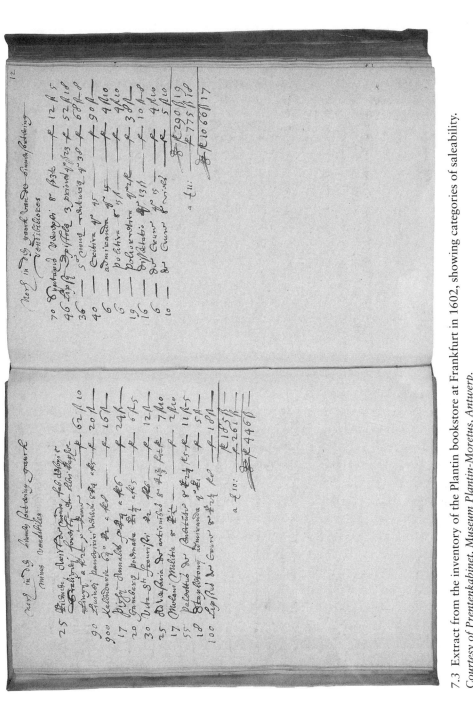

7.3 Extract from the inventory of the Plantin bookstore at Frankfurt in 1602, showing categories of saleability. *Courtesy of Prentenkabinet, Museum Plantin-Moretus, Antwerp.*

IVSTI LIPSI
DE CRVCE
LIBRI TRES

Ad sacram profanámque historiam vtiles.

Vnà cum NOTIS.

Editio vltima, serió castigata.

ANTVERPIAE,
EX OFFICINA PLANTINIANA,
Apud Ioannem Moretum.
M. DC. VI.
Cum Priuilegiis Cæsareo & duorum Regum.

7.4 The title page of Justus Lipsius's *De cruce* of 1606, making the false claim that it is a new and improved edition ("editio ultima, serio castigata"). *Courtesy of All Souls College, Oxford.*

non vendibiles" are largely imperfect copies. Some of these and the "[libri] minus vendibiles" are valued by the ream, others by the trade price; together, they amount to about 30 percent of the total stock valuation of 32,883 guilders.

Leon Voet has suggested that 1609 represents a turning point for the Plantin house; there are various indications of this.[13] Jan I writes to his son from Frankfurt that year about the conspiracies of other booksellers and publishers against the Plantin house, and advises him to avoid conflict with them. The suggestion in the letter of 29 April 1614 that their Catholic books were deliberately omitted from the official fair catalogue in 1614 may be more evidence of this.[14] The figures produced by Leon Voet suggest that after that year, the house looked more to its retail sales in the Netherlands and other zones where they were active than to the trade at the fair, and increased their direct trading with German booksellers in Cologne, Dantzig, Emmerich, and Cracow through an agent called Jacques de Jode.[15] By the beginning of the 1600s, *Tauschhandel* had dropped to a mere 12 percent of all sales.[16] As a consequence, in 1609, 11,500 books were sold to Germany altogether, against 49,500 to the southern Netherlands.[17] When the Plantin presses gave up the printing of Greek books after 1623, Balthasar Moretus refers only to the small interest in Greek in the southern Netherlands, where his commercial enterprise lay: the Frankfurt learned market has been forgotten.[18] The growing number of presses active in Antwerp (from three to six in the period 1577–1609, to seven to eleven for the next thirteen years) seems to suggest that the printing house was expanding; but the increase of sales of liturgical books to the Iberian peninsula is probably the decisive factor here, not the extension of activity to new areas of scholarship.[19] Jan I Moretus was able to renew trade with the peninsula in 1609 after declaration of a truce with the Dutch Republic, and his son Balthasar made Spain the biggest customer again outside the Low Countries over the next decade.[20] Nevertheless, the declarations of books by the Plantin house at the fair doubles between 1614, the year of the gloomy prognoses given above, to 1621. How much of this is disposal of stock sitting in the Frankfurt warehouse and shop is not clear.[21] The evidence from the cahiers and carnets suggest a dropping off of trade in the late 1610s, and a retraction of credit conceded to German booksellers such as the Willers. They confirm, therefore, that the gloomy prognoses of 1614 with which I began this chapter were more than the usual complaints of a merchant about the market.

In my chapter title I have suggested that there was a rise in the book trade from the 1560s, and that it suffered a serious decline after 1630. This is a long period, and it witnessed very different political and economic evolutions in various parts of Europe. While I think that the general argument I am making here is correct, I am aware how broad the canvas is. The midpoint of this period (around 1590) seems to be marked by the excellent prospects for the so-called Calvinist international, with Elizabeth on the throne of England, and the Palatinate in the hands of a Reformed ruler. Henri IV of France had still not abjured at this point. By 1622 the outlook for the Calvinists in many of these lands looked bleak.[22] Between these dates, the conflict in the Netherlands and the activities of the Spanish armies in Europe gave rise to much anxiety. Even Frankfurt and its fair was not spared, as was made clear by a letter of 1599 from Jan I Moretus to his home referring to the Diet being held in Frankfurt and the proximity of Spanish troops to the Imperial city.[23] But I don't think that the collapse of the book market was due only to external factors such as these. Nor can it entirely be attributed to the passing of the humanist printer-publisher, although the disappearance of figures in the latter part of the sixteenth century such as Henri II Estienne, André Wechel, Johannes Oporinus, and Paulus Manutius clearly left behind, if not a vacuum, then at least a much-reduced support system for scholarship.[24]

I shall first give some of the data which corroborates the story I shall set out to tell; next look at the earlier recorded collapses in the book trade from its inception, and the explanations that have been offered for them; then look cursorily at the general economic context of the trade, before passing to the external and internal causes of the rise that I shall have charted, and its decline at the end of the 1620s. I have taken as hypotheses from previous chapters (1) that the market for learned books was not a very broad one; (2) that its capacity for expansion was limited, both geographically and in terms of new classes of purchasers; and (3) that the conditions for the saturation and collapse of the market pertain before the actual collapse occurs, and were sensed by shrewd observers such as the Frankfurt and Leipzig city councils and the Plantin firm. I shall be referring here principally to the interactive markets for learned books in Europe: Germany and its fairs, Italy, France, and the Netherlands. One would not expect the decline in these different political and economic regimes to be simultaneous: nor are they.

Data

There are two points arising from the statistics which are of interest here: the first is steady increase, the second sudden decline. The figures from the Frankfurt book fairs of declarations of Latin books by German and foreign publishers reveal the following pattern (drawn from Schwetschke):[25]

1580–1589	4,076
1590–1599	5,206
1600–1609	8,139
1610–1619	9,983
1620–1629	7,506
1630–1639	4,506

Table 7.1, based on that by Alexander Dietz, tells a similar story for all declarations by country.[26]

Dietz's figures for Germany are given in five-year tranches, and show an advance from 722 (in 1580–1585) to 1604 (in 1616–1620).[27] These figures reveal the rise between the 1590s and 1620, with a falling back in the 1620s, and a more marked decline again in the 1630s. In the case of the three contributing zones, a similar percentage decline is seen in the Plantin declarations at the fair as elsewhere. Mario Infelise provides comparative interim figures for the decade 1600–1609 for declarations of books from Italy (1,082), France (564), the southern Netherlands (619), and the northern Netherlands (384).[28] The figures from France reveal a sharper rise and fall after 1610, and those from Italy a marked rise in the decades in which the importing association known as the Societas Veneta was active, and an even more dramatic collapse than France after 1620. The French figures can be broken down again between Paris and Lyon, the two largest exporting centres. They reveal that the presence of Lyon gradually fell away, whereas that of Paris rose dramatically after the treaty of Vervins in 1598 which brought to an

Table 7.1 Comparative Declarations at the Frankfurt Book Fair by Decade

	Italy	France	Belgium and Holland
1580–1589	492	464	397, of which 372 Antwerp and Leiden
1610–1619	559	908	1,579, of which 1,127 Antwerp and Leiden
1620–1629	34	252	1,151, of which 834 Antwerp and Leiden

end Franco-Spanish hostilities and opened the trade routes to the east, and fell away sharply at the inception of the Thirty Years' War, as is also the case with Italy.[29] The decline after 1630 relates very directly to the occupation of Frankfurt by Gustavus Adolphus from 1629 to 1633.[30]

In Frankfurt itself the number of books imported for the fair rose fourfold between 1561–1570 and 1611–1620, and the number of resident presses increased from 20 to 45 (this does not take into account the presses in satellite locations around the city which were discussed in Chapter 2).[31] Between 1560 and 1619, however, the percentage of foreign books declared fell from 40 percent to 20 percent.[32] In the early years of the seventeenth century, there were increasing difficulties with transport to the city by water through the rising cost of tolls, as well as other local economic problems arising from population growth, the activities of immigrant artisans and traders from the southern Netherlands, and the consequences of the city's hard line policy on the practice of the Reformed faith, which led to a loss of tax revenue through the desertion of printers and publishers to neighbouring territories such as Hanau, which actively encouraged their secession.[33] All of these factors were exacerbated by the Fettmilch uprising in 1612–1614. Their effect on the book trade might not have been immediate, but they may well have played a delayed role in the disastrous decline of the 1630s. In Saxony (and hence Leipzig) the 1594 ordinances governing the book trade make specific mention as threats to the stability of the market of the greed of publishers and the excessive desire of authors to be published.[34] There are a number of indications of financial difficulties for, or bankruptcies of, publishers (Feyerabend 1597; Bassée's heirs 1611; Richter 1616; Schönwetter 1617–1620; Vögelin 1625; Kopf 1633; Aubry 1630s).[35] One reason this may not be as widespread as might be expected is the perennial survival of publishers through the use of illiquid sureties of one kind or another. They were used to holding vast stocks of books which in commercial terms would have brought down many mercantile ventures, through which they were able to weather periods of difficulty for some of the reasons set out in previous chapters. But the fact of holding large stocks, which leads inevitably to ever greater illiquidity, leads to the risk of problems of cash flow, unredeemable debt, and with it generalised bankruptcy.[36]

A shift of production after 1600 is said to see Leipzig outproduce Frankfurt, and causes one Leipzig printer (Henning Grosse) to boast that there had been an effective *translatio imperii* at that time.[37] This does not, however, take into account the proportion of vernacular books printed at Leipzig. In terms of twice-yearly declarations from all publishing houses, Leipzig remained the "German" fair, and Frankfurt the "international fair" until after 1630.[38] The declaration figures for the Leipzig fair reveal the same configuration as for Frankfurt after 1600: a rise up to the decade 1610–1619; a decline of about 20 percent during the 1620s; a collapse after 1630.[39] In Kapp's history of the German book trade, there are a number of graphs which confirm this, and show the different figures for various disciplines. They reveal that theology's decline began at the end of the 1620s, but law fell off sharply a decade earlier, with history and medicine having a more modest rise around 1590 and a decline around 1630.[40] The length of decline can be measured by the decision of some printing houses active in the 1610s and 1620s to reissue the stock produced at the end of the 1610s with "refreshed" title pages in the 1640s and 1650s, after the Peace of Westphalia.[41] The number of Latin books declared after 1630 never again approached the same level as in the halcyon days of the 1610s.[42]

Beyond Germany, the picture is very mixed. Mario Infelise reports that the major producers of Italian books suffered a general crisis which affected the book trade in the decade 1620–1630, after which the plague which affected northern Italy at the end of the 1620s had a further deleterious effect on trade; but as the table given above shows, the decline in declarations predates these events.[43] Earlier examples of decline and insolvency are found in the entrepreneurial figures (both involved in the international book trade) of Robert Meietti, who had recourse to reissuing books or seeking finance from partners from the 1590s onward, and Giovanni Baptista Ciotti, who suffered a similar fate in the period 1608–1612.[44] In Nuovo and Sandal's history of Italian printing, the decline in the book trade is attributed to a number of factors: the issuing of the *Index* and the beginning of book-burning in the late 1550s (in Venice alone, ten to twelve thousand books were said to be burnt in one year—1559); the decline in the number of active presses in Venice (1588: 70; 1596: 40; 1598: 30); and the sharp rise in the proportion of books produced for the Counter-Reformation as opposed to humanist scholarship or the higher disciplines of law and medicine.[45] By 1600, Italy seems to have been almost a closed market. It is therefore unlikely that competition from northern presses was a contributory factor in the Italian decline, although other, local, forms of interference in sales may well have been. Forbidding Catholic laity to read the Bible had deleterious financial consequences.[46] There were also problems in financing publication in Rome in spite of its monopoly of liturgical printing. These are evinced by the fortunes of Paulus Manutius and the Vatican presses which have already been mentioned (above, page 50).[47] As I indicated in Chapter 5, the decline in intellectual life may have less to do with embargos on the importation and ownership of books than the manifest repression of heterodox ideas, and the fate suffered by thinkers such as Giordano Bruno and Galileo.[48]

In France the situation regarding learned books is somewhat different. The Lyon trade had struck crisis in the late 1580s because of the activities of publishers who turned to Geneva rather than Lyon to have their works printed. The warehouse stocks of its prosperous publishers, both in the city and in Medina, had reached astonishing levels, and had either to be written off or sold at considerable discounts.[49] The situation was not made better by the imposition of new tolls in the 1590s as a consequence of the religious wars.[50] A hiatus ensued, in which one or two printers (notably Horace Cardon) successfully engaged in new market zones (Iberia) and in piracy of best-selling authors such as Lipsius both inside and outside their market sector. It was not until the late 1630s, however, with the revival of the firm of Huguetan (later Huguetan and Ravaud), that a revival of large-scale scholarly printing (Catholic theology, law, medicine) occurred.[51] In Paris, there is increased activity of publishers at the Frankfurt fair between 1600 and 1620, accompanied by renewed attempts by royal authority at home to control the printing industry, notably through a new edict of 1618.[52] The same decade saw also the refounding of prestigious national projects of scholarly publication, of which the greatest was undertaken by the royal printing house, a successor to the ones of 1552 and the 1580s, when the Compagnie des Usages for liturgy and the Compagnie du Navire for patristics were founded. The royal printing house engaged in massive folio Greek-Latin editions of Greek Church Fathers, and a few other authors: Aristotle, Strabo, and Xenophon. This had been planned in the reign of Henri IV, who had brought Isaac Casaubon to Paris partly for the purpose. Its first products appeared in 1612, and twenty-three large folio volumes had been produced before 1624. The only text which seems to have been a commercial success was the two-volume Aristotle of 1619, reprinted in 1629 (and in four volumes in 1639 and 1654). Henri-Jean Martin has argued that the crisis of the French trade occurred later in the century (in the 1630s to 1650s), due to saturation of the Counter-Reformation market for liturgy and devotional literature and political crises leading up to the Fronde.[53] But the prestigious publications already mentioned, the strong interest of Richelieu in encouraging the transmission of knowledge, and the enthusiasm for collection-building in the capital (given a powerful impetus after the arrival of Mazarin) offer a rather different picture.[54]

In Geneva, there is evidence of successful piracy of humanist and scholarly works in the first thirty years of the century, exploiting the lower labour costs and the use of cheaper paper. It tailed off toward the middle years of the century, as was the case also in Basel. In both cities, this may have been affected by the deaths of prominent scholarly publishers in the late sixteenth century, leading to a loss of momentum.[55] The war against Savoy was a factor in keeping Genevan booksellers away from Frankfurt in the period between 1593 and 1600.[56] In England, never itself a serious exporter of Latin books, there is evidence of a general expansion in the book trade in the growth in the number of bindings (of apprentices to masters) at the Stationers' Company between 1590 and 1610.[57] Thereafter, the cessation of Bill's printing of the Frankfurt book fair catalogue in 1621 and the failure of the Latin stock to make a profit for the Stationer's Company are suggestive of a saturated market for learned books.[58]

Previous Book Market Collapses

Martin Lowry and others have charted the series of crises in the book trade in Venice up to 1500, induced by ill-judged speculation, competition, and market saturation, and accompanied by banking collapses around the turn of the century.[59] It seems, however, that a relatively stable market ensued, in which local overproduction was better regulated, and transregional, if not international, distribution better organised. Other local crises occur throughout the century. In Basel one occurred in the 1550s, with a loss of freedom through censorship, an increased political sensitivity to the Catholic cantons and their power, and problems of debt management and cash flow.[60] In Lyon there was a crisis (to judge by the conduct of their heirs) after the death of Gryphius and Payen, both undercapitalised merchant publishers, in the 1560s, and again, due to conflicts between printers and publishers, in the 1580s.[61] But as I shall argue below, there are other factors at work in the Frankfurt of the 1620s.

The General Economic Context

My comments on this can only be very sketchy. Such histories that are available treat macroeconomic topics, and are very difficult to use to supply contexts for elements of the general economy such as the book market, although this is, of course, not immune to the wider economic context.[62] The period 1550–1630 is said by Kapp to have been a good period for trade in Germany, although the figures given by Dietz for the printing and paper costs suggest that there was an increase of 100 percent in paper costs and 300 percent in the costs of labour; and crises in foreign banks on German soil certainly occurred from the 1560s onward.[63] In France, the religious wars disrupted normal economic life between 1560 and the end of the century. Markets closed in on themselves, and publishers made less attempt to export their books.[64] But there was a sharp recovery in the 1600s, which the return of Parisian publishers in numbers to the Frankfurt book fair between 1600 and 1620 attest. In Italy, the major problems occurred after the 1580s, leading to a collapse of the banking system by 1620s through inflation and cash problems. The "seventeenth century crisis" did not affect France until the 1650s, according to Shelagh Ogilvie and Henri-Jean Martin.[65] In Germany there was a trade slump in 1619–1622, and a period of hyperinflation in the early 1620s of up to 300 percent, apparently not directly linked to the events of Prague and Heidelberg of 1618–1622, but clearly exacerbated by them.[66] This crisis had much to do with the Kipper-Wipper coinage crisis of the period of 1618–1623, which was brought to an end by the withdrawal of debased "kipper" coins in 1623–1624, with the losses being borne by the various issuing states.[67] Other causes cited in accounts of economic decline after 1620 are the growth of state apparatuses and taxes. All this is very broad-brush, and would have to be related to the various regions of Europe with some care if it is to count as a factor in the decline of one market sector. A point to note, however, is the deleterious effect of wars on trade of all kinds, including the book trade. In the period 1560 to 1630, nearly all the major exporting centres in France, Italy, the Netherlands, Switzerland, and Germany were subject to periods of difficulties of transport, if not isolation. In spite of this, however, scholarship remained international in character, and very few scholars were deprived of the latest writings of others for long.

Internal and External Factors for the Rise in the Market in the Second Half of the Sixteenth Century

Schwetschke's data on the declarations of Latin books at the Frankfurt book fair shows a fairly steady rise of about 10 percent from decade to decade until the period 1601–1610, when a much higher increase in the number of declarations is in evidence. This was not accompanied by a concomitant rise in the number of book merchants attending the fair, for a number of contingent reasons, such as the French wars and the practice of the Societas Veneta to send only one representative to the fair. The increase, which may well have been fueled by the growing social prestige attached to book ownership, is relatively even across all fields, with theology showing the greatest increase through the demands of confessionalised societies for the range of publications I have already discussed, namely editions of Holy Writ and the fathers, Church history, manuals for training clergy in seminaries, academies, and theology faculties, catechisms for use in schools, and liturgy. In law, medicine, and philosophy, the expansion of the market is clearly related to the foundation of new universities and other institutions of learning, and to the greater numbers attending them. The increasing frequency of editions of standard texts (Bibles for theologians, the Corpus Juris Civilis for lawyers, and Galen for physicians) is very marked after 1600.[68] There is a similar increase in the number of manuals of self-instruction (reference books, encyclopaedic works, and grammars) being published. The subject areas were expanding also: botany and anatomy, the new interest in non-Roman systems of law, the historical and philological investigations of Roman law itself. Philosophy itself was also experiencing a revival through the use of Ramist methods of textbook production and the dissemination of the commentaries of the Coimbra group of scholars. These fields of learning also were extended to new classes of reader through translations into the vernacular; and the intense interest in recent history and geography fueled a steady growth in the production of new annals and other accounts of post-Reformation Europe and the newly discovered worlds beyond. There was also a geographical expansion of the market eastward, northward, and westward, to Poland, Hungary and Bohemia, Scandinavia, and England. Howard Hotson has charted a particularly striking sector of the textbook market which reveals the optimism of publishers and its causes. Up to about 1610, the Reformed communities in central and northern Europe saw an expansion in the number of higher schools and universities under their control, with the important addition of Marburg in 1607. This was accompanied with strong rises in student matriculations in Heidelberg, Herborn, and Marburg up to 1613, followed by a collapse in 1619. To serve this community, the number of Calvinist books declared at the Frankfurt book fair doubled between 1600 and 1605, putting twice as many books in circulation per student over this short period: the publishers fueling this unsustainable expansion were to be found in Heidelberg (Vögelin, whose production increased fourfold between 1609 and 1613), Steinfurt (Caesar), Hanau (Antonius), and Herborn (Corvinus). All this occurred before the disastrous military events in Heidelberg and elsewhere of 1622, which witnessed the wanton despoiling of protestant libraries, and the reconquest of Marburg by the Lutherans in 1624.[69] A specific feature of the Calvinist university scene was Ramism. This scholarly method meant both that textbooks could be produced easily and fast by a wide range of scholars, and that such textbooks could be accumulated into conciliatory works, bringing together different approaches in compendious volumes. The most striking example of this is the commentary tradition on Ramus's brief logical textbook the *Dialectica*. This culminated in Beurhaus's edition of 1596, in which the 80 pages of Ramus's *Dialectica* had been swamped by 764 pages of notes and commentary.[70] The same process had been occurring in other areas of learning. In legal commentary, Alciato had called in 1531 not for the accumulation of opinions around a core text, but for a resolution of its sense, its "unica ratio," but as I noted above, more and more interpretative texts were produced over the period 1550–1610, ending in Kopf's warehouse full of unsellable items in 1633.[71]

These developments created a sense of optimism among entrepreneurial publishers who believed that they had seen how to generate good profits, not just from the staples of the book market, but also from the broad range of available scholarship. They were willing, as we have seen, to use strategies to widen the market by causing book owners to engage in purchases of new editions of texts they already owned (humanism, law, medicine) and new historical documents; and they competed for best-selling authors such as Lipsius. They quickly recognised through the declarations at the fair which texts were worth competing for, and then engaged in speculative reprinting, either in another market zone or by direct competition by undercutting the cost of the successful first edition. Ciotti, Zetzner, Kopf, the later Wechel presses, and Schönwetter all exploited the market in these ways, as we have seen. Unauthorised reprinting or actual piracy of both small- and large-scale works occurred very widely; alternative editions were produced in quick succession, often determined by the rhythm of the fair. Basel was a frequent victim of these initiatives: witness the Lyon reprinting of Arnau de Vilanova, or the Parisian publishers' appropriation of Church Fathers. The unscrupulous Frankfurt publishers we have already met in these lectures had a broader range of targets: England, Lyon, Venice, Antwerp.

There were other commercial factors at work too. The memoirs of Thomas Platter reveal that in Basel, at least, it was not difficult to acquire loans as an aspirant printer, and it seems that those who had spare capital were happy to put it to work.[72] Whether this liberal culture of lending and borrowing was widespread is not clear, and may be related to the relative stability of the zone in question. Christophe Plantin seems to have encountered greater difficulty in finding loans in war-torn Antwerp, but even there, debtors seem rarely to have enforced bankruptcies, and were willing to renegotiate loans. Such evidence of bankruptcies as there is shows them to begin somewhat later. I shall return to this point below.

External Causes for the Decline in 1630

The facts of the decline of the Frankfurt market have long been known. The traditional account of this is heavily influenced by the figure of Leopold von Ranke, who in spite of his famous claim that he took the job of the historian strictly to be that of showing the past "wie es eigentlich gewesen," espoused a version of providential history with a strong Lutheran bias.[73] In his wake, Kapp and Schröder mention a panoply of factors, beginning with the evils of "Jesuitismus," laying great emphasis on their conspiratorial behaviour in the Imperial Chancery, and their influence in Frankfurt (although not in Leipzig) on the Imperial Book Commission.[74] The evidence they adduce includes direct accusations by the territorial rulers of the Palatinate and Saxony of the sinister meddling of the Jesuit order in the financial and censorship arrangements of the book fairs and book trade in Leipzig and Frankfurt through the pursuit of free copies of books for their educational establishments and attempts to impose much stricter censorship provisions on Reformed and Lutheran publishers.[75] These historians give much less prominence to the damage done to the Frankfurt printing trade by the intransigent attitudes of the Lutheran city fathers toward Calvinists (see above, page 12). They also mention other, related, factors which we have encountered before. There was the increasing demand for *Pflichtexemplare* extending beyond the initial two or three copies of books carrying privileges to all new publications, which strained the relations between the Holy Roman Empire, its free cities, and territorial rulers. A factor of a different sort was the rise of the vernacular, and its invasion of the intellectual territories previously occupied uniquely by Latin. Humanist editions of the classics were clearly not affected by this rise, but some very important areas of scholarly endeavour were: mathematics, philosophy, medicine, the study of all aspects of the natural world, and certain parts of law.[76] It is worth remembering that Latin remained an international language even for mathematics until the eighteenth century, which leads me to conclude that the undoubted rise of the vernaculars is to be seen as a parallel, rather than a competing, phenomenon in the period of interest to us here. Another alleged factor we have met is the expansion in Dutch entrepreneurial publishing and the Dutch style of mercantilism, which did not engage in the barter which had been such a feature of the heyday of the market, disqualifying thereby book stocks as currency, and encouraged the second-hand market, and specifically auctions, which reduced the field for new printing. The disappearance of the humanist printer-publisher is also mentioned (unfairly, I believe) as an effect of Dutch hardheadedness and tendency to subject scholarship to mercantile practices.[77] The reasons for the Dutch attitude to barter are not easy to gauge, but they may include some, if not all, of the following: Dutch publishers subscribed to the policy of the Bank of Amsterdam formulated around 1609, and they tried to reduce all their transactions to monetary credits and debts; there may have been a sharp distinction in the Netherlands between publishing and retailing books, which made Dutch publishers unwilling to return from the market with quantities of books for retail sale; successful retailers such as Claesz in Amsterdam may have been adept at securing a supply of books from the international market through different channels; Dutch publishers may have objected to the six-monthly settlement arrangements at the twice-yearly fair, and wanted to obtain immediate settlement for their goods.[78]

More strikingly, German historians record a fall in quality of German book production, possibly a result of having recourse to the satellite towns around Frankfurt, or of using cheap production methods in Frankfurt itself. This was also a feature of the use of Geneva by Lyonnais printers, at least until the introduction there of measures designed to improve the quality of paper.[79] Worn typeface, dirty printing, cheap paper, and poor levels of textual accuracy are all said by the Jesuit Adam Tanner of Ingolstadt in 1630 to be features of protestant books.[80] Even the books printed by the prestigious Wechel house declined in quality during this period, according to one historian, and became more overtly political in nature.[81] German historians of the nineteenth century charted the loss in Frankfurt of the international character of its market and shops, its desertion by authors and foreign publishers during the period of the Thirty Years' War, and the development of national protectionism. This was associated by them with the rise of Leipzig, where there was no Book Commission, and which was shielded at least from the worst effects of the Thirty Years' War, if not the concomitant problems of inflation, disturbance to distribution networks, crises of cash flow, and shortage of food.[82] The remnant of the Wechel firm, Jean II Aubry, claimed that his father had been ruined by the war, not only indirectly by the loss of external trade, but also by being forced to accept the billeting of troops in his house. At one point he had ten soldiers and ten horses imposed on him, at a time when his presses were at a standstill.[83] The recatholicisation of important printing centres at Heidelberg, Lauingen, and Lich should also be mentioned, as well as the continuing rise in national scholarly traditions which exploited the vernacular.[84] All of these factors are in some sense external to the market. It is time now to look to what in my view is the most striking internal factor, one that nineteenth-century German book historians omitted to mention.

The Abuses of Scholarly Publication

It is clear from case histories throughout Europe that publishers with monopolies of liturgical or school books, or those who acted as printers for state administrations, were not affected by the vagaries of trade, since their work consisted principally in staples. It is also clear that the publication of vernacular works was not affected by the same factors as those which obtained in the learned market. So what internal factors contributed to the decline noted above in the trade in learned books in Latin? I am going to suggest that this was affected by selling strategies and editorial policy; but if this is the case, it is incumbent upon me to find contemporary testimony of the claim. There are indications in various legislative acts. I have already mentioned the Frankfurt ordinance against piracy of 1588, and the ordinance controlling the book trade issued in Electoral Saxony in 1594, which makes specific reference to the greed of publishers and authors publishing too much and too often. Testimony of a different sort is found in a satire of the book trade which appeared in 1590 in "Nirgenheim" (i.e., Strasbourg) from the pen of Johann Fischart, one of the most original and pungent writers in German at the end of the sixteenth century. He was a satirist of the intellectual, religious, and literary world around him, with an intimate knowledge of the world of books. He worked for his brother in law, the prominent Strasbourg printer-publisher Bernhard Jobin, as corrector.

His burlesque of Frankfurt book fair catalogue, entitled the *Catalogus catalogorum perpetuo durabilis,* owes much to a previous satire by François Rabelais of a scholastic library in Paris of the 1520s—the Bibliothèque de St. Victor—but he also was prompted by Gessner's *Bibliotheca universalis* and its continuations to attack the indiscriminate listing of books.

It is a striking fact that only seventy years after the lampooning of scholastic academia in the name of humanism, humanism itself suffered the same indignity. Fischart's short introduction indicates that there are too many books and too much trade in them. The catalogue of titles which follows, some real but most fictional or semi-fictional, throws doubt on the validity of all of human intellectual endeavour. Among his specific targets are Catholic doctrines, rites, and practices (fasts, pilgrimages, relics, saints, inquisition); but his satirical knife cuts much deeper than mere sectarian polemic. He implies with some of his titles that much religious polemic is pointless hair-splitting (*Clypeus Thomistarum et quod Thomistae ac Albertistae non multum differant* per M Iohan. Crabacium Noribergensem: an author's name borrowed from Ulrich von Hutten's *Epistolae obscurorum virorum*). He then goes on to mention the genres (*Sammelbände,* epitomes, commentaries) and sales techniques (improved editions, different formats) we have already encountered above. He exposes dangers of unbridled human curiosity and pursuit of novelty, and he engages in the parody of aspects of the publishing world, such as the advertising of books to implausible groups of readers through the title page, uncritical inventorising and the collecting of information for the sake of collecting, and, most tellingly, the boom in some of the genres which I listed in Chapter 3 as a means of stimulating sales in a narrow and saturated market: complete works; epitomes *(Thesaurus thesaurorum thesaurizatus ex multis thesauris)* and the issuing of fresh editions based on new commentaries *(Commentaria commentariorum cum additionibus additionum et annotationibus super annotata).*[85] Like Sir Thomas Browne a half-century later, he implies that books are printed for no other reason than to keep printers and hack writers in business.[86] His near contemporary in France Michel de Montaigne had made the same point about legal and theological books in his day: "Il y a plus affaire à interpreter les interpretations qu'à interpreter les choses, et plus de livres sur les livres que sur autre subject: nous ne faisons que nous entregloser."[87] Humanist scholars aspired to restore all texts to their first and authoritative state by palingenesis, to provide them once and for all with wholly adequate critical

Catalogus Catalogorum perpetuo durabilis.

Das ist.

Ein Ewigwerende/ Gordiani-

scher/Pergamenischer vnd Tirzanino-
nischer Bibliothecken gleichwichtige vnd rich-
tige verzeichnuß vnd registratur/

Aller Fürnemer außbündiger/fürtreff

licher nützlicher / ergetzlicher schöner nicht jeder-
man gemeiner/getruckter vnd vngetruckter Bücher vnd
Schrifften/Operum, Tomorum, Tractatuum,
Voluminum, Partium viler mancher Herr-
licher Auctorn vnd Scribenten.

Allen Lustgirigen rhum vnd klugheit nachstellen-
den Gesellen/zu Dollen Polemischer Tractätlin/ vnge-
treumter/vnerzahtener Namentäuffung/ vnd Tit-
tulzierung/dienstlich/nutzlich/hüsflich
vnd entwürfflich.

Vormals nie außkomen / sondern vor den Sinnarmen
vnd Buchschreibreichen / an starcke Ketten bißher ver-
wart gelegen/Newlich aber durch Artwisum
von Fischmenzweiler/ erditricht/ab-
gelöst/vnd an Tag gebracht.

Gott lob durch vnser fleiß vnd groß müh/
Ists Catalogi erst theil allhie/
Drumb laßt euch nit so fast verlangen/
Der ander kompt hernach mit brangen.

Getruckt zu Nienendorff/bei Nirgendsheim/
im Menzergrund.

M. D. XC.

7.5 The title page of Johann Fischart's satirical *Catalogus catalogorum perpetuo durabilis* of 1590.
Courtesy of Universitätsbibliothek, Leipzig.

apparatus, and to place them at the appropriate point, on the appropriate shelf, under the appropriate rubric which itself formed part of the ideal encyclopaedia. Fischart sees all this in a cynical commercial light, however. The scholarly texts and critical apparatus were not immaterial idealities, but the very life blood of the publishing industry, and were reproduced as much for financial as for scholarly ends. Palingenesis—the perfect restitution of texts—could never be allowed to come about, because it would make redundant new "improved" editions, with the protection they enjoyed by privilege, and bring an expanding market to a premature end. Yet this market was the culmination of the marriage of humanism and Christian ethics that marked Erasmus's works and was greeted with such enthusiasm at the beginning the sixteenth century. The Plantin polygot Bible was in one way a fruit of this marriage, as would be the Paris and London polyglot Bibles in their turn. Elsewhere in the scholarly world, such Erasmian enterprises increasingly became victims of both commercial and confessional pressures. Moreover, fields of knowledge were no longer ideal categories belonging to a closed and sufficient system of categories. Instead, they were, at best, a crude reflection of the contemporary state of learning in existing academic institutions, and at worst a means by which potential purchasers could be attracted to the parts of a sale catalogue most likely to be of interest to them. Fields of knowledge became fragmented through the abandonment of an overarching Aristotelian framework and the changes brought about by empirical discoveries. The book became, furthermore, an object to be preserved and catalogued for itself, thus making the fact of publication culturally significant no matter by what means or in whose interest it first came about. The book became also an object to be collected as a potentially valuable possession, as a token of social or intellectual prestige, as an item of exchange, and not just the physical manifestation of a message to be consumed by an intellect. Part of this development can be ascribed to the technology of printing, which facilitated the production and distribution of texts, and part can be laid at the door of the laws governing publishing in Europe at this time; part can be seen as the logical extension of bibliographical activities which encourage the production of books on books. But whatever causes one ascribes to the publishing boom, and especially the boom in the interpretation and mediation of texts, after 1560 it seems difficult to deny it a role in the decline and eventual demise of the world of humanism and scholarship of which it was the material expression.

CHAPTER EIGHT

Postscript: Then and Now

This book has been about the late Renaissance market for scholarly books; it is appropriate to end it by looking at how that market evolved from the early years of the sixteenth century, by charting the changes that occurred in the transmission of knowledge in terms of both content and manner; and by sketching a comparison of the learned book market of 1560 to 1630 to that of the present day.

One way to look at the question of evolution is to ask what would have surprised the denizens of the market around 1520 (the point at which it became relatively stable) if they had been brought back to revisit it a century later. Authors like Erasmus, promoters of scholarship like Peutinger, publishers like the Kobergers, booksellers like the Giunti and the Birckmanns, purchasers like Fernando Colón, would have found much that was familiar. Authors' negotiations with publishers, and the rewards they might expect from their books, were very much the same. The involvement of scholars in the production process as correctors and castigators was no different; it continued to ensure that they were not alienated from the market for books, even if they had little taste for its commercial ideology. The perpetual revision and re-edition of texts, which was an important component in sustaining a potentially saturated market, was already practised in the 1520s. In Erasmus's day, recovered knowledge—humanist texts and the monuments of the higher faculties of theology, law, and medicine—constituted the bulk of all publications; by the end of the century, the percentage of new writings by contemporaries in all these fields, as well as that of natural philosophy and the literature of discovery, had increased. Elizabeth Eisenstein has argued convincingly that this increase allowed for a broader range of views to achieve dissemination, and reflects the growing self-confidence among authors and editors, and a concomitant rise in their status.[1] The development of the title page and paratext as modes of self-advertisement and self-promotion provides evidence of this. The republic of letters had also grown in efficiency and geographical spread, transmitting the news of discoveries and rediscoveries (of ancient texts, of historical documents, of new parts of the globe) even across religious and political divides. The community of scholars had much more of an international flavour in 1620, and its centre of gravity had moved decisively from Italy to the north of Europe; it also had to contend with a much more obvious set of fault lines. It is true that Johannes Reuchlin and Ulrich von Hutten struggled against the established academic world's resistance to humanism, but they were not yet operating in a confessionalised Europe in which Church institutions, states, and other political entities intervened actively to control the flow of knowledge. In 1517, Erasmus expressed his willingness to submit his writings to the Church, but confessed (somewhat disingenuously, it has to be admitted) to his friend Wolfgang Capito that he didn't know where the Church was (see above, page 153). By 1620 there could be no doubt about the answer to this question. The Western Church had split into powerful opposing factions; these had had a massive impact on the market for learned books, duplicating efforts at recovering Church history and doctrines, and allowing ideology to infiltrate the free flow of information and the unbiased production of documents. In this respect, the generations of scholars and editors who wrote their works after the 1560s found themselves in a quite different world.

The print shop of 1620 would not have surprised Erasmus and his publishers. By 1520 it had been given a shape by the constraints of material production that it was to keep until the end of the hand-press era in the early nineteenth century. But the figure of the publisher had evolved somewhat by 1620. He (or she, in a small minority of cases) was still driven by the same version of economic rationality. Insofar as one can talk of a publishing policy or business model, this seems to have been to remain in business at all costs, and to attempt to pick products that would generate profit. This policy or model determined not just the choice of copy, but also the material presentation of it to the prospective buyer. Publishers played the role akin to modern desk editors in seeking to ensure that the texts they produced were of the best quality possible. In 1520, publishers specialising in scholarship and new learning adopted the persona of the servant of humanism. This persona was still in place a century later, but there were many fewer who deserved the title of humanist printer-publisher. The Alduses, Estiennes, Frobens, Oporinuses, Wechels whose workshops were "veritable homes to cultural and social exchange between scholars, correctors and book producers"[2] had given way to a new breed of entrepreneurs who were not so much involved in the production of knowledge as in its marketing: Peter Kopf, Johann Theobald Schönwetter, Horace Cardon, Giovanni Battista Ciotti, Roberto Meietti. But the high aspirations of their scholarly predecessors were still expressed in the rhetoric of the paratext and title page, and in the claims of scholarly editions to be "emendatior, correctior, locupletior." To find denunciation of the more commercial and venal face of publishing, one has to look at the private correspondence of scholars such as Melchior Goldast, as I did in the second chapter of this study. It would be unfair not to concede that in many cases, the quality of scholarly publication was a major concern of entrepreneurial publishers, in spite of their reputation for venality among authors. But the financial interests which led them to seek profit did eventually filter through to the books they produced, just as did the ideological interests of confessional groups. They were merchants as much as (if not more than) they were servants of culture, and they connived in the perpetual revisionism of the market even more than their predecessors a century earlier, just as they slaked its perpetual thirst for news and works on recent history. On the other hand, some aspects of their trade led them to support scholarship in unexpected ways. The *Tauschhandel* in which they engaged made them active in the diffusion of knowledge of all kinds through their interaction with booksellers and publishers across Europe. The backlists they maintained produced reservoirs of learning in the major fair cities, kept alive the scholarship of previous generations, and were as much a service to scholars as were the grand libraries and collections that were emerging by this date under the patronage of Sir Thomas Bodley, the monarchy in France and territorial rulers in the Empire.

The distribution of books through fairs and retail outlets had not changed greatly in nature over the century in question. In the early years of the sixteenth century, the Kobergers were already engaged in selling through the Hansa model and the branch system described above in Chapter 6. Where a nation depended on the branch system of distribution, there were greater problems for scholars in obtaining the latest publications, but these were not insurmountable, even in parts of Europe where the censorship measures posed yet further obstacles. The trade routes on which such distribution was based hardly changed over the course of the century, but the information about what books were available certainly did. The development of catalogues and finding tools, and the efficiency of the book fairs, ensured a very good level of dissemination. This was broader both in geographical spread and (through the availability of translations into various vernaculars) in terms of categories of reader, although it should be said that a humanist school education, and a fortiori the possession of an arts degree, were prerequisites for most branches of knowledge discussed in this book.[3] It does not seem, however, to be the case that there was reader demand which led to the composition of learned works: the initiative for the production of books rested with authors, promoters, and occasionally patrons, and insofar there was feedback which provoked new works, it came principally from other scholars or the denizens of the publishing world. The appetite for books in courts and among urban elites as well as in universities and scholars' studies was very strong, especially for vernacular literature and works revealing the secrets of nature and the new global and cosmological discoveries. These found their way also into the collections of scholars with working libraries, which tended to be quite diverse; theology broadly understood is a frequently encountered component. And there were more humble collections of books, into which the element of scholarship had penetrated. Book ownership in the private space of the home created also a private mental space— what Montaigne called his "back-shop"—where a new kind of reader could exercise his private judgement or a "Freiheit der Rezeption," that fostered in turn more individual and heterodox thinking, although whether this was necessarily more skeptical of religious truths is open to question.[4] Works of piety and devotion abound in this period, and form a significant component of the book market. Although not directly relevant to the learned book under discussion here, they are a useful reminder of the importance of personal faith to nearly all people of this period. In the realm of publishing, the fact that private accounts kept by book merchants opened and closed with short prayers or divine invocations is an indication of this.

The modes of the transmission of knowledge and the content transmitted also evolved over the sixteenth century. The material transfer of a book from its printer or publisher to its purchaser is most of interest to this study, but one may also think of the transmission of content from the author or editor to the reader. Both can be described in Jakob-sonian terms, as processes which involve a code (Latin, for the most part, and a given genre or field); a contact (the material support, in respect of format, quality of paper, and apparatus such as title page, contents page, and index); a message (the content of the book); and a context (the set of social, religious, political, and commercial determinants accompa-nying the sale of the book or its reception by a reader).[5] In an ideal world—one consisting of only immaterial concepts—the physical fea-tures of the book would count for nothing; but they are in fact noticed and commented on by authors and editors, who demanded good-quality paper, decent-size typeface, a pleasant *mise en page,* and (in most cases) a generous format size, for their works. These act homologically as vi-sual guarantors of the quality of the content.

The fields I discussed above may be separated into humanistic, his-torical, professional, and more general learning or knowledge. The larg-est component of this is composed of works in the field of religion and theology. This reflects the confessionalisation of the European world, and the duplications it produces in all areas: authoritative sacred texts, the Fathers, liturgy, devotional literature, exegesis, accounts of heresy, and polemical assaults on rival doctrines. The size of this field has everywhere been noted, but the publications serving the profes-sional requirements of the law faculty have not. These constituted a substantial market sector until the 1620s, when the market for them shows signs of having collapsed. Historical writing (often connected with religious strife) and commentary on the political state of the world also grew as a market sector, as did the fruits of humanistic research. Humanism is used to describe a somewhat broad category here, em-bracing school curricula, parts of the arts course, and moral writing. It was a profitable market sector in the area of textbooks, but unprofit-able in the prestigious but poorly selling area of Greek.

There are two other aspects of transmission which deserve mention here. The first is the relative efficiency of various parts of the market. I noted above that Paris does not seem to have distributed its learned books in the same manner as elsewhere in Europe (perhaps because there was not a commercial imperative to do so), and that the Hansa system in place in northern and western Europe fared better than the branch system in Italy. Other interferences came from war and plague, both of which were perpetual threats to the free movement of merchan-dise. They affected distribution and availability much more than import controls and other forms of censorship. I myself doubt whether these repressive measures prevented access to ideas whose circulation various authorities sought to suppress, but that is not to say that they did not have a very marked effect on the free discussion and development of heterodox ideas in environments where the Inquisition or its confessional equivalent was a potent force.

Modern Parallels

A number of works have appeared in the last decade which survey the modern field of academic and literary publishing with varying degrees of alarm; as this study has charted a crisis in the same field in the early years of the seventeenth century, it is pertinent to draw some parallels with the present, although this must be done with great caution. The modern study which is most illuminating in this regard is that by J. B. Thompson, entitled *Books in the Digital Age,* which appeared in 2005. Thompson uses various models to investigate the modern state of academic publishing; the one he draws from sociology is that of Pierre Bourdieu, and it is useful to begin with an account of this, to show how it might be employed to analyze the much earlier period under consideration here.[6] Bourdieu argues for a holistic approach to culture which transcends the dichotomy between "objectivism" (the grounding of all explanation of social behaviour in determinant objective social conditions) and "subjectivism" (the attribution to the human subject of agency and critical judgement). Bourdieu wanted his human agents to be neither voluntarist not idealist, and his objective social conditions not to be mechanistically causalist. To avoid such pitfalls, he developed the operative concepts of "habitus" and "field." The former term connotes a system of "durable transposable dispositions" which allow the agent to structure his experience, but which also structures him. The habitus constitutes, not the nature of the human agent, but rather his *altera natura,* incorporating objective social conditions in him in the form of custom. In the way in which Goldast interacted with publishers and colleagues, we can see something of this two-way dynamic (above, pages 22–43). What is impressive about Goldast is the degree to which he shows himself to be aware of being constrained to behave in certain ways by the publishing world in which he operated on his own behalf and on behalf of others.

Bourdieu's term "field" refers to a "separate social universe," an area of the social world characterised by hierarchical organization and by internal relations of force and regulatory mechanisms, physically located in the agents who both bring it into being by their struggle to dominate it, and modify it by their actions. Its structure is objective, and is related by homology to the general field of society (which includes the political and economic fields). Like a habitus, therefore, it has a relation to a greater unit; and just as any habitus relates to the field of power which incorporates, so any field relates to the field of power in which it is situated by homology. The field of the Renaissance publishing world fits this model quite well, in that it was generated and kept in existence by the interaction between political and religious forces and the publishers who situated their activities in respect both of these forces and of their authors, colleagues, and clients. Bourdieu's sociological concepts as employed by Thompson are informed by a sustained analogy with economics. The publishing chain is a supply chain leading from author to reader, and a value chain, in which each passage to the next link adds value. For the publisher, it represents economic capital (money), human capital (editorial staff), symbolic capital (prestige), and intellectual capital (ownership of copyright). In Bourdieu's account, culture is mapped onto a vocabulary of commerce: writers have "specific capital" (the recognition of their peers), which they "invest" in order to derive maximum benefit from it. They employ "strategies of accumulation," and rely on "cultural bankers" (publishers) as "producers" of symbolic goods to be enjoyed by "consumers" (readers). The analysis works at its best when applied to nineteenth-century cultural and literary production, as it is constructed on a conflictual model of human social interaction. The field of cultural production was at that time inversely related to economic and class interests. It was situated between the field of power whose values it inverted and the habitus of those who contributed to it as artists and writers. It was subdivided into a field of restricted production (high art) and a field of large-scale production (mass literature and popular literature). In the former of these, the "economic" stake was "symbolic capital" which could take the form of prestige, celebrity, honour, or consecration; the most successful artists or writers in this subfield might be those who earned the least. The field of large-scale production offered straightforward financial rewards, and as such was closer to the values of the field of power.

This aspect of the model fits the world of academic publishing in the Renaissance much less well. The habitus of the writers I have been discussing was rarely explicitly opposed to religious or political values around them; but it was clearly inimical to the economic realities with which publishers have to grapple, as we saw in the second chapter.

Thompson also sets aside the ideological content of the habitus and field in his analysis of the present state of scholarly publication, and instead looks upon it as a "structured space of social positions [. . .], of resources and power with its own forms of competition and reward." Markets are an important part of fields, "but fields are much more than markets: they are also made up of agents and organisations and the relations between them, of networks and supply chains." Each field has a distinctive dynamic—what Thompson loosely calls "the logic of the field." This is "the outcome of a specific set of forces and pressures and which shapes the activities of particular agents and organizations. The logic of the field defines the conditions under which agents and organizations can participate in the field and flourish or falter within it."[7]

Thompson places academic books in the broader context of changing markets, globalisation, and the new technologies that are emerging. He outlines the function of publishers in this context, and distinguishes between the fields of academic publication (roughly scholarly monographs) and that of higher education publishing (roughly textbooks). He examines separately their operation in the United States and the United Kingdom. Having looked at the impact of the globalisation of the market, he turns to the digital revolution and the Web, and assesses its impact on the fields he has been discussing.

My brief résumé does not do justice to this complex survey; but it will allow me to look at his (and others') accounts of authors, publishers, purchasers, and libraries in it with a view to drawing some comparisons and contrasts with the field I have surveyed in this book. No one in the late Renaissance obtained professional validation in a university through publication with prestigious publishers or in reputed journals as is done now: academic presses in our period were not purveyors of academic credentials, except as commissioned publishers of disputations, and rarely produced scholarship other than in the form of textbooks. The pressure scholars felt to achieve publication, if it did not arise from their desire to promote themselves and their subject, was rhetorically attributed to their patron, whose prestige they enhanced directly in the paratext, or less directly by editing manuscripts from their library.

Just as much of this study has concerned the interaction of author and publisher, so also Thompson and others have discussed modern aspects of this relationship at length. The ominous phrase "the death of the monograph" comes first to mind; it records various aspects of the relationship which are now in crisis. Harvey Waters has recently inveighed against the link between academic survival and publishing, accusing the imperative "publish or perish" of creating a bloated assembly line fueled in large part by mediocrity.[8] There has indeed been a boom in interpretative literary and historical academic books since the Second World War; whether this is similar to the abuses identified by Fischart in 1597 is not clear. At that time, the motor driving the practices in the market comparable to the explosion of monograph publication was commercial as much as it was a desire to serve the truth. The modern excessive growth (and potential collapse) of monographs is driven by a concatenation of forces, including the function of academic validation they fulfil and the willingness of university libraries, and the private and public institutions supporting those libraries, to purchase them in economically viable numbers.[9]

Other aspects of publishing are also more divergent than similar. There was no phenomenon at the end of the Renaissance akin to the present-day trend toward larger and larger publishing houses, and the possible threat that this may pose both to the ability to be published and to freedom of expression.[10] This has led to studies expressing nostalgia for the passing of the small, independent, cultured publisher; perhaps Goldast's disgust at the mercantilism of the publishers of his day incorporates a similar nostalgia for the demise of humanist scholar-publishers like Henri II Estienne, some of whose letters he edited in a volume he published in 1610.[11] Nor was there a Renaissance equivalent of the "library sale," that is, the strategy of producing a small print run at a high price for sale to institutions as a way of ensuring a profit, and a willingness to remainder unsold copies a few years later for purchase by the less affluent (principally, the academics working in the relevant field). Modern publishers of law are able through a related strategy to charge exorbitant prices for their publications, knowing that half of their market (the practitioners) can afford them, as they can pass the costs of them on to their clients (unlike academics). Another area in which the monopolistic control of a market has led to extraordinary prices is found in those learned journals in which appear up-to-the-minute peer-reviewed articles that are deemed indispensable to the academic sector to which they relate. Robert Darnton has been active in campaigning for a new approach to scholarly publication to ensure that all knowledge is freely accessible by all: we are back to the ideal of "scientia" as a gift of God with which I began the second chapter of this study.

These publishing strategies are now complicated by electronic publication, on the one hand, and print on demand, on the other. They coincide with other aspects of the new world of publishing, including the counter-intuitive perception that having a very long list of books achieving low sales can be profitable policy. This phenomenon is a feature of the .com era; it presupposes inexpensive marketing, international credit card facilities, and efficient distribution.[12] In all these cases, the question of the costs of storage and distribution are crucial. We have seen that sixteenth-century publishers treated a press run of about 1,000 as a default position, and looked upon the resultant unsold stock as a necessary liability. The maintenance of stocks over a very long period clearly had cost implications, but these seem to have been readily borne by publishers for reasons of intellectual property and prestige. Other tactics in the modern market—for example, the selling of hardback and paperback editions of the same book at different prices, at different times in the life cycle of the book, and in different proportions—do not apply very readily to the early modern world, in which the vast majority of books were sold unbound; but the tactic of printing on different qualities of paper was pursued, which is similar in effect.[13] Print on demand (enabling modern publishers to maintain a prestigious back list at very little cost in the way of storage or frozen assets) could not, of course, have an early modern parallel in the printing shop, because of the costs of composition and the tying-up of type and formes.[14] But the practice of scribal publication (commissioning single copies from an exemplar) resembles print on demand, and one can find examples of its use even after the period under discussion here.[15]

The publisher and his role are discussed by analysts of the modern printing industry in terms of a number of separate functions: finding talent, supporting talent, editing talent, exposing and marketing talent, and paying talent (Gomez); acting as gatekeepers, controlling the flow of knowledge (Darnton); acquiring content, taking financial risks, developing the content as desk editors and ensuring its quality, managing and coordinating the stages of production, and seeing to marketing and sales (Thompson).[16] In the specific case of academia, the book is a low-volume, high-price product which has to be sold at a considerable discount to retail outlets; publishing is a business with low margins.[17] We can certainly hear echoes of the early modern world in these functions. The initial decisions about the market, the maintenance of workshops with distinguished correctors, the efforts of those in both the Hansa system and the branch system to find efficient means of distribution, and the high discounts offered to retailers of various kinds have been examined in this study, and mark a strong point of continuity. Another tactic practised both then and now was diversification: not, in the early modern period, by combining staples with marginals, but by engaging in a variety of fields (including that of textbooks) with the hope of achieving a sufficient cash flow from each to ensure survival in the trade.[18] There is even a parallel which could be drawn between the present-day practice of obtaining subsidies for academic books, and the use of patrons in the early modern period, although, as became clear above patrons rarely produced material support in advance of publication.

The most dramatic differences between the early modern world and the present day are all connected with the Internet. This has allowed one commentator (Gomez) to declare that just as modern secular society killed God in 1900, so cinema, television, and the Web have killed print a century later.[19] Electronic publication has solved the problem of the person who believed that he was conspiratorially excluded from the world of publication, and was forced to become a self-financed author: anyone can become a blogger. It has dispensed with the need to maintain stocks; it has solved some of the problems of scholarly editions by allowing digitised images of a great quantity of historical documents, or of a number of manuscripts or printed versions of the same work, to be linked virtually and to coexist with any amount of scholarly apparatus in massive hypertextual files, all updatable when new information comes to light, and all simultaneously consultable in a way that could not even be dreamed of by early modern scholars, who were wedded to the aspiration of achieving the palingenesis of a given text.[20] There is now no longer any need for the monograph to die, as theses of all kinds, and even drafts of articles and books, can be made available on the Web in electronic form. As well as individual works, whole libraries can now be made widely available in various forms and to various bodies (the virtual library, the digital warehouse, the scholarly corpus, the scholarly community), whose teething problems (such as divergent modes of encryption, simultaneous access, the ways of charging users, and the sharing of royalty pools) are gradually being dealt with.[21] The Google library could soon be, if it is not already, the greatest collection of books the world has ever seen, more easily accessed and searched than any library before it.[22]

This is a brave new world; but it is still dominated by the metaphors and language of economics. Such an association has very recently been vigorously rejected by Martha Nussbaum in her book *Not for Profit: Why Democracy Needs the Humanities*. She deplores the way in which the humanities and liberal arts are being increasingly undermined and undervalued in the face of "the unquenchable thirst for economic growth that drives education policy round the world." The humanistic disciplines of the nineteenth century, let alone the early modern world, are now valued only to the extent that they can sell themselves as tools of a growing economy.[23] If we look back to Goldast and his generation, they were not driven by such goals, even if they may have been more dependent on economic factors than they were willing to admit, and more enslaved to ideology, at least at the level of the motivations that led them to engage in academic research of various kinds. The publishers that served them were not the paragons of Adrien Baillet, embodying the virtues of "knowledge, fidelity, precision and impartiality" (above, page 10); the books they printed were not exempt from commercial dealings, and they implicitly treated knowledge to some degree as a commodity, and submitted it to the rules of the mercantile world. But the technology which produced their books was still a liberal art; the metaphors which surrounded their production still were informed by the culture of the free gift, and the contents of the books were infused with symbolic, not commercial, value.[24] Rebuffi's book (above, page 9) was an embodiment of Erasmus's humanistic ideals: a source of wisdom, a humane companion, a partner in conversation, a preserver of the past and its monuments, a fount of virtuous pleasure, and above all else a "temple of justice," If there is a dominant word-group which surrounds the book of the late Renaissance, it is that which expresses fairness, truth, righteousness, veracity, and the pious obligation to pursue these as goals. As the Basel publisher Michael Isingrin put it in 1540, author-scholars are "the priests of the republic of letters, whose names are to be held famous above all others in our day for their scholarship."[25] They may not have lived up to this ideal, but they certainly articulated it, and their aspiration to scholarly probity has induced some recent disabused commentators on the world of learning to look back nostalgically to them while claiming that "we will probably continue to see the world of scholarship degenerate towards being the mask for other interests."[26] If there is any light that can be thrown on the scholarly world of 2012 by that which existed four centuries earlier, it may be that its ideology of truth is still a worthy aspiration, no matter how imperfectly it was achieved in all aspects of the publications of the day, and that figures like Goldast were right to try to eliminate from their writings the taint of protocapitalist mercantilism, as Martha Nussbaum has tried to do in her recent defence of the arts and humanities.

Notes
Bibliography
Index

Notes

1. Setting the Scene

1. I should like here to record my debt to a number of nineteenth-century and early twentieth-century German book historians: Kirchhoff 1853a, von Hase 1885, Kapp 1886, Könnecke 1894, Goldfriedrich 1908, Dietz 1970 (first published 1910–1925). Their works are still valuable, not only because of the clarity of their writing, but also because they exploited several very rich archives which have since been lost or destroyed, most notably those of the town of Frankfurt. I have not followed them in all their *parti-pris*. Several were disciples of the German historical school of Leopold von Ranke, and their works are suffused not only with methodological individualism, that is, a commitment to explaining and understanding social phenomena as the results of the aggregation of the intentions and actions of individuals, but also a Lutheran-inspired providentialism and the promotion of a national history in which the triumph of the vernacular over Latin (not entirely divorced from that of protestant over Catholic parts of the German-speaking lands) plays an explicit role. Kapp certainly noted, as I have done, the importance of legal publications to the late Renaissance book market, deriving his account from the survey undertaken by the legal historian Roderich von Stintzing, but he paid less attention to the production of Roman law books, concentrating instead on those written in the vernacular and concerned with German law. Several of these historians are at pains to highlight the struggles of certain staunchly Lutheran towns and territories against the evils of Imperial administration and the baleful effects of "Jesuitismus," seen most notoriously in the operation of the Frankfurt Book Commission from the early years of the seventeenth century onward. This, according to them, was the principal factor in the collapse of the

Frankfurt book market. As I shall argue in this study, this collapse is attributable to intrinsic as well as extrinsic forces. This tendency in German historical writing is not entirely absent from more modern accounts. Giesecke 1991, for example, treats the rise in vernacular literature as much more important than the continuing commitment to the Latinate world, and associates it with a new free mercantile spirit, the nationalisation of knowledge, the criteria of fashion and novelty, the development of public opinion, the emergence of the author as the owner of intellectual property, and the emergence of the bourgeois reader as a figure possessing independence of mind.

2. E.g., Johns 1998 , who does not note in his discussion of English book markets the precedents for a wide range of practices in continental Europe that were well known to the denizens of the trade.

3. Some attempts have been made to produce data on the basis of the printing of sheets (e.g., Chrisman 1982, for Strasbourg), but the uncertainties of press runs and ghosts (to name but two of the obvious problems) make results very speculative. In Chapter 4, I shall also mention another impediment to the production of accurate data, namely, the deliberate element of imprecision in accounting.

4. Maclean 2009.

5. This distinction has recently been made by Thompson 2005. I shall return to it on page 60 and in the Postscript to this study.

6. *Times Literary Supplement*, 23 September 1994, p. 20: a review of an exhibition in the Libreria Sansoviniana at the Marciana Library in Venice: "Aldo Manuzio e l'ambiente veneziano (1495–1515)."

7. McKitterick 2000: 13. Eisenstein 1979: 169 makes a similar point in comparing the bookish culture of the centuries 1350–1450 and 1450–1550.

8. See, for example, Richardson 2004, 2009. Manuscripts were still traded at the Frankfurt after the introduction of printing: see Schröder 1904: 4. On the case of the University of Bologna, see Kirchhoff 1853a: 65–66.

9. Corsten 1981, 1987; Bühler 1958. But Lowry 1979: 35–36 points out that two-fifths of all books printed in the early years of printing in Italy were written by either Dominicans or Franciscans; the religious orders clearly saw the benefits of the new medium.

10. Vespasiano da Bisticci is one example which has been cited: see de la Mare 1965. I am grateful to Martin Davies for this reference, and for suggesting also a second name—that of Diebold Lauber of Hagenau—on whom, see *Allgemeine Deutsche Biographie* 1883: 18.22–25. See also Bühler 1960 and Rouse and Rouse 1988.

11. Davies 1995: 8. Scapecchi 1990 attributes the overproduction of books to the quest for ever more correct texts. Pettegree 2010: 43–62 argues that the application of the model of production of manuscripts contributed to the crisis in the book trade.

12. See Martin 1982a: 161.

13. See also Künast 1997: 197.

14. Pettegree 2010: 268. Künast 1999: 252 claims that by 1500, 12 places (including all of those named here) controlled 80 percent of all European book production. On Basel, see Teuteberg 1986: 153–187; on Paris, Babelon 1986: 75ff. (with some comparative data); on Lyon, Pelletier and Rossiaud 1990: 382–385, Bayard 1997: 94–102; on Strasbourg, Crisman 1977, 1982; on Cologne, Corsten 1981.
15. Data extracted from http://vd16/17.de.
16. de Roover 1956: 231; Künast 1999: 252.
17. Pettegree 2010: 357; Barbier 2008: 69, recording the following figures for the production of folios in the fifteenth century: Venice 1764, Lyon 483, Strasbourg 445, Paris 324, Milan 480, and Basel 313.
18. Künast 1999. The traveling time from Venice to Augsburg was twelve days; from Augsburg to Frankfurt, seven days: see Sardella 1948: 57; Wittmann 1999: 63. On trade routes in general, see Fudge 2007: 10–31.
19. See Pettegree 2010: 268 for a useful map showing the advantageous placing of a small number of centres distributed in a square of Europe whose corners were Antwerp, Leipzig, Venice, and Lyon, and whose internal places (Cologne, Frankfurt, Strasbourg, Basel; Nuremberg and Augsburg) were linked by well-established trade centres. Paris is the one significant centre omitted from the map. See also Meder 1558; Gail 1563 in Krüger 1974; Harreld 2006.
20. See the Adage "festina lente," quoted by Crousaz 2005: 119–120: "non licet cuivis pistorem esse, typographia quaestus est nulli mortalium interdictus"; the adage contains much interesting commentary on printing. See also Lehne 1939:430, 403; Schottenloher 1935. Gadd 1999: passim (on the Stationers' Company), and ibid., 209ff,, on the arrangements in Antwerp, Lyon, Strasbourg, Milan, Venice, Madrid, and Salamanca. For Venice, see Dondi 2004; for Basel, Koelner 1935.
21. Pettegree 2010: 357.
22. Scribner 1996: 13–23, 160–166.
23. Davies 1995: 7, 20 (Aldus Manutius); Mouren forthcoming.
24. Erasmus 1906–1947: 2.494 (23 February 1519, no. 919: the prefatory letter to *Titus Livius duobus libris auctus,* ed. Ulrich von Hutten, Mainz, Johann Schoeffer, 1518): "huius poene divini opificii"; Erasmus CWE (1982) 6. 253.
25. These responses are collected by Gilmont 1990: 9–11; see also Sohn 1590–1591: 1.2.130f.
26. MacCulloch 2003: 317–399.
27. A confessional grouping that was very active in various fields of scholarship was constituted by Philippists—followers of the theology of Philip Melanchthon, the architect of the "confessio variata" of 1540. The Philippists were in one sense the heirs of Erasmus, with his more inclusive and tolerant approach to religious belief, and his marriage of learning and piety. As protestants, they found themselves after 1580, together with others of similar mind, squeezed between the strict Lutherans, on the one hand, and more

radical Reformers, on the other, but continued to espouse an irenic ideology that informed their scholarship.

28. Lotz-Heumann and Pohlig 2007.

29. Mulsow 2007:171 (Goldast's *Petronius* of 1610 and Schoppe's *Priapea* of 1606).

30. Lotz-Heumann and Pohlig 2007: 38 record the claim that the following elements of intellectual life are altogether immune to confessionalisation: Roman Law, certain aspects of matrimonial law, scholarly relations within the republic of letters, the mystical-spiritual tradition, alchemy, and astrology. Chapter 2 will throw doubt upon the claim in respect of the republic of letters.

2. In Media Res

1. Rebuffi 1540:118: "Liber est templum iustitiae, per l. 2 § per autem C. de veteri iure enucleand[o] [C 1.17.2.20] vel est lumen cordis et speculum corporis, virtutum repertorium, vitiorum confusorium, corona prudentum, diadema sapientum, honorificentia doctorum, clarificentia rectorum, comes itineris (ergo studiosus in itinere debet portare libros), domesticus fidelis, socius colloquentis, collega praesidentis, vas plenum sapientiae, via recta eloquentiae, hortus plenus fructibus, principium intelligentiae, fundamentum memoriae, hostis oblivionis, amica recordationis."

2. "scientia donum dei est, unde vendi non potest": see Post, Giocarinis, and Kay 1955; cf. Davis 1983: 87: "in a century in which the book was being produced by one of the most capitalistic industries in Europe, it continued to be perceived as an object of mixed not absolute property, of collective not private enterprise, despite the unequal distribution of monetary rewards. This happened not only because the facts of collaboration were displayed on the title page, but because of the persistence of a powerful tradition for understanding what a book was and what it embodied: something not just created by us, but inherited, given by God, given by others. The book was a privileged object that resisted appropriation and which it was especially wrong to view only as a source of profit." See also Proverbs 23: 23: "veritatem eme, et noli vendere sapientiam et doctrinam et intelligentiam."

3. Baillet 1723: 345: "jugemens des principaux imprimeurs qui se sont signalés par leur savoir, par leur fidelité, par leur éxactitude [*sic*], et par leur désintéressement, qui sont les quatre principales qualités necessaires pour les bonnes impressions des Livres." The next forty pages name printers who qualify for this description, principally in Italy, France, and Catholic Germany.

4. The first three of these figures were named (together with "molti nostri Italiani in Vinegia") in Lodovico Domenichi's *Dialogo della stampa* of 1562 as outstanding scholarly practitioners of the art of printing: see Rozzo 2008: 122–123.

5. I have used extensively both Thülemeyer 1688 and Goldast 1600–1613.

6. Evans 1975: 43. David Pareus's *Irenicum* of 1615 (a plea for an ecumenical council to unite Calvinists and Lutherans) is often cited to support this view. See Milton 2010.
7. Kühlmann 2005 (Gruter and Freher); Walter 2004 (Lingelsheim); Kohlndorfer-Fries 2009 (Bongars); Goldast 1600–1613: *passim*.
8. On Goldast, see Schecker 1930, Schecker 1931, Baade 1992, Mulsow 2001: 308–347, Caspary 2006, Mulsow 2007: 143–190.
9. Schwetschke 1850–1877: 30, 59–60.
10. Frankfurt declared itself for the reformation in 1535 and joined the Schmalkaldic League a year later. It became strictly Lutheran (close to "Gnesiolutheran") after subscribing to the Formula of Concord of 1577. Its Lutheran consistory was opposed to the followers of Philip Melanchthon ("Philippists"), whom they frequently accused of being Crypto-Calvinists. For the period in question, see Dingel 1996. On the later allegiance of the City Council, see Matthäus 2009.
11. See Kapp 1886: 448–755; Dietz 1970: 3: *passim*.
12. Flood 2007: 12 (quoting Henri II Estienne 1968); Matthäus 2009: 174–176 (on the Council's attempt to find a mediator outside the context of the court).
13. Brückner 1961a. On the rise in the power of the Book Commission, see below, pages 138–139.
14. Cited by Brückner 1962: 78. See also Dietz 1970: 2.11ff.
15. This is not to say that there was no attempt at this time of achieving harmony between the denominations: see Mulsow 2001: 345.
16. Evans 1975; Könnecke 1894: 124–125. After a protest from the Wechel presses, the printing of all but the title page and last page was allowed to proceed in Frankfurt, to prevent job losses.
17. Meyn 1980: 228–233. See also Kapp 1886: 609, 629, 645.
18. Data extracted from Benzing 1977.
19. Starp 1958: 50. Könnecke 1894: 126–145 records the negotiations of the Wechel firm with the Hanau authorities, and their pleas for exemptions to offset the high cost of transport. Evidence of the need for citizenship to sell books is found in the formula "venales habentur [. . .]" in imprints or in sale catalogues: e.g., Draut 1625: 1279: "Virginea narratio de commodis et ritibus incolarum Virgineae ab Anglicis qui a D. Rich. Grenville [. . .] deducti sunt [. . .], Francofurti Theodor de Bry. Venales habentur in officina Sigismundi Feyerabend, 1590, in fol."
20. Freher in Thülemeyer 1688: 256 (5 August 1608), where he describes Mannheim as a "locum ipsa novitate commendabilem"; on Hofmann, see Benzing 1977.
21. Brückner 1962; Brauer 1979 (on the first resident Catholic printer in the city).
22. Starp 1958 points out that Schönwetter behaved as a Catholic in Mainz and a protestant in Frankfurt. Other publishers who deal with various denominations are Egenolff Emmelius, Johannes Berner, Vinzenz Steinmeyer

(works by both Calvin and the Lutheran David Chytraeus appear in his broadsheet catalogue: see Coppens 2001), and Zacharias Palthen, who published works by the Reformed writer Otto Casmann and the Lutheran Johann Gerhard, as well as documents for the Catholic Church. The printer Michael Forster had to satisfy both his Calvinist territorial ruler and the Lutheran Council of Amberg: see Paschen 1995: 43–52. On Emmelius, see Thülemeyer 1688: 408 (Raphael Egly, 4 July 1610): "Noster Egenolphus plus justo Lutheranizans quia Giessensibus et genere illic cogitur placere difficultates nexuit."

23. Thülemeyer 1688: 254–255 (5 August 1608: Lingelsheim), quoted below, note 135.

24. See Starp 1958: 43–45 (Schönwetter); Dietz 1970: 3.35 (Episcopius and Brambach). Goldast 1600–1613: 32v alleged that the Council's hostility toward Calvinists was motivated by their fear of the Jewish Community. See also ibid.: 52r (on the burning down of a house in the Jewish Quarter).

25. Kapp 1886: 484; Starp 1958: 53. Schönwetter complained that he had to pay Dr. Schacher 120 guilders to have Goldast's *Imperatorum [. . .] constitutiones* (3 vols., 1607–1610) pass the censor.

26. Friedrichs 1986.

27. Nicolaus Taurellus, professor of natural philosophy at Altdorf, is reported to have done this: see Zedler 1731–1754: s.v. A frequent visitor to the fair was Adriaan van Roomen, a mathematician and professor of medicine of Würzburg, who sought out books for his Italian correspondents: van Roomen and Bockstaele 1967. Estienne 1968 lists the Universities of Vienna, Wittenberg, Leipzig, Heidelberg, Louvain, Padua, Oxford, and Cambridge, pointedly leaving out Paris, which had been implicated in his family's exile from that city. He claims that it was the presence of authors at the fair which made it "Athenian." See also Johann Lautenbach's poem in praise of the fair of 1596, quoted by Flood 2007:10.

28. Nelles forthcoming b; Kohlndorfer-Fries 2009: 9.

29. Erasmus 1906–1947: 5.610 (no. 1528, to Johannes Caesarius, 16 December 1524); Erasmus CWE 10.466; Goldast 1600–1613: 14v (27 December 1605).

30. Goldast dedicated his edition of Ovid and his *Manuale Biblicum,* both published in 1610, to the Prior, Johannes Myntzenberger, whom he describes as a friend.

31. *Messrelationen* were first issued in 1583 by Michael von Aitzinger. Kapp 1886: 473ff. records that other ephemeral literature also circulated: "Flugschriften, Neue Zeitungen, Mord- und Wundergeschichten, Kalender, Lieder." These were sold by street salesmen known as "Hausierer": Schröder 1904: 12.

32. On Bellarmine and supremacy debate, see Mulsow 2007: 150–154; on the complex debate of 1609–1611, see Herrman de Franceschi 2009: 236ff. See also Simon Stenius, *Orationes duae quarum prima est de nefario facinore per Sicarios Venetiis perpetrato [. . .] altera de duobus brevibus a Paulo V*

Pontifice Romano ad Romano-Catholicos in Britan[n]nia missis, Heidelberg, Johannes Lancelottus, 1608. On the related controversy involving Bellarmine over the issue of papal supremacy in the transfer of the Empire from Byzantium to the Franks, see Whaley forthcoming.

33. See Kapp 1886; Goldfriedrich 1908; Niemeier 2003; Weidhaas 2003; Estienne 1968. On the colloquy, see Cosmas Morelles, *Relatio colloqui francofurdensis inter nonnullos Calvinianae Religionis ministros et Cosmam Morelles,* Cologne, 1610; it was translated into French and German in the same year, and published in Cologne. It inevitably provoked a riposte (*Anti-Morelles,* Hanau: for Conrad Biermann, 1611), and a counter-riposte by Morelles (*Jocularis [. . .] refutatio,* Cologne, 1611).

34. The spring fair took place during the eight days before Palm Sunday; the autumn fair, the eight days after St. Giles's Day (1 September). See Griffin 2005 for dispensation from work on holy days in Catholic countries.

35. Starp 1958: 39; Pallmann 1881: 44 (the Buchdruckerordnung, planned in 1563, first enacted on 5 March 1573).

36. Weidhaas 2003: 30 records that in 1488, books represented about one-twelfth of the revenues of the fair. In 1509, the Fugger bought one diamond at the fair for 20,000 ducats (many times the revenues from books): Thiel 1991: 75. On the sale of punches and other printing equipment, see Nelles forthcoming b.

37. Some examples from the exchanges between Goldast and his correspondents include a London publication of Anglo-Saxon laws of 1568 *(Archaionomia)* which Georg Michael Lingelsheim had only located in Freher's library (Thülemeyer 1688: 185: May–June 1607), and three books mentioned by Goldast to Freher: an edition of Plautus of 1513/1514; the Laws of the Emperor Frederick II published in Venice in 1477; and Saxon laws published in Cracow in 1505/1506: see Goldast 1600–1613: 18r, 50r, 97r. The mathematician Adriaan van Roomen performed the office of book hunter for the Italian Jesuit Christopher Clavius: van Roomen and Bockstaele 1967: 119.

38. Nelles forthcoming b.

39. Nelles forthcoming b records that in 1565, there were 107 members of the trade attending from 50 locations: in 1579, 119, from 42 locations, of which one-fifth was local (within two days' travel), one-third 150–250 kilometres distant, and 40 percent from yet further afield.

40. Nelles forthcoming b.

41. Erasmus 1906–1947: 3.252 (no. 797, 13 March 1518, to John Oecolampadius): "sordida illa hominum colluvie"; CWE 5 346; Erasmus, *Dialogus bilinguium et trilinguium,* in Erasmus 1933: 207: "rem bene fortunem furibus, impostoribus, periuriis, foeneratoribus, et nuguiendis"; CWE 7 336.

42. Goldast 1600–1613: 32v (19 July 1606).

43. Ibid.: 14r (27 December 1605).

44. Thülemeyer 1688: 102 (1 March 1603).

45. See Mulsow 2001: 341n.

46. Caspary 2006: 33–35 takes a lenient view of this affair.
47. See Pettegree 2010: 42 on Schedel's Nuremberg chronicle as "a statement of German self-belief." The pride in medieval German, which a correspondent of Schobinger averred was in its rhetoric and richness the equal, if not the superior, of Latin ("ornatu et copia Latinam, si non superat, attamen, aequat"), is clearly expressed in the preface to the *Paraenetica* of 1604 published by Schobinger and Goldast: see Baade 1992: 60.
48. Goldast 1600–1613: 35v (26 August 1606): "inhumanitas doctorum." The exception was the jurist Jacques Lectius.
49. Mulsow 2001: 301ff., 339–341 argues convincingly that Goldast did not forge this document, although he certainly forged at least one other.
50. Thülemeyer 1688: 47 (Waser to Goldast on Schoppe, 21 March 1601); also referred to in Waser's letters to Goldast is the "detestabilis apostasia" of Théodore, son of Denis Godefroy: Thülemeyer 1688: 365 (17 November 1609): see also ibid.: 267 (1 September 1608, concerning Lorhardus or Lothardus of St. Gallen); ibid.: 330, 335. See also Kohlndorfer-Fries 2009: 125–126.
51. Thülemeyer 1688: 42 (Johannes Jacobus Frisius, November 1600): "Indicare tibi debeo V. ornatissime K[i]ngium Bibliopolam attulisse Francofurtum Orationem Lipsii de concordia: advolasse Typographum Plantinianum, negasse esse genuinam Lipsii Orationem: coemisse omnia quae habuit exemplaria (habuit autem pauca non ultra 100) et pro maculaturis usurpasse: addidisse etiam minas, fore ut literae mittantur ad Magistratum Tigurinum, et lis intendatur authori tam editionis quam impressionis. Necesse igitur est, ut tu probes orationem esse Lipsii. Id quoniam poteris praestare, ut ad nos perscribas rogo." Frisius clearly thought that Goldast was not the author of the text. Johann Huldrich Wolf, the publisher resident in Zürich, refused to be associated with the publication, probably under pressure from the city authorities or from Caspar Waser, the Censor of the City: see Thülemeyer 1688: 44 (Johannes Jacobus Frisius, 14 December 1600: "Noster typographus Wolfius, elegantissimae illius Lipsii orationis ne unicum quidem exemplum secum Francofurtum avehere voluit." Waser asked Goldast twice to confirm that it was genuine: see ibid., 43 (1 December 1600), 47 (21 March 1601, which refers also to the lawsuit in Zürich). See also Baade 1992: 34.
52. See Garber 2003; for a different view, see Papy 2003: 523–538; Völkel 2001: 127–140; Gier 2008: 156–159 (on the collaboration between Welser and his protestant fellow townsmen David Hoeschel and Johann Wegelin, and the scholars Janus Gruter and Joseph Scaliger), and Evans 1984; also ibid.: 258: "scholars tended to be accommodating, often eirenical in their opinions. Thus, despite rising confessional antagonisms in politics and society, educated Germany remained a single open community, from sternly Lutheran Holstein in the far north, to re-catholicised Bavaria in the south." Erich Trunz 1931 sees late-Renaissance German humanism as a "Standeskultur," which fits well with their anti-mercantile attitudes, but does not

take account of the confessionalised divisions in the republic of letters. See also Mulsow 2007: 159 (Welser making documents advantageous to the Catholic side available to Gretser); Goldast 1600–1613: (3 March 1611): "nondum scis Welserum esse hominem nequam, sed coram docebo, uti scias." There were strong factions within the Catholic Church who were opposed to the Jesuits as much as were protestants: see Wilding forthcoming, and Gier 2008: 149 (on Munich in the early seventeenth century).

53. Cf. Elie Vinet's use of a printer in Poitiers from Bordeaux: Nelles forthcoming b.

54. Thülemeyer 1688: 108 (January 1609).

55. The Willers were reputed to be as good a source of rare books as was Frankfurt itself, or even possibly better: Thülemeyer 1688: 434 (Conrad Rittershausen, 8 January 1611) and 456 (Fredericus Guillimannus, 16 March 1611), in which the writer reports that booksellers from Rosenheim prefer to go to their shop in Augsburg than to the Frankfurt fair.

56. Goldast 1600–1613: 28v (29 June 1606).

57. Mulsow 2001: 325–327; Goldast 1600–1613: 32v (19 July 1606) "exsul sum, sed nulla mea culpa"; see also Mulsow 2007: 184–185. In Goldast 1600–1613: 14r (27 December 1605), written from St. Gallen, Goldast blames the Jesuits for his local problems.

58. The City Council forbade Giordano Bruno to lodge with his publisher Johann Wechel in 1590, and sent him off to lodge in the Priory: Matthäus 2009. The letters in Thülemeyer 1688: 246, 254, 288 (dating from April to November 1608) give Goldast's address as "bei H[err]n Steinheimer." His dedication to the *Manuale biblicum* which he published in 1610 ends with the words "Francofurdiae [. . .] ex museo meo a.d. IV Kal. Iun. MDC." It is not clear where this "study" was. On the Carmelite House as a place of warehousing and selling, see Weidhaas 2003: 39.

59. Schecker 1931: 232. See also Thülemeyer 1688: 291 (2 December 1608, when Goldast was "bey H[errn] Palthenio"); also ibid., 375, 489. He was in contact with Jungermann, the corrector of the Wechel presses, and the publisher Thomas de Villiers: ibid., 154, 243–245, 476. It seems that correctors moved freely from one printer to another.

60. Goldast 1600–1613: 34r (July 1606): "si stoicus essem, impromptu foret remedium voluntarium, huic remedio"; ibid., 75r (1 February 1608): "amisi omnem scribendi libidinem"; ibid., 35v (August 1606).

61. Ibid., 95v (late 1610); ibid., 97r (3 February 1611); see also Caspary 2006: 39.

62. Goldast 1600–1613: 43r–v (30 November 1606): "nullus Princeps, nullus Dominus, nulla Respublica, nulla alia persona opera mea postulet uti"; he goes on to ask Freher to look around "an apud ullum Principem, Comitem, Baronem locus esse aliquando possit".

63. Thülemeyer 1688: 311 (Caspar Waser, 18 March 1610), 456 (Georg Michael Lingelsheim, 15 March 1611).

64. See Caspary 2006: 38–39 and Goldast 1600–1613: 71r, 73r, 106r, 108r and 75v, where Goldast claims that it would cost him 70 florins to pay for the

dedicatory copy to the Elector of Saxony. An interesting light is thrown upon the returns received by authors from presenting copies to potential patrons in England by the account given by Richard Robinson of the monies he received from the copies he offered to noblemen, merchants, and others between 1576 and 1603: see Vogt 1924.

65. He was not alone in this: Bartholomäus Keckermann had to ask his students in Dantzig to transport the manuscripts of his works to Wilhelm Antonius, his printer in Hanau: Hotson 2007: 155–156.

66. *Iusti Lipsii ad C. Suetonii Tranquilli tres posteriores libros commmentarii eiusdem epistolarum praetermissarum decades sex. Nunc primum editae, partim ex primis editionibus retractae,* Offenbach: Conrad Neben for Peter Kopf, 1610. The commentaries are a transcription from a student listener, who changed Lipsius's first-person references to himself into the third person. They appeared also in Paris (Adrien Beys) in the same year. For another example of collecting letters without the appropriate authority, see Johann Manlius's *Epistolarum D. Philippi Melanchthonis farrago,* which appeared in Basel in 1565: Maclean 2009: 122–123. Goldast acted as corrector for Bongars: Mulsow 2007: 163. The *Orationes* of Lipsius (including the *De duplici concordia*) had been published in 1607 by Balthasar Hofmann of Darmstadt for Johann Jacob Porss in Frankfurt; Freher favoured using the same publisher for the letters he had received from Lipsius which he sent to Goldast: Thülemeyer 1688: 249–250 (24 June 1608). On Goldast's attempt to locate other letters, see ibid., 390 (Quirinus Reuter, asked to mention the matter to Janus Gruter, 12 January 1610), 391 (25 January 1610, Georg Michael Lingelsheim), and 392 (Fridericus Taubmann, 17 January 1610).

67. Goldast 1600–1613: 95v (27 August 1612), on the usefulness of Freher's collection of Frankish documents for a consultation.

68. E.g., Thülemeyer 1688: 369 (Georg Michael Lingelsheim, 15 September 1609): "Vides qua libertate in te utar, tu vicissim mihi ne parce, si qua in re usui tibi esse possum." But see Thülemeyer 1688: 253 (23 May 1608), where Jungermann offered payment for a book in either money or books. Some correspondents tried to achieve "aequalitas" in their exchanges (ibid., 127: Caspar Waser, 31 October 1605); others acknowledged with gratitude Goldast's noble generosity (ibid., 120: Friedrich Taubmann, 9 March 1605).

69. Goldast 1600–1613: 112r; cf. ibid., 32v (19 July 1606): "Bernerus typographus disseminavit ex ore his nescio quae de oblata mihi a principe tuo conditione"; also ibid., 112r (28 November 1612), where he indignantly proclaims that he only received twenty copies of his edition of Georg Sigismund Seld's 1556 *Consilium* as recompense.

70. Starp 1958: 53; Goldast 1600–1613: 40r (18 November 1606). The title page of Goldast's *Rationale* of 1607 carried a reference to the Cologne approbation; for the cost implications of this (in respect of Frankfurt, but not Cologne), see above, page 254n25. Thülemeyer 1688: 436 (Johann Rudolph Lavater, 10 January 1611): "Cuperem quoque titulum abs te formari, sed,

ut nosti, valde vendibilem." Ibid.: 474 (20 January 1610) (on Suizer's uneasy relationship with the local printer Wolf); ibid.: 272 (22 September 1608; on acting as corrector for a work by Egly). He was not alone in acting in this capacity in Frankfurt: the pastor of the city, Oseas Hala, represented at least one Lutheran scholar, Martin Crusius, in the same way: see Widmann 1967–1969: 1550–1551.

71. Thülemeyer 1688: 453 (8 March 1611): "Rogo juves bonum virum Schönfeldium consilio tuo fideli, quo pacto commodissime quam plurima possit exemplaria distrahere, ut aliquid pro impensis meis recuperem pecuniae. Nam et illa editio mihi magno constat. Consignavi eidem unum et alterum librum, quem ex off. Dn. Pet. Kopfii desidero, ut Tob. Baurmeisteri de Jurisdict. etc. Et Catalogum Catalogorum. Si fieri possit permutatio cum exemplaribus aliquot Malchi, tanto gratius haberem, quam si pecunia esset mihi eroganda." One of the books Ritterhausen wanted to acquire by barter was Draut's *Bibliotheca classica* published by Kopf in 1611: ibid., 425 (17 October 1610). The work edited by Rittershausen was Malchus, *De vita Pythagorae*, Altdorf: Cunradus Agricola, 1610. Kirchhoff 1853a: 102 claims on the basis of the above texts that Schönfeld would not take Rittershausen's work to the Frankfurt fair, but it seems that he organised its transport, and set the price, leaving Goldast to distribute it..

72. Mulsow 2007: 184–185.

73. Engelsing 1967–1969, 1971; Coppens 2001. The library holds eighty-eight items in whose publication Goldast was involved, many from Goldast's own library. Unfortunately, the library does not hold the originals of the letters in the Thülemeyer publication of 1688, in which there are clearly a quite high number of mistranscriptions. I am grateful to Dr. Thomas Elsmann of the Bremer Staats- und Universitätsbibliothek for informing me about the library's manuscript holdings relating to Goldast.

74. Goldast 1600–1613: 38r (2 November 1606); 61v (28 April 1607). On the importance of the Strasbourg fair, see also Thülemeyer 1688: 267 (Caspar Waser, 1 September 1608); ibid., 366 (Quirinus Reuter, 15 November 1609).

75. Thülemeyer 1688: 338 (Hieronymus Curio, 6 July 1609): "Vale Eruditissime Goldaste et quod feliciter coepisti, lucubrationibus tuis doctissimis, Reipublicae Christianae inservire perge."

76. For the list of his achievements, see Mulsow 2007: 148.

77. Frankfurt: Wolfgang Richter for Conrad Neben, "1506".

78. See Schecker 1931: 233; Starp 1958: Schönwetter was a Catholic who married the daughter of a prominent protestant printer (Johann Spiess), and kept a foot in both camps; he worked for Kopf in 1602–1603. On Jesuit-inspired attacks on protestant scholarship, see Garber 2003. The sequence of polemical works was as follows: [Schoppe], *Scaliger hypobolimaeus*, Mainz: Johannes Albinus, 1607; *Hercules tuam fidem, sive Munsterus hypobolimaeus, id est satira menippea de vita origine et moribus Gasparis Scioppi Franci*, Leiden: Joannes Patius, 1608 (two editions): Oporini Grubini

[i.e., Gasparis Scioppi] *Amphotides Scioppianae: h. e. Responsio ad Sa-tyram Menippæam Jos. Burdonis Pseudo Scaligeri pro vita et moribus Gasp. Scioppii: item responsio ad confutationum fabulæ Bardoniae*, s.l. 1608, Paris (no name of printer), 1611: thereafter Ingolstadt, 1611.

79. Goldast 1600–1613: 32v–33r (19 July 1606): "et semper existimavi mer-canariam illam prudentiam viro ingenuo ac nobilo indignam"; ibid., 75r (1 February 1608): "talia honeste quidem accipi, sed non probe peti [Ul-pian]"; "magno emitur quod precibus emitur" [Seneca]. Also ibid., 107r–v (27 August 1612), expressing outrage that privileges were granted on the same conditions to "honoratos and bene meritos" such as himself and "viles mercaenarios et lucripetas propolas"; see also the negative reference in ibid., 35v, to "astutia typograph[orum]."

80. Goldast 1600–1613: 92v (23 November 1610).

81. Ibid.: 19r (13 April 1606).

82. Lingelsheim, in Walter 2004: 363: "et quia sumptus in me saepius fecisti subministatis variis libris, ego autem hactenus nummario pretio tuam in me munificentiam dehonestare nollem, iam dum pandis arcane tua, pro meo modulo, mitto tibi paucillos istos aureos rogoque ne aspernis"; for another gift of money from the same source, see Mulsow 2007: 162, 277.

83. Goldast 1600–1613: 85r (3 December 1609) acknowledges that Kopf is his "hospes," and hopes that he will accept payment for his hospitality in services.

84. The relevant parts of the letter are reproduced in Mulsow 2007: 184–185 (a claim not borne out apparently by the title page of the work which ap-peared in 1611, unless Goldast was one of the "consorts" who paid for the edition together with Conrad Biermann). His Catholic enemies were not an anonymous group; he listed their names in the dedication to his *Monarchia*: ibid.: 164. On the Jesuit attack on his claim to noble birth, see Goldast 1600–1613: 32v (19 July 1606). It is of note that Goldast did not contrib-ute a poem to the memorial volume for Jungermann entitled *Lachrymae super immaturo obitu Godofredi Jungermanni* which appeared in 1611, al-though nearly all his close friends did.

85. See notes 137 and 138; Goldast 1600–1613: 28r (29 June 1606): "homine fidei non optimae, et perfrictissimo tricone." These attitudes and the rheto-ric which supports them are reminiscent of that employed by the nobility of early modern France.

86. Kühlmann 2005.

87. Goldast 1600–1613: 2r (23August 1600): "me clientium tuorum numero adscribe"; ibid., 12r (7 November 1603): "vale et me ama."

88. Thülemeyer 1688: 250–251 (24 June 1608): a request that Goldast should return two books or manuscripts to Freher, and his offer to add another text to Goldast's *Rerum suevicarum* if he planned to republish it. Goldast 1600–1613: 99v (10 February 1611) makes it clear that the meetings at the fair were opportunities for Goldast to pass on information and opinions that he was unwilling to set down in a letter. See also ibid., 100r (3 March 1611).

89. Ibid.: "verum quia tu Aulicus es, vix poteris eorum hominum [the Jesuits in Mainz] opera abstinere, quos ego nanci non facio." The word "aulicus" has a clear negative connotation here.

90. Goldast 1600–1613: 37r (19 October 1606), referring to the delay in the delivery of the Frankish documents.

91. Mulsow 2007: 153, where the antiquarian revolution is described as a combination of "kirchlichem Befehl, intellektueller Motivation, gelehrter Hilfe und kuratorialen Interessen." See also Trunz 1931, who argues that humanism in Germany in late sixteenth century was "remote from the real world," and Whaley forthcoming. Goldast 1600–1613: 101r (28 April 1611) declares his triple loyalty to his "patriam tam coelestem quam terrenam" and "amicitiam." It would appear that he is referring to the Empire in the second of these loyalties.

92. Cf. Thülemeyer 1688:143 (15 May 1606), where Freher offers to secure for Goldast a post in Hanau.

93. Schecker 1930: 16; Thülemeyer 1688: 226 (23 January 1608): "Jammodo accepi (nam propter multitudinem aliquandiu domi me continui) in Cancellaria a quaestore utriusque Principis munus tibi decretum Electoris 50. fl. in 20. Ducatis, Junioris 30. fl. in 20. taleris: quos ita ab incude recentes oblata ista occasione ad te mitto, et te pro tempore boni consulere iubeo; a nobis quoque IIII. Viris, ubi Hippolytus redierit, donarium pro nostra copia te sperare; Neque etiam gnadenpfenningum desperare. Caeteros quoque Proceros, quos exemplaribus donasti, gratos habebis, non dubito." Goldast 1600–1613: 73r–v (6 January 1608) records the cost of the presentation copies (150 florins, plus postage). The issue of the cost of postage arises again in these letters; see ibid., 108r (3 October 1612). See also ibid., 362 (3 November 1609), where Lingelsheim congratulates Goldast on receiving 80 guilders from Württemberg. Goldast was persuaded to make a presentation in 1610–1611 to King James I and VI (ibid., 423 (26 October 1610), 455 (13 March 1611). Goldast's contemporary, the Tübingen professor Martin Crusius, listed in his diary the returns he had received from various dedicatees (his own University and its philosophical faculty, various cities, towns, and individuals); the results were very mixed: Widmann 1967–1969: 1538.

94. Goldast 1600–1613: 30r (6 July 1606): "Roga Musas tuas, an suo munere Alemannica mea velint cohonestare. Carmen abs te volo in commendationem operis. Quod si idem possis a Grutero impetrare, rem fecisset et mihi gratum." See also Thülemeyer 1688: 150 (19 August 1606). Janus Gruter turned down Goldast's request for a liminary poem: ibid., 149 (Marquard Freher, 11 July 1606).

95. Goldast 1600–1613: 100r (3 March 1611). Walter 2004: 277 refers to Freher as "a humanist and a scholar before he was a Calvinist."

96. Thülemeyer 1688: 256 (5 August 1608): Freher refers here to the Theophrastian character "mempsimoiria."

97. Goldast 1600–1613: 67r (6 September 1607): "neque mihi citius rescribere, neque typographo licuit tua excudere per longissimam tuam

procrastinationem, nullis nunc proelis vacantibus"; ibid., 112r (28 November 1612), on the commercial damage to the Wechel presses as a result of Freher's failure to deliver the copy of his Frankish documents, which were eventually published in 1613. Goldast acknowledged, however, that Freher's court appointment left him little time for scholarship: ibid., 38r (2 November 1606): "ego sane ociosus sum, nec ullum mihi onus publicum, praeterquam voluntarium: tu contra adstrictus haeres et tener[is] occupationibus plurimorum negotiorum."

98. Ibid., 37r (19 October 1606) and 97r (3 February 1611: on having a "voluntas verbalis" rather than "realis").

99. Goldast 1600–1613: 90r (14 April 1610): "Nam si aliquid abs te petam, scio me frustra fore. Et frustra tentatur, forte communia studia partiri, quibus diversi fines propositi sunt: mihi solus publicus, tibi solus privatus."

100. Goldast 1600–1613: 31r (mid-1606): "illud ipse scis, nec apicem quidem mearum rerum clam habuisse, quem non tecum participarem"; Thülemeyer 1688: 273 (Marquard Freher, 14 October 1608) (on the Palatine privilege).

101. Ibid., 185 (20 May 1607): "scribe quaeso de variis, illis [our mutual friends], aliis." E.g., Goldast 1600–1613: 68v (25 November 1607). He did this also for others: Thülemeyer 1688: 256 (June 1608: Jungermann asking Goldast to find out whether there was a published Greek text of Oribasius); ibid., 453 (8 March 1611: Rittershausen asking for information about publications of or about Salvianus of Marseilles). He even was asked to obtain the missing sheets from publications purchased by his contacts: ibid., 329 (Caspar Waser, 18 June 1609); ibid., 467–469 (7 September 1611, Paulus Matthias Wehner). Goldast 1600–1613: 89v (18 March 1610), 100r (3 March 1611).

102. Meul was a bookseller, creditor, and collaborator of Schönwetter; see Starp 1958: 45. On these figures, see Benzing 1977. They justify the description "entrepreneurial," as they sought out profitable market sectors: alchemy, the occult, and contemporary history. Emmelius even founded a journal in Frankfurt in 1615. He acted as publisher for Goldast in 1610 of the *Manuale biblicum* and the *Philologicarum epistolarum centuria*. It is likely that Richter and Schramm also engaged in publication, although the title pages on which their names occur do not state this explicitly. Conrad Neben sold off his privilege and stock of two works by the jurist Peter Gilhausen and the natural philosopher Johannes Magirus to the Frankfurt booksellers Peter Musculus and Ruprecht Pistorius on 22 July 1609; this probably marks the end of his activity as a printer-publisher, although he continued printing for others until 1610: HHStA 51.1, Koppitz 2008: 389. Engelsing 1967–1969 reproduces the broadsheet catalogues of Antonius Hummius of Frankfurt, a friend of Schramm, and Johannes Carlus Unckelius, a Frankfurt bookseller and publisher who had his books printed in Bremen, Steinfurt, and Neustadt an der Haart.

103. Respectively, Nicholas Schramm of Neustadt and Mannheim, Michael Forster of Amberg, and Sebastian Henricpetri of Basel: Thülemeyer 1688:

250, 256, 180. On Forster, see Paschen 1995. It may not be a coincidence that all three printer-publishers named are members of the Reformed community, and that their religious faith is being praised as much as their professional virtues.

104. Ibid., 296a (27 January 1609): "satis me offendunt Typographorum tricae"; ibid., 372 (8 December 1609).

105. He required the copies in which he was paid to be printed on "Schreibpapier" (ibid., 193–194, 5 September 1607; 226–227, 23 January 1608). Starp 1958: 48 lists the costs of paper as follows: normal: 12 batzen a ream; "Sachsenschild" (used for title pages): 13 batzen; Schreibpapier: 19 batzen; "Grosspostpapier": 2 gulders 7 batzen. His local printer, Gotthard Vögelin, was congratulated by Quirinus Reuter for having produced a book for Vögelin "saneque eleganter": Thülemeyer 1688: 389 (28 December 1609). It is striking how often in these letters the epithet "elegans" is associated with book production. Freher requested a text layout "like Martinus Polonus" (in synchronic parallel columns): see Thülemeyer 1688: 169 (10 March 1607); on Roman versus Arabic numerals, see ibid., 159 (14 December 1606); on "Mittelschrift," see ibid., 147 (27 July 1606).

106. Thülemeyer 1688: 251 (4 July 1608); "Ecce generosos Dominos Fiolejoscum praefecto suo D. Salomone Neugebauer, viro mihi a multis annis familiariter noto et comperto, qui te alloquetur. Est ei aliquid cum Bryanis liticulae, ut intelliges: neque injuria reposcere suum Exemplar videtur, sive illi non possint seu nolint excudere. Juva quaeso ut suum recipiat authoritate et tua et Burgimagistri tui Priorisque et mea interposita, ne ad Magistratum sit eundum." The work by Freher published by de Bry was his *Sulpitius sive de aequitate commentaries ad L 1 C De legibus* (Matthias Becker for Joannes Theodor et Joannes Israel de Bry, 1608); for Goldast they published the *Hodoeporicon* (same imprint).

107. Payment per folio sheet printed (i.e., 4 printed pages of folio, 8 printed pages of quarto, 16 printed pages of octavo, etc.) was offered by various publishers; it was often expressed in different currencies. Kapp 1886: 316–317 records that the figures offered to Reuter for the same work were a half [Reichs]thaler (by Kopf) and the higher offer of a half guilder or florin by Emmelius.

108. Thülemeyer 1688: 179 (7 April 1607), on Freher's plan to publish short works from Pirckheimer's Nachlass in his possession, possibly using "noster typographus" (either Schönwetter or Berner). For this he wanted 100 copies on higher-quality paper ("Schreibpapier"), but "si quid insuper extorquere poteris, tibi cedam sinam." The work eventually appeared in 1610, edited by Freher's relation Johannes Imhof, printed by Johann Bringer at the expense of Jacob Fischer. Goldast did not have a high opinion of Imhof: see Goldast 1600–1613: 101r (18 April 1611).

109. Thülemeyer 1688: 152 (30 August 1606): "transtuli ego nonnulla de hac lite ex Italico in Germanicum, et misi ea Hanoviam ad Magnificum Brederodium. Si impressa sunt, ut fore imprimenda spes mihi facta est, pete meo

nomine exemplum a Typographo." A number of such documents appeared in Frankfurt and Hanau in 1606 and 1607 either without the name of publisher or published by Goldast's contacts Kopf and Neben. Also ibid., 394 (23 December 1609) on the publication in Venice of James I and VI's contribution to the debate about the loyalty of subjects.

110. Goldast 1600–1613: 28v (June 1606): "de Venetis amo te. Nihil mehercle illis libris hac calamitosa aestate utilius"; 38r (2 November 1606): "cur non pugnemus adversus hanc bestiam, contra quam Salvatoris nostris fidem dedimus [. . .]?"

111. On the problems with this proposed publication, see Thülemeyer 1688: 169–170 (10 March 1607), 176 (30 March 1607), 177 (10 April 1607), 182–183 (21 April 1607), 294 (6 January 1609), 298 (10 February 1609), 309 (10 March 1609). Goldast 1600–1613: 61v (26 April 1607) wondered why the Valla refutation was not going to be reprinted with the text.

112. Goldast 1600–1613: 75v (31 January 1606): "nec alia ratio [for accepting to publish the work] fuit, quam temporis illius occasio concinnaverat."

113. Thülemeyer 1688: 177 (10 April 1607) has Freher offering Goldast not 20, but 25, copies of the Heimburg.

114. The full range of negotiations, over a period of ten months, is found in ibid., 147–176, and Goldast 1600–1613: 28v–61v. Freher also wanted a free copy of a folio book on privileges (Marco Antonio Peregrini, *Opus materiarum, iurium, dignitatum, privilegiorum, immunitatum, praerogativarum*), published by Schönwetter in 1607. The publisher promised to supply the book, but was in no hurry to keep his promise: see Goldast 1600–1613: 50v: "nosti hoc genus hominum, si quid promittunt, pro spisso evenit."

115. Goldast 1600–1613: 50v (27 January 1607). The same letter settled the final details of the contract with Schönwetter.

116. Thülemeyer 1688: 166 (23 January 1607), 170 (13 March 1607), 176 (30 March 1607); in the last letter, Freher asked for some copies to be bound and sent to Jean Mareschal in Heidelberg. See Goldast 1600–1613: 46v (14 November 1606), 52r (8 March 1607), 54r (15 March 1607), on the publisher's problems with Freher's tardy delivery of copy.

117. "Appelationes Theodori Laelii Episcopi Feltrensis a Pii Papae II Excommunicatione iniusta Sigismundi Archiducis Austriae, &c. Nunc primum e M. SS. erutis discussae & illustratae &c. Francof. Ap. Schonvvet. 4." Both this and the definitive title are totally unlike the snappier titles of the other fourteen contributions to the debate. See Goldast 1600–1613: 59v (26 April 1607).

118. Ibid., 75v (31 January 1608).

119. The withdrawal of Schönwetter from the publication of the third volume of German documents was solved in 1610, after difficult negotiations with the Wechel house, who agreed to give half an Imperial Thaler for each folio sheet of published text. Out of this, Freher assured Goldast, he would have his usual percentage: Thülemeyer 1688: 431–432 (22 December 1610).

120. Goldast 1600–1613: 43v ((30 November 1606) mentions the problem that Schönwetter had with the title: "Heimburgicarum titulum [. . .] causatur Typographus periisse." Thülemeyer 1688: 232 (20 February 1608): "typographus, qui distrahat Heimburgiaca felicius, rationem reperi. Mutato titulo, et quibusdam, quae habeo, additis, antea ineditis." For another case (that of Adriaan van Roomen) where a publisher changed the title to secure greater sales.

121. The Andlo text, for example, first published in Strasbourg with Rihel in 1603, later discussed in Goldast 1600–1613: 31r (in an undated letter probably written in 1610), was reissued in a different form in 1612.

122. Petro von Andlo, for example, was first published by Freher in 1603, later discussed with Goldast (see Goldast 1600–1613: 31r), and republished by Freher acting alone in 1612.

123. E.g., Conrad Memmius's *Calendarii historici continuatio. Unparteyschye unnd wahrhaftige Beschreibung [. . .]*, Lich Kezelius 1603; and the works by Christoph Wilhelm Walpurger about the towns of Donauwerdt (1608) and Frankfurt (1620). In Pinelli and Dupuy 2001: 55 (15 August 1572) there is a reference to a book of contemporary history "qui veut sembler neutre et non partial."

124. Grafton 1990.

125. Herrman de Franceschi 2009: 228ff.; Lepri forthcoming; Grendler 1978.

126. Kohlndorfer-Fries 2009: 122.

127. See Herrman de Franceschi 2009: 228–241, esp. 237: "le catholicisme anti-romain va acquérir droit de cité en catholicité parce qu'il est seul susceptible de se poser en garant suffisant de la sécurité des princes."

128. Mastellone 1974: 229. The *Monarchia* contained Gallican texts as well.

129. Thülemeyer 1688: 32–34 (undated).

130. Thülemeyer 1688: 288 (Johannes Bockstadius, 16 November 1608).

131. Conrad Rittershausen reported that Goldast was credited with these additions: ibid., 387–388 (7 September 1609); but Quirinus Reuter suggests that he himself was their author (ibid., 283, 25 November 1608).

132. These passages appeared together with an anecdote about Cosimo I Medici's implication in the death of his son, omitted by de Thou; material was added without de Thou's permission to his biography of the German scholar Janus Gulielmus. See Kinser 1966: 45–46, 47–51. The documents relating to the publication of the *Historiae* are found together in the London, 1731 edition of de Thou's *Opera*, section VII.6, pp. 47–51. See also Kinser 1966: 18–20, 143–144. Reuter planned to publish the omissions sent to Lingelsheim as an appendix to his edition of Dudith: see Thülemeyer 1688: 335–336 (6 July 1609).

133. Even Cardinal Cesare Baronio was subjected to the practice of tampering with authors in this way: his Antwerp publisher Moretus was forced to omit a passage from his *Annals* in which the Spanish claims to Sicily were rejected as a forgery, but obliging issued it in 1609 with the title *Tractatus*

de monarchia Siciliae (printed by Adrien Beys in Paris): Voet 1969–1972: 1.194–195; Imhof 2008: 365–366.

134. Kinser 1966: 47 cites two letters from Lingelsheim to Goldast (1 December 1608 and 9 December 1608) in which he attempts to dissuade Goldast from going ahead with the de Thou edition. Kohlndorfer-Fries 2009: 122 cites a letter dated 18 December 1608 from Lingelsheim to Jacques Bongars, reporting that Goldast was not able to stop the edition proceeding, together with the offending marginalia. Kinser 1966: 45–47 refers to a Frankfurt undated edition of late 1608 which Kinser infers to exist from these letters and de Thou's prefatory remark in the Paris 1609 edition (below, note 137). I think that no such edition exists; it seems to have been confused with the Offenbach, Neben edition of 1609.

135. Thülemeyer 1688: 254–255 (Georg Michael Lingelsheim, 5 August 1608): "cum Frehero locutus sum de Typographi Palatini nomine tibi usurpand[o] [. . .] Ille existimat, nihil rem habere difficultatis, et posse te audacter Schrammi Neostadiani nomine uti, atque in se recepit rem confectam dare"; ibid., 278 (Quirinus Reuter, 14 October 1608): "malim autem hic a Lancelloto [Johannes Lancellotus, the University printer in Heidelberg], vel Manhemii a Schrammio excudi, tum ob viciniam, et meam praesentiam ac inspectionem, tum securitatis causa: quia Kopffio posset aliqualis moveri a Pontificiis, quorum concilium perstringitur"; ibid.: 273 (14 October 1608) "de Thuanicis quod quaeris, ita habe, ut excudendi ea in Palatinatu ubivis locorum facultas patet, ita nomen Manhemii simulato commodare Principi displicet." For other cases of a local authority refusing to allow publication with an address which it saw as compromising, see above, page 165 (Geneva, van Roomen, and Théodore de Bèze).

136. Ibid., 353 (Quirinus Reuter, 19 October 1609): "Lingelsh. adhuc nihil succenset quod amisso frontispicio liber sit inutilis."

137. de Thou 1609: a3r: "Quod harumce historiarum scriptor in operis limine nuper edici voluit, non placere sibi miseram ardelionum, qui in alienis scriptis ingeniosi videri cupiunt, ambitionem, idipsum heic etiam iterandum venit, ob inofficiosissimam male feriati cuiusdam typographi sedulitatem, qui superioribus nundinis editos Francofurti ad Moenum praecedentes libros minime ad postremam Parisiensem editionem, quod saltem debuit, expressos notis conspersit ineptis et frivolis, sane hominem ut ab incepto desisteret, viri probi et graves in Germania passim hortati fuerant, quibus ille, si pudore si otio consuluisset, parere necesse habebat. Sed is fuit ververci capitis stupor, ut prudentissimis monitis pervicaciter obsurduerit. Itaque, quando facta infecta fieri nequeunt, satis vindicata videbitur iniuria, si nugatoris illius marrucinitas quasi Marsyae cutis ad ludibrium proposita ceteros huiusmodi nebulones absterreat et cispellat." Thülemeyer 1688: 288 (Johannes Bockstadius, 16 September 1608); Kinser 1966:20.

138. Kinser 1966:52–55. Goldast continued to be associated with editions of de Thou's *Historiae* until 1625.

139. Maclean 2009: 181; Evans 1984.

140. Reuter was privy to the financial conditions of such publications: see Thülemeyer 1688: 277–278 (14 October 1608). Rhodius paid 12 batzen per folio sheet to David Pareus for his commentaries on Corinthians and Genesis; Emmelius offered half a florin per folio sheet (ibid., 361–362, 3 November 1609).

141. Thülemeyer 1688: 287 (14 October 1608).

142. Ibid., 299 (13 February 1609): "Cum Voegelino nostro de Duditianis imprimendis amplius egi. Pollicetur se diligenter et pulcre quamprimum opus aggredi et perficere velle, quot exemplatia D. Kopf, quem humanissime saluto, velit; 1200 ipse suadet; nullumque se retenturum, aut sibi vendicaturum, sed omnia Francofurti bona fide traditurum. Postulat für ein Ballen 8 3/4. fl. Er wolle auch eine lineam weiter drucken, als im nechst geschickten Format gewesen. Si igitur D. Kopfio persuadeas assensum, mitte quaeso cum isto auriga exemplar Duditianum."

143. Ibid., 319 (4 April 1609): "quid Petrus Kopfius noster, de Duditii scriptis statuerit, aveo scire. Caesareum quoddam Mandatum, isthic acceptum ajunt, quo Pontificiae censurae, libri Reformatorum subjiciantur. Illud si fortassis impediat Kopfium, Schrammius Manheimensis, vel Lancellotus noster operam suam obtulerunt, ad im primendum illud opusculum.

144. In the event, Schramm died in 1609 in Hummius's house in Frankfurt: Reske 2007: 253. See also Reuter in Thülemeyer 1688: 335 (14 July 1609).

145. Ibid., 333–334 (30 June 1609): "Ceterum de Duditianis et Cisnerianis quid P. Kopf tandem statuerit, quaeso diserte perscribas. Si conditionibus iis, quibus anno Superiori mecum egit, non volet jam Duditiana imprimere, mihi velim remittat, ut hic vel Manheimii edantur citius. Sin velit isthic; mittat mihi specimen, ut videam, qua forma et litera etc. Cuperem enim eleganti typo et charta imprimi. Cisneriana, sane bella opuscula, si Lancelloto vel Schrammio daret imprimenda, gratum mihi foret. Expectabo planum responsum, ut ne diutius in suspenso haeream"; ibid., 335 (14 July 1609); ibid., 342–343 (18 August 1609): "Duditiana novae Budingensium censurae subjecta fuisse, vix aequo animo ferre queam."

146. Ibid., 410–412 (24 August 1610).

147. Ibid., 299 (13 February 1609); 336 (14 July 1609): "Opera Sadoleti sunt ante paucos annos edita Moguntiae, a Rhodio vestro: in quibus epistolae ad Sturmium nullae: ad Genevenses una longa: cui olim respondit Calvinus. Ideo ego ante sesquiannum Schrammio dedi excudenda utraque."

148. Ibid.; also 454 (12 March 1611).

149. Ibid., 335 (14 July 1609); 352 (19 October 1609); 361 (3 November 1609); 389 (28 December 1609).

150. Mulsow 2001: 310; Thülemeyer 1688: 44 (Johann Jacobus Frisius, 14 December 1600), who names him as censor.

151. He also asked Goldast to find out whether Frans Raphelengius of Leiden had Syriac characters, and would be able to publish his introduction to that language (ibid., 311, 18 March 1610). Evidently Goldast did establish this; Waser's *Grammatica syra* was printed by Raphelengius's presses in 1619.

152. Ibid., 290–291 (2 December 1608). It was not uncommon for university printers to lack Hebrew characters: it was also the case with Joseph Barnes of Oxford (Bodley 1926: xxv).

153. Thülemeyer 1688: 267 (1 September 1608); ibid., 314 (18 March 1609).

154. Ibid., 267 (1 September 1608); 329 (18 June 1609).

155. Ibid., 310–311 (18 March 1610); 314 (18 March 1610); 374 (23 December 1609); 412–414 (1 September 1610); "Palthenius [. . .] exemplar reddere non vult, et tamen gravatur excudere"; 426 (3 November 1610); 458 (13 April 1611).

156. Voet 1969–1972: 1.300 (Plantin); Steinmann 1967: 44 (Oporinus).

157. Thülemeyer 1688: 465–466 (22 November 1611): "tam mascule et Helvetice."

158. A work printed in that city the year before for Hummius gives the name of the printer as Georgius Beatus.

159. E.g., ibid., 374 "volui, tecum iterum atque iterum rogare vehementer, velis apud clarissimum Palthenium studiose instare ut analysin meam imprimat ad nundinas proximas."

160. Rhodes 1987.

161. See above, note 142.

162. Thülemeyer 1688: 468 (7 September 1611); Goldast describes him as "mendax" on one occasion: Goldast 1600–1613: 59r (12 April 1607. On the financial skulduggery which led to his imprisonment from 1604–1606, see Starp 1958: 46f.

163. Thülemeyer 1688: 488–489 (21 April 1610): "Insignium Typographorum, et eorum qui opibus valent; [. . .] typographo qui valeat iudicio labore, studio industria, ut emaculatissime et elegantissime in lucem prodire hi mei quantulicunque labores possunt."

164. Ibid., 374 (22 December 1609): "nostri ordinis homines Typographis servire solemus: ipsi lucrum, nos quid habemus?"

165. Thülemeyer 1688: 73 (19 June 1601): "id hominum vulgus sibi omnia gratuito fieri vult." Thülemeyer 1688: 433 (8 January 1611) "morem mercatorum, quibus et famae et conscientiae nulla sit cura"; but Rittershausen also describes the Amberg publisher Johannes Schönfeld as a "bonum virum" (ibid., 453, 8 March 1611); also ibid., 419 (6 September 1610): "fere autem sic affecti sunt Bibliopolae nostri Germani, ut lucrum sibi reservent ex libris redactum; labores vero steriles relinquant iis, a quibus imprimenda volumina acceperunt, sive illi primi fuerint operum auctores atque inventores, sive recensitores et emendatores." Gessner made the same comment about their "avaritia" in a letter to Johann Crato von Krafftheim in 1564: Gessner 1577: 22r.

166. See Wendt 1973. The accusation appeared in Regensburg in 1569 with the title *Von Buchhendlern, Buchdruckern und Buchfürern: Ob Sie auch one Sünde und gefahr irer Seligkeit Unchristliche, Ketzerische, Bepstische, Unzüchtige oder sonst böse Bücher drucken und offentlich feilhaben oder von andern kauffen [. . .] mögen.* His objections are more theological than

those of Luther himself: *Fastenpostille*, 1525, "Vorrhede und vermanung an die Drucker", A2r (*Werke*, Weimarer Ausgabe, Weimar: Böhlau, 1883–1929, 17.2, 3): "es ist yhe ein ungleich ding, das wyr arbeyten und kost sollen drauff wenden, und andere sollen den genies und wyr den schaden haben."

167. Crusius's diary quoted by Widmann 1967–1969: 1529: "miseri est cogi nos ad voluntates typographorum." Goldast certainly knew of Crusius, and may have been in contact with him: Goldast 1600–1613: 47v (21 October 1606).

168. E.g., the mathematician Adriaan van Roomen, who complained in 1597 that "Francofurtani [typographi] me luserunt spe," including in that number Nicolas Bassée, to whom he had previously dedicated a book: van Roomen and Bockstaele 1967: 127.

169. See also Freher's attempt to recover the Heimburg text: Thülemeyer 1688: 183 (21 April 1607), and those of Constantianus and Ottoniana: Goldast 1600–1613: 81v, 82r (16 July 1608, 23 July 1608). Kopf admitted that he had them, but could find them among his papers. See also note 169 above (Waser's dealings with Palthenius over the manuscript of his *Analysis*). Thülemeyer 1688: 305 (Gothofredus Jungermannus 1 March 1609, on "indiligentis typographi [. . .] manus"

170. Ibid., 180 (7 April 1607): "cum ultimo Francofurti fuissem, sermo mihi de his legibus fuit cum Sebast. Henric. Petri, Basiliensi Typographo, viro optimo, e cujus officina illae primum prodierunt curante Basil. Heroldo, et pauca forte 50. vel circiter exemplaria supersunt." Not surprisingly "is se recudere nolle profitebatur": Johannes Heroldus, (ed.) *Originum ac Germanicarum antiquitatum libri : leges uidelicet Salicae, Allemannorum, Saxonum, Angliorum, Thuringorum, Burgundionum, Francorum, Ripuriae, Boioariorum, Vuestphalorum, Vuerinorum, Frisionum, Langobardorum, Theutonum,* Basel: Heinrich Petri, 1557.

171. Magdeburg: Mulsow 2001: 339–341. See Thülemeyer 1688: 348 (2 September 1609, concerning a manuscript source from Bullinger's library), where Goldast is urged by Waser "imprimis, quod maxime cautum velimus, si quid in praejudicium Reipublicae Tigurinae ab eo scriptum reperias, ut reperies in Historia Vitodurensi, pag. 24. 25. 29. et 58. Id pro tua dexteritate, ac benevolentia in Rempublicam nostram, modereris: ut et plurima superstitiosa in nimiam commendationem fratrum Minorum, prudenter temperes aut tollas: sicut et quae de Friderico Imperatore scribit, pagina 4 et 6.".

172. Thülemeyer 1688: 91, 152. I am grateful to Professor Theodor Mahlmann for identifying the Lutherans in question as the pupils and followers of Aegidius Hunnius, the predecessor by more than a decade of the Calvinist Raphael Egly, who became professor of theology in Marburg in 1606.

173. Baronio, who professed to delight in "a true and severe corrector" (referring to the Proemium to the third book of St. Augustine, *De trinitate*: "liberum correctorem desiderem") might be exempted from this charge.

As Casaubon prepared his refutation of Baronio's *Annals,* he was warned (by the French savant Nicolas Fabri de Peiresc) not to impute bad faith to him: see Mulsow 2007: 170. Baronio did not call into question the premise of papal supremacy to the extent of accepting the Donation of Constantine as authentic, and so his work also can be said to be ideologically coloured. On the Spanish suppression of the material relating to papal and Spanish claims to the two Sicilies in Baronio, see Voet 1969–1972: 1.194–195; Imhof 2008: 365–366. On the doctoring of the reference to Montmorency's treason by Giovio, see Pinelli and Dupuy 2001: 182 (4 September 1575). James 1605: A2r–v claims that both Baronio and Bellarmine engage in misrepresentation: see Nelles 2007: 32. See also Flacius 1556 and Eisengrein 1565. The phenomenon of "witnesses to the truth" is linked to I Kings 19:18 (where their number is set at 7,000) and Romans 11:4.

174. Mulsow 2001: 342: "ein Gewirr von gelehrtem Austausch, Beleidigung und Ironie, Manuskriptsuche, konfessionellen Strategien und publizistischen Taktiken"; ibid., 345: "Autorität, Legitimation und Glaubwürdigkeit."
175. Mulsow 2007: 171.
176. Ibid.: 174–176 has a subtle and convincing analysis of this.
177. Grafton 1990: 43–45.

3. Authors, Fields, and Genres

1. Quoted by Widmann 1967–1969: 1539.
2. See Maclean 2009: 133 ("deerat occasio edendi"); Magnien 1982.
3. http://www.zinoviev.ru/en/writings/zinoviev-interview-nijmegen.html: "Let us consider democratic societies. Apparently, there is no censorship. You are free to write whatever you want. The publisher is free to publish that book or not. The publisher has anyway certain opinions. And if your book does not meet the demands of the publisher ideology, or of society from the publisher's point of view, the book won't be published. Let us imagine instead that your book meets that demand and gets published, then this book must reach the readers. For this a distribution is needed, and distributors are said to be free as well. If the book does not meet the demands of the distributor it won't be distributed. Eventually, if your book is bad from the point of view of the booksellers, your book won't be sold. Every year, in the Western world about one million of new books appear but it is impossible to know about their existence. Newspapers, magazines, and TV programs decide which books are going to be presented to the public. So, publicity is fundamental. They are free to report about your book. As a result many books are ignored. It is as if they disappear." I am grateful to Grahame Lock, one of the interviewers, for this reference. See also Jansen 1991 and Keene 1991, for the claim that economic forces determine what information is reaching the public. See Darnton 2009: xvi for a much more kindly formulation: "publishers are gatekeepers, who control the flow of knowledge."

4. E.g., Zoltán Hunnivári, *The final countdown: Chronology of eclipses from Julius Caesar to Diocletian. Hungarian Calendar. Archaeoastronomy* (Budapest: Transtrading Edition, 2007). The motive of the modern self-payer may be cultural: Mikhail Saltykov-Schledrin's *History of a Town* (Oxford: W. A. Meeuws for I. P. Foote, 1980) was deemed worthy of publication in English by the distinguished Russian specialist I. P. Foote, its translator, but not by the commercial presses to which it was submitted.

5. Richardson 2004, 2009.

6. Brunet 1876; an additional monastic institution is found in Dupont 1854: 148 (the Monastère Saint-Denis in Paris). On Monserrat, see Roure 2007: 94. See also Morison 1963.

7. Brunet 1876: 12; on this practice, see Simonin 2004: 727–746.

8. Zeeberg 2004 (a full account, including details of Rantzau's handwritten dedications and special binding). The privilege of Parisano's *De subtilitate* specifies that the work was produced "eius studio labore et sumptibus"; see HHStA Impressoria 56,17 (29 May 1620); Koppitz 2008: 419. Parisano's book was reissued 1623, and received a second, enlarged, edition in 1635 (probably with reissued sheets for the first volume). These facts suggest that it did not enjoy commercial success.

9. See Lenk 1989: 161–175. The project was formed in part as a way to publish the Greek MSS which the Town Library had acquired in 1544. It was protected by an Imperial privilege: HHStA Impressoria 77, 6 (29 November 1594); Koppitz 2008: 593.

10. The claim is made in a letter to Georg Rehm: see Mulsow 2007: 184–185.

11. Mosley 2007; Wilding forthcoming. Galileo's *Le operazioni del compasso geometrico et militare* was produced in Padua in 1606 by Pietro Marinelli in a press run of sixty.

12. A full bibliography is in Maclean 2006b: 75. See also Jütte 2004.

13. Serjeantson 2001: 219; Herbert of Cherbury 1778: 172, who prayed aloud to God for a sign from heaven: "I had no sooner spoken these words, but a loud tho' yet gentle Noise came from the Heavens which did so comfort and cheer me, that I took my Petition as granted, and that I had the sign I demanded, whereupon also I resolved to print the Book."

14. Marr 2006.

15. Pettegree 2010: 75.

16. Gehl online 8.01.

17. Thülemeyer 1688: 424 (17 October 1610): "assentiris [Rittershausen is addressing Goldast] procul dubio mihi, post sacras literas vix ullum extare scriptorem, qui corruptos ac vitiosos hominum mores et gravius castiget, et felicius corrigere possit, quam hic ipse Salvianus: quem scis et a Cujacio aliisque JCtis idcirco saepe allegari, quod non pauca ad Jus civile et historiam antiquitatesque pertinentia complectatur."

18. Thülemeyer 1688: 425 (17 October 1610); "Malchi mei exemplaria 144. quae Francofurtum destinaram, audio ex Schonfeldio [the Amberg printer] meta tēn hēortēn advecta esse. Facio tibi potestatem aperiendi vasculum

etiam ante futuras nundinas vernas, et distrahendi de illis per amicos vel proxenetas quicquid poteris, vel etiam permutandi in meum usum. Typographus unum exemplar aestimavit 20. cruciferis. Ist ein gedoppelt unzertheiltes Exemplar zehen Batzen. Et sane magno mihi haec constat editio supra qua credas, ut aequum sit, me aliquo modo saltem consequi expensas"; ibid., 453 (8 March 1611): "abrumpere cogit me festinatio Schönfeldii, cui velim tradas distrahenda exemplaria Malchi nostri, cum designatione numeri exemplarium, quae meo permissu inde praelibasti danda amicis. Rogo juves bonum virum Schönfeldium consilio tuo fideli, quo pacto commodissime quam plurima possit exemplaria distrahere, ut aliquid pro impensis meis recuperem pecuniae." He was not the only scholar to attempt to recuperate costs in this way: others who had received remuneration from a publisher in the form of copies for the manuscript that they had had printed, came to the Frankfurt fair with the intention of selling them: Flood 2007: 11.

19. Andrewes 1614: L2v: I am grateful to Noel Malcolm for this reference.
20. Zeeberg 2004.
21. Rietbergen 1983. It should be noted, however, that the Plantin Press's edition of the first volume sold so well that the price was raised by a third for the second volume two years later.
22. Pinon forthcoming a, detailing the initial outlay, the negotiations over paper and press run, the customization of copies for individual patrons, and the slow sales.
23. E.g., Waser 1611a, 1611b. The Chaldean primer seems to have sold better than the Grammar: see Dyroff 1963: 1334 (1193 remaining copies of the Grammar, against 154 of the *Elementale*).
24. Erasmus 1906–1947: 10.206–207 (no. 2798, to Eustache Chapuys, 23 April 1533): "typographi sciunt vix aliud nomen est vendibilius. Crederem illos blandiri, nisi sic a me semper aliquid flagitarent, si nihil aliud, certe praefatiunculum." Confirmation of this claim by contemporary publishers comes from Pallmann 1881: 96n; Chrisman 1977: 545. Simon de Colines had a separate entry for his Erasmus publications in his catalogue of 1546: see Lesage, Netchine, and Sarrazin 2006: 252 (no. 1608).
25. Crousaz 2005; Jardine 1993.
26. Maclean forthcoming a.
27. See Maclean 2009: 131–162.
28. On Case being wooed by German publishers, see Schmitt 1982: 151. Zuber 1980: 167 suggests that Scaliger, Lipsius, and Casaubon were all best-selling authors, but as will be seen below (274n40), even a long-awaited edition of Polybius from the last-named scholar failed to sell. On Oporinus's view of Camerarius, Vives, and Rivius, see Steinmann 1967: 61.
29. Jan I Moretus, for example, produces a list of books he would prefer to publish than a new edition of the works of Benito Arias Montano, including Bibles, breviaries, missals, and the works of Baronio and Lipsius: MPM Archive 12, f. 258 (12 June 1604), quoted by Imhof 2005: 53–54.

30. Nutton 1993. See below, note 147 (the example of Giambattista da Monte); other Italian professors of medicine who are reproduced in Germany in this way are listed in note 146, below. See also Maclean 2009: 47 (Zabarella).

31. Pinelli and Dupuy 2001: 184 (on Wechel's scrupulous approach to Sigonio for permission to publish him); in Joubert's life of Guillaume Rondelet, there is a reference to an unauthorised edition of Rondelet's lecture notes in Paris, which the author deplored: Joubert 1599: 2.155–156.

32. Gessner 1966 [1545 and 1555]: *3v; Pliny the Younger, *Letters*, 3.5 (quoting his uncle): "nullus est liber tam malus, ut non aliqua parte prosit." The same quotation is used by Baronio in the preface to his *Annals*.

33. Crousaz 2005.

34. Thülemeyer 1688: 419 (6 September 1610). For the full quotation, see above, Chapter 2, note165. The meaning of "recensitores" is not clear from the context; it could refer either to those through whose initiative texts were made available, or those who revised them.

35. See http://www.termiumplus.gc.ca ("la banque de données terminologiques et linguistiques du gouvernement du Canada"), where "auteur secondaire" is defined as "la personne ou la collectivité qui a joué un rôle secondaire dans la réalisation d'un document. La nature de sa contribution est mentionnée: par exemple, on indique s'il a été 'éditeur scientifique' (celui qui a établi le texte), illustrateur, intervieweur, préfacier, rédacteur, réalisateur, traducteur, etc." In the chapter that follows, the editor and promoter are clearly "secondary authors" in this sense. The patron could also be so considered, because his input as provider of finance or of the resources of his library are conditions *sine qua non* of the eventual publication which benefits from either or both. Publishers could be patrons in this sense: see, for example, the dedication of the eleventh volume of Conrad Schlüsselburg's *Haereticorum catalogus* in 1599 to his publishers Nicolas Bassée and Peter Kopf.

36. Moss 2003.

37. See Schenker 2008: 242–249, 285–289, 774–779, on this enterprise and its difficulties for the editor Benito Arias Montano.

38. On Hebrew, see Burnett 2000; Heller 2004, 2008, 2011. Theodore Dunkelgrün has kindly informed me that a major collection of essays on early modern Hebrew printing in Italy is forthcoming from the University of Pennsylvania Press, edited by Joseph Hacker and Adam Shear. For Greek, see Lowry 1979: 53ff, 263ff; Davies 1995; on the early printing of Greek in Paris, see Barbier 2008: 96–97; on Rome, see Nuovo and Sandal 1998: 43; on Basel, see Hieronymus 1992; Steinmann 1967: 63ff. Thomas Linacre had some texts of Galen printed in Cambridge in the 1520s. Frankfurt began in the 1540s: Pallmann 1881: 47. The beginnings of Greek publication at Basel have been attributed to the importation of Aldus Manutius's books by Wolf Lachner, the father-in-law and financier of Johannes Froben: Bietenholz and Deutscher 1985–1987: 2.60–63, 279–280. Bolgar 1958: 375 states that most Greek classical texts were printed by 1520, but this is a somewhat misleading claim. On Louvain, see Pettegree 2010: 83.

39. Armstrong 1954 (on Robert Estienne); Evans 1984; Gier 2008.

40. Thülemeyer 1688: 189 (Georg Michael Lingelsheim, 9 July 1607), 194 (Marcus Welser, 22 September 1607), 269 (Fredericus Guillimannus, 18 September 1608), 304 (Lingelsheim, 2 March 1609). First published in 1610, the sheets were reissued in 1619, although advertised in the fair catalogue as though a new edition. Casaubon's partial commentary appeared posthumously in Paris in 1617.

41. Gilmont 2004: 62.

42. Maclean 2009: 179. On Greek more praised than practised, see Maclean 2001: 19–20; Nutton 1993 and 1995, and Hieronymus 1995.

43. Lowry 1979: 263ff; Davies 1995; Oporinus and Steinmann 1969: 144–145 (Oporinus's letter of 13 March 1555); Gilmont 2005b: 62 (on Henri II Estienne's struggles to get his Greek texts published, and the need for Ulrich Fugger's support); Hieronymus 1995: 96 (on the view of the Basel publisher Andreas Cratander in 1528 that few physicians possessed Greek).

44. Guthmüller 1998; Burke 2004.

45. Whaley forthcoming; Pettegree 2010: 42 (on the Nuremberg Chronicle).

46. Edwards 2003: 193. Whaley forthcoming points out that Calvinists stressed the potential of the vernacular to restore unity and harmony rather than seeing it as a means to promote a national sense of identity. See also Borst 1957–1963: 3.1, 1346–1352.

47. "Clag und Vermanung Latein ich vor geschriben hab/das war ein yeden nicht beknadt/jetzt schrey ich an das vaterland/teutsch nation in irer sprach"; cited by Wittmann 1999: 50. See also Giesecke 1991: 382–383.

48. Fuchsberger 1533: sig. 2r–v has a bibliography of early translations of works relating to the arts course. He was later, in 1536, to translate Justinian's *Institutes*. Both works enjoyed repeated editions. There was another translation of the *Institutes*, by Justinus Gobler in 1552, which was reprinted in a dual-language text in 1563: both versions enjoyed several editions. An epitome (by Heinrich Knaust) appeared in 1572 and 1574.

49. Pantin 1996 (natural philosophy); Worth forthcoming (medical works); Maclean 2009: 146–147 (Cardano translations).

50. Skalnik 2002 (on Ramus); Pantin 1996 (on scientific literature).

51. French was also recognised as the language of diplomacy: see Graf 1997.

52. On medical books being translated into English, see Wear 2000: 44; Wilding forthcoming (Meietti at the end of his career); Rhodes forthcoming (on Ciotti); Maclean 2009: 297–298. Ciotti was involved in an ambitious programme with the Accademia della Fama in Venice to vulgarise knowledge: see Lepri forthcoming. Andrew Maunsell's *The catalogue of English books*, London, John Windet for Andrew Maunsell, 1595, lists 6,000 books in English, organised by field (divinity, the sciences, the humanities).

53. See Burke 2004, who overstresses its association with the Roman Catholic Church; Bowen and Imhof 2008: on Latin as lingua franca. Sir Thomas Bodley preferred works in English to be translated into Latin: Bodley 1926: xii. See also such works as William Perkins's *Catholicus reformatus* [. . .]

primum in Hispanicum, ex Hispanico in Latinum idioma translatus, Hanau, Wilhelm Antonius, 1601; Voet 1969–1972: 2.224–226 (on Juan de Valverde's anatomy, first published in Spanish, then in Latin).

54. E.g., Melanchthon, *Corpus doctrinae Christianae* (Latin and German) (Leipzig: Ernest Vögelin, 1560); Canisius, *Epistolae et evangelia* (Dillingen: Sebald Meyer, 1570); *Evangelien* (Dillingen: Sebald Meyer, 1573); Casmann, *Gnorismata et signa scientific electionis* (Frankfurt: Zacharias Palthen, 1607); *Gnorismata [. . .] das ist gewisse und unfelhbare Warzeichenn und Versicherung der Gnadenwahl [. . .]* (Frankfurt: Zacharias Palthen, 1607). See also Bowen and Imhof 2008: 223–224, 226–227; Pierre Coustau, *Pegma cum narrationibus philosophicis* (Lyon: Macé Bonhomme, 1555); *Le Pegme, avec les narrations philosophiques* (Lyon: Macé Bonhomme, 1560). On Andreas Libavius's *Alchemia,* see Giesecke 1991: 672–678. See also Worth forthcoming (simultaneous publication of medical books in French and Latin).

55. Pettegree 2010: 357.

56. Even theologically contentious issues such as transsubstantiation, justification by faith, and predestination could be investigated through Draut's lists; the bringing together of Catholic, Lutheran, Zwinglian, and Calvinist titles on such topics suggests that Draut might have hoped for the emergence of some super-theologian who, having read all the available material, would be able to pronounce a final verdict, commanding general assent and bringing to an end all controversy. This is not as implausible as it may seem: the University of Marburg, to whom Draut dedicates his bibliography, was known for its Calvinist-inspired irenic and conciliatory attitude to philosophical and theological issues. It was led in this by the figure of Rudolph Goclenius, Draut's erstwhile tutor, whose *Conciliator philosophicus* (1609) and *Lexicon philosophicum* (1613) embody this approach to scholarship: see Bauer 1999. One of its professors of theology, Georg Sohn, clearly articulated the hope of reconciliation through dispassionate consideration of all the available literature in a work published in 1589: Sohn 1591–1592: 1.89: "Utinam vero existeret aliquis et ingenio pollens, et otio abundans, qui Theologiam in sacrae Scripturae libris disparsam lateque diffusam ad methodum revocaret accuratiorem, et in unum corpus, suis membris distinctum atque divisum contraheret: hoc est, qui omnes ejus partes, et partium partes, generaque et species continuis definitionibus, divisionibus ac regulis illustraret, ordineque suo, ac statione debita, singula collocaret." Draut's desire to include as much as he could in his *Bibliotheca classica* should remind us both of the irenic aspirations of Sohn and Goclenius, and of the all-inclusive approach to bibliography and the ideology of compendious and non-selective scholarship articulated by its founding father, Conrad Gessner, and exemplified in his *Bibliotheca universalis* of 1545.

57. Schwetschke 1850–1877.

58. Meyer 1987: 207–209.

59. E.g., Martin Crusius, a scholar *si quis alius,* was a keen collector of Amadis de Gaule: Pettegree 2010: 151–152. Nearly all scholars' libraries contain a significant component of theological and devotional literature.

60. See Jensen 1996: 63–81; Blair 2010.

61. For a bibliography of such works, see Palisca 2006: 233–240.

62. Thülemeyer 1688: 313 (Claudius Christophorus): "Proximo anno Chronicon Gronlandicum Danice, in publ. rudiorum et indoctiorum emisi"; this is *Den grønlandske Chronica* (Copenhagen: [no name of printer], 1608).

63. Kinser 1966:46.

64. Thompson 2005. For textbooks in the early modern period, see Gehl online and Campi De et al. 2008. I am using the term "field" descriptively in this chapter; for a discussion of the Bourdieusian use of the term, see below, pages 240–241.

65. One might be tempted from this to surmise that the former financed the latter and that the fields were therefore interdependent, but I shall argue against this (see below, pages 114–115. Basic grammars often have prefatory material which makes the point that Latin offers three benefits to those acquiring it (it enhances careers, it provides a key to ancient wisdom, and it affords access to morally improving works); this establishes that the grammars are preparations for entry into the learned world, and not learned works in themselves: see Gehl online 8.03.

66. Maclean 2009: 178

67. The field of natural philosophy offers a somewhat complex picture; before 1520, even medieval mathematicians were being promoted, mainly by physicians: see Maclean 2001: 171n. There are no general surveys of this field from the point of view of publishing for the later period, but see the helpful articles by Pantin 1988, 1996, 2006.

68. Plantin's 24mo series has largely not survived. Apuleius provides an example of a scholarly edition from these presses. The Leiden editions appeared from 1587 with Petrus Colvius as the editor; after 1591 he was replaced by Bonaventura Vulcanus.

69. Oporinus and Steinmann 1969: 159 (François Hotman to Oporinus, 16 May 1559), specifying 16mo and high-quality paper for an introduction to law, on the grounds of the expectations in Lyon; in fact, Herwagen produced the book in folio; Cardano 2004: 39 (Cardano and the choice of folio for his commentaries on Hippocrates). Also above, pages 29–38 (on specification of paper and format).

70. Crisman 1977 classifies the production in Strasbourg under the headings humanism, science, history, law and theology, which offers a sort of empirical confirmation of the divisions I am employing here.

71. For a bibliography covering the complex history of the printing of the Bible in this period, see Schenker 2008: 774–775. As a guide to the volume of Bible editions in theology as a whole, it represented 14 percent in Geneva, against 18 percent exegesis, 18 percent systematic theology, and 43 percent devotional and pastoral literature: Gilmont 2005b: 47. For an interesting insight into cross-confessional printing of Bible editions in 1586 involving

Nicolas Bassée, Sigmund Feyerabend, and Matthäus Harnisch of Neustadt an der Haart, see Dietz 1970: 3.34.

72. See Martin, Chartier, and Vivet 1982: 332.

73. 186 lire, according to Nuovo 2003: 148. In 1629, Naudé 2008: 156 (facsimile 72) chose Tostatus's multi-volume *Opera* as an example of a purchase made only by those seeking to make their mark as collectors by their ownership of multi-volume folio books.

74. Surprisingly, it was followed by two more editions, one at Cologne in 1613, and another in Venice in 1615. Antonio et al. 1788: 2.259 refers to an edition of 1547 "de orden de Carlos V": this is Francisco de la Fuentes, *Index operarum Alphonsi de Madrigal cognomenato Tostado* [. . .] (Valladolid: Juan de Villaquirán, 1547), fol.

75. Dietz 1970: 3.40.

76. See Flachmann 1996; Wendland 1985; Gilmont 2005a.

77. Chaix 1978: 117ff.; Dubois 2007.

78. Backus 1997.

79. Nelles 2007.

80. Kapp 1886: 327–341 has a section on pre-Reformation law publications.

81. Stintzing 1880: 60–65; Simeoni 1940: 29–32.

82. Stein 1999: 79–83, 104ff.

83. Among the fifteen or so reprinted physicians between 1640 and 1665 are Girolamo Cardano, Daniel Sennert, Wilhelm Fabry von Hilden, Johannes van Heurne, and Georg Schenck von Grafenberg. The only two jurists are Pedro Barbosa (d. ?1596) and Matteo Buratti (d. 1627).

84. The graphs in Kapp 1886 *ad fin.* show that this declines at the beginning of the 1620s, somewhat earlier than the other faculties. For a brief survey of the genres of legal writing, and an indication of their practical application through the "usus modernus" (of both civil and canon law), see Wijffels 1992: xix–xxiv.

85. Lowry 1979: 19, 22, 78. Nuovo 2003: 118 quotes a directive of the University of Bologna from the beginning of the sixteenth century controlling the prices of books, which clearly indicates that law books cost much more than those in medicine and the liberal arts. The fact that law books were aimed at both academic purchasers and practitioners can be inferred from phrases on the title page asserting the usefulness of the volume in question to both groups ("iuris studiosis et practicis").

86. A late attestation of this practice of exhibition is found in Gerhard Meurschen's preface entitled "de vana librorum pompa" to the second edition of Thomas Bardolinus, *De libris legendis dissertationes* (The Hague and Frankfurt: Nicolaus Wildt, 1711), *3ff.

87. Petrucci 1969. They are called "libri da banco" because they were suitable to be accommodated on university lecterns.

88. Labitte, Agustín, and Freymon 1585. Sebastian Gryphius apparently approached living jurists in southern French universities for copy: see Maclean 2009: 280–281.

89. Pinelli and Dupuy 2001: 162 (Dupuy to Pinelli, 25 March 1575) carries a reference to a new edition of the "Corpus Iuris Civilis avec les gloses, rouge et noir, le plus beau qui fut oncques fait." It had Accursius's gloss, Contius's scholiae, and Cujas's paratitla; its double-colour title page aped the Lyon editions of earlier in the century. On the Florentine Pandects of 1553, see Kapp 1886: 296. On clashes between publishers in the same city and between cities over legal publications, see Pallmann 1881: 67ff.; Glocke 1962; Dietz 1970: 3.35; Koppitz 2008: *passim*.

90. Hoogewerff 1926: 371. I am grateful to Angela Nuovo for this reference.

91. The full title reads *Tractatus universi iuris, duce, et auspice Gregorio XIII Pontifice Maximo in unum congesti: additis quamplurimis antea nunquam editis, hac nota * designatis: XVIII materias, XXV voluminibus comprehendens*. Another collection of almost the same magnitude is the *Repetitionum seu commentariorum in varia iusrisconsultorum responsa* published by the Compagnie des libraires of Lyon in 9 volumes in 1553.

92. De Bujanda 1985–2002: 8.182, 536.

93. The colleges in question are All Souls, Queen's, Merton, St. John's, and Christ Church, Oxford; Peterhouse, St. John's, and Trinity, Cambridge. On the lack of relevance of these volumes to English jurists, see Wijffels 1992: xix–xxiv.

94. Schönwetter set out on his publishing career by publishing almost uniquely law books in Latin. Starp 1958: 51, 84ff. Other publishers to take up law publishing include Jacob Stoer, on whom see Dubois 2007, and Beraud and Michel in Lyon, on whom see Maclean 2009: 227–272. On Feyerabend, see Pallmann 1881 and Dietz 1970: 3.32. For accounts of the earlier profitability of law in Lyon, Germany, and Italy, see Martin, Chartier, and Vivet 1982: 187, 219, 242; Kapp 1886, 327ff.; Nuovo and Sandal 1998: 43–44; Nuovo 2004.

95. Thülemeyer 1688: 468 (7 September 1611): "Cum Schonwettero mihi res adhuc est aliqua. Sed homo ille callidus et mirabilis est. Vellem absque molestia expiscari, num adhuc supersint apud eum observationes meae. Ante biennium scripsit, se eas non habere amplius. Nuper contra sibi ad 300. exemplaria restare: Et tamen petit sibi committi exemplar auctius, ultra quadruplum." Schönwetter had published his *Practicae observationes* in 1608.

96. Quoted by Glocke 1962: 88–91, and Dietz 1970: 3.35. The offending publication was Bassée's reprinting of Antoine de Harsy's *Tractatus de in integrum restitutionibus ex diversis I.V. doctoribus decerpti* of 1586, which Bassée declared in the autumn fair catalogue of 1586 with the title *Tractatus de in integrum restitutionibus selectissimorum iurisconsultorum*.

97. Azpilcueta was printed initially in Coimbra in 1542 and 1547–1548, and then in both Venice and Lyon between 1569 and 1600. As a canonist, he also was published in Rome. Popular works by Menochio were published in Venice, Cologne, and Frankfurt (financed by the Cologne printer Johann Gymnich) between 1580 and 1605; those by Farinacci appeared in Venice,

Frankfurt, and Lyon between 1589 and 1607. In all these cases, it appears that a policy of market zoning was engaged in by the publishers concerned: see below, pages 194–200.

98. Kelley 1970.

99. Merula 1543: 19r (à propos Pylades Brixianus and Alexander de Villa Dei): "nihil est horum carminibus insulsius, barbarius, invenustius, incultius, durius, horridius. Nullus est per Germanias, Gallias, Hispaniasque typographus, quem non pudeat his duobus authoribus manus admovere." See also Naudé 2008: 90ff. (facsimile 39ff.).

100. Schottenloher 1953: 153–154 (in Flood 2007: 16) quotes the preface to *Matrimonialia consilia* edited by Giovanni Battista Ziletti, written by its German editor Nikolaus Rucker in 1580, in which he makes the point that nearly 200 such books were on offer in Frankfurt.

101. The jurists with their dates are as follows: Albericus de Rosate, 1290–c.1360; Bartolus de Saxoferrato, 1341–1357; Andreas Alciatus, 1492–1550; Baldus de Ubaldis, 1327–1400; Petrus Paulus Parisius, 1471/1472–1545; Stephanus Bertrandus, 1434–1516; Petrus Philippus Corneus, 1385–1462; Philippus Decius, 1454–1535; Bartholomaeus Socinus, 1436–1507; Marianus Socinus, 1482–1556; Andreas Barbatia, d.1479; Christophorus Porcus, 1435–1519; Ludovicus Pontanus Romanus, 1409–1439; Jason Maynus, 1435–1519; Carolus Ruinus, 1456–1530; Hippolytus Riminaldus, 1520–1589; Ioannes a Turrecremata, 1388–1468; Felinus Maria Sandeus, 1444–1503; Joannes Faber,1470–1530; Dominicus de Sancto Geminiano, d. 1424; Henricus B[o]ichus, d. 1390; Hippolytus de Marsiliis, 1450–1529; Joannes de Imola, d. 1436; Luca de Penna, B.C. 1325; Matthaeus de Afflictis, 1443–1523; Ioannes a Ripa, d. 1535; Paulus de Castro, fl. 1360; Joannes Bartachinus, B.C. 1448; Bartholomaeus de Saliceto, d. 1412; Henricus de Segusio [Hostiensis], 1200–1271; Azo, 1150–1230; Franciscus Zabarella, 1339–1417; Cyno da Pistoia, 1270–1337.

102. Dietz 1970: 3.82

103. See Maclean 2009: 59–86, for a more extensive account of medical publications.

104. Nutton 1993; Hieronymus 1995.

105. Sudhoff 1894; Hieronymus 1995: 104–109; Maclean 2009: 59–86.

106. Maclean 2009: Ibid., 85–86. On *Observationes*, see Pomata 2010; on *Consilia*, see Agrimi and Crisciani 1996.

107. From the example of Leipzig fair declarations between 1596 and 1601, the percentages of the various formats are as follows: folio 23 percent; 4 to 29 percent; 8vo 43 percent; 12mo 4.5 percent; and 16mo 0.5 percent. There were almost certainly more plain texts and basic manuals printed in the smaller formats, that were not declared at the fairs. See also Maclean 2009: 59–86.

108. The publishers who emerge from a census of Adams 1967 and the holdings of the Herzog-August-Bibliothek, Wolfenbüttel, are the following: Guillaume Roville of Lyon, Heinrich Petri and his heirs of Basel, Pietro Perna

and Conrad von Waldkirch, also of Basel; the Giunti in Lyon and Venice, and Roberto Meietti in Venice; André Wechel, his heirs in Frankfurt and Hanau, and the presses which are associated with his name although independent of him (Johann Wechel and Zacharias Palthen); and figures such as Giovanni Battista Ciotti of Venice and Jacques Chouet of Geneva, who specialised in reprinting. On Paracelsus, see Sudhoff 1894.

109. Gallus 1590; Spachius 1591; Schenck 1609. Under the rubric "medicinae scriptores," Draut 1625a: 941 also names the continuator of Conrad Gessner's *Bibliotheca universalis* of 1545, Michael Neander, whose compilation appeared in Basel in 1565.

110. See Maclean 2001: 45, on the transmission into Italy of medical ideas. See also Grafton forthcoming b.

111. Pantin 1988; Marr 2008, 2009.

112. Draut 1625: 1004–1304 ("libri, histiorici, geographici, politici"). On history, see Grafton 2007; on geography, Atkinson 1927.

113. Evans 1984: 262.

114. On Case, see Maclean 2009: 307–308; on Lipsius, see Imhof 2008: 182–189; on Botero, see Baldini 1992. Jean Bodin's *De Republica* appeared in French in 1576, and thereafter in Latin in 1586 and 1591 (two editions, one produced for the original Parisian printer Jacques Dupuys in Geneva, the other being an unauthorised reprinting by Johann Wechel and Peter Fischer for which the publishers secured an Imperial privilege: see Koppitz 2008: 149 [19.56]. Editions labelled fourth, fifth, sixth, and seventh appeared in 1601, 1609, 1622, and 1624; the last was announced in a privilege application of 1624 (Koppitz 2008: 454 [60.33]). Pierre Grégoire's work of the same name appeared in Pont à Mousson and Lyon in 1596, and in Frankfurt in 1597; his previous work, the *Syntagma iuris universi*, had appeared in Lyon in 1582 and 1587, before being reprinted by Peter Fischer in Frankfurt in 1591, protected by the same privilege as Bodin. It appeared thereafter in 1599 and 1611 in Frankfurt, and 1611 and 1639 in Geneva.

115. Grafton 1997: 140, 161ff.

116. Even James's Catalogue of MSS in Oxford and Cambridge College Libraries (the *Ecloga* of 1605) was a contribution to a historical debate (the antiquity and status of the Saxon Church).

117. A striking and almost unique feature of the *Centuries* was their collaborative nature. They were produced by what would now be called a research team: see Grafton 1997: 160–162; Hartmann 2001: 75–79; Lyon 2003. On the historical series published by the Wechel presses, see Evans 1975.

118. Steinmann 1967: 65ff.

119. Gehl forthcoming: "Various issues are of interest here. The preface expressed often the ambition to serve either the children of a patron or more generally those in schools. In Italy, the productions were aimed at a very local market, were often dedicated to the city fathers, and were sometimes financed by the pedagogues themselves. Patrons of a different kind were

often promised cultural prestige and lasting fame from their association with the textbook in question. The commercial interests of publishers were often revealed in framing narratives that were targeted at identifiable consumers of large numbers of [such] books."

120. There are many such examples, among them those of Apuleius, Ausonius, and Pomponius Mela. On this last author, see Alicke 2009; see also the helpful surveys in Kraye 1996.

121. Botfield 1861.

122. See Vanek 2007.

123. This has been charted by Jehasse 1976, Grafton 1991, and Bury 2003, inter alios.

124. See Troje 1971; Maclean 2001: 18–22.

125. Gessner 1966 [1545 and 1555]: 73r–91v (the longest entry for any author): Cranz-Schmitt 1984; Lohr 1988.

126. Gessner 1966 [1545 and 1555]: 495–497. Gessner chose to transcribe the order of works from the Herwagen edition of 1534, but was aware of the Aldine edition of earlier in the century, the Paris publication edited by Pietro Vettori, the edition by Paulus Manutius, and those by Wendelinus Rihelius of Strasbourg of the 1540s. On these competing editions, see below 286n111.

127. See, e.g., Frasca-Spada and Jardine 2000.

128. See di Filippo Bareggi 1988. Parent-Charon 1982: 242 claims that professional authors are very rare in France at this time: not so Simonin 1992.

129. On Eck's hopes for profit, see the online edition of his letters, ed. Vinzenz Pfnür, no. 29: http://ivv/svv15.uni-muenster.de/mnkg/pfnuer/Eck-Briefe.html (17 April 1516, to Nikolaus Ellenbog).

130. Maclean 2009: 158.

131. Steinmann 1967: 61.

132. See Nuovo 2003: 45.

133. The cut-throat nature of the fair is clear also from the experience of Leonard Thurneisser, who stressed that authors needed make sure that they were the first to distribute their works at book fairs to forestall piracy: Kirchhoff 1853a: 103. On sales of Lipsius in England, see Rees and Wakely 2009: 219, 224–226; more generally, de Landtsheer 2007.

134. Privileges also protected the best-selling schoolbooks, such as the school dictionary by Henricus Decimator and the *Dialectica* of Ramus. See also Koppitz 2008 for the entries of Jacopo Menochio, Abraham Bucholzer, Jean Bodin, Paracelsus, Andreas Libau, and Johann Schneidewein.

135. Some examples of the usefulness of promoters to authors are afforded by Gretser, to Bellarmine: Nelles 2007: 36; Castelvetro, to Alberico Gentile and Erastus: Maclean 2009: 291ff; Sadoleto, to Paleario: Paleario 1992: 89–90, 93–94; Freige, to Ramus: Maclean 2009: 173–174; Silvestri, to Cardano: Maclean 2009: 149; Peucer and Manlius to Melanchthon: Maclean 2009: 121.

136. Erasmus 1906–1947: 7.119–120 (no. 1855, to Jan Łaski, 13 August 1527): "alioqui quum nunc novorum librorum gargara, ut habet vetus comoedia,

pene nos obruant, mihi praeclarius esse facinus videtur veterum autorum monumenta temporum iniuria scribarumque temeritate collapsa restituere, quam nova cudere volumina; praesertim quum quod sua aetate vere dixit Ecclesiastes, 'nihil esse novum sub sole', et 'scribendi plures libros nullum esse finem', in hoc seculum multo verius dici possit"; Erasmus CWE 13.234–235; Gessner 1966 [1545 and 1555]: *3v.

137. Naudé 2008: 171–187 (facsimile 79–87). He singles out at one point Richard Suiseth or Swineshead, the medieval mathematician known as the "Calculator," whom the two philosophical rivals Girolamo Cardano and Julius Caesar Scaliger had both admired.

138. Over one-third of Aldus's publications were by fourteenth- and fifteenth-century authors: Lowry 1979: 218.

139. Labitte, Agustín, and Freymon von Randeck 1585.

140. Maclean 2009: 87–106; Maclean 2001: 171 (Oxford calculators).

141. E.g., Arnaldus Arlenius acting as a scout looking for Basel printers seeking Greek MSS: Wellisch 1975: 159. Elie Vinet sought out manuscripts of Ausonius: Nelles forthcoming b.

142. Peutinger 1923: *passim.*

143. Gilly 1979.

144. Jardine 1993 (on Erasmus's use of the figures of his countryman Rudolph Agricola and St. Jerome for self-promotion); Dodoens 1581: a6–7.

145. HHStA 62, II, 20; Koppitz 2008: 471.

146. Another example is provided by Ercole Sassonia, whose *Tractatus triplex, de fe[b]rium putridarum signis et symptomatibus, de pulsibus et de urinis* was edited by Peter Uffenbach, the town physician of Frankfurt, and produced in 8vo at the expense of Johann Theobald Schönwetter in 1600. Three years later Uffenbach brought out, at the expense of the publisher, Zacharias Palthen, the *Pantheum medicinae selectum* of Sassonia in folio, inspired, as he says, by four other Germans (Johannes Hartmann Beyer, Johannes Baumann with Johannes Munster, and Peter de Spina), who had edited the lecture notes of Hieronymus Capivaccius, Antonio Massaria, and Girolamo Mercuriale, respectively. A further folio volume by Sassonia (the *De pulsibus*) was edited by Uffenbach in 1604, following its appearance in Padua in 1603. Part of these works, all based on lecture notes, then appeared in folio, also from the Palthen presses, in 1610, with the title *Prognoseon practicarum,* edited this time by an ex-student from Cremona, Leander Vialatus, with an introduction by Johann Jessen of the University of Wittenberg. In 1620, the Venice publisher Francesco Bolzetta reprinted this volume in Vicenza, in folio.

147. The promoters of da Monte include Valentinus Lublinus of Poland, the Italian Girolamo Donzellini, the Imperial physician Johann Crato von Krafftheim, and the Silesian Martin Weindrich. There are also various editions of individual works in Vienna and Augsburg from 1551 onward. On Paracelsus, see Gilly 1979: 134–135; Maclean 2009: 70, 98

148. Maclean 2009: 72. There is no composite guide to the diffusion of Paracelsianism after 1580.

149. On the interest in Basel in Lull, and its relationship to Paracelsianism, see Gilly 1985: 123ff.

150. After their first edition in 1534 in Paris, Clichtove's sermons continued to be published in Cologne up to 1572 (six editions), but his philosophical works were not reprinted.

151. Gessner 1966 [1545 and 1555]: 197v–204r; Kumaniecki, Mynors, Robinson, and Waszink, 1969: vi–x. In January 1536 the Portuguese humanist Damião de Goís offered to finance the publication of Erasmus's *Opera omnia*, but withdrew the offer soon after Erasmus's death.

152. The Cologne editions predate the Council of Trent; the first edition of the expurgated edition appears in 1574. There are Paris editions from the 1570s, and editions from the Wechel presses from 1599 (it seems that the 1617 reprint was thereafter remaindered in 1629, 1643, and 1646).

153. Maclean 2009: 107–130.

154. Maclean 2009: 173–178.

155. On the necessity of a clear and unambiguous copy, see Plantin 1883–1918: 1.131–132 (Plantin to Pamelius, 19 July 1567).

156. Voet 1969–1972: 2.286–289; Maclean forthcoming a (Alciato); Hotson 2007: 155ff. (Keckermann).

157. Voet 1969–1972: 2.292–293 (Plantin's letter to Jacobus Strada, October 1578).

158. Rantzau may be an exception: see Zeeberg 2004: 50–59.

159. Shevchenko 2007: 194; Vogt 1924; Maclean 2009: 296 (Leicester).

160. See Kapp 1886: 314; Zeeberg 2004: 46 (on the medical professor Heinrich Meibom's complaints concerning his poverty); Widmann 1967–1969: 1551–1552 (Crusius).

161. Imhof 2005 (on Luis Perez's support of Arias Montano). The *Martyrologium Romanum* was published "by order ("iussu") of Pope Gregory XIII"; this formula usually indicates financial support, as in the case of Francisco Suarez's *De legibus* of 1612, published in Coimbra "iussu ac ductu" of the Bishop of Egitania.

162. Zeeberg 2004: 78, 241.

163. An exception are the introductions to the books of Gessner's *Pandectae*, published in 1548. A rare example of dedication to printers is Charles de Sainte Marthe, *La poesie françoise* (Lyon: Le Prince, 1540–1541).

164. Goldast approached Freher and Gruter to supply these for his *Alemannicarum rerum scriptores* of 1606: see above, note 94.

165. van Roomen and Bockstaele 1967: 122–123.

166. The Imprimerie Royale can also be considered an institutional press: see Pallier 2000. In England, Archbishop Laud employed Richard Badger as his house printer: McCulloch 1998. There was also a Typographia regia in Spain.

167. Maclean 2009: 320–321 (on confessional allegiance of publishers). Giovanni Argenterio's decision to spurn offers from "excellent printers in Lyon, Basel and Venice" and be published in Florence was presumably motivated by his desire to please his patrons in the University of Pisa: Sirasi 1990: 177. See

also Erasmus 1906–1947: 1.439 (on elegance of presentation); Gier 2008: 149 (Peter Canisius's choice of Cologne); Evans 1975 (Wechel's authors); Maclean 2009 (Gentili and Antonius).

168. van Roomen and Bockstaele 1967: 126–129 (September 1597). This is presumably also why he had another work printed in part in Louvain by Johannes Masius, and finished off not by his contact Jan I Moretus, but another Antwerp printer, Johannes Keerberghen: ibid., 99–100 (7, 10 January 1593). But he instructed Moretus to see to the distribution of the work.

169. Bowen and Imhof 2008: 60 (Hieronymus Cock); Nuovo 2003: 92–93 (Perna and Ziletti).

170. Paleario 1992: 89–90, 93–94; Maclean forthcoming a.

171. For examples, see Voet 1969–1972: 2.283–295; Zeeberg 2004: 45; Simonin 1992.

172. Plantin 1883–1918: 1.98 (22 June 1567), and ibid., 4.88 (19 May 1574).

173. See Erasmus 1906–1947: 1.439 (on Aldus's elegance of presentation).

174. See Thülemeyer 1688: *passim,* for the importance of the criterion of elegance.

175. Comparative judgements can be found: e.g., Gilly 2001: 15 (Hieronymus Wolf rating Oporinus higher than Gryphius, Stephanus and Aldus). See also Paleario 1992: 89 (Sadoleto's praise of Gryphius in 1536): "noli enim putare non apud Italos omnes tuum esse nomen in magna gratia. Quicquid prodit ex officina tua, id ita demum et rectum et probatum habetur omnibus, si in eo tuum nomen sit praescriptum. Nota est enim probitas, et diligentia tua, nota eruditio." On Wechel's high editorial standards, see Maclean 2009: 182. On Alciato and his choices of publisher, see Maclean forthcoming a.

176. Widmann 1967–1969: 1531–1532; Voet 1969–1972: 2.279; Cardano 2004: 102 (on the *De utilitate ex adversis capienda*); Maclean 2009: 148 (Cardano), 179 (Wechel and Camerarius).

177. The leaders of the various confessions had a very shrewd knowledge of the book market: most secured very rich returns for their printers. Erasmus, a clear best-seller, required only to be paid in house and board. Luther and Theodore de Bèze as reformers did not require any payment as authors: Wittmann 1999: 51–52; but Calvin and Zwingli did: Kapp 1886: 312ff. Steinmann 1967: 48–49 records that Hieronymus Wolf was not paid by Oporinus, but simply enjoyed "the honour of being published." Kirchhoff 1853a: 109 records that a copyist earned more per word than an author: this relationship is analogous to that between the creator of a book illustration and the woodcutter or engraver, who earned more: Kusukawa 1997: 406. On losing a deal through too hard bargaining, see Hieronymus 1995: 101 (Janus Cornarius and Johannes Herwagen in 1553).

178. See above, page 38. Oporinus also made such contracts with his potential authors: see Oporinus and Steinmann 1969: 195–196. Rantzau as a self-financed author had to pay a similar sum to the publisher to have his books printed: Zeeberg 2004: 42–43.

179. Burchill 198: 203. For Cardano's claims about his earnings, see Maclean 2009: 158. Oporinus and Steinmann 1969: 172–173 (letter of 20 April 1563) records that two Oporinus authors were disappointed to be paid not in cash but in copies. See also Oporinus and Steinmann 1969: 195–196 (13 July 1554: contract with Hieronymus Massarius for a medical *Sammelband* including Celsus and Aretaeus).

180. Maclean 2006a: xli; Kirchhoff 1853a: 110–111 (two examples of unsuccessful negotiations); Maclean 2009: 314 (Alberico Gentili); Allen 1916: 14–17 (Erasmus).

181. Kopf: see above Chapter 2, note 107.

182. Imhof 2008: 221f.

183. Voet 1969–1972: 286–289.

184. See above, 264n114.

185. Kapp 1886: 312ff.

186. Maclean forthcoming a.

187. Quoted by Voet 1969–1972: 2.284–285.

188. Gilmont 2003: 47. Epstein 2001: 136 points out that in the case of the series of literary texts entitled "Library of America," their founder planned them to be "irreproachable [. . .] complete, without footnotes or introduction."

189. Grafton 1977: 152ff.

190. E.g., the edition of Juvenal, published by Bade at Lyon in 1498 with commentaries by himself and by Antonio Mancinelli. In the same year, a Venice edition appears with four advanced humanist commentaries (by Mancinelli, Domizio Calderini, Giorgio Valla, and Giorgio Merula).

191. For examples, see Mouren 2010 (Vettori on Cicero); Grafton forthcoming a (Erasmus on More's *Utopia*).

192. See Thülemeyer 1688: 296a–b (27 January 1609, Marquard Freher): "interea commentariolus ille meus [on the Donation of Constantine] (ut spero) distrahi, et secunda editio auctior et completior istis accedere poterit." Another example is found in ibid., 101 (20 June 1603, Helias Putschius), referring to his edition of the *Opera omnia* of Sallust (Leiden: Frans Raphelengius, 1602), and the second edition he envisages as necessary. In fact, another edition appeared at Frankfurt (edited by Janus Gruter, and published by the Palthen presses at the expense of Jonas Rhodius or Rosa in 1607), before the anticipated second edition appeared, edited by Putschius's relation Andreas Schott (Leiden: Frans Raphaelengius, 1613).

193. For an example of a publisher who, to the surprise of the author, wanted to print a second edition even though many copies of the first remained, see Thülemeyer 1688: 468 (Paulus Matthias Wehner, 7 September 1611).

194. Erasmus 1906–1947: 2:351 (no. 472, 29 September 1516): "Ea de te est mortalium opinio ut, si recognitum quodvis operum tuorum a te praedices, etiamsi nihil addideris, prius impressum nihili aestiment; quam iacturam in Copia linguae Latine. in Panegyrico, in Moria, in Enchiridio (nam quingenta redemeram volumina) et in Adagiis, quorum 110 emeram, facere coactus sum."

195. Vespasiano da Bisticci 1997: 421–422. I am grateful to Anthony Grafton for this reference.
196. Rosenberg and Grafton 2010: 27.
197. Oporinus remarked on the success of such publishing strategies: see Steinmann 1967: 45.
198. Bolgar 1958. On one pursuit of "typographica palingenesia" for a modern author, see Maclean 2009: 175 (Freige and Ramus).
199. "qui tum incuria temporum, tum incuria calceographorum penitus obsolescerat, summa fide recognita, pristini integritati restituta in lucem educta est cum indice principalium sententiarum."
200. Naudé 2008: 97 (facsimile 43) separates straight editions from editions with commentaries, or commentaries that have been separately published.
201. On these editions, see Hieronymus 1992: 648–667 (nos. 410, 414, 416).
202. Grafton 1983–1993. The Pontac edition (about which I learned from Anthony Grafton) contains the texts of Prosper Aquitanus and Sophronius Eusebius Hieronymus, all "infinitis locis emendata."
203. Maclean 1992: 37–50.
204. Scapecchi 1990.
205. Maclean 2009: 71–72. Repeated editions could be motivated by theological considerations as well as commerce: see Visser 2011: 51.
206. Jan I Moretus protested to the Book Commission in Frankfurt in 1598 about the translation of Baronio's *Annals* by some of his Cologne colleagues and rivals: Imhof 2008: 345–355.
207. On the Plantin polyglot and the input of Benito Arias Montano, see Tejero and Marcos 2008: 242–249; on the Articella, see Arrizabalaga 1998.
208. Trithemius 1494; Fichard and Rutilus 1539; Champier 1506.
209. Allen 1916: 25–26; Coppens forthcoming; for another early example, see Maclean in Cardano 2004: 13–16. I am grateful to Anthony Grafton for pointing out the existence of the Campano *Opera* to me. It is preceded by a life, as are many subsequent examples of the genre. The publisher Joannes Amerbach was the motive force behind the publication in 1505 of Augustine's *Opera Omnia*, after having undertaken some market research though the Kobergers: see von Hase 1885:XVII, and Visser 2011: 14-20.
210. Adam's volume cover in turn philosophers and humanists (1615), non-German theologians (1618), German theologians, jurists and physicians (1620, three separate volumes). All were published by the Frankfurt bookseller and publisher Johannes Rosa. See also Siraisi 2007; Coppens forthcoming on the tradition of autobiobibliography, which begins in the fifteenth century with Giovanni Vincenzo Biffi of Milan.
211. A particularly interesting case is that afforded by Cicero and the competition to bring out his works in the 1530s, with editions by Manutius (1533), the Giunti (1534–1537), Herwagen (1534), Robert Estienne (1539), and Rihel (1540), on which see Gessner 1966 [1545 and 1555] : 495–497 and Mouren 2010.
212. Naudé 2008: 165 (facsimile 76): "tel negligera les oeuvres et opuscules de quelque auteur, pendant qu'elles sont éparses et séparées, qui brûle par

après du désir de les avoir quand elles sont recueillies et ramassées en un volume."

213. Lowry 1979: 31

214. Aldus, in Perotti 1513: 1123–1124. Epitomes and anthologies were not scorned in all disciplines. It had been recognized from the time of Isidore of Seville in the early middle ages that some authors were too copious to read, and that as a result, epitomes and anthologies were justified. For a bibliography of this very popular genre, see Lane 2003; see also Visser 2011: 65–82.

215. See Hotson 2007: 63.

216. The compendium is a genre inherited from the Middle Ages: see Grafton forthcoming a.

217. Gessner 1577: 139v (to Melchior Guilandinus, no year date given), quoted by Reeds 1991: 261; Kapp 1886: 314 (quoting a letter from Gessner to Heinrich Bullinger of 1558).

218. Braida 2009; Grafton forthcoming a.

219. See van der Haeghen 1886.

220. Giunti 1604.

221. Naudé 2008: 90ff. (facsimile39ff.).

222. Oxford Dictionary of National Biography, s.v. Fludd (Maclean)

223. Widmann 1967–1969: 1543. The Prolegomena to Homeric Studies had been delivered in Tübingen by Crusius in November 1581, and the Commentary itself on 15 July 1594. The edition is dedicated by Gotthard Vögelin to Johann Georg I, Elector of Saxony, who had acquired the MS from Crusius's Nachlass, the author having died in 1607.

224. See Dyroff 1963.

4. Labor, Impensa, Emolumentum

1. See Steinmann 1967: 132–151 for Oporinus's various engagements with these risks. There are many cases of commercial dealings between learned publishers of all religious persuasions (e.g., Plantin and the Wechel house: Kapp 1886: 471–472), and strife between publishers of the same persuasion: see Banderier 2000. So the interference at this level of confessional issues should not be exaggerated.

2. Pettas 1980 claims that the Giunti were poor, but it is very difficult to match this claim with their survival as a diversified international firm holding very large stocks of books: Nuovo and Sandal 1998: 49ff. A piece of evidence a negativo is provided by the supplication to Venice for a privilege by Vincent Vaugris (later known as Vincenzo Valgrisi) dated 13 October 1554, in which he specifies that he only engages in publication ('ho gran numero di figliuoli, e grande familia in casa, la quale co'l mezzo di questa mia industria (che altra mercatantia non faccio) sostento, pago le mie angarie, et passo la vita mia sotto ombra di questo Serenissimo Dominio': Archivio di Stato di Venezia, Senato Terra, Suppliche, filza n. 19 (1554). I am

grateful to Angela Nuovo for having supplied me with this reference. Even newcomers to publishing traded in other commodities: for other publishers, see Starp 1958: 46, on Schönwetter, who was certainly not rich, but had a reputation of being so: Goldast 1600–1613: 28v: (to Marquard Freher, about his collection of Frankish documents): "typographus, opinor, facilis est, qui sumptus suppedidat"; Grotefend 1881: 22 (on Egenolff); Voet 1969–1972: 2.245 (on Plantin); Pallmann 1881 (on Feyerabend); Lowry 1979: 9 (Aldus Manutius compared to spice merchants); Dietz 1970: 3.36 (Nicolas Bassée); Maclean 2009: 419f (Cramoisy); Matthäus 2009 (Johann Wechel). There are cases of authors marrying into publishers' families: e.g., Johann Heinrich Alsted (the son-in-law of Christophorus Corvinus of Herborn). Andreas Aurifaber married a daughter of Hans Lufft of Wittenberg: see Seebass 1985: 133. On Adam Lonitzer and Christoph Egenolff, see Pinon 2008: 444–445. For an account of the close family ties between publishers in Paris and Lyon, see Morisse 2000: 72. German printers had a reputation for being undercapitalised and in too much of a hurry: see the warning in Thülemeyer 1688: 32–34 (the open letter by Jacques-August de Thou): "ne typographi nimis festinent, aut sumptibus parcant, ut saepe fit in Germania."

3. These phrases are drawn from HHStA: 2.34, ff. 245, 252; 56.3, f. 25: (Jean Aubry, Zacharias Palthen) "acerrimo labore maximoque sumptu"; "necnon magno sumptu" "sinistribus machinationibus"; "vitiosa imitatione vel aliis sinistribus artibus."

4. See Maclean 2009: 227–250 (on the estates of Filippo Tinghi, the Giunti family, and Symphorien Beraud of Lyon); Goldast 1600–1613: 28v.

5. Dietz 1970: 3.33, 37

6. Fraeb 1931: 18–19; Könnecke 1894: 156.

7. As in the case of Lorenzo Torrentino and the Medici of Florence: Nuovo and Sandal 1998: 46.

8. Arbour 1992: 137–156; it appears that the provisions in much of Europe concerning bankruptcy resemble Chapter 11 of U.S. bankruptcy code, which offers the debtor a number of mechanisms to restructure his business.

9. Voet 1969–1972: 391, 451, 459, 525; see also Steinmann 1967: 54 (Oporinus in 1566). Debts as well as assets were inherited with the estate. It is not clear what percentage of a press run was thought to represent a successful sale: in the English case of Brooke's *A discoverie of errors* printed in 1594, a remainder of 40 percent of the original press run of 500 over twenty-eight years was seen as a failure: Augustine Vincent, *A discoverie of errors in the first edition of the Catalogue of Nobilitie published by Raphe Brooke* (London: William Jaggard, 1622), sig. ¶6v. I suspect that on the continent such a percentage, admittedly over a shorter time scale, would represent success, given the size of stocks and the use of unsold copies as a form of currency.

10. Starp 1958: 56 records that in 1627, Schönwetter had to confirm that he had not used the same stock for surety in other cases ("welcher sonst niemandt verpfendet oder verfegt ist in keiner Weise"). Ciotti acted as guaran-

tor of a Giunti debt: see Camerini 1963: 213. See also Clair 1976: 161 (the Plantin house's use of punches as surety in 1588); Steinmann 1969: 134 (Oporinus's use of a precious vase as surety); Dietz 1970: 3.35 (Eusebius Episcopius and Hans Brambach's use of their Frankfurt warehouse as surety for Nicolas Bassée, who stood guarantor for them in the sum of 2,250 fl. owing to a Frankfurt Jewish moneylender called Isaak zur goldenen Stelze). See also Maclean 2009: 237–242, showing the overvaluation of stock used as surety. Some of these cases reveal the internationalisation of finance brought about by attendance at fairs.

11. Voet 1969–1972: 1.166–167, 2.425, records that Plantin left 47,830 florins in money (included in this figure are chattels and houses), and estate worth 175,775 florins in the form of books.

12. Dietz 1970: 30–31.

13. Platter 1964: 111ff. Yet in the same city and within a decade or so of Platter's experience, Oporinus was unable to raise money from his fellow citizens to in order to secure an edition of Girolamo Zanchi for his presses: Steinmann 1969: 179–180 (10 June 1563).

14. Könnecke 1894: 142 (Tossanus in Heidelberg, who was eventually paid by being given the bookshop in Frankfurt); Voet 1969–1972: 2.457–458, quoting a letter of 22 December 1572 from Plantin to Çayas: "car l''imprimerie est ung vray abisme ou goufre auquel par ung labeur assidu et une constance ferme et asseurée il convent perpétuellement entendre luy jecter en la gueule et fournir tout ce qu'il est necessaire ou autrement il devore et engloustit son maistre et tous ceux qui s'en meslent avec luy."

15. Oporinus and Plantin printed works on their own initiative, for authors, for ecclesiastical and secular authorities, for other printers, and also employed other printers to produce works for him: Steinmann 1967: 58–59; Voet 1969–1972: 1.68–75.

16. Koppitz 2008: 292 (38, 38–40): applications to the Imperial Chancery for privileges dated 14 April 1597 and 11 April 1608.

17. Brauer 1974: 34–35.

18. Feyerabend began his career as a wood engraver: Schröder 1904: 6. Berner was a typefounder. The grocer Alexandre de Villeneuve became a publisher through the payment of an inheritance in books: Maclean 2009: 242. It seems likely that Dirk Martens had his dedicatory letters written for him: Adam and Vanautgaerden 2009:105ff.

19. Plantin 1883–1918: 8–9.54–55: (4 October 1586, no. 1149): "besogner aux despens des libraires de Paris, de Lyon, de Cologne et d'Italie qui font ainsi leur profict de mes labeurs d'imprimerie et de mon nom." He complained in 1586 that he once was able to print big books at his own expense, but now will not even undertake little ones without an assured sale of at least a hundred copies: Zeeberg 2004: 43. The only other enterprise on the scale of Plantin was the Kobergers at the beginning of the century, with 24 presses and 100 journeymen: see Niedermeyer 1967.

20. Steinmann 1967: 58–59.

21. Matthäus 2009.

22. Dietz 1970: 17, 37 records the tax paid by the Feyerabend and Wechel houses, but it is not clear that this is a very reliable indication of wealth as a publisher: Meyn 1980: 90 points out that many merchants paid a high sum to avoid declaring the extent of their wealth. Filippo de Vivo has informed me that Roberto Meietti is one of the lowest-assessed publishers in Venice, but on the evidence of his international trade, he does not seem to justify this position.

23. Erasmus, *Ratio seu Methodus compendio perveniendi ad veram theologiam* (Louvain: Dirk Martens, November 1518) (dedicatory letter of Martens to Erasmus): "tot typographos alit Basilea, prorsus infrequens frigidaque Academia, si ad Lovaniensem conferatur."

24. On Bourges, see Jenny 2007. Millanges was given money to set up a press in Bordeaux for the same reason: Nelles forthcoming b.

25. But see Ercole Sassonia, *Luis venereae tractatus,* Padua "apud Laurentium Pasquatum, typographum almae Universitatis Iuristarum," 1597. Through the good offices of Angela Nuovo, I have learned from Marco Allegari that the title seems to have been self-attributed by Pasquato.

26. Juan Luis Vives to Juan de Vergara (1527), quoted by Gilly 1985: 135.

27. Gier 2008.

28. Moxon's *Mechanick exercises* of 1683, and the seventh volume of the *Recueil de planches* of the French *Encyclopédie* of 1769 are two comprehensive and much-used sources for information about the printing shop in the hand-press era. See also McKenzie 2002 and Gilmont 1980 on these issues.

29. de Roover 1956: 242: "in printing, there were probably no economies of large-scale production in the sixteenth century." Martin 1982b: 379 records that 46 percent of Parisian printers (35 out of 76) in 1644 were operating with two presses.

30. Rietbergen 1983 records a figure of five sheets a day by the Vatican Presses; Melchior Goldast's correspondent Schobinger reports that his printer managed four sheets a day (Thülemeyer 1688: 113); see also Pettegree 2002. Pallmann's claim (1881: 17) that one press could produce 10,000 sheets in six months must refer to the press runs, not the composition of pages.

31. See Gilmont 1980; printing regulations were produced in Lyon in 1539, Paris in 1539 and 1571, Geneva in 1560, Frankfurt in 1573, Leipzig in 1594. Individual houses such as the Plantin presses and the Wechel presses also produced them: see Voet 1969–1972: 2.309–310 and Könnecke 1894: 30–33.

32. André Wechel does not seem to have played any part in the relevant guild and confrérie while in Paris between 1558 and 1572, whereas his contemporary Thomas Brumen was active in the parish, in the local watch, and in the confrérie: Guilleminot-Chrétien 2008.

33. In Venice, the guilds were organised by locality: Lowry 1979: 8. In Basel, by hierarchy (the Safranzunft being less senior than the Zunft zum Schlüssel): Koelner 1935.

34. Von der Linde 1882: 32 (printing regulations of 1591).
35. See Maclean 2009: 273–274; Pettas 1997: 177–178.
36. See the helpful account in Nuovo 2003: 120–123.
37. Voet 1969–1972: 2.appendices; Wackernagel 1881.
38. Voet 1969–1972: 2.459.
39. Maclean 2009: 227–250; Pettas 1997: 186–187 (Jacqueline Giunti's attempts in 1580 to recover small sums from over two hundred debtors).
40. Pallmann 1881: 77–79 offers an example of this.
41. See above, page 183: also Gilmont 1995: 276.
42. Wackernagel 1881.
43. Voet 1969–1972.
44. Ibid.: 2.44.
45. The relevant account is illustrated in Voet 1969–1972: between 8–9 (plate 3).
46. The Vatican even charged its own presses rent on the room occupied by correctors: Rietbergen 1983: 99.
47. See Elder 1937; de Roover 1956; and Voet 1969–1972: 2.382–384, 440–442. See also Kapp 1886: 307ff. on variable discounts. In the case of commissioned books, printers were sometimes paid in free copies, and then made to share in the commercial risk: Voet 1969–1972: 2.286; Zeeberg 2004: 44.
48. Maclean 2009: 242–243.
49. They also acted as agents for bookbinders: Nelles forthcoming b (Millanges); Pallmann 1881 (Feyerabend). Claude de Marne attended Leipzig fair and acted as postman (Thülemeyer 1688: 101 [20 July 1603, Helias Putschius]). See Pinelli and Dupuy 2001: *passim;* Perini 2002: 301 (Perna); Maclean 2009: 170 (Wechel); and Kapp 1886: 468 (Konrad König of Jena) for other examples of publishers being employed as postal agents. Ciotti transported plant bulbs (Nuovo 2003: 93f.), and Carolus Clusius asked publishers to do the same for him: Hunger 1927–1943: 2.75. See also Schröder 1904: 4–5 (on printers combining the tasks of bookbinding and brewing); Banderier 2000: 574, 594 (Simon Goulart as purveyor of current news). On diversification, see Nuovo 2004: 159 (on the Giolito presses): "their production of books could not have existed without continuous and well-defined financing from other sources which is poorly documented." Angela Nuovo kindly sent to me an image of the contract drawn up in 1539 between the Giovanni Giolito and Vincenzo Portonari of Lyon (now preserved in the Archivio di Stato, Alessandria) which covers not just books but "other trading" (possibly cloths such as canvas).
50. von Hase 1885: 336–340 reports that Luther thought that no more than a 5 percent profit margin was justifiable, but the fact that book traders were given a 20 percent discount against the retail price indicates that his figure was unrealistic.
51. Maclean 2009: 141: "egregios procrastinatores." But for their part, publishers also had to put up with procrastination on the part of authors. Freher, for example, took six years to produce the copy of his Frankish documents for the Wechel presses: see above, 261n90.

52. Schröder 1904: 14.
53. Maclean 2009: 229; Pettas 1997: 181ff. There were also cases of the imitation of a more prestigious printer's mark as a strategy to secure better sales: see Baudrier and Baudrier 1964–1965: 6.438, quoting the case of Filippo Tinghi and the Giunti, and the comment by the King's Attorney General Barnabé Brisson: "les marques des imprimeurs sont de grande importance pour le bruit et cours des livres, parce que la réputation d'un bon imprimeur se recongnoist par la marque." See also Nuovo 2003: 182ff.; Lepri forthcoming: 3–4 on Ciotti's use of the marks of Johann Wechel and Francesco de' Franceschi.
54. Paschen 1995: 43–60.
55. Gilmont 1995: 275
56. Guilleminot-Chrétien 2007, 2009.
57. Nuovo and Sandal 1998: 44; Baudrier and Baudrier 1964–1965: 2.213–217; Maclean 2009: 146–147. Associations could publish in their name, or in the individual names of its members, giving rise to multiple imprints of the same edition with no more than a standard press run. This has not always been taken into account, with the result that the number of editions of a given text have been overestimated by assuming that all variant imprints represent separate press runs.
58. Erasmus 1906–1947: 5.542 (no. 1494, to Polydore Virgil, c. 6 September 1524): "est triplex excudendi ratio. Nonnunquam totum negocium Frobenius sisucipit suo periculo: hoc aliquoties facit in minoribus voluminibus, in quibus minus periculosa est alea. Nonnunquam tota res agitur periclo alieno, ipse tantum pro opera sua paciscitur mercedem. Nonnunquam res fit communi periculo sociorum." See also Erasmus CWE : 10.374–375.
59. Pallmann 1881; Starp 1958: 39–40, 49, 52 (Schönwetter's associations with Spiess, Tambach, Richter, Meul, Kopf, and Rhodius). Michael Forster tried to circumvent the problems of paper costs and delivery by setting up a paper mill of his own in Amberg: Paschen 1995: 43, 52.
60. See Pettas 1997 for the Lyon and Italian associations; on the earlier association between Arrivabene, de Tortis, the Giunti, and Scoto, see Lowry 1979: 16–17; for Paris associations, see Parent-Charon 1996.
61. Lowry 1979: 16–17 (Venice, 1507).
62. Kapp 1886: 292ff. (Augsburg); Parent-Charon 1996 (Paris); Wackernagel 1881 (Basel); Nuovo and Sandal 1998: 44 (Rome).
63. Baudrier and Baudrier 1964–1965: 7.27.
64. Financial problems could arise from the wayward behaviour of one partner. Gaspar Trechsel's association with a group of Salamanca booksellers in the 1530s led to his being accused of speculating on exchange rates with the association's money, making unauthorised use of letters of credit and notes of debt, and withholding profits from his partners: see Morisse 2000: 80. Pallmann 1881: 21ff. has charted the problematic relationship between the Feyerabend house and Simon Hüter.

65. Camerini 1963: 213. The agreement also specifies staggered payments for the debt owed by Mariolesco to the Giunti.
66. Pettegree 2010: 73 quotes the case involving Rusch and Amerbach. Lehne 1939: 369 quotes the case a pact between author and publisher Christoph Egenolff over the unauthorised publication of a student copy of Lagus's *Methodus iuris publici* of 1539. For the case of Roville and Plantin, see Plantin 1883–1918: 1.47–48 (26 December 1565, no. 19).
67. Maclean 2009: 282–284 (Gryphius and the Grande Compagnie). Gryphius was financially dependent on Hugues de la Porte, a member of the Compagnie des Libraires: see Davis 1982: 262. On Wechel, Bishop, Antonius, and Palthen, see Maclean 2009: 320–322.
68. Imhof 2008: 348f.; Rietbergen 1983; Wygant 2002: 76. The Cologne edition was in smaller format and character. Moretus protested first to Hansenius, then, in 1600, to the Imperial Commissioner Valentin Leucht and finally to the Frankfurt City Council. He printed the Plantin 1565 general Imperial licence in the following volumes of Baronio, and set about protecting his right to publish an epitome. On his knowledge of Hierat's plans, see Imhof 2008: 356. Moretus also had conflicts with his brother-in-law Adrian Périer in Paris over the sale of Lipsius in Frankfurt: ibid., 407.
69. The collaboration between Moretus and Raphelengius was made along confessional lines: Raphelengius undertook humanist publications, and Moretus liturgy. Imhof 2008: 91,378. Morisse 2000 gives an account of the complex relations linking publishers in Lyon, Paris, and Geneva. See also Maclean 2009: 233. Dietz 1970: 3.38 records the collaboration between Wechel and Gymnich in a case against the heirs of Sigmund Feyerabend in 1594.
70. The privilege is recorded on the title page as lasting six years, but the extract on the verso of the title page records it as lasting ten years. For the eager anticipation of the edition, see Thülemeyer 1688: 303–304 (Georg Michel Lingelsheim, 2 March 1609); ibid., 311 (Caspar Waser, 18 March 1610, on Henri IV's gift of 1000 crowns to Casaubon); ibid., 388 (Franciscus Guillimannus, early 1610); ibid., 456 (Lingelsheim, 15 March 1611). Drouart did, however, sell books directly at the fair.
71. Lowry 1979:13.
72. Baudrier and Baudrier 1964–1965: 7.373–374 records the interesting case of the Lyon merchant publishers Jean and Claude Senneton paying for the loan of the Law Faculty of Avignon's copy of the Pandects with the Accursian gloss, in return for a caution of 500 écus and the promise of twenty-one free copies of the printed version (in six folio volumes!) to go to the members of the faculty; ibid., records a similar contract with the Couvent des Jacobins of Avignon for two patristic manuscripts (of works by Augustine and Ambrose). The contracts date from the 1540s; the books to which they relate were published in 1550, 1555, and 1556, respectively. Also Voet 1969–1972: 2.292–293 (Plantin's letter to Jacobus Strada, October 1578).
73. Voet 1969–1972: 1.213–215.

74. Dyroff 1963: 1324–1325.
75. See Gilly 1979: 64; and Gilly 2002 (the printing of anti-Aristotelian works by Doni and Patrizzi in Basel under the influence of Theodor Zwinger); Maclean 2009: 51 (the case of the Wechel presses); Kemp 2008: 156–159 (Sebastian Gryphius publishing both Erasmus and anti-Erasmian works).
76. Dubois 2007: 82; Dubois 2008; for other cases of publishing policy, see Voet 1969–1972 (Plantin and his successors); Rudolphi 1963 (Froschauer); Mouren 2008 (Gryphius); Rhodes forthcoming (Ciotti); Maclean 2009: 33–34 (Gilles Beys). On the practice of issuing new editions to stimulate sales, see above, pages 84–91.
77. Kingdon 1957.
78. See Dyroff 1963 (on Vögelin); Maclean 2009: 182; Gehl online.
79. Above, 258n76 and page 176 (on "libri minus vendibiles" and "vendibiliores"); Goldast 1600–1613: 31r (July 1606?), on making the medieval historical document of Petrus de Andlo a more saleable edition by adding other documents to it.
80. Maclean 2009: 181–182; I have already pointed out that even presses specializing in Greek, such as the Wechels, were reluctant to take risks in that area.
81. Maclean 2009: 197, 279. Theodore de Banos's decision to finance the publication of Ramus's *Commentarii de religione Christiana* in 1576 was probably motivated by a desire to commemorate his dead friend: it turned out to be a commercial success, leading to republication within the year, in spite of an initial press run of 2,000: see Guilleminot-Chrétien 2009: 70.
82. Petri refused to print Cardano's revised versions of his works, although they were submitted to him: see Baldi and Canziani 2004. Grendler 1977: 29 surmises that the press runs of first editions were small and reprints larger; but I believe that the organization of workshops has more to do with maximising the efficiency with which press runs were produced.
83. See the case of Basilius Johannes Heroldus's *Originum ac germanicarum antiquitatum libri[. . .]* printed by Heinrich Petri in 1557 and sought by Freher from his successor, above Chapter 2, note 17. It may also be the case that holding stock rather than disposing of multiple copies at the end of the fair was a commercial strategy designed to depress the expectations that bargains were to be had at such times.
84. Even prestigious houses did this, as in the case of the Wechel presses' reissue of Casaubon's Polybius in 1619.
85. Maclean 2009: 288, 326.
86. There is another practice which may involve a reprinted first gathering. It appears that compositors sometimes recovered rejected sheets and assembled them into books, which they then sold cheaply on their own behalf: see Grafton forthcoming a; Ross 2009: 186–187 (a passage from a letter addressed to Christian Daum of Zwickau by Johannes Sextus, referring to the Entner house in Nuremberg in the seventeenth century). This practice, which is fully attested in this passage, may explain in part the many states in which books from this period are found.

87. Maclean 2009: 114–121.
88. Kapp 1886: 513 also refers to a case involving Thurneysser and Gymnich, and to the Elzevier's similar practice of adding one or two pages to an existing edition and then claiming it to be new.
89. An early protest against the practice was made by Aldus Manutius in his Admonition of 1503: see Lowry 1979: 155–156. Luther also protested about it: Wittmann 1999: 52.
90. Goldfriedrich 1908: 176–177 (a ruling of 1606). For an example of such reprinting with a local privilege, see Peter Fischer's editions of Jean Bodin's *De republica* of 1591 and of Pierre Grégoire's *Syntagma iuris universi* of 1597.
91. Maclean 2009: 307 (Joseph Barnes, who was forced by "Nachdruck" to petition the University of Oxford in 1590 to require every bachelor of arts supplicating for his degree to buy a copy of his printing of John Case's *Sphaera civitatis;* see also the legal struggles between Oporinus and Egenolff over the printing of Melanchthon's Latin grammar: Oporinus and Steinmann 1969: 160–161 (letter to Joachim Camerarius, 29 May 1560).
92. Feyerabend suggested that the practice of "Nachdruck" had become so common that it should be disregarded: Maclean 2009: 116. For the Frankfurt Council's *Ordnung gegen den Nachdruck,* see Pallmann 1881: Beilage XIX. Among its prescriptions was the requirement to declare prospectively publications due to appear in the next six months. For examples of Feyerabend's many brushes with litigation, see Pallmann 1881: 56 (involving Bassée) and 67ff. (Aubry). Both cases had compromise outcomes, probably because Feyerabend was a local patrician, and at least one of his litigants (Aubry) a member of the Reformed community. For a case involving Bassée and the Wechel presses together, see their reprinting of the 1583 edition of Scaliger's *Opus novum de emendatione temporum* by Sébastien Nivelle in Paris. See also Dietz 1970 3:35 on Harsy's complaint; Crousaz 2005: 110–112 (Amerbach versus Holzhorn of Cologne); Maclean 2009: 308 (Barnes and Wechel); Steinmann 1967: 58 (the reprinting in Lyon and Paris of Froben's edition of Wolfgang Musculus).
93. Johann Wechel's Lipsius publications in 1590 are the following: *Epistolarum centuria prima; De Constantia; Politica.* The latter two were reprinted in 1591, together with *Epistolarum centuriae duae; Mellificium duplex ex media philosophia petitum; Adversus dialogistam liber de una religione; Epistolica institutio.* In 1592 the *Epistolarum centuria secunda* appeared from his presses, claiming to be a first edition.
94. Bowen and Imhof 2008.
95. Baudrier and Baudrier 1964–1965: 4.40–76; Maclean 2009: 229–230.
96. Another case in the Catholic sphere was the reprinting of the Moretus edition of Stapleton's *Promptuarium morale* in Cologne and Lyon: Imhof 2008: 439f.
97. Maclean 2009: 176–178, on Perna's attempt to challenge Wechel's monopoly of Ramus editions. Wechel reacted by aggressive reprinting of his own

editions in this case, and in the cases of Jean Fernel and Nicolas Clénard. On switching format, see Maclean 2009: 53 (Piccolomini). On the excuses offered for "Nachdruck," see Gilmont 2006 a: 19–39.

98. Goldfriedrich 1908: 171; Lehne 1939: 365 (referring to Sigmund Feyerabend on 15 November 1588).

99. Lehne 1939: 390, 405: "Nachdruck" is described as a "falsum," "actio iniuriarum," and those engaging in it as "stelliones" (see D 47.200). Lehne 1939: 359 (giving the text of Episcopius's application for a privilege 6 June 1553): "alii ex alterius commodo suum parare commodum student." The Frenchman Denis Godefroy, professor in Heidelberg, applied unsuccessfully for an Imperial privilege for his editions of the Corpus Juris Civilis and Cicero which appeared in Lyon in 1588–1589: ibid.: 364.

100. Pinelli and Dupuy 1991: 162 (4 September 675): "Vechel n'eust voulu imprimer les livres du Sr Sigonio de antiquo iure populi Romani nisi cum bona ipsius gratia." See also Voet 1969–1972: 2.290–291 (Plantin's assurance that he republishes only with the permission of the author and first printer). Plantin 1883–1918: 1.47–48 (no. 19, to Guillaume Roville, 26 December 1565); Voet 1969–1972: 2.291.

101. A similar justification was offered by André Wechel in the preface to his reprinting of Paulus Manutius's edition of Cicero; he claimed that he was motivated to do so by his desire to serve the republic of letters by making available good editions. Another case of such justification is found in Roberto Meietti's preface to a work of the Spanish physician Luis de Lemos: Maclean 2009: 70.

102. Steinmann 1967: 48.

103. Plantin 1883–1918: 8–9.422 (no. 1394, to Petrus Pantinus, 6–22 August 1588); the presses benefiting from the concessions were the Wechel house and Paolo Meietti. On Utopia, see Cave 2008: 16–19. See also Maclean 2009: 52–53 (on scholarly works and schoolbooks produced cheaply for local consumption in Marburg).

104. Gilmont 2005 b: 68, 112–113; Maclean 2009: 272–273. Rhodes 2005 records Francesco de' Franceschi using printers in Bergamo, Pavia, Ferrara, and Bologna. Other printers who use a variety of printing houses include Ciotti (see Rhodes 1987), Lazarus Zetzner (see Maclean 2009: 45) and Gotthard Vögelin (see Dyroff 1963: 1263). The contracts with printers were often very detailed: see, for example, Baudrier and Baudrier 1964–1965: 7.218, 221 (the de Gabiano-Michel contract). The practice of using printers living outside the kingdom of France was specifically prohibited in royal legislation on 10 September 1572; it is striking that it was both frequently reiterated in lettres patentes and edicts after this date, but was never able to be enforced: see Dupont 1854: 2.522f. On methods of charging for printing in the Plantin presses, see Bowen and Imhof 2008: 449.

105. Sturlese 1991; Maclean 2009: 49.

106. It has been claimed that Italian books were more expensive to produce than German books (Kapp 1886: 312), which may account for the use made of Cologne and Frankfurt printers by Giovanni Battista Ciotti.

107. Dietz 1970: 3.71; Maclean 2009: 272–273.
108. Voet 1969–1972: 2.162–163; Maclean 2009: 170 (on specimen pages); Hotman in Oporinus and Steinmann 1969: 159.
109. Kirchhoff 1853 a: 110. Paschen 1995: 153–154 records that the inventory of Michael Forster's printing shop in 1622 divided works according to the quality of paper on which they were printed. On the costs of different grades of paper, Starp 1958: 48.
110. Geneva was known to have poor quality of paper in comparison to Lyon and Paris: Chaix 1978: 47. Dubois 2007 (chapter 5) refers to legislation under which Jacob Stoer in Geneva was made inspector of the quality of paper in 1595. Angela Nuovo has been unable to find records of paper dealing in Italy, and has surmised that at least some of the publishers and printers owned shares in paper mills. Rietbergen 1983: 98 records the different qualities of paper used in the printing of Baronio's *Annals*. This was the case in Amberg, where Forster had to sell his paper mill at a moment of financial difficulty: Paschen 1995: 52. On qualities of paper, see Starp 1958: 48.; Kirchhoff 1853 a: 97, and Kapp 1886: 309.
111. Voet 1969–1972 2.19ff., gives the figure as 60–65 percent; Hirsch 1967: 38–40 as 33 percent.
112. Steinmann 1967: 46 (Oporinus).
113. Bowen and Imhof 2008: 180 (quoting Plantin writing in 1580 about clients "qui raris cupiunt ornare suas bibliothecas").
114. On the rather special case of the Bible, see Engammare 1994.
115. Eisenstein 1979: 56; Wilson 1976; Reske 2000.
116. Alciato 1953: 151 (letter 89, 12 May 1534); van Roomen and Bockstaele 1967: 127.
117. Kunze 1993: 224–244; Nissen 1951: 1.42, 49; Reeds 1991: 127–129.
118. Kusukawa 2000: 108; see also Johann Huttich to Willibald Pirckheimer in 1524 (about a planned edition of Ptolemy's *Geography*), quoted by Grafton forthcoming a: "magis oblectari librariam ineptis picturis quam diligenti cura." See also MPM 12, 3 (Jan I Moretus to Justus Lipsius, 5 January 1595), quoted by Grafton forthcoming a.
119. Frangenberg 1994; Kusukawa 2000; Kusukawa and Maclean 2006; Woodward 2007; Bowen and Imhof 2008; Kusukawa forthcoming.
120. Wittmann 1999: 49–50 attributes the move to octavo to the "Luther effect"; Maclean 2009: 179 (Wechel).
121. Plantin 1883–1918: 8–9.36–37 (no. 1137, to Charles de Tisnac, 13 September 1586); ibid., 8–9.346–347 (no. 1359, to Cornelius Prunius, 1587).
122. Dubois 2008: 8: "il a tout misé sur une politique de petits formats."
123. Maclean 2009: 63ff.
124. Gessner 1577: 139v (Froschauer); Maclean 2009: 47 (Mareschal); ibid., 73f (medical works).
125. Imhof 2008: 120–126; it should be noted, however, that octavo, with 33 percent of all titles, remained the dominant format. See also Voet 1969–1972: 164ff.
126. Pottinger, quoted by Voet 1969–1972: 167.

127. Zeeberg 2004: 15n records that Rantzau had recourse to short press runs to avoid the toil of making many copies by hand; this is also the case with Jacques-Auguste de Thou (Pinelli and Dupuy 2001: 1.363). See also Sabbatino 1986: 84 (Scipione Ammirato) and Simonin 2004: 727–747 (on "éditions à l"essai").

128. There are many examples of scribal publication in the period: see Zanier 1991 (Pomponazzi); Maclean2006a: lvii (pamphlets on the materiality of the soul circulating in Paris around 1630); Maclean 2004: 414n (scribal publication of Cardano's *Metoposcopia* and other texts); Popkin 1990: 5–6 (on the circulation of Bodin's *Heptoplomeres*); Serjeantson and Woolford 2009: 148–149 (on Francis Bacon and semi-scribal publication). Simon Forman owned a manuscript copy of Agrippa's *De occulta philosophia* at the end of the sixteenth century: Feingold 2005: 545. On multiple manuscript editions in the scribal age, see Kirchhoff 1853b.

129. For examples of smaller figures (on commission), see Plantin 1883–1918: 8–9.68–69 (no. 1158, to Heinrich Rantzov, 22 October 1586). The greatest claim for numbers of copies printed of a single work that I have encountered is 32,000, made by Pietro Matthioli in respect of ten editions of his commentary on *Dioscorides*, which equates to an average press run for each edition of 3,200. Press run estimates are found in Voet 1969–1972: 2.20, 169–171; Nuovo and Sandal 1998: 49; Febvre and Martin 1958: 308ff; Kapp 1886: 323ff.

130. E.g., Wechel in Alciato 1536: A1r: "Quod cum ego in animo cogitationeque versarem, circumspicere coepi, si quam mihi viam ipse communire possem, qua et vitam honeste tuerer, et mei usum aliquem Reipublicae adferrem. Delegi itaque ex tanta exercitationum universitate artem excudendorum librorum, quam passim incultam et pene abiectam iacere videbam. Vanus sim, nisi id quam plurima Autorum monumenta, Typographorum incuria misere contaminata palam testentur." For a more amusing and world-weary formulation, see Du Fresne in Leonardi da Vinci 1651: R3r: "L'opera essendo italiana, si perdoneranno gli errori a gli stampatori Francesi, e poi sono stampatori." A typical example of a title is afforded by Pietro d'Ancharano, *Super Clementinis facundissima commentaria. A quamplurimis erroribus, quibus antiquorum impressorum incuria erant obruta, nunc expurgata, et qua maiori fieri potuit diligentia ad veram, germanamque lectionem restituta* (Bologna: Societas typographia, 1580).

131. Kumaniecki, Mynors, Robinson, and Waszink 1969: 1.1, vi–x.

132. I am much indebted in all this section to Anthony Grafton for allowing me to see the manuscript of his forthcoming *The Culture of Correction*, from which this reference is taken.

133. "si non ab omnibus, certe ab innumeris mendis repurgatae." Grafton forthcoming a; Maclean forthcoming.

134. Davies 1995: 22, 25; Grafton forthcoming a.

135. Thülemeyer 1688: 27 (Johannes Guilielmus Stuckius, 27 March 1600): "Me inscio prelo subjecta et excusa est D. Frisii et Eglini opera Iusti Lipsii

Oratio de duplici concordia cum insigni et turpi mendo, quod extat in ipsius limine. Nam pro illis verbis, quae meo judicio poni debuerunt mihi causa fuit de re gravissima dicendi, ipsi posuerunt mihi causa suit de re pravissima dicendi"; ibid., 373 (15 December 1609) and 366 (15 November 1609).

136. Cardano found himself in trouble with the Dominican order because of marginalia added to one of his texts: see Maclean 2009: 145. Plantin filed author's copy as a safeguard against accusations of carelessness: Plantin 1883–1918: 1.16, 2.242, 264–268, 7.201.

137. See Thülemeyer 1688: 32 (Jacques-Auguste de Thou, undated, on the importance of accurate correctors). On Rome and the requirement of accuracy, see Rietbergen 1983: 83; on Heidelberg, see Junius's preface to the *Index expurgatorius* of 1586.

138. Grafton forthcoming a on the correctors' chapel in Plantin presses (a threnody about declining wages). On Plantin's corrector Cornelius Kiliaan, see van den Branden, Cockx-Indestege, and Sills 1978. Zwinger was a proofreader for Waldkirch: Gilly 1979: 134–135; Claude Baduel for Gryphius: Maclean 2009: 279; Franciscus Modius for Feyerabend: Pallmann 1881: 181–183. See also Kapp 1886: 308ff. On Bruno, see the prefatory letter by Johann Wechel to Julius von Braunschweig, in Bruno 1591 and Lepri 2008: 370. See also Voet 1969–1972: 2.288 (on payments to Dodoens and L'Obel). Oporinus acted on occasions as his own corrector: Steinmann 1967: 47. See also de Frede 2006: 50.

139. See Wackernagel 1881: 38, 40, 56, 72, 74.

140. Erasmus 1906–1947: 5.202 (27 January 1522, to Wilibald Pirckheimer): "Frobenius immensam pecuniam impendit in castigatores."

141. Quoted from the preface to Janus Cornarus's *Opus medicum practicum* of 1537 by Hieronymus 1995: 100.

142. Grafton forthcoming a; Plantin 1883–1918: 8–9.523 (no. 1464, 24 May 1589, to Cornelius Schutting): "correctore non uno utor, sed tribus quatuorve." Grafton forthcoming a records that Robert Estienne employed ten correctors. On Moretus's instructions, see Vervliet 1959. The Vatican charged rent on the room they made available to their printer for his correctors: Rietbergen 1983: 99.

143. Plantin 1883–1918: 1.50 (no. 20, 19 December 1566); Grafton forthcoming a

144. Gerritsen 1991.

145. This is particularly noticeable in the correction of vernacular texts: see Richardson 1994. Plantin clearly stated that he treated the author's text as authoritative, and would not alter it without his consent: Plantin 1883–1918: 5.87, 6.61–62, 264. He was particularly praised by Scaliger for his fidelity to this principle: see Grafton forthcoming a. See also Mouren 2010: 125 ("correctio ope codicis" and "correctio ope ingenii").

146. Grafton forthcoming a.

147. Payments for such services are found in publishers'accounts: see Wackernagel 1881: 98–99. Gessner wrote the preface to the Froben-Episcopius

edition of Galen, and received 15 livres; Coccius undertook the index to Eusebius.

148. Ibid.; Nelles 2010.

149. Dubois 2008: 68n, on Henri II Estienne's loss of books in the sinking of a barge; see also Steinmann 1967: 175–180 (on Oporinus's problems in 1563 in transporting money to the fair, hidden among old matrices and punches). See also Voet 1969–1972: 429–430. Pettas 1997: 189–190.

150. Kapp 1886: 502–505; Morisse 2000.

151. Könnecke 1894: 142ff.

152. See Pinelli and Dupuy 2001: *passim*. The time taken to transport books from Antwerp to Rome was nine months: it took more than a year for goods to be transported to Spain; Voet 1969–1972: 429–430.

153. Starp 1958: 46, where a bale of new books is valued at 22 fl, and old stock at 14 fl. Maclean 2009: 271. Pettas 1980: 137 records that after six years, the Giunti remaindered 771 out of 1,275 copies of Cervini at half price.

154. For a case of rarity, see the Estienne Bible of 1546 used in an exchange by John Norton (below, page 184. Dubois 2008: 67 gives an example of a price rising as a result of a failed first sale and re-advertisement, but this seems to be exceptional. John Wolfe's decision to advertise his editions of Machiavelli and Aretino at the Frankfurt book fair in the early 1580s suggests that he was trading on the notoriety of these figures: see Maclean 2009: 298. Basel's printing of Spanish authors who had been forced to leave Spain (Vives, Furio Ceriol, Fox Morcillio) provide another case of opportunism; see Gilly 1985: 185ff. The edition of Agrippa von Nettesheim's *Opera* with a false imprint by Thomas Guarinus is another case in point; ibid., 64n.

155. Dubois 2008: 67.

156. This seems to have been the case for the Milanese Girolamo Cardano published by Henri Petri in Basel, and the London resident Alberico Gentili, published by Wilhelm Antonius in Hanau: see Maclean 2009: 314. A press run of 2000 of Ramus's *Commentarii de religione christiana* took between seven and eight months to complete: Guilleminot-Chrétien 2009: 70. A useful set of calculations is found in Voet 1969–1972: 2.302–305. On the constraint placed upon publishers by the dates of the fairs, see Jakob Wimpheling, *Epithoma rerum Germanicarum* (Strasbourg: Matthias Schürer, 1505), colophon, quoted by Grafton forthcoming a.

157. Plantin 1883–1918: 1.221–224 (July 1571, no. 280)

158. Olson 2002: 98 (Flacius); Maclean 2009: 333–334 (Gentili).

159. See Smith 2000; Rautenberg 2008; Gilmont and Vanautgaerden 2008.

160. van Roomen and Bockstaele 1967: 127 (17 September 1597): "existimant enim eum titulum nimis esse vilem." The work in question was the *In Archimedis circuli dimensionem expositio et analysis*.

161. Maclean 2009: 371–402.

162. Matthioli 1565. I am grateful to Neil Kenny for drawing my attention to this title page. See also Mouren forthcoming; Gilmont and Vanautgaerden 2008.

163. Sixtus Senensis, *Bibliotheca sacra* (1566), quoted by Zedelmaier 1992: 171: "novos quotidie librorum foetus emittunt [typographi] adulterinos, suppositicios, pseudoepigraphicos, et nothos, praepositis absque ullo iudicio et pudore in frontispiciis operum, quo ipsa et charius et citius vendant, falsis illustrium autorum inscriptionibus."

164. Maclean 2009: 197; Gilmont 2005a: 57.

165. Rees and Wakely 2009: 104ff.

166. Blair 2010.

167. See, for examples, Kolb 1976 (on the library of Caspar Peucer); and Agasse 2002–2003 (the library of Girolamo Mercuriale); also Maclean 2009: 22.

168. Pettas 1997: 184–185. On the protection of trader's marks in general, which is a feature of medieval law, see Lehne 1939: 329.

169. Nuovo 2003: 181–190; Pettas 1997: 185.

170. Rhodes 1987, 2005.

171. Maclean 2009: 249–250. Chaix 1978: 66–69 (on Lyon being used as bibliographical address by Genevan publishers). The success of the ploy can sometimes be confirmed by the holdings of libraries: the Jesuit College in Alcalá de Henares, for example, possessed a copy of Martin Delrio's legal *Miscellanea* that was printed at Lyon "apud Samuelem Crespinum" (a Genevan publisher). The reverse phenomenon (Catholic works being disguised for infiltration into protestant markets) is much rarer, for obvious reasons: but it can be found in recusant literature produced in England smuggled in with false imprints, and in cases where the title disguises confessional allegiance through the use of such words as "defence" and apology." An interesting twist on the use of the alternative place name "Aureliae Allobrogum" is found in books on legal, medical, and philosophical topics imported into England between 1610 and 1620, in which the place name has been obliterated by the Genevan printer, and "Genevae" supplied above it: examples are found from the presses of Cartier (Alesius's Greek Grammar of 1613 and Antoine Fèvre's legal commentaries, 1618) and the Chouets (Jacques Fontaine's medical works of 1613 and Virgil's Bucolics of 1620).

172. On Plantin's use of "ex officina" and "in officina" to distinguish works printed with or without his consent, see Voet 1969–1972: 1.111.

173. Rott 1905: 83 (Zacharias Ursinus to Crato, 12 November 1572): Zanchi's desire to have an Imperial privilege is "propter Italiam, in qua sperat facilius admissum et lectum iri librum privilegio caesarea munitum."

174. Pantin 1988: 242, referring inter alia to Cavellat's edition of Hartmann Beyer's *Quaestiones in sphaeram* of 1562, with postdated editions of 1565, 1566 and 1569.

175. See below, 289n18. Arias Montano wrote at least one preface for Plantin: see Bowen and Imhof 2008: 291. Beatus Rhenanus wrote at least one preface for Froben, and Arias Montano at least one preface for Plantin: see Grafton forthcoming a; Bowen and Imhof 2008:291. Other printers who rely on the Latin of others include Wolf Lachner, Dirk Martens, and Aldus

Manutius the Younger: see von Hase 1885: 203; Vanautgaerden 2009; and Grafton forthcoming a, who also quotes Henri Estienne's complaint in his *Artis typographiae querimonia* that most "typographi" were incapable of understanding Latin, but still had prefatory material written by others attributed to them.

176. Shevchenko 2007: 195; Maclean 2009: 229 (Beraud and Tinghi), 293–294.
177. Simonin 2004: 761–82 ("Peut-on parler de politique éditoriale au XVIe siècle? Le cas de Vincent Sertenas, libraire du Palais").
178. Schöder 1904: 6, where Adam Lonicer of Frankfurt describes him as "virum de omnibus literarum studiosis optime meritum, et rei publicae nostrae bibliopolam laudatissimum."
179. On the seriousness (or not) of this venture, see Davies 1995: 55–60.
180. On 24 October 1595, the Prince-Bishop of Würzburg instructed his client Adriaan van Roomen to buy in future all the volumes produced by Jan I Moretus at the Frankfurt fair: van Roomen and Bockstaele 1967: 122–123: on the Wechel presses' reputation, see Maclean 2009: 163.
181. Guilleminot-Chrétien 2005; Maclean 2009: 163–226.

5. Controlling the Market

1. Cited by Pinon forthcoming a: "Ante liber non liber eram . . . sed tua me, Stephane, ut poliit, censura, labosque sum liber liber."
2. Eisenhardt 1985: 295 points out that the earliest legal codification of freedom of expression is found in the Bill of Rights for Virginia of 12 June 1776.
3. Raz-Kiakotzkin 2007: 15: where the claim is found that the erasure of words and phrases found in Hebrew books is "not an act of suppression but a consequence of print." I am not dealing in this chapter with the censorship of Hebrew books, governed in Catholic lands by the papal bull *Cum sicut nuper* of 29 May 1554 (Julius III). On this topic, see Popper 1969, Burnett 2000, and van Boxel forthcoming.
4. Erasmus pointed out that libel carried the death penalty, but adultery did not: see Crousaz 2005: 132.
5. Maclean 1992: 186–202.
6. Koppitz 2008: XI; Ehrenpreis 2006: 66–68.
7. Witcombe 2004: 21.
8. See above, page 5; the University of Ingolstadt produced guild regulations for printers in 1516, but as elsewhere, these did not generate a separate guild: see http://www.copyrighthistory.org.
9. On Aldine counterfeits, see Kemp 1997.
10. Witcombe 2004: 326ff.
11. E.g., HHStA 33.50, f. 261 (a general Imperial privilege granted to the Society of Jesus on 20 February 1620). In France, the Jesuit order held a general privilege, granted by Henri III on 10 May 1583 and confirmed by Henri IV on 20 December 1606: see Martin del Rio, *Commentarius litteralis in*

Threnos, id est Lamentationes Ieremiae Prophetae (Lyon: Horace Cardon, 1608), *3v.

12. As well as the volumes of Impressoria calendared by Koppitz 2008, there are Reichshofratsprotokolle with useful information: see Ehrenpreis 2006: 65–93.

13. For early examples of learned chancery officials (in the papal chancery of the fifteenth century), see Grafton 1993; see also Whaley forthcoming.

14. Eisenhardt 1985: 310; Gross 1933: 22ff.

15. Gessner acknowledged his help in obtaining a privilege: Gessner 1577: 18v (26 March 1564). See also HHStA 79.48 (Francesco Zoanetti to Seld, 22 May 1563); Kapp 1886: 466; Vogel 1933.

16. Gross 1933: 307ff.

17. The Diet of Worms in 1521 specified the local bishop or university as the censors. Dietz 1970: 3.65 claims that the first Imperial controls were enacted at the Diet of Nuremberg in 1524. For these texts, see Kapp 1886: 775ff. The earliest ordinances deal with scurrilous literature ("Schmähschriften" directed against individuals or on political issues); thereafter, they cover protestant literature, pre-censorship (as in Speyer in 1529), clandestine printing houses (1548), restrictions on locations for presses, punishments for printers in violation of Imperial ordinances, extension of Imperial powers to territories in which the Ruler was not sufficiently active in suppressing forbidden categories of books (1577) and bookselling. See Eisenhardt 1970: 58–60.

18. Evans 1986: 266.

19. On the Augsburg Confession in its "variata" form, see Cameron 1991: 370–372. http://www.copyrighthistory.org claims that applications for privileges fall off after the Peace of Augsburg, but offers no authority for this claim, or supporting statistics. The Imperial ordinance of 9 November 1577 (Kapp 1886: 783; also ibid.: 778 [30 June 1548]) refers to the definition of "christliche Kirchen" in the Peace of Augsburg and before; see also Eisenhardt 1970: 32. Kapp 1886: 713 refers to an attempt by Lutherans in Frankfurt to argue that Calvinists were not included in the concessions of the Peace of Augsburg. The first formal recognition of the Reformed Churches in Germany was at the Peace of Westphalia in 1648.

20. Schröder 1904: 19; Dietz 1970: 3.66; Schottenloher 1933: 91 (on the misuse of "kaiserliche Freyheit"); Brückner 1961a. Publisher also had to bear the not-inconsiderable cost of transport of the "Pflichtexemplare" to Vienna or Prague: see Kapp 1886: 472.

21. Schröder 1904:10.

22. Eisenhardt 1970: 64ff. argues that the real foundation of the Commission was in 1597. See also Brückner 1962: 79.

23. In 1614 Johannes Berner was fined 30 thalers by Leucht for being found in possession of scurrilous literature: Kapp 1886: 638. In 1628 Kopf's copies of de Thou's *Historiae* were confiscated on the grounds that they were on the Roman Index: ibid. The Council did, however, argue on 3 March 1609

that the existing provisions under the Ordinances of 1577 were adequate to control the problem: Kapp 1886: 620–627.

24. They were right to fear the measures taken against them; in 1628 the Book Commission finally managed to have Calvinist theology excluded from the fair catalogue on the grounds it was not protected by the provisions of the Peace of Augsburg: Kapp 1886: 645.

25. Pallmann 1881: 44 (the Buchdruckerordnung, planned on 22 April 1563, enacted on 5 March 1573, and revised in 12 March 1588); Kirchhoff 1853a: 38 ("Pflichtexemplare"); Dietz 1970: 66 (the Predigerministerium demanded that "keine verführerische, päpstliche, kalvinistische und sektirerische Bücher der Schwenckfelder, Enthusiasten und Weigelianer allhier gedrückt würden"); Kapp 1886: 620ff.; Brückner 1962; van Groesen 2008: 283. The Commissioner was given the title of Imperial counsellor (Rat) in 1613. In 1625, the number of "Pflichtexemplare" to be given to the Book Commission was raised to four: Kapp 1886: 345.

26. Kapp 1886: 610ff.

27. There are very many such cases recorded in Koppitz 2008, involving a number of the printers whom we met in Chapter 2: Neben, Schönwetter, Wechel, Bassée, and Feyerabend. The documents in the Impressoria very rarely record the outcomes of these complaints. The Chancery also regulated the export of printing presses: e.g., HHStA 42.29, ff. 187–189 (to Thomas Loncius, 27 November 1600, to Moscow). On the early history of grants of privileges, see Schottenloher 1933.

28. Lehne 1939: 385ff.

29. There are many examples of privileges granted to authors not resident in the Empire, but also a few of foreign authors living in the Empire who were refused privileges on the grounds of their foreign status: e.g., Denis Godefroy, professor of law at Heidelberg, who applied for protection against Lyon printers: Lehne 1939: 364. See also Ehrenpreis 2006: 65–66. There were two sections in the Chancery, one of which received requests in Latin and replied in that language ("lateinische Expedition"); the other of which responded in German to German requests ("deutsche Expedition"): Gross 1933: 137f.

30. For an example of a submission on vellum, see below, note 68.

31. There are various formulae for "public good": HHStA 76.2: "coetus literarii commodum"; ibid., 56.3, f. 25r: "quantum lucis publicae rei literariae ex eiusmodi editionibus provenire soleat"; ibid., 56.38, f. 243: "ad communem Reipublicae utilitatem"; ibid., 56., f. 34v: "Nos [the Emperor Matthias] pro benigna nostra in rem litterariam affectione precibus istius gratiose annuendum duximus, uti vigore praesentium annuimus." See also Lehne 1939: 350–354.

32. In requests for privileges to cover composite volumes, this is not necessarily the case: see HHStA 56.3. f. 28 (16 December 1603), where the justification for republishing is the "ingens precium" of existing editions, and Zacharias Palthen's desire to produce a "modicum volumen." Lehne 1939: 387 claims

that fewer applications were made to renew old privileges than to seek protection for new works.

33. De Bujanda 1985–2002: 8.131–133, 786.

34. HHstA 56.35, ff. 241–245, 24 October 1567: the privilege covers "opera juridica, medical, philosophica, historica, mathematica, poetica, et ea quibus Hebraicae, Graecaee vel Latinae linguae studium adiuvant. Vel prius non edita, vel labore atque impensis Pernae emendatiora, locupletiora, et illustriora facta, in publicum prolata." Stephanus Laurens also intervened on behalf of Johannes Wier's *De praestigiis daemonum* and four other books on 4 November 1564: ibid., 77.48, f. 496.

35. Ibid., 2.35, f. 255r."ad historicorum et Theolog[ic]orum librorum vero editionem privilegio meo absque peculiari consensu uti non debet." For another example of sensitivity to historical titles, see Maclean 2009: 116–117 (the *Chronicon Carionis*).

36. HHStA 26.38, f. 250–251 (1 January 1601, the physician Christophorus Guarinonius), and 77.6, ff. 85–86 (29 November 1594, Marcus Welser of Augsburg). For the exceptionally generous twenty-year privilege granted on 15 June 1602 by Rudolph II to Martin del Rio, and covering all his past and future works, as well as the one in which the privilege appears, see Martin del Rio, *Disquisitionum magiciarum lbiri sex* (Lyon: Jean Pillehotte, 1608), ††1r. I am grateful to Jan Machielsen for this reference.

37. E.g., Leonhard Fuchs, who in 1544 wrote a pamphlet against Christian Egenolff's copying of his illustrations entitled *Adversus mendaces et Christiano homine indignas, Christiani Egenolphi Typographi Francoforti suique architecti calumnias responsio*: see Kusukawa forthcoming.

38. Cf. Blackstone 1977: 2.405–406: "Now the identity of a literary composition consists entirely in the *sentiment* and the *language*; the same conceptions, clothed in the same words, must necessarily be the same composition"; see also Flachmann 1996: 36–45 (Luther on books).

39. Brown 1891: 79; Witcombe 2004: 54–56.

40. Fritschius 1675. For the documents relating to the emergence of intellectual property, see http://www.copyrighthistory.org.

41. On Laurens, see note 34 above. Direct evidence of Crato's influence is found in HHStA 26.30 (14 October 1574: the application of Barthélémy Vincent and Antoine Gryphius of Lyon, which is annotated with the words "ad sollicitationem Dr. Cratonis bewilligt"; Zanchi had approached Crato on behalf of the Lyon printers of Sanctes Pagnini's *Thesaurus linguae sanctae*, which appeared in 1574: see Rott 1905: 91. See also Gessner 1577: 1–22v; Kapp 1886: 464 (Henri II Estienne); Perini 2002: 316–319 (Vittorio Trincavelli).

42. Whaley forthcoming; on the assistance given by Crato to André Wechel in 1574, see Maclean 2009: 169.

43. Steinmann 1967: 93 (Christoph von Württemberg for Oporinus, 1557); HHStA 56.27, ff.200–207 (Archduke Ferdinand of Austria for Hans Paur, 1586); ibid., 14.38, ff. 248–253 (Elector of Brandenburg for Johannes Eichorn); Ehrenpreis 2006: 65 (the Dukes of Jülich and Bavaria).

44. "Exhibeat librum." The annotation "apponat exemplum" is found on many of the applications, and may indicate that privileges would be only granted after the book in question had appeared in print.

45. Rott 1905: 83 (12 November 1572, no. 26): "sine mentione privilegii prodiit liber, quia [Zanchius] metuebat, ne vestros [i.e., the Imperial Chancery] offenderet. Misi autem antea ipsius literas cum meis, quibus petit etiamnum privilegium impetrari, si ullo modo potest. Vult enim curare, ut primae paginae hac de causa recudantur potissimum propter Italiam, in qua sperat facilius admissum et licetum iri librum privilegio caesario munitum." Also ibid., 84 (26 November 1572, no. 27): "De privilegio tibi magnae aguntur gratiae a Zanchio et amicis, etiam a me. Quod solvendum fuit Zanchius, paratus est vel mihi vel cui volueris." This latter phrase suggests that Crato had not only used his influence, but had also advanced the money for the privilege himself.

46. *De tribus Elohim,* Neustadt an der Haart: Matthaeus Harnisch, 1589, a1v: "Summam [privilegii] hanc ideo subiicere voluimus, ut omnes intelligant hoc libro non contineri doctrinam, quae non ipsi etiam Romanae Ecclesiae probetur: quando ea ab ipsis Caesareae Maiestatis Theologis post diligentem examinationem pia et orthodoxa esse iudicata fuit, et vero etiam testimonio, Privilegioque Caesaris confirmata et obsignata." The work eventually enjoyed some success, being reprinted in 1597–1598, 1600–1601, and 1604.

47. "Dummodo tamen libri illi nihil in se contineant scandalosum aut orthodoxae Religioni Catholicae sacrique Romani Imperii constitutionibus adversum sive in praefatione sive in textu, aut alias quoquomodo contineant": after 1600 the clause "vel bonis moribus contrarium" was added at the end: see Lehne 1939: 377. In Egenolff's privilege of 4 May 1555, the requirement to conform to the "constitutiones imperii de re impressoria" is also found. The "clausula religionis" is not found, for example, in Bassée's privilege of 12 July 1576: HHStA 3.68, f. 512–513). An early example of its Rudolphine use is found in HHStA 3.65, ff. 493–496 (Bassée, 16 July 1583).

48. HHStA 56.43, ff. 253–254 (18 April 1566, renewed 7 February 1570).

49. Schröder 1904: 19.

50. HHStA 79.1.25, f. 183r : Valerio Polidoro and Girolamo Mengo's *Thesaurus exorcismorum et coniurationum* (a compendium of the former's *Practica exorcistarum* (1582) and the latter's *Flagellum Daemonum* (1577), published by Lazarus Zetzner in Cologne in 1608. The publication follows the third edition of the *Practica exorcistarum* by Roberto Meietti in 1606, and is evidently an example of "Nachdruck."

51. Lehne 1939: 366 (Nicolas Bassée, 11 December 1582); Ehrenpreis 2006: 65–66.

52. Pallmann 1881: 44 (Frankfurter Buchdruckerordnung of 12 March 1588); Schottenloher 1933: 91–92; Witcombe 2004: 58. In some cases in Venice and France, the fine was shared three ways, between the issuing authority, the holder of the privilege, and a local charity; in others, between the holder

of the privilege and a local charity: Witcombe 2004: 30; and Maclean 2006a: xliii.

53. von Hase 1885: 229; Steinmann 1967: 57. Erasmus was able to secure exemption: see Erasmus 1906–1947: 5.201–202, 228–234 (nos. 1341 to Willibald Pirckheimer 28 January 1523, and 1344 from Pirckheimer, 17 February 1523); also Erasmus CWE 1989: 9.289–290, 402–408.

54. HHStA 2.35, f. 256v (24 May 1582).

55. Schröder 1904: 24.

56. Ibid., 14.16–20, ff. 130–152.

57. HHStA: 3. 70, ff. 521–526 (9 July 1597, Nicolas Bassée).

58. Pallmann 1881: 56–60; HHStA: 56.5 (ff. 28f (Zacharias Palthen, 16 December 1603); HHStA 3. 52.70, ff. 458–526 (518–519) (Nicolas Bassée and his heirs).

59. Ibid. The Cologne publisher Johann Gymnich asked for a privilege in "forma Bassaeae" in 1600 to protect his publication of Baronio: ibid., 26.59, ff. 434–436.

60. HHStA 77.50–52, ff. 503–521; the last document is written on vellum on behalf of the city of Augsburg.

61. HHStA 79.3.48, ff. 367–373, 1 June 1563.

62. Koppitz 2008: 204 (26.58, ff. 426–433): *Index chronologicus*, Görlitz: by and for Johannes Rhamba, 1599. Previous editions had appeared in 1577, 1580, and 1584.

63. HHStA 56.18, ff 116–119 (Georg Parreuter); ibid., ff. 210–212 (Jeremias Pepfenhauser).

64. Koppitz 2008: *passim;* among the printer-supplicants who specialized in law were Nicolas Bassée, Sigmund Feyerabend, and Zacharias Palthen of Frankfurt, and Johann Gymnich and Antonius Hierat of Cologne; the Catholic theologians whose names most often occur in Koppitz's calendar are Robert Bellarmine and Caesar Baronio.

65. But authors believed that obtaining a privilege encouraged a printer "ut melius atque ornatius excudat": Imhof 2008: 347 (Leonardus Lessius's letter to Moretus dated 16 January 1609).

66. See Nuovo forthcoming.

67. Simonsfeld 1887.

68. Kirchhoff 1853a: 92, quoting Joannes Cotovicus, *Synopsis Reipublicae Venetae* (Leiden: Elzevir, 1628), p. 16.

69. Brown 1891: 79; Witcombe 2006: 54–56.

70. Witcombe 2004: 1–35; Woodward 1996: 67.

71. Witcombe 2004:62.

72. Lowry 1979: 155.

73. Nuovo 2003: 205–206; www.copyrighthistory.org (where the "proprio motu" document is reproduced with a transcription).

74. Herrman de Franceschi 2009: 231ff.

75. Lowry 1979: 32–33; Witcombe 2004: 62. Early examples of offending images were the nude figures in the Giunti's edition of Ovid of 1497.

76. De Vivo 2007: 201, referring inter alia to Brown 1891: 205–234.

77. Oporinus and Steinmann 1969: 117–118.

78. Grendler 1977.

79. Wilding forthcoming; Ciotti 1602. Meietti was involved in anti-papal publication during the Interdict, and was excommunicated for a time. On censorship in general in Italy, see Stango 2001. A number of northern publishers, including Gotthard Vögelin and Hieronymus Commelinus, printed title pages without mention of the location of the presses in question.

80. *Colloquia obscurorum theologorum* "Roma, stampato con privilegio del Papa", 1560, quoted by Schottenloher 1933: 93: "Tenor privilegii: Sanctissimus papa prohibuit sub poena excommunicationis longae et brevis, altae et profundae, ne quis hunc librum per totam Italiam, Galliam vel Hispaniam imprimat, sed Germanis, quia sunt pessimi Lutherani, non possumus prohibere."

81. The relevant instrument was the constitution *Inter sollicitudines:* De Bujanda 1985–2002: 11.27–28.

82. Erasmus 1906–1947: 3.163–164 (no. 734, 9 December 1517): "puto neminem bonum virum non hoc animo scribere quin ab Ecclesiae iudicio pendeat: verum ubi sit Ecclesia non satis aliquoties liquet"; also Erasmus CWE 5 (1979): 231–233.

83. Bonnant 1969: 611 points out that episcopal censorship dates from the Council of Nicea (325 AD).

84. Witcombe 2004: 45ff.

85. Baldini 2001; Baldini and Spruit 2009; Hermann de Franceschi 2009: 238.

86. De Bujanda 1985–2002: vols. 1–9.

87. Van Groesen 2008: 286–287.

88. Bonnant 1969: 618.

89. De Bujanda 1985–2002, vol. 5.

90. A striking case is that of the expurgation of the Talmud, undertaken by the Inquisitor Marco Marino on the 1546–1550 edition: see James Hastings, *Encyclopaedia of Religion and Ethics,* s.v. Talmud. Marino signed every page as he expurgated it.

91. Warren Boutcher has kindly informed me that the Francesco Maria II della Rovere, Duke of Urbino (1549–1631), assiduously applied for licences to hold copies of forbidden books, and kept them apart from the rest of his extensive library.

92. Bonnant 1969: 614 claims that this formula was first employed in the Roman Index of 1596. There is a long commentary on these rules in Reusch 1883–1888: 1.330–341.

93. Protestant churches also engaged in excommunication for publishing offenses, as in the case of a printer in France who agreed to publish Bellarmine, and refused to destroy his copies when asked to do so by the Consistory of Charenton in 1609: Herrman de Franceschi 2009: 235–236.

94. Rietbergen 1983.

95. Voet 1969–1972: 2.277.

96. E.g., Latino Latini, on whom see Petitmengin 2004.
97. A similar index was planned in Rome between 1596 and 1607, but the initiative was never carried through to fruition: see De Bujanda 2002: 32–33.
98. Plantin 1883–1918: 86 (Pierre d'Overloepe, 19 September 1571, no. 372); Bonnant 1969: 612–628.
99. For the obliteration of a portrait (of Erasmus), see Bethencourt 2009: 224.
100. Voet 1969–1972: 2.277.
101. Giunti 1604: preface.
102. Fragnito 2001; Truman forthcoming.
103. Pettegree 2010: 225 points out that compendia and anthologies posed a particularly difficult problem for Catholic authorities, given the scattered nature of references to forbidden authors and topics. For an example of triviality, see van Groesen 2008: 291. Grafton forthcoming b points out that Baronio makes use of the scholarship of Joseph Justus Scaliger without acknowledgement in his *Annals*.
104. Turretini 1619: 14. See also Truman forthcoming.
105. Turretini 1619: preface; Germann 1985: 209; Bonnant 1969; van Groesen 2008: 620; Nelles 2007: 34–35.
106. The 1611 edition published in Hanau by Wilhelm Antonius refers to the work's contents as "testes fraudum et falsificationum pontificiarum."
107. Eisenstein 1979: 416–417.
108. Cited by Truman forthcoming.
109. "il piu bell'arcano per adoperare la religione a far gli uomini insensati": quoted in Gilly 1985: 140.
110. Herrman de Franceschi 2009: 66.
111. Nuovo 2003: 182ff., 206–207. For its importance in Germany, see Lehne 1939: 329.
112. Hoogewerff 1926.
113. Banderier 2000: 589 (quoting a letter of 1599 from Simon Goulart to Schobinger); Grendler 1978.
114. Perini 2002: 233–245. Paracelsus was subject even in the Empire to examination by an expert before a privilege was granted: Lehne 1939: 360 (Reichshofratsprotokolle, 23 November 1575, application of Leonhard Thurneysser).
115. An example of medical citation are given in Maclean 2001: 45 (Franciscus Bartolettus alluding to Paracelsus). See also Grafton forthcoming b (Baronio citing Scaliger silently).
116. Rebuffi 1540; Dupont 1854: 129.
117. Dupont 1854: 131ff (17 January 1538, on Greek studies), 110 and 141 (31 August 1539, on the role of correctors and printer's marks), 138 (8 December 1536, on legal deposit).
118. Armstrong 1990; Armstrong 1993; Witcombe 2004: 336ff.; Parent-Charon 1982; Parent-Charon 2005; Fritschius 1675: sig. K3v. This measure, whose text is given by Fritschius but whose original grant I have not been able to

trace, was reaffirmed in 1583: see Dupont 1854: 111, 150. It may be in the Lettres patentes granted by Charles IX in March 1560 and confirmed by the Parlement on 3 May 1561: see ibid., appendix.

119. Martin 1999: 1.50–57. The 1618 legislation was published in 1621 in a pamphlet with the title *Lettres patentes du Roy pour le reglement des Libraires Imprimeurs et Relieurs de cette ville de Paris*.

120. Dupont 1854: 131–132.

121. Dupont 1854: 2.522 records lettres patentes relating to printing in Lyon.

122. Watson 1999; cf. Dupont 1854: 2.522 (the declaration of 10 September 1572 requiring all printing to be carried out in France, which never was able to be enforced).

123. Maclean 2009: 229, 246–248.

124. The privilege, dated 21 February 1578, specifies that the book "a esté visité par les Docteurs de la faculté de Theologie."

125. Martin, Chartier, and Vivet 1982: 332.

126. Pallier 1982; Pallier 2000; Desmars 1994; Guilleminot-Chrétien 2008; *Indices* 1611: 10–11 (Franciscus Junius on the experience of a corrector in Lyon in 1559, cited by Grafton forthcoming a).

127. Chaix 1978: 85.

128. Shuger 1994: 14 (Sedan).

129. Herrman de Franceschi 2009: 232–238.

130. Cressy 2005; Vallée 2008: 199.

131. Hermann de Franceschi 2009: 235.

132. Cited by ibid., 230.

133. Kapp 1886: 785 ff. has an appendix with the relevant texts; see also Lehne 1939; Koppitz 2008: ix. There are some cases of local town privileges: e.g., Breslau in 1590 for a schoolbook by Georg Baumann der Ältere (Kirchhoff 1853a: 152–153). It was confirmed by the Imperial Chancery on 25 January 1596.

134. For a comprehensive archive of relevant documents, see Kapp 1886: 785ff.

135. Künast 1977: 197–201.

136. Gier 2008: 151; on censorship in Bavaria, see Wittmann 1999: 69ff. Documents relating to Ingolstadt, Wittenberg, Leipzig, and Marburg are to be found on www.copyrighthistory.org. On Strasbourg, see Schottenloher 1933.

137. Eisenhardt 1985: 295; Gier 2008: 151–152.

138. See *Realencyclopädie der protestantischen Theologie und Kirche* (1898: 4:441–445, Walter Goetz), s.v. Brendel von Homburg.

139. Flachmann 1996.

140. Brückner 1961b: 1635.

141. Lehne 1939: 361 (on quality of paper).

142. Goldfriedrich 1908: 159ff.

143. Kolb 1977; Crusius 2008.

144. Ehrenpreis 2006: 65; Brauer 1974: 37 (Henning Grosse). Ernest Vögelin had already been forced to flee to Heidelberg because of his Calvinist beliefs: see Kirchhoff 1853a: 93.

145. Goldfriedrich 1908: 168ff.

146. Dyroff 1963: 1280.

147. Kinser 1966: 30, records the privilege granted to Kopf or Goldast for the publication of de Thou in 1609; but no mention of this appears on the relevant title page. Other title pages do, however, carry a reference to a Palatine privilege: e.g., Caspar Waser, *Grammatica hebraea*, [Heidelberg]: typis Gotthardi Voegelini, "cum priv. Elect. Palat." 1611, 8vo. See also Könnecke 1894: 75; Dietz 1970: 3.75 (a twelve-year Palatinate privilege for 56 books granted to Daniel and David Aubry of Frankfurt on 8 July 1619).

148. Goldast 1600–1613: 107r (27 August 1612).

149. Pallmann 1881: 31–33, 56–58, 60ff. (on Feyerabend's many brushes with the law); Pöllmann 1966 (Feyerabend); Schottenloher 1933: 91 (Egenolff); Starp 1958 (Schönwetter). This last case is particularly interesting, as it concerns the unauthorised publication of restricted legal documents (the *Consultationes Saxonicae*) in 1599, and their prosecution by the Saxon authorities in Frankfurt. Later editions were published in Mainz and Oberursel, beyond the control of the Frankfurt City Council.

150. Fritschius 1675. There is a section devoted to booksellers which begins with their eulogy. References to ecclesiastical censorship are scarce in this work

151. Gilmont 2005b: 41; Chaix 1978: 86; Dubois 2008.

152. Grafton forthcoming a.

153. Gilmont 2005b: 49 (quoting a letter written by Calvin to Claude Baduel): "tu connais la vie et les moeurs des imprimeurs, combien ils sont dissolus, querelleurs, prompts à toute débauche et à tout forfait."

154. Chaix 1978: 17–18.

155. Ibid., 20–24. The measures were to be enforced by three supervisors appointed by the Council.

156. Gilmont 1995.

157. Chaix 1978: 73–74, 53; Dubois 2008.

158. Crousaz 2005: 142–156.

159. Roth 1914.

160. See, e.g., the edition of the works of Nicephorus by Oporinus, which were granted a Louvain "censura" in 1551, and printed in 1553.

161. Steinmann 1967: 94–95. In practice, the different faculties granted approbations for works in their purview, as in Johan Georgius Grossius, *Compendium quatuor facultatum* (Basel: Ludwig König, 1620).

162. Oporinus and Steinmann 1969: 155–156 (letter of 13 February 1558); ibid., 175–180 (letter of 10 June 1563); ibid., 164 (on the duties of the Council of Thirteen).

163. Steinmann 1967: 23–25, 97–98. Oporinus must have also regretted the loss of trade he suffered after having been cited in the Roman Index of 1559: see De Bujanda 1985–2002: 5.131–132, 786.

164. Reyes Gómez 2000: vol. 2 contains in full all legislative acts for this period.

165. Van Groesen 2008: 285.
166. Reyes Gómez 2000: 2.795.
167. For an example, see Heitjan 1969; for the French practice, see above, page 161. James I and VI ordered the burning in Oxford and Cambridge of a book on the rights of magistrates under an unjust monarch: Milton 2010: 159–160.
168. Voet 1969–1972: 2.259; Truman 2004, 2009, forthcoming.
169. Duke 1990.
170. Witcombe 1991; Voet 1969–1972: 2.468.
171. Clair 1960: 57–82; Simpson 2009.
172. Voet 1969–1972: 274ff.
173. Imhof 2008: 281–287.
174. Imhof 2008: 267, 315–338 (the Van Keerberghen cases in the period 1598–1603). Imhof's work contains a very thorough account of all the privilege issues encountered by Moretus.
175. Pettegree 2008 points out that the same number of presses was operating in the whole country as in the City of Geneva (around 34).
176. Roberts 1997: 320.
177. Pettegree 2008. The powers conferred by the Charter of 1557 were extended in 1559.
178. Gadd 1999.
179. Oxford Dictionary of National Biography, s.v. (Gadd)
180. Rees and Wakely 2009; Barnard 2002, 2005.
181. Gilly 1977: 109–110 (quoting a letter from Moffet to Theodor Zwinger in December 1578).
182. Roberts 1997.
183. On other effects of standardisation, see Eisenstein 1979: 80–88.
184. Ross 1998. In 1605 the Stationers' Company was granted a monopoly over the publication of common law texts.
185. In the southern Netherlands, the Jesuit Andreas Schott arranged for forbidden books to be sent to him via Amsterdam to evade the censorship regulations: Hessels 1887: 1.510–512.
186. See above, note 128.
187. Maclean 2009: 183; MPM Archive 12.48, quoted by Grafton forthcoming a; van Boxel forthcoming
188. See Grafton forthcoming a.
189. Ibid.
190. See Maclean 2006a: xxxiv–xl.

6. Sellers and Purchasers

1. von Hase 1885: 263 (May 1500): "es ist ein jämmerlich Ding geworden mit unserem Handel: ich kann kein Geld mehr aus Büchern lösen und geht allenhalben grosse Zehrung und Kosten darauf"; see also Kapp 1886, quoting Christoph Foschauer in 1526: "verkouffens halb hab ich nit ein bösse

meßt gehapt, aber böse bezahlung"; also Oporinus and Steinmann 1969: 111 (Oporinus, 15 September 1536); Nuovo 2003: 92 (Pietro Perna's difficulties with the absence of money at the fair in 1575).

2. Imhof 2008: 39. He joined Plantin in 1559, married his daughter in 1570, and was appointed "en la boutique pour nos comptes et marchandises." Between 1571 and 1576 he attended the fair by himself, or with his brother-in-law Frans Raphelengius, according to Kapp 1886: 505. In 1588 he became "directeur de la trafficque de librairie."

3. I have conferred the carnet for 1587 (MPM Archive 861) with the cahier for 1586 (MPM Archive 965); there are a number of discrepancies, and some adjustments to the carnet, indicating recent settlements.

4. Maclean 2009: 76 (on Heidelberg professors being required to attend the fair); Kapp 1886: 466 (same requirement imposed on the Librarian of Strasbourg); Nelles forthcoming b (on the Imperial Librarian Hugo Blotius). The few sales made to individuals at the fair for cash are recorded in the MPM cahiers under the heading "vendre contans a menu" (e.g., Archive 962: 28r); for other records of retail sales, see Kirchhoff 1853a: 49ff.; and Dyroff 1963: 1612.

5. MPM Archive 849: 1v–2r: "Auec Po di Longi passè quelques foires ne ay fait conclusion de compte et je trouue que je luy doibs enuiron 28 ou 30 fl en liures. Nota que ledit m'a ioue ung tour la foire prochaine c'est que je luy ay baillèe 40 escus en argent la foire passee pour ung op[er]a Tostadi lesquels ie debuois receuoir bien tost (comme il disoit) car la balle estoit en chemin et deuroit estre en Anvers avant mon retour de francfort. memes me bailla en note les liures qui estoient pacquez auec lesdittes oeuures en la dite balle dont est la facture copiee sur mon cahier de francfort de la foire passee. Et iusques a present n'ay rien receu, et ay rescript plus de 15 fois a Venise pour entendre quelque chose de luy de laditte balle, Et iamais il n'a respondu ung seul mot. Tant il y a que ie veulx quil rende les 40 [ecus] et me face bon interest auec la perte et la honte que ien ay eu de auoir si asseurement promis veu que ne pensois nullement de me trouuer ainsi totalement trompè." The previous fair's cahier does not appear to survive in the archive.

6. Lepri 2008: 379; Kapp 1886: 772–774. From the Pinelli-Dupuy correspondence (Pinelli and Dupuy 2001), it is clear that he had a connection to the Wechel house.

7. Antonio et al. 1786–1788: 2.259 refers to the commissioning by Charles V of an edition in 1547; two folio volumes of an index to his works by Franciscus Fontanus appeared in Valladolid, from the presses of Juan de Villaquiràn. See also Nuovo 2003: 148, on the monumental edition of 1596.

8. MPM 760: f. 1–10 contains the list of bad debts (i.e., ones not settled at the following fair): the smallest figure recorded is 3 guilders, and the oldest debt dates from 1589.

9. Maclean 2009: 227–250.

10. Buhl 1879: 10.

11. Kapp 1886; Goldfriedrich 1908; Nuovo 2003.

12. von Hase 1885: 267–272; Pettegree 2010: 80–81. On the routes used by those espousing this model of trade, see Krüger 1974. Book trading at the Frankfurt fair was active from the end of the fifteenth century: some publishers attended the fair as much as one hundred times: Maclean 2009: 142 (Heinrich Petri of Basel).

13. Nuovo 2003: 75, 210–227.

14. Johannes Froben both sold through the Frankfurt fair, and also used the Johann Schabler and Franz Birckmann consortium of booksellers: see Bietenholz and Deutscher 1985–1987: 2.60–63.

15. Flood 2007: 8, citing Richter 1985: 54–5.

16. Nelles forthcoming a; Orthez, Agen, Pau, La Rochelle, Saintes, Limoges, Cahors, Poitiers, Lyon (the Pillehotte family, who were involved in international trade, as was Millanges himself).

17. Dubois 2008: 69.

18. Nuovo 2004: 153: "by the beginning of the sixteenth century it became necessary to have a vast stock of books on hand that came from various sources in order to be able to barter them. But only booksellers who had a stock of good books could hope to barter them with other good books. At this time, it was not possible to produce books without having also a network of exchange and a distribution and sales operation." Rees and Wakely 2009: 169–184 point to the importance of demonstrating continuity of stocks to satisfy and retain customers. Künast 1997: 120 shows that even middle-order publishers and booksellers had depots of books in a number of cities. Millanges's stock at his death was 97,000 volumes (Nelles forthcoming a); for other examples, see Griffin 1998 (Cromberger in Seville); Weidhaas 2003: 40 (Plantin in Frankfurt).

19. MPM Archive 490: 10v ff.

20. Maclean 2009: 230. Pettas 1995: 187 records the attempt of another member of the family around the same time to sell off her father's immense stocks in Lyon.

21. Pettas 1995: 250–276; Pallmann 1881: 122–188 (Beilagen 2, 7, 11, 15, 18: the stocks of David Zöpfel, two members of the Gülfferich family, Simon Hüter, and Peter Brubach, as well as Feyerabend's bookstore); Dyroff 1963; Camerini 1963: 213 (the stock held by the Giunti in their Lanciano warehouse).

22. Weidhaas 2003: 39

23. Giunti 1604; Pettas 1995 (the Giunti shop in Burgos).

24. Claesz 1604; Nelles forthcoming a (Millanges and Toulouze).

25. The data is taken from Giunti 1604 and James 1620. See also Schottenloher 1953: 153–154.

26. Oporinus and Steinmann 1969: 181–182; and Gilly 2001: 17.

27. Könnecke 1894: 156

28. Dietz 1970: 3.83.

29. Gehl 1997.

30. Nuovo 2003: 177.
31. Maclean 2009: 227–250.
32. Oporinus and Steinmann 1969: 54 (1 September 1560).
33. Kapp 1886: 507; Clair 1976: 220; Voet 1969–1972: 2.419–420.
34. Perini 2002: 271–272 [1559]: "mitto ad te Clarissime Vir, hos libros quos e Francfordia attuli, non ut eos emas, nisi velis, sed ut eos videas. Et si quis inter eos tibi arrideat ut accipias, utarisque. Mitto etiam adnotata pretia, ut si maveris emere quam dono accipere scias me nunquam emisse cariores libros, non ultra septem folia pro duobus batziis habere potui ab nova Academia veneta." On the Accademia Veneziana, see Bolzoni 1981.
35. Ciotti 1602. Warren Boutcher has kindly communicated to me his transcription of a letter from Ciotti to the Duke of Urbino (Archivio di Stato di Firenze, Ducato di Urbino, classe I, divisione G, filza 219 "Venezia e suo Dominio Diversi 1590–1629", fol. 554r) dated 17 March 1601 in which the publisher offers to procure desiderata for the ducal library without any mention of payment ("m'offerisco di fare havere al suo bibliotecario tutti que più rari libri, che da lui mi sien domandati").
36. See Pollard and Ehrman 1965; Richter 1974; Engelsing 1967–1969, 1971; Wittmann 1985; Amelung 1985; Serrai 1993: 16ff.; Richter 1997; Coppens 2001; Nuovo 2003: 228ff; Lesage, Netchine, and Sarrazin 2006; Myers, Harris, and Mandelbrote 2007.
37. Lesage, Netchine, and Sarrazin 2006: 18 (nos. 20–22, dated 1558–1559) record the catalogues of the Accademia Veneziana, which were designed for different purposes (local advertisement in Italian and Latin, and distribution at the Frankfurt book fair).
38. Ibid., 240 (no. 2283).
39. Early examples with prices include the 1498 Aldus Manutius catalogue, illustrated in Davies 1995: 21; and that of Jean Louys Tiletan (1546), illustrated in Barbier 2008: 120. See also Hellinga 2009.
40. See Leonnard 1902; Richter 1974: 326–329.
41. The asterisk is employed in this way by the Plantin house: Voet 1969–1972: 2.424. Henning Grosse uses it in his catalogue of 1596 to mark books obtained from other booksellers, and distinguishes those he has bought from those he has swapped ("ab aliis bibliopolis partim redemit, partim commutavit"): Kirchhoff 1853a: 90; Buhl 1879: 23. See also Richter 1997: 205–206 (Andreas Cratander's catalogue of 1534, which distinguishes his own publications from books of other presses, whose source is identified).
42. Engelsing 1967–1969, 1971; Fabian 1972–2001; Pollard and Ehrman 1965; Richter 1974; Wittmann 1985. See also Lesage, Netchine, and Sarrazin 2006: 252 (no. 1314, dated 1608) for the example of the bookshop of Giovanni Battista Ciotti, Bernardo Giunti, and their associates.
43. Imhof 2008: 357 (referring to the Schönwetter Bible of 1608); Wilding forthcoming (referring to Giovanni Antonio Magini's *Primum mobile* of 1603).
44. Kapp 1886: 304, 468 wrongly claims that "Tauschhandel" was not a feature of the sixteenth-century book market.

45. Buhl 1879: 24–28.
46. www.Eckbriefe/html (18 March 1517) to Johann Vadian: "mitto Lucae Alantsee x diaria [*Disputatio Viennae Pannonae habita,* Augsburg, ex officina Millerana, 1517, 4to], ut ipse invicem rependat XIX Orationes contra philosophos [*Oratio adversus priscam et ethnicam philosophiam,* Vienna, Johann Singrener, 1516, 4to], sic enim charta aequabitur chartae." Eck also demonstrates his financial acumen by offering Alantsee a discount if he will undertake to buy one or two hundred copies of the relevant work.
47. Kirchhoff 1853a: 40.
48. Plantin 1883–1918: 1.47 (no. 19, to Guillaume Roville, 26 December 1565): "je receuz votre lettres du 12 octobre avec la balle de livres que m'avez envoyez montant 142 fl. 8, que j'ay mys à l'encontre de ce que me deviez."
49. MPM Cahiers de Francfort 962 s.v. Guarin (who trades in a number of titles which he himself had not printed, as well as those that he had), including two copies of Cardan's *De subtilitate,* and six copies of the banned anonymous pamphlet *Vindiciae contra tyrannos*). In various accounts, books printed by the Plantin presses that had been returned are entered as credits.
50. "Pay[é] Sept. 1612 a p[a]rte 2 Corpus d'accord fl 38; En Quaresme 1613 resconta la reste."
51. MPM Archive 189: 69r describes it as "Arte de Cavalleria."
52. Flood 2007: 24.
53. Voet 1969–1972: 2.448. For the problem of the diverse currencies used to settle accounts, see ibid., 2.446.
54. E.g., Henning Grosse of Leipzig: see above, note 41.
55. But see Imhof 2008: 404, quoting MPM Archive 126 f. 114r (Jan I Moretus's letter of 18 August 1598), on Moretus's alarm when it was discovered that Adrian Périer of Paris "a envoyé en une balle divers entre lesquels aulcuns qui ne nous duisent pour estre suspects."
56. I am grateful to Anthony Milton for drawing my attention to this feature of the reception of English theology.
57. Voet 1969–1972: 2.417–419.
58. Kapp 1886: 500.
59. Myers, Harris, and Mandelbrote 2001.
60. Pettegree 2008 attributes the success of the Dutch printing industry to "a paradoxical relationship between concentration of production and diversity of output," and stresses their place at the hub of European commerce and their experience in financial transactions. See also de Vries and van der Woude 1997: 131, on the policy of the Bank of Amsterdam after 1609: "the great concern of the city fathers was to protect and enlarge the supply of good, full-valued coin. This they regarded as far more important to the prosperity of a commercial economy than the proliferation of circulating bills."
61. Vilvain 1654: a4v–a5r: "My memory cannot reach to remember every Patient or Party of my antient acquaintance, to whom I am engaged in amity

or courtesy: but my desire is to gratify ech, and send 400. Copies (som bound, som unbound) to dispers in free gift (without any fee to sender or bringer) that none may be forgotten. Thos that are omitted, may repair to Mr *Hooper* Apothecary in *Exceter* neer S. *Martins* Lane; who wil deliver one *gratis* to any man of quality my familiar Friend."

62. See Findlen 1991; Goldgar 1995: 15–53 (for a later manifestation of the same ethos).

63. Coppens 2009; Post, Giocarinis, and Kay 1955; Davis 1983, 2009; Bepler 2001; Shevchenko 2007: 19, 145–158.

64. Gobiet 1979: 23, 338 (4 July 1613, 6 December 1617).

65. Verstegan 1618: 67: "Van Franckfort wordt gheschreven [. . .] dat de Mert die men daer tweemaels 'sjaers is houdende, is ghelijck de Arca van Noé, die alderley reyne ende onreyne beesten was begrijpende, het welck gethoont wordt uyt den Catalogus van Lutersche, Catholijcke, ende Calvinische boecken, daer de Luterschen de precedentie oft voor-plaets inghenomen hebben, niet door antiquiteyt, maer door hun eyghen aenghenomen authoriteyt. Dat de winckels van d'Apothekers ende de boeck-vercoopers, zijn voor de zielen en voor de lichamen van de menschen goet ende quaedt." I am grateful to Paul Arblaster for this reference. See also Weidhaas 2003: 58.

66. Schröder 1904; Eisenhardt 1985: 311; see also Kapp 1886: 489ff.; Goldfriedrich 1980: 149–164, who correctly sees Frankfurt as the major international fair with the greater proportion of Latin books. See also Brübach and Schneider 1994.

67. Vasquez de Prada 1991 (Medina); Clair 1976: 219; Brübach and Schneider 1991 and Pettas 1995: 169 (Lyon); Racine 1991 and Nuovo 2003: 95–98 (Italian fairs). Kapp 1886: 307 records that Vincent Vaugris of Lyon attended fairs in Geneva, Paris, Strasbourg, Frankfurt, and Basel in 1524. There was also a fair at Nördlingen in the early years of the sixteenth century: Dietz 1970: 1.58.

68. Pettegree 2010: 79. The Strasbourg fair was in November. Lorenz Meder's *Handel Buch* of 1558 (lxv ff.) sets the dates out in such a way that it is plausible to see it as a mutually beneficial agreement between the cities involved.

69. Schröder 1904: 4, 12–13.

70. Voet 1969–1972: 2.500–506. Christoph Froschauer of Zürich sold all 2,000 copies of one book he took to Frankfurt (the *Epitome trium terrae partium*) in two successive fairs in 1534: Clair 1976: 221. On Oporinus's experience of the fair, see Steinmann 1967: 50–56.

71. Voet 1969–1972: 508–517 (the fair accounts for 1609).

72. Kapp 1886: 478.

73. Schwetschke 1850–1877: 21–82; Schröder 1904: 16. The Accademia Veneziana of 1558–1559, just prior to the first index of forbidden books to be published in Italy, was founded with the specific ambition to create ties with the German book market through the Frankfurt fair: see Bolzoni 1981.

74. Kapp 1886: 471: from Plantin, Willer received 20–25 percent, Herwagen's heirs received 12.5 percent, Plantin's London agent (Ascanius de Renialme) 40 percent, and his Frankfurt agent (Jean Dressler) 30 percent; the standard rebate was 25 percent. See also Plantin 1883–1918: 8–9: 147–152 (no. 1207, to Jean Dresseler, 5 February 1587); Voet 1969–1972: 2.405; Schröder 1904: 10; Dyroff 1963: 1325–1327 (Vögelin); Wittmann 1999: 64.

75. Gilmont 2010. The early years of the catalogue listed editions of venerable age, such as the 1542 edition of Alciato's *Emblems* published by Wechel in Paris (advertised in the spring catalogue of 1570).

76. Voet 1969–1972: 2.422; Imhof 2008: 357; Bowen and Imhof 2008: 67–84 (Juan de Valverde); Simpson 2009: 44–50.

77. Jean Calvin, *Defensio . . . adversus calumnias Alberti Pighii* (1543), in Opera, ed. Karl Gottlieb Bretschneider (Halle 1839), 6. 404: (a reply to Pighius which is incomplete because of the short time available to Calvin to write it): "alterius vero tractationem ad proximas usque nundinas differendum censui"; Lane 1999: 179–180 (Calvin and Pighus); Maclean 2009: 66. The theologians and Ramists Heizo Busch and Johannes Piscator engaged in a polemic in the 1590s following the rhythm of the book fair. See also Flood 2007: 6–7 on the pressures imposed on publishers by fair deadlines.

78. Sohn 1591–1592: 2.sig.):(4v (Corvinus to the reader); Kirchhoff 1853a: 36 (Casaubon's Polybius).

79. Simpson 2009: 68–72.

80. Gilmont 2005a: 15; Johann Schönberger of Augsburg had branches or depots in Zwickau, Nuremberg, Frankfurt, Linz, Vienna, and Speyer in 1523: Flood 2007: 14.

81. Voet 1969–1971: 1.77, 115, 402–403 (where the "Salamanca branch" is discussed).

82. Evans 1975: 77. Aubry also operated out of Basel, where he was a member of the Safranzunft.

83. Nuovo 2003: 200ff.

84. Kirchhoff 1853b: 50; Kapp 1886: 477.

85. Thülemeyer 1688: 434 (Conrad Rittershausen, 8 January 1611); ibid., 456 (Franciscus Guillimannus, 16 March 1611): "Bibliopolae Oenipontani Francofurtenses nundinas haudquaquam frequentant, Augustanis contenti."

86. Kirchhoff 1853a: 48; Blum 1959: 237.

87. Ibid., 49–50.

88. Voet 1969–1972: 2.292.

89. Pettegree 1994; Claesz 1604 (whose listing under "auctores qui de coena Domini scripsere" includes Catholic, Lutheran, Calvinist, Melanchthonian, and Zwinglian entries), The Cloet bookshop of 1543 also stocked a wide selection of books, but that was less surprising before the deliberations of the Council of Trent: Delsaert 2001.

90. Kapp 1886: 466–467.

91. A copy of this catalogue located in the Escorial Library suggests that it was used by Spanish purchasers: Morisse 2000: 94.

92. Roville 1604; Giunti 1604: sig. 2r: "oramus, ut si quis Auctor aut Titulus, inter legendum in unaquaque scientia occurrerit, quem numquam tua [sci. Alessandro Borgia's] percurrerit indefessa lectio (quod plane incredibile videtur) illum ad te iubeas adduci, omnes enim quotquot sunt ut nostra omnia, tuae amplitudini impense subijci volumus."

93. Borraccini and Rusconi 2006.

94. Kapp 1886: 302, 470; Nuovo 2003: 103ff. states that the wares of the "venditori ambulanti" in Italy were most often in the vernacular.

95. Some examples in Plantin 1883–1918: 7. 204–206 (no. 1043, to Henricus Wittemius, 4 November 1585); Kapp 1886: 471 (Plantin and Moretus); Voet 1969–1972: 2.412. Rees and Wakely 2009: 216ff., 227 point out that John Bill and John Norton were commissioned to buy books on behalf of the Bodleian Library.

96. Banderier 2000; Pinelli and Dupuy 2002: 18–19, 120, 160, 162–163, 175–176, 180, 308–309 (1574–1584).

97. Lepri forthcoming. For the earlier period, the Fondaco dei Tedeschi in Venice was a strong point of contact between German printers and Venice: see Simonsfeld 1887: 2.287–289. Künast 1997: 156 makes the point that few Italians bothered to take their trade to Germany.

98. Nuovo 2003: 260f.; Nuovo and Sandal 1998: 83–91; Kapp 1886: 301 (on the Paris shop of Jean Petit in 1516).

99. See above, 254n27.

100. Garber 1987; Martin 1982b: 388–390.

101. Thülemeyer 1688: 185: (Georg Michael Lingelsheim, May 1607): "Leges veteres Londini editos obtinere non potui, quas vidi apud Freherum." This could be either the *Archionomia, sive de priscis Anglorum legibus libri* of 1568 or George Salteren's *Of the antient laws of great Britain* of 1605.

102. The works in question were *Novellae constitutiones, Libri feudorum, Codicis libri x–xii*, Venice, Jacobus Rubens, 1477 (Goldast 1600–1613: 50r), and *Libri duo iuris civilis Magdeburgensis et privincialis Saxonici cum tertio libro iuris feudalis*, Cracow, Jan Haller, 1506 (ibid., 97v).

103. Gessner 1966 [1545 and 1555], with continuations in 1555, 1574 (by Josias Simler), and 1583 (by Johann Jakob Fries); see Widmann 1966; Constantin 1555.

104. Hornung 1626: 387; Crato and Monavius 1591–1595: 2.234–235, 5.394–399.

105. Maclean 2009: 241; Naudé 2008: 173 (facsimile 84).

106. Nuovo 2003: 179–181. Ibid., 170, and Kirchhoff 1853a: 104 for the remaindering of editions by booksellers to create cash flow. According to Nuovo and Sandal 1998: 75, this practice began in the fifteenth century.

107. Shevchenko 2007: 126ff (the library of Albrecht von Brandenburg); Bowen and Imhof 2008: 180.

108. There are exceptions: Steinmann 1967: 53 records that Oporinus send bound books to the Frankfurt book fair.

109. Nuovo 2003: 124ff; Nuovo and Sandal 1998: 86; Pallmann 1881: 75.

110. Purcell 1999: 142–143; Leedham-Green 1986.
111. One such example is Helmstedt: see Nelles 2001.
112. Welti 1985: 35.
113. Gilly 2001: 21–24.
114. Nuovo 2005; Stevens 2005.
115. Naudé 2008: 229 ff. (facsimile 108ff.).
116. Künast 1997: 166; Lehmann 1956–1960; Naudé 2008: 223f. (facsimile 105f.).
117. Bepler 2001.
118. Van Selm 1986.
119. Lowry 1979: 14–15.
120. Nuovo 2003: 165–176.
121. In the declaration of this book in the Frankfurt book fair catalogue of autumn 1586, the bibliographical address is given simply as "Lugduni."
122. Zabarella 1586–1587: 1.sig.)(3r: "non esse verendum, ne Meietus typographus de hac editione, quae non lucri, sed publici boni causa instituta est, conquereretur; novi eius mores et probitatem, potius putabit se a Mareschallo adiutum in tua praeclara doctrina disseminanda: ipse enim poterit in Italia et vicinis locis exemplaria distrahere, nec moleste fieret, quod alia in Germania vendantur, quo paucissima ab ipso edita perveniunt." The *Tabulae logicae* of 1589 published by Meietti in Venice have the same pagination, but they are not a reissue.
123. Nuovo 2003: 227 argues that Italy depended on imports from and exports to northern Europe, but that the bookselling systems in place prevented this happening efficiently. On Venice's links to Frankfurt and Paris, see Lepri 2008.
124. van Roomen and Bockstaele 1976: 103.
125. Bologna, Bibliotheca Universitaria, Fondo Aldrovandi, MS 38 ii–iii, f. 11 r: Fenari to Aldrovandi, 8 December 1571; http://disc.leidenuniv.nl, Clusius Correspondence VUL 101: Pieter Garret to Carolus Clusius, 9 December 1591 (asking for a Spanish edition of Nicolás Monardes's *Historia medicinal* (presumably the Seville edition of either 1574 or 1580). I am grateful to Valentina Pugliano for these references. Clusius was one of the few scholars to have an account with the Plantin presses at the Frankfurt book fair: see MPM Archive 964: 80r (September 1587).
126. Osler, Campanella and Viola 2006 (on Teramo); Osler 2005 (on the Biblioteca di Scienze Sociali, University of Florence); Sbordone 2006 (on the Biblioteca dei Caracciolini in Naples). But Starp 1958: 51 shows the Societas Veneta to be the best client of Schönwetter in 1604–1605. For the ownership of legal books, see Aquilon 1988 (Angevin private libraries 1586–1592) and Mantese 1968 (a Vicenza library of 1608).
127. Borraccini and Rusconi 2006.
128. Voet 1969–1972: 2.397–402; Guilleminot-Chrétien 2008, 2009.
129. This appears to be the case even in Toulouse, where booksellers were the clearing house for distributing books to the southwest, and where Lyon

books dominate the market: Nelles forthcoming a; Pettegree 2010: 87 deduces from the fact that Fernando Colón bought his Paris books outside France that they circulated freely in Europe up to 1540; but it might also be inferred that the distribution was inefficient even inside France, as it was successful enough not to have to bother with external sales. A recent study of a library in Bourges in 1568 shows that Parisian books are well represented: Le Clech-Charton 1996.

130. E.g., Rondelet's *Methodus curandorum morborum,* which first appeared in Paris in an unauthorised edition of 1562, but enjoyed simultaneous editions in Paris and Lyon in 1575.

131. The works in question are the *De dosibus* (Venice 1562, Padua 1566) and the *De ponderibus* (Antwerp, 1561, Padua 1563).

132. On Valgrisi's activities in transmitting French books to Italy, see Baudrier and Baudrier 1964–1965: 10.457–464; Rinaldi 2009: 36, 40–46. The works of Rondelet include his *De ponderibus* and *De dosibus.*

133. Bodley 1926: 53, 57, 178 (1602–1608) records John Bill's purchases for Sir Thomas Bodley in Paris; he also went to Italy, Spain, and Lyon in this period. It seems as if most of the later Parisian purchases for the library came through London and the Latin stock of the Stationers' Company, and possibly Henry Featherstone of London (after 1620–1621), who preferred to obtain such books in Paris than through Frankfurt: Roberts 1997 and 2000. Evidence *ex nihilo* is always difficult to evaluate, but it is striking that John Foster's inventory of books at York in 1616 contains very few books from Paris or Lyon: Barnard and Bell 1994.

134. Maclean 2009: 288; Gilly 1985: 263; Pantin 1988: 243.

135. Imhof 2008: 348–355.

136. There has been no separate study of the activities of the printer Esaias Mechler, who in the space of less than a decade reprinted such European authors as Levinus Lemnius, Joannes Olearius, Nicodemus Frischlin, Emilio Ferretti, and Fredericus Beurhaus.

137. Desgraves 2000 (on Bordeaux and Toulouse). See Nelles forthcoming a on the contract for Foix's Pimander, which distinguishes between local sales and regional sales.

138. Tübingen University Library shows, however, that a policy of obtaining the best editions from all European printing centres was in force: see Brinkhus 1985. On Lyon's success in Naples, see Sbordone 2006. On Filippo Tinghi of Lyon's outlets, see Maclean 2009: 229. See also Morisse 2000.

139. Serrai 1993: 34; Ciotti 1602. The latter catalogue was sent to the Duke of Urbino for him or his librarian to mark up with crosses for desiderata. The list contains two purportedly London publications: "Biblioteca Collegii Osonii" (i.e., Thomas James's *Ecloga Oxonio-Cantabrigiensis,* 1600) and "Diarium nauticum in 4 Londini." This latter is either Edward Wright's *Certain errors in navigation [with] the Voyage of the right Ho[n]. George Earle of Cumberl[and] to the Azores* of 1599 or Gerrit de Veer's *Diarium nauticum,* printed in Arnhem and Amsterdam in 1598, of which Ciotti himself published

a translation in 1599 in a *Sammelband* entitled *Tre navigationi fatte dagli Olandesi e Zelandesi al Settentrione della Norvegia, Moscovia e Tartaria* [. . .]. The catalogue also contains some early material (e.g., Edward Wotton's *De differentiis animalium* of 1552), twenty-two books in Spanish (four attributed to Salamanca as a place of publication), and a 24mo Plantin Bible. On the Spanish elements in the catalogue, see Rhodes 2011.This is not to say that protestant theology failed to reach Italy: on clandestine importation, see Grendler 1978, 1980; Woodward 1996: 67.

140. Quoted by Kirchhoff 1853a: 95: [Chiocci] "quanquam existimo Typographi et Bibliopolas Italos potius nostram expectationem fallere"; [Macei]: "sed defuit mittendi facultas [. . .] isti enim bibliopolae ex propria consuetudine multa pollicentur, sed nihil unquam faciunt."

141. Nuovo 2003: 226–267

142. Maclean 2009: 180.

143. Maclean 2009: 250; a sample survey for the years 1600–1620, and for one Genevan printer, Samuel Crespin, in the Catálogo Colectivo of Spanish Libraries at http://www.mcu.es/patrimonio bibliografico revealed that there were 43 relevant entries, of which 34 either did not state a place of publication, or used designations for Geneva which did not fall foul of the Inquisition (Aureliae Allobrogum and Coloniae Allobrogum). See also Föhl and Berger 1986: 458–462, 467, with examples from the Catholic Stiftsbibliothek in Xanten of the same practice relating to Geneva and Heidelberg imprints, including Gruter's edition of Seneca by Commelinus of 1604, and Freher's edition of the Alemannic creed by Vögelin of 1609.

144. Sardello 1948: 57 points out that the traveling time from Venice to Augsburg was no more than twelve days. Flood 2007: 23 records the declarations of Ciotti at the Frankfurt fair between 1599 and 1605: the most successful years were 1600–1602.

145. Nuovo and Sandal 1998.

146. MPM Archive 964, f. 49v–50r.

147. See Maclean 2009: 291–370 for a fuller account.

148. Barker 1985: 262.

149. On Norton, Bill, and the English trade, see Rees and Wakely 2009. Graham Rees kindly sent me the following note about Bill's involvement with Frankfurt and the Officina Plantiniana: "When John Norton died, Bill took sole charge of the continental dealings on behalf of his partnership with Bonham Norton. And in the Plantiniana records and Frankfurt catalogues he appears to be by far the most important Englishman involved in the Latin trade. In 1617 he started publishing his own versions of the official Frankfurt catalogues, and continued to do so until 1621/2 when, in order to pay off debts to Bonham Norton, he sold his stock of Latin-trade books to the Stationers' Company for its ultimately unsuccessful Latin Stock. The book trade evidently abhors a vacuum: in the years when Bill was not producing catalogues (mid-1621 to spring 1628) and/or not dealing with the Plantini-

ana (mid-1622 to spring 1629), others rushed in to take his place. As one might expect, the Stationers' Company did business with the Plantiniana at the Frankfurt fairs of autumn 1621, and spring 1622. But then we hear nothing at all about the Company until autumn 1626 when we find a page of the *Cahier* documenting sales to 'Compag. Anglicane Simon Waterson'. For a number of years Waterson and Clement Knight seem to have been acting as Stationers' Company Agents at the fair. The Stationers' Company's unsuccessful Latin Stock was not real heir to John Bill during the years of his retreat from Antwerp and Frankfurt. His real heir was the enterprising erstwhile apprentice of Bonham Norton, Henry Featherstone. Featherstone did his first deal with the Plantiniana in the autumn of 1621; a second was concluded in the spring of 1622, and there were a further ten visits before Bill resumed his connection with Antwerp and Frankfurt in 1629. When the Stationers' Company's Latin Stock was wound up, Bill bought back a lot of the stock he had sold to it, produced another catalogue (spring, 1628), and had further dealings with the Plantiniana (spring, 1629). Bill's re-emergence was brief. He died in 1630."

150. See Rees and Wakely 2009; and Plantin-Moretus Archive 189 "Germani et Basilienses et Hispani", f. 69r–v. I am grateful to John Barnard for drawing my attention to this document.

151. MPM Archive 189 f. 69r–v and 1012 f. 23; Voet 1969–1972: 2.443; Kapp 1886: 471, who points out that Ascanius benefited from very favourable discount rates; Rees and Wakely 2009: 219–233.

152. Roberts 1997; Rees and Wakely 2009: 41–44, 178ff, 190ff.

153. Voet 1969–1972: 2.379–438.

154. Cardano 2004: 333 (*De libris propriis,* 1562): "itaque mihi sane satis felix esse visus sum, tametsi paupertate tanta premerer quandoque, ut emptis libris nec obolus superesset, multique maledicerent, plures etiam contemnerent."

155. E.g., Thülemeyer 1688: 194 (Marcus Welser, 21 September 1607).

156. E.g., Plantin 1883–1918: 1.47–48 (no. 19, 26 December 1565); Voet 1969–1972: 291.

157. Maclean 2009: 92–93; Hotson forthcoming.

158. Naudé 2008: 241–242 (facsimile 114–115) is particularly scathing about a "certain King of France" in this regard.

159. Pesenti 2000: 75.

160. Pettegree 2010: 87–88. John Dee and Belisario Bulgarini of Siena are later examples of private collectors with similarly extensive libraries: see Roberts and Watson 1990; Rhodes 1967; and Danesi 2008. Among the largest collections held by territorial rulers are the Bibliotheca Palatina at Heidelberg and the library of Francesco Maria II della Rovere, Duke of Urbino, on which see Mittler 1999 and Boutcher 2011. The Ambrosiana Library in Milan, founded by Federico Borromeo in 1607, is another very extensive collection: see Jones 1993 and Buzzi and Ferro 2005. The Escorial (1563–1584),

the Vatican Library under Sixtus V (1587–1589), and the Bodleian Library, Oxford, were three other ambitious library projects of this period. On French libraries, see Jolly 1988; on British Libraries, see Leedham-Green and Webber 2006. These and other libraries are discussed by Naudé 2008: 319–321 (facsimile 153–154).

161. Mandelbrote 2008.

162. Lehmann 1956–1960. From the inventory of books he sold to the ruler of the Palatinate in 1569, it can be seen that Ulrich Fugger purchased multiple copies of certain genres, including herbals, which can most easily be explained as a speculative investment.

163. Luther, *An die Ratsherrn aller Städte Deutschlands: dass sie Christliche Schulen aufrichten und hallten sollen* (1524), in *Werke*, (Weimar, 1906–1961), 15: 9–53; Wendland 1985; von Schade 1985: 150–151.

164. Beaujean 1985.

165. Germann 1985.

166. Eisenstein 1979: 97.

167. Nelles 2010.

168. Mattaire 1725: 3.147–497.

169. Thülemeyer 1688: 424 (17 October 1610); 433 (8 January 1611).

170. Fichard and Rutilus1539: preface. Goldast 1600–1613: 21v (17 April 1606) knew of the holdings of the library in Vienna.

171. Evidence cited in Kirchhoff 1853a: 31 (Alfonso Ciaconi's letter from Rome to Paulus Manutius): "Antonius Gomezius Lusitanus [. . .] te meo nomine salutavit, plurimumque a te contendit, ut duos indiculos librorum, qui nundinis Francofurdensibus autumnalibus anni 1579 et vernalibus anni 1581 venales exponi solent, mihi impartiri velles."

172. Bassée 1592; Grosse 1600; Clessius 1602.

173. In Oxford alone, a copy of Draut now in the library of the Queen's College was annotated by Thomas Barlow, Bishop of Lincoln, who was associated with the Bodleian Library for a period after 1652, and another interleaved and copiously annotated copy was bequeathed to Wadham College by a former undergraduate Philip Stubbs: see Birrell 2001: 60.

174. Draut 1625a: 1045–1046.

175. Schenck 1609: 88

176. Sixtus Senensis 1575 (further editions in 1575 [Frankfurt: Nicolas Bassée], 1576, 1586 [Cologne: Maternus Cholinus], and 1610 [Paris: Rolin Theodoricus]); Possevino 1593, 1597, 1603–1606 (further editions in 1608 [Cologne: Johannes Gymnich] and 1609 [Ferrara: Vittorio Baldini 'typographus episcopalis']).

177. The model of this is Galen, *De ordine librorum suorum,* first printed in Greek in 1525 in the Venice edition of his works; Johann Fichard produced a Latin translation of the work in 1531 for the edition of Galen's works published in Basel by Andreas Cratander.

178. Nuovo 2007; Maclean 2009: 428.

179. Naudé 2008: 237–242 (facsimile 112–115).
180. Ibid., 243 (facsimile 115): "j'adjoute qu'il serait aussi besoin de savoir des parents et héritiers de beaucoup de galants hommes s'ils n'ont pas laissé quelques manuscrits desquels il se veulent défaire, parce qu'il arrive souvent, que la plupart d'iceux ne font pas imprimer la moitié de leurs oeuvres, soit qu'ils soient prévenus par la mort ou empêchés de ce faire, par la dépense, l'appréhension des diverses censures et jugements, la crainte de n'avoir pas bien rencontré, la liberté de leurs discours, le peu d'envie de paraître, et autres raisons semblables."
181. Naudé 2008: 89 (facsimile 38).
182. Naudé is often heralded as the pioneer of open access libraries, but he does in fact recommend that the Librarian should act as a gatekeeper of contentious material, and effectively restrict access to it in various ways: Naudé 2008: 291–293 (facsimile 139–140).
183. Nuovo 2007.
184. Pinelli and Du Puy 2001: 51 (19 July 1572).
185. See above, note 125 (Fenari and Clusius).
186. Pettas 1995: 1–21 discusses inventory of 15,827 volumes in the bookshop of Juan de Junta of Burgos drawn up in the 1550s; he refers also to the Cromberger bookstock of 1529 in Seville, and the Juan de Ayala inventory of 1556 in Toledo.
187. Morisse 2000: 91; Truman 2004, 2009.
188. Grendler 1977, 1978, 1980.
189. Kirchhoff 1853a: 51–52 gives an example of letters traveling between Frankfurt and Leipzig in 1592 in a week.
190. See above, note 124.
191. Arbenz 1894: 248 (no. 169, 24 September 1519). On the related topic of a sense of exclusion felt in Spain from the latest humanist medicine, see Oroscius 1540: aa 5–7. I am grateful to Vivian Nutton for both of these references.
192. Stevenson 1966–1969: 1.16ff. (the relevant books are all marked as "APG").
193. It is worthy of note that provincial France (Bourges) was considered by Andrea Alciato in 1530 as a better place for the sustaining international communications than northern Italy: Maclean forthcoming.

7. The Rise and Fall of the Learned Book Market, 1560–1630

1. MPM Archive 89 f. 411: "Charissime frater, nundinas flaccessere coram experior et timidos emptores. Breviaria pauca in f° petunt, ob Veneta aut Kerbergi quae vilia habent; cum tempore haec magis innotescent et expetentur, uti Lipsiana Opera, quorum ut plerique per partes olim habuere, solum titulum plures eam quam opera integra expetunt; et licet nulla hic prostent Lugdunensia, alibi tamen necessario latent, vel praeteritis nundinis fuere qui ea ementes, inter caetera G. Willerus et alii nullum e nostris sumunt: ferendo vincendum [...] Antonium Hierat de Annalium numero quem

haberet conveni, sexcenta adhuc integra supersunt et recusis 9° 10° 11° 12° facile adhuc bis centum perficiet."

2. Voet 1969–1972: 267, 412, 472, 483; Imhof 2008: 267, 315–338, 477.

3. The edition was protected with a French royal privilege dated 22 October 1611, and carried a number of approbations, including one lifted from a Moretus edition of Lipsius's life by Aubert Miraeus. Moretus had protected his Lipsius publications with Lipsius's own French privilege in 1605; that had lapsed with the death of the author: see Imhof 2008: 361.

4. See above, note 0.

5. Imhof 2008: 348–355 gives a very full account, including the complex issue of Moretus's privileges.

6. MPM Archive 89 f. 411: "Pro multitudine librorum allatorum minorem prospicio venditionem, parem mutationem et emptionem [instituere?] nolo. hic sequentes nundinas expectent, quam inaequali permutatione vilipend-ere, et de plerisque nobis satis prospectum domi: ita ut parata emere multi-tudinem librorum haud necessarium putem."

7. MPM Archive 89 f. 413: "Catalogi 10 exemplaria mitto editionis Franco-furdensis, Moguntinis, qui catolicorum, [libros] nostros non inserunt vel pauciores tantum [. . .] Nundinae lente procedunt [. . .] frigida distribu-tio Breviarii f[olio] et Lipsii operum, emptor[es] hebebunt ubi magis innotescent."

8. Imhof 2008: 355; see also Heitjan 1974.

9. MPM Archive 89 f. 415; "videbo num quid cum Mylio de Promptuario in reditum transigam, non enim differet vendere, et studebit quantum pot-erit correctissime nostrum noc novum exemplar sequuturus, et si pretio solito foreni hic vendat vix nostra hic petentur"; see also Imhof 2008: 439f.

10. MPM Archive 89 f 491–492; Pallmann 1881: 195ff (on Willers' purchase of the Feyerabend presses in 1600). There is reference also to the Willers' absence from the fair in April 1614, suggesting that they too were finding sales difficult.

11. MPM Archive 490, f. 10–11.

12. Imhof 2008: 124 records the cost of the 4to edition of 1593–1594 as 18 stuivers and that of 1595 in octavo as 11 stuivers.

13. Voet 1969–1972: 2.406–408; cf. Imhof 2008: 76–79, 103–104 (declining editions of classical authors), 113–114 (decline in Greek publications).

14. MPM Archive 89 f. 143r: "Catalogi 10 exemplaria mitto editionis Franco-furdensis, Moguntinis, qui catolicorum, [libros] nostros non inserunt vel pauciores tantum."

15. Imhof 2008: 280.

16. Voet 1969–1972: 2.417–419.

17. Voet 1969–1972: 406.

18. Balthasar Moretus to Erycius Puteanus February 1623, quoted by Imhof 2001: 187.

19. Voet 1969–1972: 1.209–210.

20. Ibid., 1.213.
21. Kapp 1886: 508.
22. Cohn 1985.
23. MPM Archive 89: 391–392.
24. Febvre and Martin 1958: 233ff., 331ff.
25. Schwetschke 1850–1877.
26. Dietz 1970: 3.70.
27. Ibid.; Kirchhoff 1853a: 129–130 shows the yearly declarations of two Cologne houses: Mylius (1586–1605) and Birckmann (1606–1633), which broadly confirm Dietz's figures. It would now be possible with the help of vd. 16/17 to provide the same (probably more complete) figures for many German printing houses.
28. Infelise 1996.
29. Schnapper 1995: 87–99 on the disruptions in Lorraine and the Franco-Spanish war. Febvre and Martin 1958: 329; Jacob 1646: sig. i2r (the claim that more books were published in Paris alone than in the whole of Germany in any one year).
30. Dietz 1970 4. 2ff. ("Pest und Hungerjahre 1632–7"); Weidhaas 2003: 60.
31. Dietz 1970: 3.71.
32. Flood 2007: 25–26.
33. Meyn 1980: 134, 143–149, 201–210. The city council did not help to stimulate the foreign book trade by insisting in 1621 on the delivery of two *Pflichtexemplare* to the Ratsbibliothek: Dietz 1970: 3.70.
34. Gieseke 2006.
35. On these figures, see Dietz 1970: 3, 36, 75ff; Starp 1958; Könnecke 1894; Reske 2007, *sub nominibus.*
36. For a case history, see Maclean 2009 227–250.
37. Brauer 1974: 38
38. Goldfriedrich 1908: 153–155; Schröder 1904: 17 (arguing that Leipzig was no more important a book market than Augsburg, Nuremberg, Strasbourg, and Wittenberg in the sixteenth century); Dietz 1970: 3.72 (reporting that in the decade 1610–1619, Leipzig printed 2,296 books to Frankfurt's 1,799); Wittmann 1999: 68.
39. Schröder 1904: 40–48.
40. Kapp 1886: appendix.
41. Two examples are the reissue by Johannes Pressius (the purchaser of the Wechel presses) in 1643 and 1646 of the *Adagia* of Erasmus, first printed in 1617; and by Eberhard Zetzner of various works by Jacopo Zabarella first printed in 1619–1623 in 1654, on which see Maclean 2009: 58. Cf. also the application in 1624 for an Imperial privilege to protect the new edition of Jean Bodin's *De republica* by the widow of Jonas Rosa; it did not appear until 1641.
42. Schröder 1904: 28.
43. Infelise 1996.
44. Wilding forthcoming; Rhodes forthcoming.

45. Nuovo and Sandal 1998: 95ff.; Nuovo 2003: 203ff. (arguing that Counter-Reformation liturgical printing compensated for the loss of northern European trade after 1550).
46. Eisenstein 1979: 415.
47. On Manutius's crisis in the period 1568–1573, see Nuovo 2003: 203.
48. Nuovo and Sandal 1998: 96 argue that the "paese cattolici si trovarono esclusi e private di un grandissimo numero di contribute erudite scientifiche letterati di primo ordine"; see also Kirchhoff 1853a: 64 (on the severe punishments meted out to Italian booksellers for possessing forbidden books after the introduction of the Roman Index).
49. See Maclean 2009: 274 (on trade practices) and 239–250 (on warehouse stocks and their disposal).
50. Lignereux 2003: 85–89.
51. The list of their publications includes folio editions both contemporary or recently dead authors (Johann Fabry von Hilden, Daniel Sennert, Kaspar Hoffmann, Georg Schenck von Grafenberg, Zacutus Lusitanus, Johann Heinrich Alsted, Galileo Galilei), those of previous generations (Cardano, Barthélémy de Chasseneux), and medieval theologians (Albert the Great, Bernard of Clairvaux).
52. Barbiche, 1982: 367–345.
53. Martin 1999: 40–44.
54. Maclean 2009: 417–421.
55. I am referring to such figures as Thomas Guarin (d. 1592), the presses of Nicolaus Brylinger (last printing in 1600), Conrad von Waldkirch (d. 1616), and Sebastian Henricpetri (bankrupt in 1626). For Geneva, see Dubois 2008: 57 (Jacques Stoer, d. 1609); also Eustache Vignon (d. 1588) and Simon Goulart (d. 1628).
56. Dubois 2008: 70.
57. Gadd 1999: 68.
58. Rees and Wakely 2009: 179.
59. Lowry 1979: 13–14; Pettegree 2010: 42.
60. Steinmann 1967: 88ff.
61. See Maclean 2009: 280; and above, pages 104 and 118.
62. See, e.g., Kellenbenz 1976: 75–88, 124–125; de Vries 1976; van Zanden 2001; Buringh and van Zanden 2009, who set out to explain the growth in book production in the whole period of the Middle Ages and early modern times.
63. Dietz 1970: 1.63, 3.71; Kapp 1886: 316.
64. Mellot 1996.
65. Ogilvie 1992 (who sees economic decline in Italy in the 1580s, in Germany and Austria in the 1620s, and in France and the Baltic in the 1650s); Martin 1987: 44–45, who associates the crisis with market saturation and the failure to maintain sales of Counter-Reformation literature.
66. Gould 1954; Bepler 2001: 963 (on the effect of inflation on book selling).
67. Schneider 1990; Kindleberger 1991; Roth 1993; Rosseaux 2001.

68. For example, between 1550 and 1593, there were six editions of the Corpus Juris Civilis published in Lyon, and one in Geneva; between 1598 and 1621, there were a further five published in Lyon, and four in Geneva. The last edition of the Tremellius Bible appeared in 1622–1624; of Galen's complete works in Latin, in 1625; of the Corpus Juris Civilis, in 1628. See also Deutscher 2002, for evidence of market demand stimulated by seminaries.

69. Hotson forthcoming records the distressing stories of the crude destruction of "heretical books" by the occupying forces in the period 1620–1622.

70. See Ong 1958: no. 345; Beurhaus 1596; Hotson 2007: 101–126; Hotson forthcoming.

71. Maclean forthcoming a. It does not seem to be the case that Lutheran textbook publication suffered the same decline, at least before 1630, if the very buoyant production figures for Wittenberg, Tübingen, and Jena are a true reflection of the state of affairs. Kopf was Nicolas Bassée's son-in-law and heir: on his father-in-law. See also Dietz 1970: 3.82–83. Stintzing 1880: 527–532 identifies the period 1570–1630 as the high point of the production in Germany of consilia and other Latin legal texts.

72. Platter 1964: 105–111; Steinmann 1967: 104 (on Oporinus and debt).

73. See Iggers 1990; Kirchhoff 1853a; von Hase 1885; Kapp 1886; Goldfriedrich 1908; 1853 Dietz 1970 (first published 1910–1925).

74. Jesuits were hated as much by certain Catholics as by protestants: see Garber 2003; Whaley forthcoming, citing the case of Kaspar Schoppe; Kapp 1886: 485, 509; Schröder 1904: 18ff.; Brückner 1961. Dietz 1970: 3.63–64 believes that the deleterious effect of the Book Commission has been exaggerated. For a contemporary attack on Jesuits in the wake of the assassination of Henri IV in Paris, see *Von den Jesuiten wider König und Fürstliche-Personen Abschewliche/ Hochgeführliche Pratiken/Anschlägen/ und Thaten: Etliche schöne herrliche Politische une Historische Tractätlein [. . .] in Frantzösisch und Teutsch beschrieben/ und jetzund alles in Hochteutsch ubersetzt*, printed in 1611 by Goldast's publisher contact in Hanau, Thomas de Villiers.

75. Kapp 1886: 608–654.

76. Burke 2004.

77. Kapp 1886: 500, who records that in bartering, the Dutch publishers wanted to exchange one sheet for three or four (at a somewhat later date).

78. de Vries and van der Woude 1997: 131. The Dutch also objected (as did the Venetians) in 1608 to the delivery of Pflichtexemplare: Dietz 1970: 3.70. A possible factor is the collapse of the Italian banking system (seen clearly in the fate of Piacenza after 1608) and the rise of the Amsterdam and London banks: Racine 1991.

79. Dubois 2007 (chapter 6, on Jacob Stoer as inspector of paper in Geneva).

80. Quoted by Kapp 1886: 500: "charta nigra, bibula, sordida, flaccida [. . .] atramentum sutorum infiguratum, maculosum: typus et impressio neglectissima."

81. Evans 1975: 5; Evans 1985: 266.

82. Attestation of the falling off of production by the end of the Thirty Years' War comes from Louis Jacob, *Catalogus omnium librorum per universum Regnum Galliae 1643. 1644 et 6145 excusorum* (Paris: Rolet Le Duc, 1646), sig. i2r, where the French bibliographer claims that more books were published in Paris alone that in the whole of Germany in one year.

83. Könnecke 1894: 156f: "gänzlich verarmt und ruiniert."

84. Though even Catholic centres such as Dillingen and Lauingen encountered severe problems if not collapse in the period 1610–1620: see Gier 2008: 163.

85. Fischart 1993 [1597].

86. *Religio medici*, §24, quoted by Eisenstein 1979: 18.

87. Montaigne 1992: 1045 (3.13). The high number of commentaries on Cicero's speeches alone led to the production of a bibliography of such works: Johannes Baptista Helius, *Bibliotheca commentariorum in Orationes Ciceronis* (Basel: Episcopius Press, 1594).

8. Postscript: Then and Now

1. Eisenstein 1979: 229ff.

2. Martin, Chartier, and Vivet 1982: 228–229: "entrepreneurs et savants tous ensemble, leurs ateliers sont de véritables foyers de l'échange culturel et social entre auteurs de passage, correcteurs d'épreuves et artisans du livre."

3. Fremmer 2001: 25 refers to this ability as "Abstraktionsvermögen."

4. Ibid., 24; Montaigne 1992: 241A (1.39).

5. For this adaptation of Jakobson's model, see Scholar 2006: 5–6.

6. The following account is taken from Maclean 1993.

7. Thompson 2005: 6–7.

8. Waters 2004.

9. Darnton 2009.

10. Schiffrin 2000.

11. Epstein 2001; *Philologicarum epistolarum centuria* 1674: 299–318 (nos. 72–77).

12. Anderson 2004.

13. Thompson 2005: 118–125.

14. Ibid.: 419ff.

15. Love 1993; Maclean 2009: 414–417.

16. Gomez 2008: 187ff.; Darnton 2009: xvi; Thompson 2005: 24–26.

17. Thompson 2005: 26–28.

18. Ibid., 195ff.

19. Gomez 2008: 39.

20. Darnton 2009: 63ff.

21. Thompson 2005: 330ff.

22. Ibid.; Darnton 2009: 29; most recently, Robert Darnton's article on the legal struggles over copyright and access in the *New York Review of Books*, April 28–May 11, 2011, pp. 10–12.

23. Nussbaum 2010.
24. Shevchenko 2007.
25. Manardo 1540: a2–3; "reipublicae literariae mystas [. . .] viri qui nostra hac aetate et studiorum nomine et vitae commendatione in repub. literaria prae caeteris clari haberentur."
26. Charlton 2009.

Bibliography

a. Manuscripts

Goldast 1600–1613: Bayerische Staatsbibliothek [BSB] Clm 10389: Melchioris Haiminsfeldii Goldasti epistolae (86 numero) ad Marquardum Freherum.

HHStA: Haus, Hof-, und Staatsarchiv, Vienna: Impressoria. For details of the contents of this archive, see Koppitz 2008.

MPM: Plantin Moretus Museum, Archive. For details of the contents of this archive, see Denucé 1926 and Coppens 1998–1999.

b. Books before 1801; and Editions of Authors Writing before 1801

Alciato, Andrea. 1536. *Les Emblemes*. Paris: Chrétien Wechel.

———. 1953. *Le Lettere*. Edited by Gian Luigi Barni. Florence: Le Monnier.

Amerbach, Boniface. 1973. *Die Amerbachkorrespondenz*, Vol. 7. Edited by Alfred Hartmann and Beat Rudolf Jenny. Basel: Universitätsbibliothek.

Andrewes, John. 1614. *Christ his Crosse*. Oxford: Joseph Barnes.

Antonio, Nicolás, Rafael Casalbón y Geli, Juan Antonio Pellécer y Pilares, and Tomás Sánchez. 1783–1788. *Bibliotheca hispana nova*. Madrid: Heirs of Joachin de Ibarra.

———. 1788. *Bibliotheca hispana vetus*. 2 vols. Madrid: Widow and Heirs of Joachimus de Ibarra.

Arbenz, Emil. 1894. Die Vadianische Briefsammlung, II. *Mitteilungen zur väterlandische Geschichte* 25.2: 193–486.

Baillet, Adrien. 1723. *Jugemens des savants sur les principaux ouvrages des auteurs*. Vol. 1. Edited by Bernard de la Monnoye. Paris: Charles Moette et al.

Bassée, Nicolas. 1592. *Collectio in unum corpus omnium librorum Hebraeorum, Graecorum, Latinorum nec non Germanice, Italice, Gallice et Hispanice scriptorum, qui in nundinis Francofurtensibus ab anno 1564 usque ad nundinas autumnales anni 1592 partim novi, partim nova forma, et diversis in locis editi, venales extiterunt: desumpta ex omnibus Catalogis Willerianis singularum nundinarum* [. . .] *meliori ratione quam hactenus disposita.* 3 vols. Frankfurt: Nicolas Bassée.

Beurhaus, Friedrich. 1596. *Ad P. Rami Dialecticae praxin generalis introductio.* Cologne: Gosvinus Cholinus.

Blackstone, William. 1977. *Commentaries on the laws of England.* 2 vols. Oxford: Clarendon Press.

Bodley, Sir Thomas. 1926. *Letters to Thomas James,* ed. G. W. Wheeler. Oxford: Clarendon Press.

Bruno, Giordano. 1591. *De triplici minimo* [. . .]. Frankfurt am Main: Johann Wechel.

Cardano, Girolamo. 2004. *De libris propriis,* ed. Ian Maclean Milan: FrancoAngeli.

Catalogus authorum. 1578. *Catalogus authorum qui in Sacros Biblicos Libros Veteris et Novi Testamenti iam iterum, post G. Theophili Itali aeditionem, ex variis Bibliothecis collectus, et plus quadringentis Authoribus, recentioribus maxime, auctus.* Wittenberg: Clemens Schleich and Anton Schöne.

Champier, Symphorien. 1506. *Libelli duo . . . Primus de medicine claris scriptoribus* [. . .]. Lyon: J. de Campis.

Ciotti, Giovanni Battista. 1602. *Catalogus eorum librorum omnium, qui in ultramontanis regionibus impressi apud Io. Baptistam Ciottum prostant.* Venice: Giovanni Battista Ciotti.

Claesz, Cornelis. 1604. *Catalogus librorum, qui apud Cornelium Nicolai venales reperiuntur, quorum partem Francofurti, partem aliis locis advehi curavit, et quotidie ex diversis regionibus accessere jubet, praeter innumera alia variarum editionum volumina, in hoc elencho non comprehensa* [. . .] *sunt et nobis alii, cuiuscunque facultatis compacti, quorum cum sit ingens multitudo, nec nomen, nec numerum his adiungere quivimus.* Amsterdam: Cornelis Claesz.

Clessius, Joannes 1602. *Unius seculi: eiusque virorum literatorum monumentis tum florentissimi tum fertilissimi: ab anno* [. . .] *1500 ad 1602 nundinarum autumnalium inclusive elenchus consummatissimus librorum : Hebraei, Graeci, Latini, Germani, aliorumque Europae idiomatum, typorum aeternitati consecratorum, quo quicquid in rebus divinis et humanis a magni nominis theologis, jureconsultis, medicis, philosophis, historicis, etc. literis demandatum est, commodissima methodo deprehendere licet* [. . .] *elenchus* [. . .] *librorum.* Frankfurt: Joannes Saur for Peter Kopf.

Constantin, Robert. 1555. *Nomenclator insignium scriptorium quorum libri extant vel manuscript vel impressi ex bibliothecis Galliae et Angliae.* Paris: André Wechel.

Coustau, Pierre 1555. *Pegma, cum narrationibus philosophicis.* Lyon: Macé Bonhomme.

———. 1560. *Le Pegme, avec les narrations philosophiques.* Lyon: Macé Bonhomme.

Crato von Krafftheim, Johann, and Petrus Monavius. 1591–1595. *Consilia et epistolae medicinales.* 5 vols. Frankfurt am Main: Wechel Presses.

da Vinci, Leonardo. 1651. *Trattato della pittura di, nuovamente dato in luce, con la vita dell'istesso autore, scritta da Rafaelle du Fresne. Si sono giunti i tre libri della pittura, ed il trattato della statua di Leon Battista Alberti con la vita del medesimo.* Paris: Langlois.

De Thou, Jacques-Auguste. 1609. *Historiarum sui temporis libri cxxv.* Paris: Jerôme Drouart.

Dodoens, Rembert. 1581. *Medicinalium observationum exempla rara.* Cologne: Maternus Cholinus.

Draut, Georg. 1625a. *Bibliotheca classica.* Frankfurt am Main: Balthasar Ostern.

———. 1625b. *Bibliotheca classica Germanica.* Frankfurt am Main: Balthasar Ostern.

———. 1625c. *Bibliotheca exotica.* Frankfurt am Main: Balthasar Ostern.

du Verdier, Antoine. 1585. *La Bibliotheque, contenant le catalogue de tous ceux qui ont escrit, ou traduict en françois.* Lyon: Jean d'Ogerolles and Barthelemy Honorat.

Eck, Johannes and Vinzenz Pfnür, ed. Online. *Briefwechsel.* At http://ivv7srv15 .uni-muenster.de/mnkg/pfnuer/Eck-Briefe.html.

Eisengrein, Wilhelm. 1565. *Catalogus testium veritatis locupletissimus, omnium orthodoxae Matris Eccelsiae Doctorum extantium et non extantium, publicatorum et in Bibliothecis latentium.* Dillingen: Sebald Mayer.

Erasmus, Desiderius. 1523. *Catalogus omnium lucubrationum.* Basel: Johannes Froben.

———. 1537. *Catalogi duo operum ab ipso conscripti et digesti.* Basel and Antwerp: Johannes Froben and Nicolaus Episcopius.

———. 1906–1947. *Opus epistolarum.* 12 vols. Edited by P. S. Allen. Oxford: Clarendon Press.

———. 1933. *Opuscula.* Edited by Wallace K. Ferguson. The Hague: Nijhoff.

———. 1974–present. *CWE* [Complete Works in English]. Toronto: Toronto University Press.

Estienne, Henri II. 1968. *Francofordiense Emporium. Der Frankfurter Markt. The Frankfurt Fair, La Foire de Francfort.* Frankfurt am Main: Frankfurt am Mainer Buchmesse.

———. 1969. *Francofordiense emporium; the Frankfurt Book Fair.* Edited and translated by James Westfall Thompson. Amsterdam: Gerard Th. van Heusen.

Fichard, Johann, and Bernardinus Rutilus. 1539. *Iurisconsultorum vitae veterum* [. . .] *recentiorum vero ad nostra usque tempora.* Basel: Robert Winter.

Fischart, Johann. 1993. *Catalogus catalogorum perpetuo durabilis.* ed. Michael Schilling. Tübingen: Max Niemeyer.

Flacius Illyricus, Matthias. 1556. *Catalogus testium veritatis, qui ante nostram aetatem Pontifici Romano eiusque erroribus reclamarunt,* Basel: Michael Stella for Johannes Oporinus.

Fritschius, Ahasuerus. 1675. *Tractatus de typographis, bibliopolis, chartariis et bibliopegis, in quo de eorum statutis et immutatibus abusibus item et controversiis, censura librorum, inspectione Typographiarum et Bibliopoliorum ordinatione Taxae etc. succincte agitur. Pro usu Reip[ublicae] Literariae.* Jena: Zacharias Hertelius; and Hamburg: Samuel Adolf Müller.

Fuchsberger, Ortholff. 1533. *Ein gründlicher klarer anfang der naturlichen und rechten kunst der waren Dialectica.* Augsburg: Alexander Weissenhorn.

———. 1536. *Justiniansicher Instituten warhaffte dolmetschung.* Augsburg: Alexander Weissenhorn.

Gallus (Le Coq), Pascalis. 1590. *Bibliotheca medica.* Basel: Conrad von Waldkirch.

Gessner, Conrad. 1548–1549. *Pandectarum sive partitionum universalium libri xxi.* Zürich: Christoph Froschauer.

———. 1577. *Epistolarum medicinalium libri tres.* Edited by Caspar Wolf. Zürich: Froschauer Presses.

———. 1966 [1545 and 1555]. *Bibliotheca universalis, sive Catalogus omnium scriptorum locupletissimus: in tribus linguis, Latina, Graeca, et Hebraica: extantium et non extantium, veterum et recentiorum in hunc usque diem, doctorum et indoctorum, publicatorum et in bibliothecis latentium* [facsimile edition of Zürich: Christoph Froschauer, 1545, with *Appendix:* ibid., 1555]. Osnabrück: Otto Zeller Verlagsbuchhandlung.

Giunti, heirs of Filippo. 1604. *Catalogus librorum qui in Iunctarum bibliotheca Philippi haeredum Florentiae prostant.* Florence: Heirs of Filippo Giunti.

Glareanus, Heinrich. 1516. *Isagoge in musicen.* Basel: Johannes Froben for his wife Gertrude Lachner.

———. 1547. *Dodecachordon.* Basel: Heinrich Petri.

Goldast, Melchior, ed. 1674. *Philologicarum epistolarum centuria una diversorum a renatis literis doctissimorum virorum: in qua veterum theologorum, jurisconsultorum, medicorum, philosophorum, historicorum, poetarum, grammaticorum libri difficillimis locis vel emendantur vel illustrantur; insuper Richardi De Buri Episcopi Dunelmensis etc. Philobiblion et Bessarionis Patriarchae Constantinopolitani et Cardinalis Nicaeni epistola ad Senatum Venetum ex Bibliotheca Melchioris Haiminsfeldii Goldasti.* Leipzig: Johann Köhler for Johann Bartholomäus Oeler.

Grosse, Henning. 1600. *Elenchus seu index generalis, in quo continentur libri omnes, qui [. . .] post annum 1593 usque ad annum 1600 in sancto Romano imperio et vicinis regionibus novi auctive prodierunt.* Leipzig: Henning Grosse.

Grossius, Johannes Georgius. 1620. *Compendium quatuor facultatum.* Basel: Ludwig König.

Herbert of Cherbury, Edward Lord. 1778. *The life.* London: J. Dodsley.

Hornung, Joannes. 1626. *Cista medica, qua in epistolae clarissimorum Germaniae medicorum, familiares, et in re medica, tam quoad hermetica et chymica [. . .] potissimum ex posthuma clarissimi quondam philosophiae et medicinae doctoris d[omini] Sigismundi Schnitzeri Ulmensis bibliotheca.* Nuremberg: Simon Halbmayr.

Jacob, Louis. 1646. *Catalogus omnium librorum per universum Regnum Galliae 1643, 1644 et 1645 excusorum.* Pris : Rolet Le Duc.

James, Thomas. 1600. *Ecloga oxonio-cantabrigiensis.* London: George Bishop and John Norton.

———. 1605. *Catalogus Bibliothecae publicae quam vir ornatissimus Thomas Bodleius Eques Auratus in Academia Oxoniensi nuper instituit.* Oxford: Joseph Barnes.

———. 1620. *Catalogus universalis librorum in bibliotheca Bodleiana.* Oxford: I. Lichfield and I. Short.

Joubert, Laurent. 1599. *Operum tomus primus.* Frankfurt am Main: Wechel Presses.

Junius, Franciscus. 1586. Introduction. In *Index expurgatorius.* [Heidelberg]: Jean Mareschal.

Indices. 1611. *Indices expurgatorii duo textes fraudum ac falsationum Pontificarum.* Hanau: Wilhelm Antonius.

Labitte, Jacques, Antonio Agustín, and Johann Wolfgang Freymon von Randeck. 1585. *Indices iuris varii ad Pandectarum et Codicis leges huc et illuc dispersas suis authoribus ac libris coniunctim restituendas: temporum, quibus veteres illi iuris authores vixerunt, aut leges promulgarunt, ratione servata: anno, mense ac die adiectis; singulis authoribus praefixae sunt eorum vitae. Adiecta et etiam Brevis interpretum iuris, qui ab Irnerio vixerunt, enumeratio.* Geneva: Jacques Chouet.

La Croix du Maine, François Grudé de. 1584. *Premier volume de la bibliotheque [. . .] qui est un catalogue general de toutes sortes d'Autheurs, qui ont escrit en françois depuis cinq cents ans et plus [. . .].* Paris: Abel L'Angelier.

Lautenbach, Konrad, *alias* Marx Mangold. 1965. Marckschiff oder Marckschiffergespräch von der Frankfurter Messe. In *Der deutsche Buchhandel in Urkunden und Quellen,* ed. Hans Widmann. Hamburg: Hauswedel.

Manardo, Giovanni. 1540. *Epistolae medicinales.* Basel: Michael Isingrin.

Mattaire, Michel. 1725. *Annales typographici [tomus tertius] ab anno M D XXXVI ad annum M DLVII.* The Hague: Frères Vaillant and Nicolas Prevost.

Matthioli, Pierandrea. 1565. *Commentarii in sex libros Pedacii Dioscoridis Anazarbei de medica materia, iam denuo ab ipso autore recogniti, et locis plus mille aucti. Adiectis magnis, ac novis plantarum, ac animalium iconibus, supra priores editiones longe pluribus, ad vivum delineatis.* Venice: Vincenzo Valgrisi.

Meder, Lorenz. 1558. *Handel Buch.* Nuremberg: Johann vom Berg and Ulrich Neuber.

Merula Gaudenzio. 1543. *Terentianus dialogus,* Borgolavezzaro: Betaceus Tortelius. Meurschen, Gerhard. 1711. De vana librorum pompa. In Thomas Bardolinus, *De libris legendis dissertationes.* sig *. The Hague and Frankfurt: Nicolaus Wildt.

Monnoye, M de la, ed. 1772. *Les bibliothèques françoises de la Croix de Maine et de Du Verdier.* Paris: Saillant; and Nyon: Lambert.

Montaigne, Michel de. 1992. *Les Essais.* 3 vols. Edited by Pierre Villey. Paris: Quadrige/Presses Universitaires de France.

Naudé, Gabriel. 2008. *Advis pour dresser une Bibliotheque.* Edited by Bernard Teyssandier. Paris: Klincksieck (includes a facsimile of the second edition of 1642).

Oporinus, Johannes and Martin Steinmann. 1969. Aus dem Briefwechsel des Basler Druckers Johannes Oporinus. *Basler Zeitschrift für Geschichte und Altertumskunde* 69: 103–203.

Oroscius, Christophorus. 1540. *Annotationes in interpretationes Aetii medici.* Basel: Robert Winter, 1540.

Otto Brunfels, Otto. 1533. *Neotericorum aliquot medicorum in medicinam practicam introductiones.* Strasbourg: Johannes Albert.

Paleario, Aonio. 1992. *De animorum immortalitate.* Edited by Dirk Sacre. Brussels: AWLSK.

Parisano, Emilio. 1621. *Nobilium exercitationum libri xii de Subtilitate.* Venice: Evangelista Deuchino.

Perotti, Niccolò. 1513. *Coruncopiae sive linguae latinae commentarii.* Venice: Aldus Manutius and son-in-law.

Peutinger, Konrad. 1923. *Konrad Peutingers Briefwechsel.* Edited by Erich König. Munich: Beck.

Pietro d'Ancarano. 1580–1581. *In quinque Decretalium libros facundissima commentaria: a plerisque erratis, quibus veterum typographorum incuria erant oppressa, nunc liberata, pristinoq[ue] suo, ac innato candori, qua fieri potuit diligentia, restituta.* Bologna: Societas Typographia Bononiensis.

Pinelli, Gian Vicenzo, and Claude Dupuy. 2001. *Une Correspondance entre deux Humanistes.* Edited by Anna Maria Raugei, ed. Florence: Olschki.

Plantin, Christophe. 1883–1918. *Correspondance.* 9 vols. Max Rooses and Jean Denucé, eds. Nendeln: Kraus [Antwerp: J. E. Buschmann].

Platter, Thomas. 1964. *Autobiographie.* Translated by Marie Helmer. Paris: Armand Colin.

Possevino, Antonio. 1593. *Bibliotheca selecta, qua agitur de ratione studiorum in historia, in disciplinis, in salutem omnium procuranda.* Rome: Vatican Press.

———. 1597. *Apparatus ad omnium gentium historiarum et methodus ad geographiam tradendam.* Venice: Giovanni Battista Ciotti.

———. 1603–1606. *Apparatus sacer.* 3 vols. Venice: Altobello Salicato.

Rebuffi, Pierre. 1540. *De scholasticorum, bibliopolarum, atque ceterorum universitatum ministrorum juratorumque privilegiis.* Paris: Pierre Vidoue.

Riswick, Otto. 1593. *Elenchus continens libros protestantium et pontificorum theologorum. Frankfurter Messe 1569–Leipziger Neujahrsmess 1593.* Erfurt: Esaias Mechler for Otto Riswick.

Roomen, Adriaan van, and Paul B. Bockstaele. 1967. The correspondence of Adriaan van Roomen. *Lias* 3: 85–129.

———. 1992. The correspondence of Adriaan van Roomen (1561–1615): Corrections and additions, 1594–1615. *Lias* 19: 1–20.

Roville, heirs of Guillaume. 1604. *Catalogus librorum Lugduni, Parisiis, Italiae, Germaniae, et Flandriae, excussorum. Qui reperiuntur Lugduni in aedibus haeredum Guilielmi Rovilli.* Lyon: Heirs of Guillaume Roville.

Schenck von Grafenburg, Johannes Georg. 1609. *Biblia iatrica.* Frankfurt am Main: Johann Spiess for Antonius Hummius.

Simler, Josias. 1574. *Bibliotheca instituta et collecta a Conrado Gesnero* [. . .] *recognita.* Zürich: Christoph Froschauer.

Sixtus Senensis. 1575. *Bibliotheca sacra.* Venice: Francesco de' Franceschi.

Sohn, Georg 1591–1592. *Methodus theologiae.* In *Opera.* 3 vols. Herborn: Christophorus Corvinus.

Spachius, Israel 1591. *Nomenclator scriptorum medicorum, hoc est, elenchus qui artem medicam suis scriptis illustrarunt, secundum locos communes ipsius medicinae conscriptus.* Frankfurt am Main: Marin Lechler for Nicolas Bassée.

———. 1598. *Nomenclator scriptorum philosophicorum et philologicorum.* Strasbourg: Antonius Bertramus.

Thülemeyer, Heinrich Günther. 1688. *Virorum Cl[arissimorum] et Doctorum ad Melchiorem Goldastum JCtum et Polyhistorem celebratissimum Epistolae ex Bibliotheca Henrici Günteri Thülemarii, JC. editae.* Frankfurt am Main and Speyer: Christoph Olffen.

Trithemius, Johannes. 1494. *Liber de scriptoribus eccelsiasticis.* Basel: Johann Amerbach.

Turretini, Benedetto. 1619. Preface. In *Index librorum prohibitorum et expurgatorum.* Geneva: Jacques Crespin.

Verstegan, Richard. 1618. *Gazette van Nieuwe-maren van de gheheele wereldt. Ghemenght met oude Waerheden.* Antwerp: Hieronymus Verdussen.

Vespasiano da Bisticci, 1997. *The Vespasiano Memoirs: Lives of Illustrious Men of the XVth Century,* trans. William George and Emily Waters. Toronto: University of Toronto Press, in association with the Renaissance Society of America.

Vilvain, Robert. 1654. *Enchiridium epigrammatum Latino-Anglicum. An epitome of essais, englished out of Latin: without elucidat explications.* London: R. Hodgkinsonne for Robert Vilvain.

Waser, Caspar. 1611a. *Elementale chaldaicum.* Heidelberg: Gotthard Vögelin.

———. 1611b. *Grammatica hebraea.* Heidelberg: Gotthard Vögelin.

———. 1612. *Analysis psalmi XC regii prophetae Davidis.* Offenbach: Antonius Hummius.

Zabarella, Jacopo. 1586–1587. *Opera logica.* Frankfurt am Main: Johann Wechel for Jean Mareschal.

Zedler, Johann Heinrich. 1731–1754. *Grosses Universal-Lexicon.* 68 vols. Leipzig and Halle: Johann Heinrich Zedler.

c. Books and Articles after 1801

Adam, Renaud, and Alexandre Vanautgaerden. 2009. *Thierry Martens et la figure de l'imprimeur humaniste.* Brussels-Turnhout: Brepols.

Adams, H. M. 1967. *Catalogue of books printed on the continent, 1501–1600, in Cambridge libraries.* 2 vols. Cambridge: Cambridge University Press.

Agasse, J.-M. 2002–2003. La bibliothèque d'un médecin humaniste: L'*Index librorum* de Girolamo Mercuriale. *Les Cahiers de l'humanisme* 3–4: 201–253.

Agrimi, Jole, and Chiara Crisciani. 1996. *Les Consilia médicinaux.* Translated by Caroline Viola. Turnhout: Brepols.

Alicke, Gerhard. 2009. Vadians Pomponius Mela: Ein Stück Buchgeschichte. *Daphnis* 29: 379–412.

Allen, P. S. 1916. *Erasmus' relations with his printers.* London: Blades, East and Blades.

Amelung, Peter. 1985. *Johannes Zainer der Ältere und Jüngere.* Translated by Ruth Schwab-Rosenthal. Los Angeles: Kenneth Karmiole.

Anderson, Chris. 2004. The long tail. *Wired* 12.10, October.

Aquilon, Pierre. 1988. Quatre avocats angevins dans leurs librairies (1586–1592). In *Le livre dans l'Europe de la Renaissance,* ed. Pierre Aquilon, Henri-Jean Martin and François Dupuigrenet-Desroussilles, 503–552. Paris: Promodis.

Arbour, Roméo. 1992. *Un éditeur d'œuvres littéraires au XVIIe siècle: Toussaint du Bray (1604–1636).* Geneva: Droz.

Armstrong, Elizabeth. 1954. *Robert Estienne, royal printer.* Cambridge: Cambridge University Press.

———. 1990. *Before copyright: The French book-privilege system, 1498–1526.* Cambridge: Cambridge University Press.

———. 1993. Quelques privilèges du règne de Henri II. In *Parcours et rencontres: Mélanges de langue, d'histoire et de littérature françaises offerts à Enea Balmas,* ed. Paolo Carile et al., 29–35. Paris: Klincksieck.

Arnold, Werner, ed. 1997. *Bibliotheken und Bücher im Zeitalter der Renaissance.* Wiesbaden: Harrassowitz.

Arrizabalaga, Jon. 1998. *The Articella in the early press, 1476–1534.* Cambridge: Wellcome Unit; Barcelona: Department of the History of Science.

———. 2007. De la copie à l'édition: Francesc Argilagues et les manuscrits médicaux aux premiers temps de l'imprimerie (fin XVe- début XVIe siècle). *Médiévales* 52: 119–134.

Ascarelli, Fernanda. 1972. *Le cinquecentine romane: Censimento delle edizioni romane del XVI secolo possedute dalle biblioteche di Roma.* Milan: Etimar.

Ascarelli, Fernanda, and Marco Menato. 1989. *La tipografia del '500 in Italia.* Florence: Olschki.

Atkinson, Geoffroy. 1927. *La littérature géographique française de la Renaissance.* Paris: Picard.

Baade, Anne A. 1992. *Melchior Goldast von Haiminsfeld: Collector, commentator and editor.* New York: Peter Lang.

Babelon, Jean-Pierre. 1986. *Nouvelle histoire de Paris au XVIe siècle.* Paris: Hachette.

Backus, Irene, ed. 1997. *The reception of the Church Fathers in the West: from the Carolingians to the Maurists.* 2 vols. Leiden: Brill.

Baldi, Marialuisa, and Guido Canziani. 2004. *Cardano: De utilitate ex adversis capienda, "secunda editio."* Varese: University Press.

Baldini, A. Enzo. 1992. *Botero e la "ragion di stato": Atti del convengo in memoria di Luigi Firpo.* Florence: Olschki.

Baldini, Ugo. 2001. Die römischen Kongregationen der Inquisition und das Index. In *Inquisition, Index, Zensur: Wissenskulturen der Neuzeit im Widerstreit,* ed. Hubert Wolf, 229–278. Padeborn: Schöningh.

Baldini, Ugo, and Leen Spruit, eds. 2009. *Catholic Church and modern science: Documents from the Archives of the Roman Congregations of the Holy Office and the Index*. Rome: Libreria Editrice Vaticana.

Balsamo, Luigi. 1997. Vicende censorie in Inghilterra tra '500 e '600'. In *La censura libraria nell'Europa del secolo XVI*, ed. Ugo Rozzo, 31–51. Udine: Forum.

Banderier, Gilles. 2000. Documents sur Simon Goulart. *Bulletin de la Société d'Histoire du Protestantisme en France* 146: 571–606.

Barberi, Francesco. 1986. *Tipografi romani del cinquecento*. Florence: Olschki.

Barbiche, Bernard. 1982. Le régime de l'édition. In *Histoire de l'Edition française, vol. 1: Le livre conquérant*, ed. Henri-Jean Martin, Roger Chartier, and Jean-Pierre Vivet, 367–377. Paris: Promodis.

Barbier, Frédéric. 2008. *Paris capitale des livres: le monde des livres et de la presse à Paris, du Moyen Age au XXe siècle*. Paris: PUF.

Barker, Nicolas. 1985. The importation of books into England, 1460–1526. In *Beiträge zur Geschichte des Buchwesens im konfessionellen Zeitalter*, ed. Herbert G. Göpfert, Peter Vodosek, Erdmann Weyrauch, and Reinhard Wittmann, 251–266. Wiesbaden: Harrassowitz.

Barnard, John. 2002. Politics, profits and idealism: John Norton, the Stationer's Company and Sir Thomas Bodley. *Bodleian Library Record* 17: 335–408.

———. 2005. The financing of the Authorised Version 1610–12: Robert Barker, and "combining" and "sleeping" stationers. *Publishing History* 57: 5–52.

Barnard, John, and Maureen Bell. 1994. *John Foster's inventory of 1616*. Leeds: Leeds Literary and Philosophical Society.

Baudrier, Henri-Louis, and Julien Baudrier. 1964–1965. *Bibliographie lyonnaise*. 13 vols. Paris: de Nobele.

Bauer, Barbara, ed. 1999. *Melanchthon und die Marburger Professoren (1527–1627)*. 2 vols. Marburg: Universitätsbibliothek.

Baumeister, Ursula. 1979. Gilles Beys, 1541/2–1595. In *Imprimeurs et libraires parisiens du XVIe siècle: Ouvrage publié d'après les manuscrits de Philippe Renouard*, vol. 3, 312–372. Paris: Bibliothèque Nationale.

Bayard, Françoise. 1997. *Vivre à Lyon sous l'ancien régime*. Paris: Perrin.

Beaujean, Marion. 1985. Die Bibliotheca Senatus Hanoverensis im Zeitalter der Reformation. In *Beiträge zur Geschichte des Buchwesens im konfessionellen Zeitalter*, ed. Herbert G. Göpfert, Peter Vodosek, Erdmann Weyrauch and Reinhard Wittmann, 213–228. Wiesbaden: Harrassowitz.

Bécares Botas, Vicente, and Alejandro Luis Iglesias. 1992. *La Librería de Benito Boyer: (Medina del Campo, 1592)*. Salamanca: Junta de Castilla y León.

Benzing, Josef. 1958. Matthäus Harnischs Söhne zu Neustadt an der Haart und ihre Nachfolger. *Archiv für Geschichte des Buchwesens* 1: 582–589.

———. 1977. Die deutschen Verleger des 16. und 17. Jahrhunderts: Eine Neubearbeitung. *Archiv für Geschichte des Buchwesens* 18: 1077–1322.

———. 1980. Die Hanauer Erstdrucker: Wilhelm und Peter Antonius (1593–1625). *Archiv für Geschichte des Buchwesens* 21: 1005–1126.

———. 1983. *Die Buchdrucker des 16 und 17 Jahrhunderts im deutschen Sprachgebiet*. Wiesbaden: Harrassowitz.

Bepler, Jill. 2001. Vicissitudo temporum: Some sidelights on book collecting in the Thirty Years' War. *Sixteenth Century Journal* 32: 953–968.

Bethencourt, Francisco. 2009. *The Inquisition: A global history, 1470–1834.* Cambridge: Cambridge University Press.

Bietenholz, Peter G. 1954. *Der italienischer Humanismus und die Blütezeit des Buchdrucks in Basel: Die Baseler Drucker italienischer Autoren von 1530 bis zum Ende des 16. Jahrhunderts.* Basel: Helbing und Lichtenhahn.

———. 1971. *Basel and France in the sixteenth century: The Basel humanists and printers in their contacts with francophone culture.* Geneva: Droz.

Bietenholz, Peter G., and Thomas B. Deutscher. 1985–1987. *Contemporaries of Erasmus.* London: Toronto University Press.

Birrell, T. A. 2001. Books and buyers in seventeenth-century English auction sales. In *Under the Hammer: Book Auctions since the seventeenth century,* ed. Robin Myers, Michael Harris, and Giles Mandelbrote, 51–64. New Castle, DE: Oak Knoll Press; London: British Library.

Blair, Ann. M. 2010. *Too much to know: Managing scholarly information before the modern age.* New Haven: Yale University Press.

Blum, Rudolf. 1959. Vor- und Frühgeschichte der Allgemeinbibliographie. *Archiv für Geschichte des Buchwesens* 2: 233–303.

Boghardt, Martin. 2008. Hieronymus Hornschuch und seine Orthotypographia (1608/1634). In *Archäologie des gedruckten Buches,* ed. Paul Needham and Julie Boghardt, 195–216. Wiesbaden: Harrassowitz.

Bolgar, R. R. 1958. *The classical heritage and its beneficiaries.* Cambridge: Cambridge University Press.

Bolzoni, Lina. 1981. L'Accademia Veneziana: Splendore e decadenza di una utopia enciclopedica. In *Università accademie e società scientifiche in Italia e in Germania dal cinquecento al settecento. Annali dell'Istituto Storico Italo-Germanico,* ed. Laetitia Boehm and Ezio Raimondi, 9: 117–167.

Bonnant, Georges. 1969. Les Index prohibitifs et expurgatoires contrefaits par les protestants aux XVIe et XVIIe siècles. *Bibliothèque d'Humanisme et Renaissance* 31: 511–540.

Borraccini, Rosa Marisa, and Roberto Rusconi, eds. 2006. *Libri, biblioteche e cultura degli Ordini regolari nell'Italia moderna attraverso la documentazione della Congregazione dell'Indice. Atti del Convegno internazionale, Macerata, Università degli studi di Macerata, Dipartimento di scienze storiche, documentarie, artistiche e del territorio, 30 maggio–1 giugno 2006.* Studi e Testi 434. Città del Vaticano: Biblioteca Apostolica Vaticana.

Borsa, Gedeon. 1980. *Clavis typographorum librariorumque Italiae, 1465–1600.* Baden-Baden: Koerner.

Borst, Arno. 1957–1963. *Der Turmbau von Babel.* 4 vols. Stuttgart: Hiersemann.

Botfield, Beriah. 1861. *Praefationes et epistolae editionibus principibus auctorum veterum.* Cambridge: Cambridge University Press.

Boutcher, Warren. 2011. Collecting manuscripts and printed books in the late Renaissance: Naudé and the last Duke of Urbino's library. *Italian Studies* 64: 206–220.

Bowen, Karen L., and Dirk Imhof. 2008. *Christopher Plantin and engraved book illustrations in sixteenth-century Europe.* Cambridge: Cambridge University Press.

Braida, Lodovica. 2009. *Libri di lettere: Le raccolte epistolari del Cinquecento tra inquietudini religiose e "buon volgare."* Bari: Laterza.

Brauer, Adalbert. 1974. Henning Groß (Grosse), der "Erste" Buchhändler in Leipzig und seine Bedeutung für den deutschen Buchhandel. In *Beiträge zur Geschichte des Buches und seiner Funktion in der Gesellschaft: Festschrift für Hans Widmann,* ed. Alfred Swierk, 34–43. Stuttgart: Hiersemann.

———. 1979. Die kaiserliche Bücherkommission und der Niedergang Frankfurts als Buchhandelsmetropole. *Deutschlands Genealogisches Jahrbuch* 19: 185–199.

Breugelmans, R. 2003. Fac et spera: Joannes Maire, publisher, printer and bookseller in Leiden, 1603–1657. t 'Goy-Houten: Hes and de Graaf.

Brinkhus, Gerd. 1985. Stadt-Universität-Bibliotheken: Zur Tübinger Bibliotheksgeschichte im 16. Jahrhundert. In *Beiträge zur Geschichte des Buchwesens im konfessionellen Zeitalter,* ed. Herbert G. Göpfert, Peter Vodosek, Erdmann Weyrauch and Reinhard Wittmann, 179–188. Wiesbaden: Harrassowitz.

Brown, Horatio. 1891. *The Venetian printing press.* London: Nimmo.

Brübach, Niels, and Jürgen Schneider. 1991. Frankreichs Messplätze. In *Brücke zwischen den Völkern: zur Geschichte der Frankfurter Messe,* 3 vols., ed. Rainer Koch, 171–190. Frankfurt am Main: Historisches Museum.

———. 1994. *Die Reichsmessen von Frankfurt am Main, Leipzig und Braunschweig (14–18. Jahrhundert).* Stuttgart: Franz Steiner.

Brückner, Wolfgang. 1961a. Der kaiserliche Bücherkommissar Valentin Leucht. *Archiv für Geschichte des Buchwesens* 3: 97–180.

———. 1961b. Eine Messbuchhändlerliste von 1579 und Beiträge zur Geschichte der Bücherkommission. *Archiv für Geschichte des Buchwesens* 3: 1630–1648.

———. 1962. Die Gegenreformation im Kampf um die Buchmessse. *Archiv für Frankfurter Geschichte und Kunst* 48: 67–86.

Brunet, Gustave. 1876. *Recherches sur les imprimeries imaginaires, clandestines et particulières.* Brussels: Gay et Doucé.

Buhl, Heinrich. 1879. *Zur Rechtsgeschichte des deutschen Sortimentshandels.* Heidelberg: Carl Winter's Universitätsbuchhandlung.

Bühler, Curt F. 1958. *The university and the press in fifteenth-century Bologna.* Notre Dame, Indiana: Mediaeval Institute, University of Notre Dame.

———. 1960. *The fifteenth-century book: The scribes, the printers, the decorators.* Philadelphia: University of Pennsylvania Press.

Burchill, Christopher. 1984. Girolamo Zanchi: Portrait of a Reformed theologian and his work. *Sixteenth Century Journal* 15: 185–207.

Buringh, Eltjo, and Jan Luiten van Zanden. 2009. Charting the "Rise of the West": Manuscripts and printed books in Europe—A long-term perspective from the sixth through eighteenth centuries. *Journal of Economic History* 69: 409–445.

Burke, Peter. 2004. *Languages and communities in early modern Europe.* Cambridge: Cambridge University Press.

Burnett, Stephen G. 2000. Christian Hebrew printers in the sixteenth century: Printers, humanism and the impact of the reformation. *Helmantica* 51: 13–42.

Bury, Emmanuel. 2003. La philologie dans le concert des savoirs: Mutations et permanences de l'*ars critica* au XVIIe siècle. In *Le Savoir au XVIIe siècle,* ed. John D. Lyons and C. Welch, 17–33. Tübingen: Narr.

Buzzi, Franco, and Roberta Ferro. 2005. *Federico Borromeo fondatore dell'Ambrosiana: Atti delle giornate di studio 25–27 novembre 2004.* Milan: Biblioteca Ambrosiana/Rome: Bulzoni.

Camerini, Paolo. 1963. *Anni dei Guinti.* Florence: Sansoni.

Cameron, Euan. 1991. *The European Reformation.* Oxford: Clarendon Press.

Campi, E., S. De Angelis, A. S. Goeing, and A. T. Grafton. 2008. *Scholarly knowledge: Textbooks in early modern Europe.* Geneva: Droz.

Caspary, Gundula. 2006. *Späthumanismus und Reichspatriotismus: Melchior Goldast und seine Editionen zur Reichsverfassungsgeschichte.* Göttingen: Vandenhoeck und Ruprecht.

Cave, Terence, ed. 2008. *Thomas More's Utopia in early modern Europe: Paratexts and contexts.* Manchester: Manchester University Press.

Chaix, Paul. 1978. *Recherches sur l'imprimerie à Genève de 1550 à 1564.* Geneva: Slatkine.

Charlton, Bruce C. 2009. Are you an honest academic? *Oxford Magazine,* 0th week, Trinity Term, 8–10.

Chartier, Roger. 1982. Pamphlets et gazettes. In *Histoire de l'Edition française,* vol. 1: *Le livre conquérant,* ed. Henri-Jean Martin, Roger Chartier and Jean-Pierre Vivet, 405–425. Paris: Promodis.

Chrisman, Miriam Usher. 1977. L'imprimerie à Strasbourg. In *Strasbourg au coeur religieux du XVIe siècle,* ed. Georges Livet, 539–550. Strasbourg: Istra.

———. 1982. *Lay culture, learned culture: Books and social change in Strasbourg, 1480–1599.* New Haven: Yale University Press.

Clair, Colin. 1960. *Christopher Plantin.* London: Plantin.

———. 1976. *A History of European Printing.* London: Academic Press.

Clegg, Cyndia Susan. 1997. *Press censorship in Elizabethan England.* Cambridge: Cambridge University Press.

Cohn, Henry J. 1985. Germany, 1559–1622. In *International Calvinism,* ed. Menna Prestwich, 135–165. Oxford: Clarendon Press.

Coppens, Christian. 1998–1999. The Plantin Moretus Archives: An index to Juan Denucé's inventory of 1926. *De Gulden Passer,* 76–77: 333–360.

———. 2001. Five unrecorded German bookseller's catalogues, end 16th–early 17th century. *Archiv für Geschichte des Buchwesens* 54: 157–165

———. 2009. Et amicorum: Not just for friends. In *Syntagmata: Essays on neo-Latin literature in honour of Monique Mund-Dopchie and Gilbert Tournoy,* ed. Dirk Sacré and Jan Papy, 9–18. Leuven: Leuven University Press.

———. [forthcoming]. Autobibliography and the market for books.

Corsten, Severin. 1981. Universität und Buchdruck in Köln: Versuch eines Überblicks für das 15. Jahrhundert. In *Buch und Text im 15. Jahrhundert,* ed. Lotte Hellinga and Helmar Härtel, 189–199. Hamburg: Hauswedell.

———. 1987. Universities and early printing. In *Bibliography and the study of fifteenth-century civilisation*, ed. Lotte Hellinga and John Goldfinch, eds., 83–123. London: British Library.

Cranz, F. Edward. 1984. *A bibliography of Aristotle editions, 1501–1600*. Edited by Charles B. Schmitt. Baden-Baden: Koerner.

Cressy, David. 2005. Book burning in Tudor and Stuart England. *Sixteenth Century Journal* 36: 359–374.

Crousaz, Karine. 2005. *Erasme et le pouvoir de l'imprimerie*. Lausanne: Antipodes.

Crusius, Irene. 2008. Nicht calvinistisch, nicht lutherisch: Zu Humanismus, Philippismus und Kryptokalvinismus in Sachsen am Ende des 16. Jahrhunderts. *Archiv für Reformationsgeschichte* 99: 139–174.

Danesi, Daniele. 2008. I prezzi dei libri veneziani nelle note di acquisto di Bellisario Bulgarini, 1570–1620. In Lisa Pon and Craig Kallendorf, eds., *The Books of Venice / Il libro veneziano*. *Miscellanea Marciana* (2005–2007) 20: 301–326.

Darlow, T. H., and H. P. Moule. 1903–1911. *Historical catalogue of the printed editions of Holy Scripture in the library of the British and Foreign Bible Society*. London: Bible Society.

Darnton, Robert. 2009. *The case for books: Past, present, future*. Cambridge, MA: Perseus.

Davies, Martin. 1995. *Aldus Manutius: Printer and publisher of Renaissance Venice*. London: British Library.

Davis, Natalie Zemon. 1975. Strikes and salvation at Lyon. In *Society and culture in early modern France*, 1–16. London: Duckworth.

———. 1982. Le monde de l'imprimerie humaniste: Lyon. In *Histoire de l'Edition française*, vol. 1: *Le livre conquérant*, ed. Henri-Jean Martin, Roger Chartier, and Jean-Pierre Vivet, 255–277. Paris: Promodis.

———. 1983. Beyond the market: Books as gifts in sixteenth-century France. *Transactions of the Royal Historical Society* 33: 69–88.

———. 2009. *The gift in sixteenth-century France*. Oxford: Oxford University Press.

De Bujanda, J. M. 1985–2002. *Index des livres interdits*. 11 vols. Sherbrooke: CER; Geneva: Droz.

de Frede, Carlo. 2006. Gli umanisti e l'invenzione della stampa. In *Per la storia della tipogafia Napoletana nel secoli XV–XVII*, ed. Antonio Garzya, 41–89. Naples: Accademia Pontaniana.

de la Mare, Albinia C. 1965. Vespasiano da Bisticci: Historian and bookseller. PhD diss., University of London (Warburg Institute), London. 2 vols.

de Landtsheer, Jeanine. 2007. An author and his printer: Justus Lipsius and the Officina Plantiniana. *Quaerendo* 37: 10–29.

Delisle, C. 2004. The letter: Private text or public place? The Mattioli-Gesner Controversy about the *aconitum primum*. *Gesnerus* 61: 161–176.

Delsaert, Pierre. 2001. A bookshop for a new age: The inventory of the bookshop of the Louvain bookseller Hieronymus Cloet, 1543. In *The bookshop of the world: The role of the Low Countries in the book-trade, 1473–1941,* ed. Lotte Hellinga, Alastair Duke, Jacob Harskamp, Theo Hermans, Elaine Paintin, 75–86. 't Goy-Houten: De Graaf.

Denucé, Jan. 1926. *Musaeum Plantin-Moretus. Inventaris van het Plantynsch archief. Inventaire des archives Plantiniennes.* Antwerp: Plantin-Moretus Museum.

de Roover, Raymond. 1956. The business organisation of the Plantin Press in the setting of sixteenth-century Antwerp. In *Gedenkboek der Plantin-Dagen, 1555–1955,* 230–246. Antwerp: Vereniging der Antwerpsche Bibliophielen.

Desgraves, Louis. 2000. Le livre à Bordeaux et à Toulouse aux XVe et XVIe siècles. In *Le livre et l'art: Études offertes en hommage à Pierre Lelièvre,* ed. Thérèse Kleindienst. Paris: Somogy; Villeurbane: ENSIBB.

Desmars, Henri. 1994. *Histoire et commerce du livre.* Paris: GIPPE.

Deutscher, Thomas B. 2002. From Cicero to Tasso : humanism and the education of the Novarese parish clergy (1563-1663). *Renaissance Quarterly* 55:1005-1027.

de Vivo, Filippo. 2007. *Information and communication in Venice: Rethinking early modern politics.* Oxford: Oxford University Press.

de Vries, Jan. 1976. *The economy of Europe in the Age of Crisis, 1600–1750.* New York: Cambridge University Press.

de Vries, Jan, and A. M. van der Woude. 1997. *The first modern economy: Success, failure and perserverance of the Dutch economy, 1500–1815.* Cambridge: Cambridge University Press.

Dietz, Alexander. 1970. *Frankfurter Handelsgeschichte.* 4 vols. Glashütten im Taunus: Verlag Detlev Auvermann.

Dingel, Irene. 1996. *Concordia controversa: Die öffentlichen Diskussionen um das lutherische Konkordienwerk am Ende des 16. Jahrhunderts.* Gütersloh: Gütersloher Verlagshaus.

di Filippo Bareggi, Claudia. 1988. *Il mestiere di scrivere: Lavoro intellettuale e mercato librario a Venezie nel cinquecento.* Rome: Bulzoni.

Dondi, Cristina. 2004. Printers and guilds in fifteenth-century Venice. *La Bibliofilia* 106: 229–265.

Doucet, R. 1956. *Les Bibliothèques parisiennes au XVIe siècle.* Paris: Picard.

Dubois, Alain. 2007. L'éditeur réformé Jacob Stoer (1542–1610): Recherches sur son officine typographique d'après la bibliographie de ses éditions. Thesis, École des Chartes, Paris.

———. 2008. Les échanges de livres entre Genève et Anvers lors des foires de Francfort: L'exemple de Jacob Stoer et de la firme plantinienne. *Bibliologia* 3: 35–54.

Duke, Alastair. 1990. Building Heaven. In *Reformation and revolt in the Low Countries,* ed. Alastair Duke, 71–100. London: Hambledon Press.

Duntze, Oliver. 2007. *Ein Verleger sucht sein Publikum: Die Straßburger Offizin des Matthias Hupfuff (1497/98–1520).* Munich: Saur.

Dupont, Paul. 1854. *Histoire de l'imprimerie.* 2 vols. Paris: Dupont.

Dyroff, Hans Dieter. 1963. Gotthard Vögelin—Verleger, Drucker, Buchhandler 1597–1631. *Archiv für Geschichte des Buchwesens* 4: 1131–1423.

Edwards, John Richard, Graeme Dean, and Frank Clarke. 2009. Merchants' accounts, performance assessment and decision making in mercantilist Britain. *Accounting Organizations and Society* 34.5: 551–570.

Edwards, Mark U., Jr. 2003. Luther's polemical controversies. In *The Cambridge Companion to Luther,* ed. Donald K. McKim, 192–208. Cambridge: Cambridge University Press.

Ehrenpreis, Stefan. 2006. *Kaiserliche Gerichtsbarkeit und Konfessionskonflikt: Der Reichshofrat unter Rudolf II, 1576–1612.* Göttingen: Vandenhoeck und Ruprecht.

Eisenhardt, Ulrich. 1970. *Die kaiserliche Aufsicht über Buchdruck, Buchhandel und Presse im Heiligen Römischen Reich Deutscher Nation (1496–1806).* Karlsruhe: C. F. Müller.

———. 1985. Staatliche und kirchliche Einflußnahmen auf den deutschen Buchhandel im 16. Jahrhundert. In *Beiträge zur Geschichte des Buchwesens im konfessionellen Zeitalter,* ed. Herbert G. Göpfert, Peter Vodosek, Erdmann Weyrauch and Reinhard Wittmann, 295–314. Wiesbaden: Harrassowitz.

Eisenstein, Elizabeth. 1979. *The printing press as an agent of change.* Cambridge: Cambridge University Press.

Elder, Florence. 1937. Cost accounting in the sixteenth century: The books of account of Christopher Plantin, Antwerp, printer and publisher. *Accounting Review* 12.3: 226–237.

Engammare, Max. 1994. *Lire le Cantique des cantiques à la Renaissance.* La Rochelle: Rumeur des Ages.

Engelsing, Rolf. 1967–1969. Deutsche Verlegerplakate des 17. Jahrhunderts. *Archiv für Geschichte des Buchwesens* 9: 217–338.

———. 1971. *Deutsche Bücherplakate des siebzehnten Jahhunderts.* Wiesbaden: Pressler.

Epstein, Jason. 2001. *Book business: Publishing past, present and future.* New York: Norton.

Evans, R. J. W. 1975. The Wechel Presses: Humanism and Calvinism in central Europe, 1572–1627. *Past and Present Society Supplement 2.*

———. 1984. Rantzau and Welser: Aspects of Later German Humanism. *History of European Ideas* 5: 257–272.

Fabian, Bernhard, ed. 1972–2001. *Die Messkataloge des sechzehnten Jahrhunderts, 1564–1600.* 5 vols. Hildesheim: Olms.

Febvre, Lucien, and Henri-Jean Martin. 1958. *L'apparition du livre.* Paris: Albin Michel.

Feingold, Mordechai. 2005. A conjurer and a quack? The lives of John Dee and Simon Forman. *Huntingdon Library Quarterly* 68: 545–559.

Findlen, Paula J. 1991. The economy of scientific exchange in early modern Italy. In *Patronage and institutions: Science, technology, and medicine at the European court, 1500–1750,* ed. Bruce T. Moran, 5–24. Rochester, NY: Boydell.

Firpo, Luigi. 1981. Giovanni Battista Ciotti. *Dizionario biografico deglo Italiani* 25: 692–696.

———. 1993. *Il processo di Giordano Bruno.* Rome: Salerno.

Fischer, H. 1966. Conrad Gessner (1516–65) as bibliographer and encyclopaedist. *The Library* 5.21: 269–281.

Flachmann, Holger. 1996. *Martin Luther und das Buch: Eine historische Studie auf Bedeutung des Buches im Handeln und Denken des Reformators.* Tübingen: Mohr.

Flood, John. 2007. The Frankfurt Fair in the early modern period. In *Fairs, markets and the itinerant book trade,* ed. Robin Myers, Michael Harris, and Giles Mandelbrote, 1–40. New Castle: Oak Knoll Press; London: British Library.

Föhl, Hildegard, and Anita Berger, eds. 1996. *Katalog der Stiftsbibliothek Xanten.* Kevelaer: Bulzon und Bercker.

Fraeb, Walter Martin. 1933. *Hanau in der Geschichte des Buchhandels und der Druckschriften.* Hanau am Main: Verlag des Hanauer Geschichts-Vereins.

Fragnito, Gigliola. 2001. The central and peripheral organization of censorship. In *Church, censorship and culture in early modern Italy,* ed. Gigliola Fragnito, 13–49. Cambridge: Cambridge University Press.

Frangenberg, Thomas. 1994. Chorographies of Florence: The use of city views and city plans in the sixteenth century. *Imago Mundi* 46: 41–64.

Frasca-Spada, Marina, and Nick Jardine, eds. 2000. *Books and the sciences in history.* Cambridge: Cambridge University Press.

Fremmer, Anselm. 2001. *Venezianische Buchkultur: Bücher, Buchhändler und Leser in der Frührenaissance.* Cologne: Böhlau Verlag.

Friedrichs, Christopher R. 1986. Politics or pogrom? The Fettmilch uprising in German and Jewish history. *Central European History* 19: 186–228.

Fudge, John D. 2007. *Commerce and print in the early Reformation.* Leiden: Brill.

Gadd, Ian Anders. 1999. "Being like a field": Corporate identity in the Stationer's Company, 1557–1684. D.Phil. diss., Oxford University, Oxford.

Garber, Klaus. 1987. Paris die Hauptstadt des Europäischen Späthumanismus: Jacques Auguste de Thou und das Cabinet Dupuy. In *Res publica literaria. Die Institutionen der Gelehrsamkeit in der frühen Neuzeit,* ed. S. Neumeister and C. Wiedemann, 71–92. Wiesbaden: Harrassowitz.

———. 2003. Konfessioneller Fundamentalismus und späthumanistischer Nationalismus. In *Germania latina—Latinitas teutonica: Politik, Wissenschaft, humanistische Kultur vom späten Mittelalter bis in unsere Zeit,* ed. Eckhard Kessler and Heinrich C. Kuhn, 107–142. Munich: Humanistische Bibliothek.

Garzya, Antonio. 2006. *Per la storia della typografia napoletana nei secoli XV–XVII.* Naples: Gianni.

Gehl, Paul F. 1997. Credit-sales strategies in the late cinquecento book trade. In *Libri, tipografi biblioteche. Ricerche storiche dedicate a Luigi Balsamo,* ed. Arnaldo Ganda and E. Grignani, 193–206. Florence: Olschki.

———. [forthcoming]. The view from below: Textbooks, authors and markets.

Gehl online. *Humanism for sale: Making and marketing schoolbooks in Italy, 1450–1650.* At http://www.humanismforsale.org/text/.

Germann, Martin. 1985. Bibliotheken im reformierten Zürich: Vom Büchersturm (1525) zur Gründung der Stadtbibliothek. In *Beiträge zur Geschichte des Buchwesens im konfessionellen Zeitalter,* ed. Herbert G. Göpfert, Peter Vodosek Erdmann Weyrauch and Reinhard Wittmann, 189–212. Wiesbaden: Harrassowitz.

Gerritsen, Johan. 1991. Printing at Froben's. *Studies in Bibliography* 44: 144–162.

Gier, Helmut. 2008. Die ostschwäbische und altbayerische Verlagslandschaft in der Epoche des Späthumanismus: Augsburg, Dillingen, Lauingen, Ingolstadt, München, Tegernsee und Thierhaupten. In *Justus Lipsius und der europäische Späthumanismus in Oberdeutschland,* ed. Alois Schmid, 143–164. Munich: Beck.

Giesecke, Michael. 1991. *Der Buchdruck in der frühen Neuzeit: Eine historische Fallstudie über die Durchsetzung neuer Informations- und Kommmunikationstechnologien.* Frankfurt am Main: Suhrkamp.

Gieseke, Ludwig. 2006. Die kursächsische Ordnung für Buchhändler und Buckdrucker von 1594. *Archiv für Geschichte des Buchwesens* 60: 176–183.

Gilly, Carlos. 1979. Zwischen Erfahrung und Spekulation: Theodor Zwinger und die religiöse und kulturelle Krise seiner Zeit. *Basler Zeitschrift für Geschichte und Altertumskunde* 77: 57–223.

———. 1985. *Spanien und der Basler Buchdruck bis 1600.* Basel: Helbing und Lichtenhahn.

———. 2001. *Die Manuskripte in der Bibliothek des Johannes Oporinus.* Basel: Schwabe.

———. 2002. Theatrum humanae vitae di Theodor Zwinger: Da una "historia naturalis dell'uomo" al "novum organum" delle scienze. In *Magia alcimia scienza dal '400 al '700. L'influsso di Ermete Trismegisto,* ed. Carlos Gilly and Cis van Heerkum, 253–264. Florence: Centro Di.

Gilmont, Jean-François. 1980. *Printers by the rules.* The Library 6.2: 129–155.

———. 1984. Les mémoires d'Eustache Vignon (1588): Souvenirs d'un éditeur genevois du XVIe siècle. In *Palaestra Typographica,* ed. Jean-François Gilmont, 165–199. Aubel: Gason.

———. 1990. *La Réforme et le livre: l'Europe et l'imprimé 1517–v.1570.* Paris: Editions du Cerf.

———. 1995. L'imprimerie réformée à Genève au temps de Laurent de Normandie. *Bulletin du bibliophile* 2: 262–278.

———. 1997. Les centres de la production imprimée aux XVe et XVIe siècles. In *Produzione e Commercio della carta e del libro secc. XIII–XVIII,* ed. Simonetta Cavaiocchi, 343–363. Florence: Le Monnier.

———. 2003. *Le livre et ses secrets.* Geneva: Droz; Louvain-la Neuve: Université Catholique de Louvain.

———. 2004. La correction des épreuves à Genève autour de 1560. In *E Codicibus Impressisque,* ed. Elly Cockx-Indestege, 161–174. Leuven: Peeters.

———. 2005a. *John Calvin and the printed book.* Translated by Karin Maag. Kirksville: Truman State University Press.

———. 2005b. *Le livre réformé au XVIe siècle.* Paris: Bibliothèque de France.

———. 2006a. Peut-on parler de contrefaçon au XVIe siècle et au début du XVIIe siècle? La situation de Genève et d'ailleurs. *Bulletin du Bibliophile* 1: 19–40.

———. 2006b. Le "protestantisme" des libraires et typographes lyonnais (1560–1560). *Revue d'Histoire Ecclésiastique* 101: 988–1013.

———. 2007. Théodore de Bèze et ses Imprimeurs. In *Théodore de Bèze (1519–1605)*, ed. Irene Backus, 89–100. Geneva: Droz.

———. 2010. La fiabilité des notices de catalogue de la foire de Frankfurt: Les éditions genevoises signalées par les catalogues de Willer. In *Les instruments de travail à la Renaissance*, ed. Jean-François Gilmont and Alexandre Vanautgaerden, 135–1152. Turnhout: Brepols.

Gilmont, Jean-François, and Alexandre Vanautgaerden, eds. 2008. *La Page de titre à la Renaissance*. Turnhout: Brepols.

Giralt i Soler, Sebastià. 2002. *Arnau de Vilanova en la imprenta renaixentista*. Manresa: Publicacions de l'Arxiu Històric de les Ciències de la Salut, Col.legi Oficial de Metges de Barcelona.

———. 2007. La tradition médiévale d'Arnaud de Villeneuve, du manuscrit à l'imprimé. *Médiévales* 52: 75–88.

Glocke, Gottfried. 1962. *Petite chronique des relations du monde de la librairie entre Lyon et Francfort au XVIe siècle [Kleine Chronik der Buchhandelsbeziehungen zwischen Lyon und Frankfurt im 16. Jahrhundert]*. Frankfurt am Main: Waldemar Kramer.

Gobiet, Ronald, ed. 1979. *Auszüge aus der Korrespondenz Herzog August des Jüngeren von Braunschweig—Lüneburg mit dem Augsburger Patrizier Philipp Hainhofer aus den Jahren 1613–1647: Briefe Herzog August des Jüngeren von Braunschweig—Lüneburg und des Augsburger Agenten Philipp Hainhofer*. Munich: Deutscher Kunstverlag.

Goldfriedrich, Johann. 1908. *Geschichte des deutschen Buchhandels*. Vol. 2. Leipzig: Verlag des Börsenvereins der deutschen Buchhändler.

Goldgar, Anne. 1995. *Impolite learning: Conduct and community in the republic of letters, 1680–1750*. New Haven: Yale University Press.

Gomez, Jeff. 2008. *Print is dead: Books in our digital age*. New York: Palgrave Macmillan.

Göpfert, Herbert G., Peter Vodosek, Erdmann Weyrauch, and Reinhard Wittmann. 1985. *Beiträge zur Geschichte des Buchwesens im konfessionellen Zeitalter*. Wiesbaden: Harrassowitz.

Gould, J. D. 1954. The trade depression of the early 1620s. *Economic History Review* n.s., 7: 81–90.

Graf, Holger Thomas. 1997. The Collegium Mauritianum and the making of Calvinist diplomacy. *Sixteenth Century Journal* 28: 1167–1180.

Grafton, Anthony. 1977. On the scholarship of Politian and its context. *Journal of the Warburg and Courtauld Institutes* 40: 150–188.

———. 1983–1993. *Joseph Scaliger: A study in the history of classical scholarship*. 2 vols. Oxford: Oxford University Press.

———. 1990. *Forgers and critics: Creativity and duplicity in western scholarship*. London: Collins and Brown.

———. 1991. *Defenders of the text: The tradition of scholarship in an age of science, 1450–1800*. Cambridge, MA: Harvard University Press.

———. 1993. *Rome reborn: The Vatican Library and Renaissance culture.* Washington, DC: Library of Congress.

———. 1997. *The footnote.* London: Faber and Faber.

———. 2007. *What was history? The art of history in early modern Europe.* Cambridge: Cambridge University Press.

———. [forthcoming a]. *The culture of correction in Renaissance Europe* [Panizzi lectures 2009].

———. [forthcoming b]. Where did the Christian Church come from? Tradition and innovation in early modern history.

———. [forthcoming c]. How Jesus celebrated Passover: The Last Supper in early modern scholarship.

Granata, Giovanna. 2009. Le bibliothece dei Francescani osservanti alla fine del '500: Un approccio bibliometrico. In *Libri, biblioteche e cultura degli ordini regolari nell'Italia moderna attraverso la documentazione della Congregazione dell'Indice,* ed. Rosa Marisa Borraccini and Roberto Rusconi, 146–178. Città del Vaticano: Bibliotheca apostolica Vaticana.

Grendler, Paul. 1977. *The Roman Inquisition and the Venetian press, 1540–1605.* Princeton: Princeton University Press.

———. 1978. Books for Sarpi: The smuggling of prohibited books into Venice during the Interdict of 1606–1607. In *Essays presented to Myron P. Gilmore,* ed. Sergio Bertelli, 104–114. Florence: La nuova Italia.

———. 1980. The circulation of protestant books in Italy. In *Peter Martyr Vermigli and Italian reform,* ed. Joseph C. McLelland, 11–14. Waterloo, Ontario: Wilfred Laurier University Press.

Griffin, Clive. 1998. El inventario del amacén de libros del impresor Juan Cromberger: Sevilla 1540. In *Coleccionismo y bibliotecas: Siglas XV–XVIII,* ed. María Luisa López-Vidriera, Pedro M. Cátedra, and María Hernández González, 257–373. Salamanca: Universidad de Salamanca.

———. 2005. *Journeymen-printers, heresy and the inquisition in sixteenth-century Spain.* Oxford: Oxford University Press.

Groesen, Michiel van. 2008. *The representations of the overseas world in the De Bry Collection of Voyages (1590–1634).* Leiden : Brill.

Gross, Lothar. 1933. Die Geschichte der deutschen Reichshofkanzlei von 1559 bis 1806. Vienna: Selbstverlag des Haus-, Hof- und Staatsarchivs.

Grotefend, Hermann. 1881. *Christian Egenolff : der erste ständige Buchdrucker zu Frankfurt am Main und seine Vorläufer.* Frankfurt am Main: Völcker.

Guilleminot-Chrétien, Geneviève. 2005. Chrétien et André Wechel "libraires parisiens"? In *Printers and Readers in the Sixteenth Century,* ed. Christian Coppens, 27–38. Turnhout: Brepols.

———. 2007. La Société parisienne s'ouvre à l'imprimé. In *Paris capitale des livres: Le monde des livres et de la presse à Paris, du Moyen Age au XXe siècle,* ed. Frédéric Barbier, 103–139. Paris: Bibliothèque de France.

———. 2009. Fidélités à Ramus après la Saint-Barthélemy. In *Passeurs de textes: Imprimeurs, éditeurs et lecteurs humanistes dans les collections de la Bibliothèque Sainte-Geneviève,* ed. Yann Sordet, 68–73. Brussels: Brepols.

Guthmüller, Bodo, ed. 1998. *Latein und Nationalsprachen in der Renaissance.* Wiesbaden: Harrassowitz.

Harreld, Donald J. 2006. *Merchants and international trade networks in the sixteenth century.* At http://www.helsinki.fi/iehc2006/papers3/Harreld.pdf.

Hartmann, Martina. 2001. *Humanismus und Kirchenkritik: Matthias Flacius Illyricus als Erforscher des Mittelalters.* Stuttgart: Thorbecke.

Hase, Oscar von. 1885. *Die Koberger: Eine Darstellung des buchhändlerischen Geschäftsbetriebes in der Zeit des Übergangs vom Mittelalter zur Neuzeit.* 2nd ed. Leipzig: Breitkopf und Härtel.

Heitjan, Isabel. 1969. Ein Kölner Druck zur Bücherverbrennung in Madrid 1634. *Archiv für Geschichte des Buchwesens* 9: 401–419.

———. 1974. Zur Arbeit Valentin Leuchts als Bücherkommissar. *Archiv für Geschichte des Buchwesens* 14: 123–132.

Heller, Marvin. 2004. *The sixteenth-century Hebrew book: An abridged thesaurus.* Leiden: Brill.

———. 2008. *Studies in the making of the early Hebrew book.* Leiden: Brill.

———. 2011. *The seventeenth-century Hebrew book: An abridged thesaurus.* Leiden: Brill

Hellinga, Lotte. 2009. Sale advertisements for books printed in the fifteenth century. In *Books for sale: the Advertising and Promotion of Print since the Fifteenth Century,* ed. Giles Mandelbrote, Michael Harris and Robyn Myers, 1–25. New Castle: Oak Knoll Press.

Hermann de Franceschi, S. 2009. *La crise théologico-politique: Antiromanisme doctrinal, pouvoir pastoral et raison du prince: Le Saint-Siège face au prisme français (1607–1627).* (Bibliothèque des Écoles françaises d'Athènes et de Rome 340.) Rome: École française de Rome.

Hessels, John Henry. 1887. *Abrahami Ortelii et virorum eruditorum ad eundem et ad Jacobum Colium Ortelianum epistulae cum aliis epistulis.* Cambridge: Typis Academiae.

Hieronymus, Frank. 1992. *Griechischer Geist aus Basler Pressen.* Basel: Universitätsbiblithek.

———. 1995. Physicians and publishers: The translation of medical works in sixteenth-century Basle. In *The German Book, 1450–1750,* ed. John L. Flood and William A. Kelly, 95–110. London: British Library.

———. 1997. *1488 Petri: Schwabe 1988: Eine traditionsreiche Basler Offizin im Spiegel ihrer frühen Drucke.* Basel: Schwabe.

———. 2005. *Theophrast und Galen—Celsus und Paracelsus: Medizin, Naturphilosophie und Kirchenreform im Baseler Buchdruck bis zum dreissigjährigen Krieg.* 5 vols. Basel: Universitätsbibliothek.

Hirsch, Rudolf. 1967. *Printing, selling, and reading, 1450–1550.* Wiesbaden: Harrassowitz.

Hoogewerff, Godefridus J. 1926. *Laurentius Torrentinus (Laurens Leenaertsz van der Beke): Boekdrukker en uitgever van den hertog van Toscane, 1547–1563. Het boek* 15: 272–288, 369–381.

Hotson, Howard. 2007. *Commonplace learning: Ramism and its German ramifications, 1543–1630.* Oxford: Oxford University Press.

———. [forthcoming]. *The reformation of common learning: Post-Ramist method and the reception of the new philosophy, 1618–1670.*

Huffmann, Clifford Chalmers. 1988. *Elizabethan impressions: John Wolfe and his press.* New York: AMS Press.

Hunger, F. W. T. 1927–1943. *Charles de L'Ecluse, 1529–1609.* 2 vols. The Hague: Nijhoff.

Iggers, Georg G. 1990. *Leopold von Ranke and the shaping of the historical discipline.* Syracuse, NY: University of Syracuse Press.

Imhof, Dirk. 2001. Return my woodblocks at once: Dealings between Balthasar Moretus and Richard Whitacker. In *The bookshop of the world: The role of the Low Countries in the book-trade, 1473–1941,* ed. Lotte Hellinga, Alastair Duke, Jacob Harskamp, Theo Hermans, Elaine Pantin, 179–190. 't Goy-Houten: De Graaf.

———. 2005. De Spaanse koopman Luys Perez als financier van Jan Moretus' uitgaven van Benedictus Arias Montanus. *De Gulden Passer* 83: 149–155.

———. 2008. De Officina Plantiniana ratione recta: Het uitgeversfonds von Jan I Moretus (1589–1610). PhD diss, University of Antwerp, Antwerp.

Infelise, Mario. 1996. La librairie italienne (XVIIe et XVIIIe siècles). In *L'Europe et le livre: réseaux et pratiques du négoce de librairie XVIe–XIXe siècles,* ed.Frédéric Barbier, Sabine Juratic, and Dominique Varry, 81–97. Paris: Klincksieck.

Irving, David, ed. 1831. *Catalogue of law books in the Advocates' Library.* Edinburgh: Thomas Clark.

Isambert, François André. 1829. *Recueil général des anciennes lois.* Vol. 14. Paris: Belin-Prieur et Verdière.

Jansen, Sue Curry. 1991. *Censorship: The knot that binds power and knowledge.* New York: Oxford University Press.

Jardine, Lisa. 1993. *Erasmus, man of letters.* Princeton: Princeton University Press.

Jehasse, Jean. 1976. *La renaissance de la critique: L'essor de l'humanisme érudit de 1560 à 1614.* St. Etienne: Université de St. Etienne.

Jenny, Jean. 2007. L'imprimerie à Bourges jusqu'en 1562 environ: État provisoire de la question; Nouvelles recherches sur l'imprimerie à Bourges avant 1562; Notes sur l'imprimerie à Bourges de 1562 à 1600; Coup d'oeil sur les rapports entre les imprimeurs-libraires lyonnais et berruyers au XVIe siècle. In *Hommage à Jean Jenny,* 25–88. (Cahiers d'Archéologie et d'Histoire du Berry 169–170.) Bourges: Société d'archéologie et d'histoire du Berry.

Jensen, Kristian. 1996. The humanist reform of Latin and Latin teaching. In *The Cambridge companion to Renaissance humanism,* ed. Jill Kraye, 63–81. Cambridge: Cambridge University Press.

Johns, Adrian. 1998. *The nature of the book: print and knowledge in the making.* Chicago: Chicago University Press.

Jolly, Claude, ed. 1988. *Les bibliothèques sous l'ancien régime, 1530–1789.* Paris: Promodis.

Jones, Pamela M. 1993. *Federico Borromeo and the Ambrosiana: Art patronage and reform in seventeenth-century Milan.* Cambridge: Cambridge University Press.

Jütte, Robert. 2004. *"Ein Wunder wie der goldene Zahn": Eine unerhörte Begebenheit aus dem Jahre 1593 macht Geschichte.* Ostfildern: Jan Thorbecke Verlag.

Kapp, Friedrich. 1886. *Geschichte des Deutschen Buchhandels bis in das siebzehnte Jahrhundert.* Leipzig: Verlag des Börsenvereins der Deutschen Buchhändler.

Kataoka, Yasuhiko. 1998. *The first manuscript in the world on double-entry bookkeeping written by Benedetto Cotrugli.* Tokyo: Institute of Business Research, Daito Bunka University.

Keene, John. 1991. *The media and democracy.* Cambridge: Polity Press.

Kellenbenz, Hermann. 1976. *The rise of the European economy: An economic history of continental Europe from the fifteenth to the eighteenth centuries.* Rev. Gerhard Beneke. London: Weidenfeld and Nicholson.

Kelley, Donald R. 1970. *Foundations of modern historical scholarship: Language, law and history in the French Renaissance.* New York: Columbia University Press.

Kemp, William. 1997. Counterfeit Aldines and italic-letter editions printed in Lyons, 1502–10: Early diffusion in Italy and France. *Papers of the Bibliographical Society of Canada,* 4 January 1997.

———. 2008. De Laurent Hyllaire et Jacques Moderne à Sébastien Gryphe: Erasme à Lyon pendant les années 1520. In *Quid novi? Sébastien Gryphe à l'occasion du 450e anniversaire de sa mort,* ed. Raphaële Mouren, 153–180. Villeurbanne: ENSIBB.

Kindleberger, Charles P. 1991. The economic crisis of 1619–1623. *Journal of Economic History* 51: 149–175.

Kingdon, R. M. 1957. The business activities of printers Henri and François Estienne. In *Aspects de la propaganda religieuse,* ed. Gabrielle Bertoud, 258–275. Geneva: Droz.

Kinser, Samuel. 1966. *The works of Jacques-Auguste de Thou.* The Hague: Martinus Nijhoff.

Kirchhoff, Albrecht. 1853a. *Versuch einer Geschichte des deutschen Buchhandels.* Leipzig: J. C. Hinrichs'sche Buchhandlung.

———. 1853b. *Die Handschriftenhändler des Mittelalters.* Leipzig: J. C. Hinrichs'sche Buchhandlung.

Koch, Rainer, ed. 1991. *Brücke zwischen den Völkern: Zur Geschichte der Frankfurter Messe.* 3 vols. Frankfurt am Main: Historisches Museum.

Kolb, Robert. 1976. *Caspar Peucer's library.* St. Louis: Center for Reformation Research.

Koelner, Paul. 1935. *Die Safranzunft zu Basel und ihre Handwerke und Gewerbe.* Basel: Schwabe.

Kohlndorfer-Fries, Ruth. 2009. *Diplomatie und Gelehrtenrepublik: Die Kontakte des französischen Gesandten Jacques Bongars (1554–1612).* Tübingen: Niemeyer.

Kolb, Robert. 1977. Dynamics of party conflict in the Saxon late Reformation: Gnesio-Lutherans vs. Philippists. *Journal of Modern History* 49: 1289–305.

Könnecke, Gustav. 1894. *Hessisches Buchdruckerbuch*. Marburg: Elwert.

Koppitz, Hans-Joachim, ed. 2008. *Die kaiserlichen Druckprivilegien im Haus-, Hof-, und Staatsarchiv Wien*. Wiesbaden: Harrassowitz.

Kosch, Wilhelm. 1971. *Deutsches Literatur-lexikon*. Bern: Francke.

Kraye, Jill, ed. 1996. *The Cambridge companion to Renaissance humanism*. Cambridge: Cambridge University Press.

Krüger, Herbert. 1974. *Die älteste deutsche Routenhandbuch: Jörg Gails Raißbüchlin*. Graz: Akademische Druck- und Verlagsanstalt.

Kühlmann, Wilhelm. 1982. *Gelehrtenrepublik und Fürstenstaat: Entwicklung und Kritik des deutschen Späthumanismus in der Literatur des Barockzeitalters*. Tübingen: Niemeyer.

———, ed. 2005. *Die deutschen Humanisten: Die Kurpfalz*. Vols. 1.1 and 1.2. Turnhout: Brepols.

Kumaniecki, K., R. A. B. Mynors, C. Robinson, and J. H. Waszink. 1969. General introduction. In Desiderius Erasmus, *Opera omnia*. Amsterdam: North-Holland.

Künast, Hans Jörg. 1997. *Getruckt zu Augspurg: Buchdruck und Buchhandel in Augsburg zwischen 1468 und 1555*. Tübingen: Niemeyer.

Kunze, Horst. 1993. *Geschichte der Buchillustration in Deutschland*. Vol 1: *Das sechzente und siebzehnte Jahrhundert*. Leipzig: Inselverlag.

Kusukawa, Sachiko. 1997. Leonhart Fuchs on the importance of pictures. *Journal of the History of Ideas* 58: 403–427.

———. 2000. Illustrating nature. In *Books and the Sciences in History*, ed. Marina Frasca-Spada and Nick Jardine, 90–113. Cambridge: Cambridge University Press.

———. [forthcoming]. *Picturing the book of nature: The emergence of visual arguments in sixteenth-century Europe*. Chicago: Chicago University Press.

Kusukawa, Sachiko, and Ian Maclean, eds. 2006. *Transmitting knowledge: words images, and instruments in early modern Europe*. Oxford: Oxford University Press.

Labarre, Albert. 1970. Editions et privilèges des héritiers d'André Wechel à Francfort et à Hanau, 1582–1627. *Gutenberg-Jahrbuch* 46: 238–250.

———. 1971. *Le Livre dans la vie amiénoise du 16e siècle*. ParisLouvain: Nauwelaerts.

Lafond, Jean, and Andre Stegmann, eds. 1981. *L'automne de la Renaissance, 1580–1630. Actes du XXIIe colloque international d'etudes humanistes, Tours*. Paris: Vrin.

Lane, Anthony N. S. 1999. *John Calvin: Student of the church fathers*. Edinburgh: Clark.

La Perrière, Yvonne. 1967. *Supplément provisoire à la "Bibliographie lyonnaise" du président Baudrier*. Paris: Bibliothèque Nationale.

Le Clech-Charton, Sylvie. 1996. Le Cabinet de lecture de Claude de l'Aubespine à Bourges, ou la culture de la noblesse au XVIe siècle. In *Cahiers d'Archéologie et d'Histoire du Berry: Mélanges Jean-Yves Ribault,* ed.Philippe Goldman and Christian E-Roth, 221–226. Bourges: SAHB.

Leedham-Green, E. S. 1986. *Books in Cambridge inventories: Book lists from Vice-Chancellor's Court probate inventories in the Tudor and Stuart periods.* Cambridge: Cambridge University Press.

Leedham-Green, Elizabeth, and Teresa Webber, eds. 2006. *The Cambridge history of British libraries: to 1640.* Cambridge: Cambridge University Press.

Lehmann, Paul. 1956–1960. *Eine Geschichte der alten Fuggerbibliotheken.* 2 vols. Tübingen: Mohr (Siebeck).

Lehne, Friedrich. 1939. *Zur Rechtsgeschichte der kaiserlichen Privilegien.* Mittteilungen des österreichischen Instituts für Geschichtsforschung 53: 323–405.

Lenk, Leonhard. 1989. *Augsburger Bürgertum im Späthumanismus und Frühbarock (1580–1700).* Augsburg: H. Mühlberger.

Leonnard, Hans Konrad. 1902. *Samuel Selfisch.* Leipzig: Jäh und Schunke.

Lepri, Valentina. 2008. Johann Wechel, Giovan Battista Ciotti e le ultime edizioni di Bruno. *Rinascimento,* 2nd series, 48: 367–388.

———. [forthcoming]. L'editore Giovan Battista Ciotti tra mercato e politica. *Archivo storico lucchese.*

Lesage, Claire, Eve Netchine, and Véronique Sarrazin. 2006. *Catalogues de librarires, 1473–1800.* Paris: Bibliothèque Nationale de France.

Lignereux, Yann. 2003. *Lyon et le roi: De la bonne ville à l'absolutisme municipal, 1594–1654.* Seyssel: Champ Vallon.

Lohr, Charles H. 1987. *Latin Aristotle commentaries,* vol. 2: *Renaissance authors.* Florence: Olschki.

Lotz-Heumann, Ute, and Matthias Pohlig. 2007. Confessionalization and literature in the Empire, 1555–1700. *Central European History* 40: 35–61.

Love, Harold. 1993. *Scribal publication in seventeenth-century England.* Oxford: Oxford University Press.

Lowry, Martin. 1979. *The world of Aldus Manutius: Business and scholarship in Renaissance Venice.* Oxford: Blackwell.

Lyon, Gregory B. 2003. Baudouin, Flacius, and the plan for the Magdeburg centuries. *Journal of the History of Ideas* 64: 253–272.

MacCulloch, Diarmaid. 2003. *Reformation: Europe's house divided.* London: Penguin and Allen Lane.

Maclean, Ian. 1992. *Interpretation and meaning in the Renaissance: The case of law.* Cambridge: Cambridge University Press.

———. 1993. Bourdieu's field of cultural production. *French Cultural Studies* 4: 283–289.

———. 2001. *Logic signs and nature in the Renaissance: The case of learned medicine.* Cambridge: Cambridge University Press.

———. 2006a. Introduction. In René Descartes, *A discourse on the method,* trans, Ian Maclean, Oxford: World's Classics.

———. 2006b. *Le monde et les hommes selon les médecins de la Renaissance:* Paris: Editions CNRS.

———. 2009. *Learning and the market place: Essays in the history of the early modern book.* Leiden: Brill.

———. [forthcoming a]. Le séjour d'Alciat à Bourges, vu à travers sa correspondance et ses préfaces berruyères. In *ommes de lettres, hommes de loi: Bourges à la Renaissance,* ed. Stéphan Geonget.

———. [forthcoming b] Les premiers ouvrages d'Alciat. In *André Alciat: un humaniste au confluent des savoirs dans l'Europe de la Renaissance,* ed. Anne and Stéphane Rolet.

Magnien, Michel. 1982. Un humaniste face aux problèmes d'édition: Jules-César Scaliger et les imprimeurs. *Bibliothèque d'Humanisme et Renaissance* 44: 307–329.

Mandelbrote, Giles. 1995. A new edition of the distribution of books by catalogue: Problems and prospects. *Bibliographical Society of America* 89: 399–408.

———. 2008. The first printed library catalogue? A German doctor's library of the sixteenth century and its place in the history of the distribution of books by catalogue. In *Le biblioteche private come paradigma bibliografico,* ed. Fiammetta Sabba, 295–311. Rome: Bulzoni.

Mantese, Giovanni. 1968. *I mille libri che si leggevano e vendevano a Vicenza alla fine del secolo XVI.* Vicenza: Accademia Olimpica.

Marr, Alexander. 2006. The production and distribution of Mutio Oddi's Dello Squadro (1625). In *Transmitting knowledge: words, images and instruments in early modern Europe,* ed. Sachiko Kusukawa and Ian Maclean, 165–192. Oxford: Oxford University Press.

———. 2008. A Renaissance library rediscovered: The 'Repertorium librorum Mathematica' of Jean I du Temps. *The Library,* 7th series, 9: 428–470.

———. 2009. Ed. *The worlds of Oronce Fine: Mathematics, instruments and print in Renaissance France.* Donington: Shaun Tyas.

Martin, Henri-Jean. 1982a. La révolution de l'imprimé. In *Histoire de l'Edition française,* vol. 1: *Le livre conquérant,* ed. Henri-Jean Martin, Roger Chartier, and Pierre Vivet, 145–162. Paris: Promodis.

———. 1982b. Renouvellements et concurrences. In *Histoire de l'Edition française,* vol. 1: *Le livre conquérant,* ed. Henri-Jean Martin, Roger Chartier, and Pierre Vivet, 379–403. Paris: Promodis.

———. 1987. *Pour une histoire du livre (XVe –XVIIIe siècle).* Paris: Bibliopolis.

———. 1999. *Livres, pouvoirs et société à Paris au XVIIe siècle.* 2 vols. Geneva: Droz.

Martin, Henri-Jean, Roger Chartier, and Pierre Vivet, eds. 1982. *Histoire de l'Edition française,* vol. 1: *Le livre conquérant.* Paris: Promodis.

Mastellone, Salvo. 1974. Gallicans et libertins. In *Aspects du libertinisme au XVIe siècle; actes du colloque international de Sommières,* ed. Marcel Bataillon et al., 29–234. Paris: Vrin.

Materné, Jan. 1996. La librairie de la Contre-Réforme: Le réseau de l'Officine plantinienne au XVIIe siècle. In *L'Europe et le livre: Réseaux et pratiques du négoce de librairie XVIe–XIXe siècles,* ed. Frédéric Barbier, Sabine Juratic, and Dominique Varry, 43–59. Paris: Klincksieck.

Matthäus, Michael. 2009. Der Frankfurter Drucker Johann Wechel. *Gutenberg-Jahrbuch* 84: 169–183.

McCulloch, Peter. 1998. Making dead men speak: Laudianism, print and the works of Lancelot Andrewes, 1626–42. *Historical Journal* 41: 401–424.

McKenzie, D. F. 2002. *Making meaning: "Printers of the Mind" and other essays.* Edited by Peter D. McDonald and Michael F. Suarez. Amherst: University of Massachusetts Press.

McKitterick, Rosamund. 2000. Books and the sciences before print. In *Books and the sciences in history,* ed. Marina Frasca-Spada and Nick Jardine, 13–34. Cambridge: Cambridge University Press.

McLelland, Joseph C., ed. 1980. *Peter Martyr Vermigli and Italian reform.* Waterloo, Ont.: Wilfrid Laurier University Press.

Mellot, Jean-Dominique. 1996. Librairie et cadre corporatif en France à l'âge classique. In *L'Europe et le livre: réseaux et pratiques du négoce de librairie XVIe–XIXe siècles,* ed. Frédéric Barbier, Sabine Juratic, and Dominique Varry, 61–77. Paris: Klincksieck.

———. 2009. La capitale et l'imprimé à l'apogée de l'absolutisme (1618–1723). In *Une capitale internationale du livre: Paris, XVIIe–XXe siècle,* ed. Jean-Yves Mollier, 143–188. Geneva: Droz.

Meyer, Horst. 1987. Buchhandel. In *Die Erforschung der Buch- und Bibliothekgeschichte in Deutschland,* ed. Werner Arnold, Wolfgang Dittrick and Bernhard Zeller, 188–260. Wiesbaden: Harrassowitz.

Meyn, Matthias. 1980. *Die Reichsstadt Frankfurt am Main vor dem Bürgeraufstand von 1612–1614: Struktur und Krise.* Frankfurt am Main: Kramer.

Milton, Anthony. 2010. The Church of England and the Palatinate. *Proceedings of the British Academy* 164: 137–165.

Mittler, Elmar, ed. 1999. *Bibliotheca palatina: Druckschriften-stampati palatini-printed books. Katalog zur Microfiche-Ausgabe.* 4 vols. Munich: Saur.

Morison, S. 1963. The learned press as an institution. In *Bibliotheca docet: Festgabe für Carl Wehmer,* ed. Siegfried Joost, 153–179. Amsterdam Verlag der Erasmus-Buchhandlung.

Morisse, Gérard. 2000. L'activité en Espagne d'un libraire lyonnais du XVIe siècle, d'après les dossiers de la Chancellerie de Castille. *Revista portuguesa de história do livro e da edição* 4: 67–100.

Mosley, Adam. 2007. *Bearing the Hheavens: Tycho Brahe and the astronomical community of the late sixteenth century.* Cambridge: Cambridge University Press.

Moss, Ann. 2003. *Renaissance truth and the Latin language turn.* Oxford: Oxford University Press.

Moulinier-Brogi, Laurence, and Nicolas Weill-Parot. 2007. La science médiévale, du codex à l'imprimé. *Médiévales* 52: 7–14.

Mouren, Raphaële, ed. 2008. *Quid novi? Sébastien Gryphe à l'occasion du 450e anniversaire de sa mort,* 153–180. Villeurbanne: ENSIBB.

———. 2010. L'auteur, l'imprimeur, et les autres: éditer les oeuvres complètes de Cicéron (1533–40). In *Écrivain et imprimeur,* ed. Alain Ruffiaud, 123–146. Rennes: Presses universitaires de Rennes.

——. [forthcoming]. *Author, authority and modes of reference in the humanist book of the fifteenth and sixteenth centuries.*

Mulsow, Martin. 2001. Gelehrte Pratiken politischer Kompromittierung: Melchior Goldast und Lipsius' Rede "De duplici concordia" im Vorfeld der Entstehung der protestantischen Union. In *Die Pratiken der Gelehrsamkeit in der frühen Neuzeit,* ed. Helmut Zedelmaier and Martin Mulsow, 308–347. Tübingen: Niemeyer.

——. 2007. *Die unanständige Gelehrtenrepublik: Wissen, Libertinage und Kommunikation in der Frühen Neuzeit.* Stuttgart: Metzler.

Myers, Robin, Michael Harris, and Giles Mandelbrote, eds. 2001. *Under the hammer: Book auctions since the seventeenth century.* New Castle, DE: Oak Knoll Press; London: British Library.

——, eds. 2009. *Books for sale: The advertising and promotion of print since the fifteenth century.* New Castle, DE: Oak Knoll Press; London: British Library.

Nelles, Paul. 1997. The Library as an instrument of discovery: Gabriel Naudé and the uses of history. In *History and the disciplines: The reclassification of knowledge in early modern Europe,* ed. Donald R. Kelley, 41–57. Rochester: Rochester University Press.

——. 1999. L'érudition ecclésiastique et les bibliothèques de Paris au XVIIe siècle: Etude de catalogage et de classification. *Revue française d'histoire du livre* 104–105: 227–252.

——. 2001. Historia litteraria at Helmstedt: Books, professors and students in the early Enlightenment university. In *Die Praktiken der Gelehrsamkeit in der frühen Neuzeit,* ed. Helmut Zedelmaier and Martin Mulsow, 147–175. Tübingen: Niemeyer.

——. 2007. The uses of orthodoxy and Jacobean erudition: Thomas James and the Bodleian Library. *History of Universities* 22: 21–70.

——. 2010. Reading and memory in the universal library: Conrad Gesner and the Renaissance book. In *Ars Reminiscendi: Mind and Memory in Renaissance Culture,* ed. Donald Beecher and Grant Williams, 147–169. Toronto: CRRS.

——. [forthcoming a]. Stocking a library: Montaigne, the market, and the diffusion of print. In *La librairie de Montaigne,* ed. Neil Kenny.

——. [forthcoming b]. *The invention of the Renaissance library.*

Niedermeier, Hans. 1967–1969. Johannes Rynmann (1460–1522), ein Verleger theologischer Literatur. *Börsenblatt für den deutschen Buchhandel* 61: 2723-2730.

Niemeier, Sabine. 2003. *Funktionen der Frankfurter Buchmesse im Wandel von den Anfängen bis heute.* Wiesbaden: Harrassowitz.

Nissen, Claus. 1951. *Die botanische Buchillustration.* 2 vols. Stuttgart: Hiersemann.

Nuovo, Angela. 2003. *Il Commercio Librario nell'Italia del Rinascimento.* Milan: FrancoAngeli.

——. 2004. Giovanni Giolito, publisher of law books in Pavia (1503–1520). *Gutenberg-Jahrbuch* 79: 153–181.

———. 2005a. *Biblioteche private in età moderna e contemporanea: Atii del convegno internazionale Udine, 18–20 ottobre 2004*. Milan: Bonnard.

———, ed. 2005b. Dispersione di una biblioteca privata: La biblioteca di Gian Vincenzo Pinelli dall'agosto 1601 all'ottobre 1604. In *Biblioteche private in età moderna e contemporanea*, ed. Angela Nuovo, 43–54. Milan: Bonnard.

———. 2007. Gian Vincenzo Pinelli's collection of catalogues of private libraries in sixteenth-century Europe. *Gutenberg-Jahrbuch* 82: 129–143.

———. [forthcoming]. *The book trade in the Italian Renaissance: Structure and regulation*.

Nuovo, Angela, and Ennio Sandal. 1998. *Il libro nell'Italia del Rinascimento*. Brescia: Grafo.

Nussbaum, Martha. 2010. *Not for profit: Why democracy needs the humanities*. Princeton: Princeton University Press.

Nutton, Vivian. 1993. *Medicine and printing in the sixteenth century*. Bishop and LeFanu Memorial Lecture 1993, CILIP Health Libraries Section AGM.

———. 1995. The changing language of medicine, 1450–1550. In *Vocabulary of teaching and research between the Middle Ages and the Renaissance*, ed. Olga Weijers, 184–198. Turnhout: Brepols.

Offer, Avner. 1997. Between the gift and the market: The economy of regard. *Economic History Review* 50: 450–476.

Ogilvie, Sheilagh C. 1992. Germany and the seventeenth-century crisis. *Historical Journal* 35.2: 417–441.

Olson, Oliver K. 2002. *Flacius Illyricus and the survival of Luther's reform*. Wiesbaden: Harrassowitz.

Ong, Walter J. 1958. *Ramus and Talon inventory: A short-title inventory of the published works of Peter Ramus (1515–1572) and of Omer Talon (ca. 1510–1562) in their original and in their variously altered forms*. Cambridge, MA: Harvard University Press.

Osler, Douglas J. 2005. *Catalogue of books printed before 1600 in the legal historical section of the Biblioteca di Scienze Soziali dell'Università degli Studi di Firenze*. Florence: Firenze University Press.

Osler, Douglas J., Paolo Campanella, and Rita Viola, eds. 2005. *Le cinquecentine della Facoltà di giurisprudenza [dell'Università degli Studi di Teramo]*. Pescara: Edizioni Scientifiche Abruzzesi.

Paisley, David. 2003. German book fair catalogues. *The Library* 4.4: 417–427.

Palisca, Claude V. 2006. *Music and ideas in the sixteenth and seventeenth centuries*. Urbana: University of Illinois Press.

Pallier, Denis. 1982. Le livre et les propagandes religieuses: Les réponses catholiques. In *Histoire de l'Edition française*, vol. 1: *Le livre conquérant*, ed. Henri-Jean Martin, Roger Chartier and Pierre Vivet, 327–350. Paris: Promodis.

———. 2000. Les imprimeurs du roi au XVIe siècle: La constitution d'un nouvel office dans les métiers du livre. In *Le livre et l'art: Études offertes à Pierre Lelièvre*, ed. Thérèse Kleindienst, 183–202. Paris: Somogy; Villeurbanne: ENSIBB.

Pallmann, Heinrich. 1881. *Sigmund Feyerabend: Sein Leben und seine geschäftlichen Verbindungen nach archivalischen Quellen.* Frankfurt am Main: K. Th. Völcker's Verlag.

Pantin, Isabelle. 1986. *Imprimeurs et libraires du XVIe siècle: Ouvrage publié d'après les manuscrits de Philippe Renouard, fascicule Cavellat.* Paris: Paris-Musées.

———. 1988. Les problèmes de l'édition des livres scientifiques: L'exemple de Guillaume Cavellat. In *Le livre dans l'Europe de la Renaissance,* ed. Pierre Aquilon and Henri-Jean Martin, 240–252. Paris: Promodis.

———. 1996. Latin et langues vernaculaires dans la littérature scientifique au début de l'époque moderne. In *Sciences et langues en Europe,* ed. Roger Chartier and Pietro Corsi, 43–58. Paris: EHESS.

———. 1999. New philosophy and old prejudices: Aspects of the reception of Copernicanism in a divided Europe. *Studies in the History and Philosophy of Science* 30: 237–262.

———. 2006. Kepler's *epitome:* New images for an innovative book. In *Transmitting knowledge: Words, images and instruments in early modern Europe,* ed. Sachiko Kusukawa and Ian Maclean, 217–238. Oxford: Oxford University Press.

Papy, Jan. 2003. Justus Lipsius and the German republic of letters: Latin philology as a means of intellectual exchange and influence. In *Germania latina— Latinitas teutonica: Politik, Wissenschaft, humanistische Kultur vom späten Mittelalter bis in unsere Zeit,* ed. Eckhard Kessler and Heinrich C. Kuhn, 523–538 (Reihe I, 54). Munich: Humanistische Bibliothek.

Parent-Charon, Annie. 1982. Le monde de l'imprimerie humaniste. In *Histoire de l'Edition française,* vol. 1: *Le livre conquérant,* ed. Henri-Jean Martin, Roger Chartier and Pierre Vivet, 237–254. Paris: Promodis.

———. 1996. Associations dans la librairie parisienne du XVIe siècle. In *L'Europe et le livre: Réseaux et pratiques du négoce de librairie XVIe–XIXe siècles,* ed. Frédéric Barbier, Sabine Juratic, and Dominique Varry, 17–29. Paris: Klincksieck.

———. 2005. La pratique des privilèges chez Josse Bade (1510–1535). In *Printers and readers in the sixteenth century,* ed. Christian Coppens, 15–26. Turnhout: Brepols.

Paschen, Christine. 1995. Buchproduktion und Buchbesitz in der frühen Neuzeit: Amberg in der Oberpfalz. *Archiv für Geschichte des Buchwesens* 43: 1–201.

Pelletier, André, and Jacques Rossiaud. 1990. *Histoire de Lyon des origines à nos jours,* vol. 1 : *Antiquité et Moyen Age.* Lyon: Horvath.

Pérez Pastor, Cristóbal. 1895. *La imprenta en Medina del Campo.* Madrid: Sucesores de Rivadeneyra.

Perini, Leandro. 2002. *La vita e i tempi di Pietro Perna.* Rome: Edizioni di storia e litteratura.

Pesenti, Tiziana. 2000. How did early printers choose medical commentaries for the press? In *Medical Latin from the late Middle Ages to the eighteenth century,* ed. Wouter Bracke and Herwig Deumens, 67–92. Brussels: Konin-klijke Academie voor Geneeskunde van België.

Petitmengin, Pierre. 2004. Latino Latini: Une longue vie au service des Peres de l'Église. In *Humanisme et Église en Italie et en France méridionale: XVe siècle–milieu du XVIe siècle,* ed. Patrick Gilli, 381–407. (Collection de l'École française de Rome 330.) Rome: École française de Rome.

Petrucci, Armando. 1969. Alle origini del libro moderno: Libri da banco, libri da bisaccia, libretti da mano. *Italia medioevale e umanistica* 12: 295–313.

Pettas, William A. 1980. *The Giunti of Florence: Merchant publishers of the six-teenth century.* San Francisco: Rosenthal.

———. 1995. *A sixteenth-century Spanish bookstore: The inventory of Juan de Junta.* Philadelphia: American Philosophical Society.

———. 1997. The Giunti and the book trade in Lyon. In *Libri, Tipografi, Biblio-thece: Ricerche storiche dedicate a Luigi Balsamo,* ed. Arnaldo Ganda and E. Grignani, 169–192. Florence: Olschki.

Pettegree, Andrew. 1994. *Emden as a centre of the sixteenth-century book trade: A catalogue of the bookseller Gaspar Staphorst.* Quaerendo 24: 114–125.

———. 2002. Printing and the Reformation: The English exception. In *The beginnings of English Protestantism,* ed. Peter Marshall and Alec Ryrie, 157–179. Cambridge: Cambridge University Press.

———. 2008. Centre and periphery in the European book world. *Transactions of the Royal Historical Society* 18: 101–128.

———. 2010. *The book in the Renaissance.* New Haven: Yale University Press.

Pinon, Laurent. 2008. La *Naturalis Historia* d'Adam Lonitzer: Une Oeuvre mi-neure? In *Esculape et Dionysos: Mélanges en l'Honneur de Jean Céard,* ed. Jean Dupèbe, Franco Giacone, Emmanuel Naya, and Anne-Pascale Pouey-Mounou, 443–457. Geneva: Droz.

———. [forthcoming a]. *Ulysse Aldrovandi.*

———. [forthcoming b]. *Un Auteur-éditeur: Ippolito Saviani et son Historia Aquatilium Animalium (1557–1558).*

Pollard, G., and A. Ehrman. 1965. *The distribution of books by catalogue from the invention of printing to* A.D. 1800, based on material in the Broxbourne Library. Cambridge: Roxburghe Club.

Pöllmann, Hansjörg. 1966. Die Urheberrechtsstreit des Wittenberger Professors Dr. med. Kaspar Peukers mit der Frankfurter Verleger Sigismund Feyerabend. *Archiv für Geschichte des Buchwesens* 6: 594–639.

Pomata, Giovanna. 2010. Sharing cases: The *observationes* in early modern medicine. *Early Science and Medicine* 15: 193–236.

Popkin, Richard. 1990. The role of Jewish anti-Christian arguments in the rise of scepticism. In *new perspectives on Renaissance thought: Essays in the history of science, education and philosophy in memory of Charles B. Schmitt,* ed. John Henry and Sarah Hutton, 1–12. London: Duckworth.

Popper, William. 1969. *The censorship of Hebrew books.* New York: KTAV.

Post, G., K. Giocarinis, and R. Kay. 1955. The medieval heritage of a humanist ideal: Scientia donum Dei est, unde vendi non potest. *Traditio* 9: 195–234.

Prestwich, Menna, ed. 1985. *International Calvinism: 1541–1715.* Oxford: Clarendon Press.

Primary sources on copyright (1450–1900). At http://www.copyrighthistory.org.

Purcell, Mark. 1999. "Useful weapons for the defence of that cause": Richard Allestree, John Fell and the Foundation of the Allestree Library. *The Library* 6.21: 124–147.

Putnam, G. H. 1906. *The censorship of the Church of Rome and its influence on the production and distribution of literature.* 2 vols. New York: G. P. Putnam's Sons.

Racine, Pierre. 1991. Messen in Italien im 16. Jahrhundert: Die Wechselmessen von Piacenza. In *Brücke zwischen den Völkern: Zur Geschichte der Frankfurter Messe,* vol. 1, ed. Rainer Koch, 155–170. Frankfurt am Main: Historisches Museum.

Rautenberg, Ursula. 2008. Die Entstehung und Entwicklung des Buchtitelblatts in der Inkunabelzeit in Deutschland, den Niederlanden und Venedig: Quantative und qualitative Studien. *Archiv für Geschichte des Buchwesens* 62: 1–105.

Raz-Kiakotzkin, A. 2007. *The censor, the editor and the text: The Catholic Church and the shaping of the Jewish canon in the sixteenth century.* Translated by Jake Feldman. Philadelphia: University of Pennsylvania Press.

Reeds, Karen M. 1991. *Botany in medieval and Renaissance universities.* New York: Columbia University Press.

Rees, Graham, and Maria Wakely. 2009. *Publishing, politics and culture: The king's printers in the reign of James I and IV.* Oxford: Oxford University Press.

Renouard, Philippe. 1965. *Répertoire des imprimeurs parisiens.* Paris: Minard.

Reske, Christoph. 2000. *Die Produktion der Schedelschen Weltchronik in Nürnberg.* Wiesbaden: Harrassowitz.

———. 2007. *Die Buchdrucker des 16. und 17. Jahrhunderts im deutschen Sprachgebiet: Auf der Grundlage des gleichnamigen Werkes von Josef Benzing.* Wiesbaden: Harrassowitz.

Reusch, Franz Heinrich. 1883–1888. *Der Index der verbotenen Bücher: ein Beitrag zur Kirchen- und Literaturgeschichte.* 2 vols. Bonn: M. Cohen.

Reyes Gómez, Fermín de los. 2000. *El libro en España y América: Legislacíon y Censura (siglos XV–XVIII).* 2 vols. Madrid: Arco/Libros.

Rhodes, Dennis E. 1967. Per la biblioteca di Belisario Bulgarini e per la storia del mercato librario in Siena lui vivente (1539–1620). In *Studi bibliografici: Atti del convegno dedicato alla storia del libro italiano nel V centenario dell'introduzione dell'arte tipografica in Italia, Bolzano, 7–8 ottobre 1965,* 159–168. Florence, Olschki.

———. 1987. Some neglected aspects of the career of Giovanni Battista Ciotti. *The Library,* 6th series, 9.3: 225–239.

———. 2005. Notes on the expansion of business activities of Francesco de' Franceschi. *Gutenberg-Jahrbuch* 80: 133–135.

———. 2011. Spanish books on sale in the Venetian bookshop of G. B. Ciotti, 1602. *The Library,* 7th series, 12.1: 50–55.

———. [forthcoming]. *The career of Giovanni Battista Ciotti.*

Richardson, Brian. 1994. *Print culture in Renaissance Italy: The editor and the vernacular text, 1470–1600.* Cambridge: Cambridge University Press.

———. 2004. Print or pen? Modes of written publication in sixteenth-century Italy. *Italian Studies* 59: 39–64.

———. 2009. *Manuscript culture in Renaissance Italy.* Cambridge: Cambridge University Press.

Richter, Günter. 1967. Christian Egenolffs Erben, 1555–1667. *Archiv für Geschichte des Buchwesens* 7: 449–1130.

———. 1974. Bibliographische Beiträge zur Geschichte buchhandlerischer Kataloge im 16. und 17. Jahrhundert. In *Beiträge zur Geschichte des Buches und seiner Funktion in der Gesellschaft. Festschrift für Hans Widman,* 183–229. Stuttgart: Hiersemann.

———. 1985. Buchhändlerische Kataloge von 15. bis um die Mitte des 17. Jahrhunderts. In *Bücherkataloge als buchgeschichtliche Quellen in der frühen Neuzeit,* ed. Reinhard Wittmann, 33–65. Wiesbaden: Harrassowitz.

———. 1997. Humanistische Bücher in Buchhändlerkatalogen des 15. und 16. Jahrhunderts. In Fritz Krafft and Dieter Wuttke, eds., *Das verhältnis der Humanisten zum Buch,* 184–208. Bonn: Deutsche Forschungsgemeinschaft.

Rico, Francisco. 1998–2010. Historia del texto. At http://cvc.cervantes.es.

Rietbergen, Peter J. A. N. 1983. Printing Baronius' *Annales ecclesiastici. Quaerendo* 13: 87–102.

Rinaldi, Massimo. 2009. Modèles de vulgarisation dans l'anatomie du XVIe siècle: Notes sur la *Contemplatione anatomica* de Prospero Borgarucci (1564). In *Vulgariser la médecine: Du style médical en France et en Italie,* ed. Andrea Carlino and Michel Jeanneret, 35–54. Geneva: Droz.

Roberts, Julian. 1997. Importing books for Oxford, 1500–1640. In *Books and collectors, 1200–1700: Essays presented to Andrew Watson,* ed. James P. Carley and Colin G. C. Tite, 317–333. London: British Library.

———. 2000. The Latin stock (1616–27) and its library contacts. In *Libraries and the book trade,* ed. Robin Myers, Michael Harris, and Giles Mandelbrote, 15–28. New Castle, DE: Oak Knoll Press.

Roberts, Julian, and Andrew G. Watson, eds. 1990. *John Dee's library catalogue.* London: Bibliographical Society.

Rosenberg, Daniel, and Anthony Grafton. 2010. *Cartographies of time: A history of the timeline.* New York: Princeton Architectural Press.

Ross, Alan. 2009. Scholarship and education after the Thirty Years' War: Christian Daum and his pupils at the Latin School of Zwickau/Saxony. D.Phil. diss., Oxford University, Oxford.

Ross, Richard J. 1998. The commoning of the common law: The Renaissance debate over printing English law, 1520–1640. *University of Pennsylvania Law Review* 146: 323–461.

Rosseaux, Ulrich. 2001. *Die Kipper und Wipper also publizistisches Ereignis (1620–26).* Berlin: Dunker und Humblot.

Roth, Carl. 1914. Die Bücherzensur im alten Basel. *Zentralblatt für Bibliothekswesen* 31: 49–67.

Roth, Paul W. 1993. Die Kipper- und Wipper-Zeit in den Habsburgischen Ländern, 1620 bis 1623. In *Geld und Währung vom 16. Jahrhundert bis zur Gegenwart,* ed. Eckart Schremmer, 85–103. Stuttgart: Franz Steiner.

Rott, Hans, ed. 1905. Briefe des Heidelberger Theologen Zacharias Ursinus aus Heidelberg und Neustadt. *Neue Heidelberger Jarhbücher* 1905: 39–172.

Roure, Damià. 2007. *La Biblioteca de Monserrat*. Monserrat: Publicacion de l'Abadia.

Rouse, Mary A., and Richard H. Rouse. 1988. *Cartolai, illuminators and printers in fifteenth-century Italy: The evidence of the Ripoli Press*. Los Angeles: University of California.

Rozzo, Ugo. 1988. La Cultura Italiana nelle Edizione Lionese di Sébastien Gryphius. *La Bibliofilia* 90: 161–195.

———. 2008. Sébastien Gryphe, Editore di Humanisti es "Eretici" Italiani. In *Quid novi? Sébastien Gryphe à l'occasion du 450e anniversaire de sa mort*, ed. Raphaële Mouren, 113–152. Villeurbanne: ENSIBB.

Rudolphi, E. Camillo. 1963. *Die Buchdrucker-Familie Froschauer in Zürich, 1521–1595*. Nieuwkoop: de Graaf.

Sabbatino, Pasquale, 1986. *Il Modello bembiano a Napoli nel Cinquecento*. Naples: Ferraro.

Sardello, Pierre. 1948. *Nouvelles et spéculations à Venise au début du XVIe siècle*. Paris: A. Colin.

Sbordone, Silvia. 2006. Le Cinquecentine delle Biblioteche dei Caracciolini di Napoli: Studio Analytico dei Typografi. In *Per la Storia della Tipografia Napoletana nei Secoli XV–XVIII*, ed. A. Garzya, 163–193. Naples: Giannini.

Scapecchi, Piero. 1990. An example of printer's copy used in Rome. *The Library* 6.12: 50–52.

Schade, Herwarth von. 1985. Der Einfluss der Reformation auf die Entwicklung des evangelischen Bibliothekswesens. In *Beiträge zur Geschichte des Buchwesens im konfessionellen Zeitalter*, ed. Herbert G. Göpfert, Peter Vodosek, Erdmann Weyrauch, and Reinhard Wittmann, 147–178. Wiesbaden: Harrassowitz.

Schecker, Heinz. 1930. *Melchior Goldast von Haiminsfeld: Eine Studie*. Bremen: Bremer Bibliophile Gesellschaft.

———. 1931. Das Prager Tagebuch des Melchior Goldast von Haiminsfeld in der Bremer Staatsbibliothek. *Abhandlungen und Vorträge herausgegeben von der Bremer Wissenschaftlichen Gesellschaft* 5. 4: 218–280.

Schenker, Adrian. 2008. The polyglot Bibles of Antwerp, Paris and London, 1568–1658. In *Hebrew Bible/Old Testament: The history of its interpretation*, ed. Magne Sæbø, 774–784. Göttingen: Vandenhoeck and Ruprecht.

Schiffrin, André. 2000. *The business of books: How the international conglomerates took over publishing and changed the way we read*. London: Verso Books.

Schmidt, Imke. 1996. *Die Bücher aus der Frankfurter Offizin Güllferich-Han Weigand Han-Erben*. Wiesbaden: Harrassowitz.

Schmitt, Charles B. 1982. John Case e l'Aristotelismo nell'Inghilterra del Rinascimento. *Giornale Critico della Filosofia Italiana* 43: 129–152.

Schnapper, Bernard. 1995. *Les rentes au XVIe siècle: Histoire d'un instrument de crédit*. Paris: EHESS.

Schneider, Konrad. 1990. *Frankfurt und die Kipper- und Wipperinflation der Jahre 1619–23*. Frankfurt am Main: Kramer.

Scholar, Richard. 2006. Introduction. In *Transmitting Knowledge: Words, Images and Instruments in Early Modern Europe,* ed. Sachiko Kusukawa and Ian Maclean, 1–10. Oxford: Oxford University Press.

Schottenloher, Karl. 1933. Die Druckprivilegien des 16. Jahrhunderts. *Gutenberg-Jahrbuch* 8: 89–97.

———. 1935. *Der Buchdrucker als neuer Berufstand des 15 und 16 Jahrhunderts.* Mainz: Verlag der Gutenberg-Gesellschaft.

———. 1953. *Die Widmungsrede im Buch des 16. Jahrhunderts.* Münster: Aschendorff.

Schröder, Felix von. 1904. *Die Verlegung der Büchermesse von Frankfurt am Main nach Leipzig.* Leipzig: Jäh und Schunke.

Schwetschke, Gustav. 1850–1877. *Codex nundinarius Germaniae literatae bisecularis.* Halle: Schwetschke.

Scribner, Bob, ed. 1996. *Germany: A new social and economic history,* vol. 1: *1450–1630.* London: Arnold.

Seebass, Andreas. 1985. Osiander und seine Drucker. In *Beiträge zur Geschichte des Buchwesens im konfessionellen Zeitalter,* ed. Herbert G. Göpfert, Peter Vodosek, Erdmann Weyrauch, and Reinhard Wittmann, 133–147. Wiesbaden: Harrassowitz.

Selm, Bert van. 1986. The introduction of the printed book auction catalogue. *Quaerendo* 15: 16–54.

———. 1987. Een menighte treffelijcke Boecken: Nederlandse Boekhandelscatalogi in het Begin van de zeventiende Eeuw. PhD diss., HES, Utrecht.

Serjeantson, R. W. 2001. Herbert of Cherbury before deism. *Seventeenth Century* 16: 217–238.

Serjeantson, Richard, and Thomas Woolford. 2009. The scribal publication of a printed book: Francis Bacon's *Certain Considerations Touching the Church of England* (1604). *The Library* 7.10: 119–156.

Serrai, Alfredo. 1993. *Storia della Bibliografia IV: Cataloghi a stampa. Bibliografie teologiche. Bibliografie filosofiche.* Edited by Antonio Possevino. Rome: Bulzoni.

Shevchenko, Nadezdo. 2007. *Eine historische Anthropologie des Buches: Bücher in der preußischen Herzogfamilie zur Zeit der Reformation.* Göttingen: Vandenhoeck and Ruprecht.

Shuger, Debora Kuller. 1994. *The Renaissance Bible: Scholarship, sacrifice and subjectivity.* Berkeley: University of California Press.

Simeoni, Luigi. 1940. *Storia della Universita' di Bologna,* vol. 2: *L'Eta' moderna.* Bologna: Zanichelli.

Simonin, Michel. 1988. Peut-on parler de politique éditoriale au XVIe siècle? Le cas de Vincent Sertenas (1534–62), Libraire du Palais. In *Le livre dans l'Europe de la Renaissance,* ed. Pierre Aquilon, Henri-Jean Martin and François Dupuigrenet-Desroussilles, 264–281. Paris: Promodis.

———. 1992. *Vivre de sa Plume au XVIe Siècle, ou la Carrière de François de Belleforest.* Geneva: Droz.

———. 2004. *L'Encre et la Lumière: Quarante-sept articles.* Geneva: Droz.

Simonsfeld, Henry. 1887. *Zur Geschichte deutscher Geerbetriebender in Venedig, Der Fondaco dei Tedeschi in Venedig und die Deutsch-Venetianischen Handelsbeziehungen.* 2 vols. Stuttgart: Verlag der J. G. Cotta'schen Buchhandlung.

Siraisi, Nancy G. 1990. Giovanni Argenterio and sixteenth-century medical innovation, between princely patronage and academic controversy. *Osiris* 2.6: 161–180.

———. 2007. *History, medicine, and the traditions of Renaissance learning.* Ann Arbor: University of Michigan Press.

Simpson, Julianne. 2009. Selling the Biblia Regia: The marketing and distribution methods for Christopher Plantin's polyglot Bible. In *Books for sale: The advertising and promotion of print since the fifteenth century,* ed. Robyn Myers, Michael Harris, and Giles Mandelbrote, 27–55. New Castle, DE: Oak Knoll Press.

Skalnik, James Veazie. 2002. *Ramus and reform: University and Church at the rnd of the Renaissance.* Kirksville, MO: Truman State University Press.

Smith, Margaret M. 2000. *The title-page: Its early development, 1460–1510.* New Castle, DE: Oak Knoll Press; London: British Library.

Stango, Cristina. 2001. *Censura ecclesiastica e Censura politica in Italia tra Cinquecento e Seicento: VI Giornata Luigi Firpo, Atti del Convegno, 5 marzo 1999.* Florence: Olschki.

Starp, Hildegard. 1958. Das Frankfurter Verlagshaus Schönwetter, 1598–1726. *Archiv für Geschichte des Buchwesens* 1: 38–113.

Stein, Peter. 1999. *Roman law in European history.* Cambridge: Cambridge University Press.

Steinmann, Martin. 1967. *Johannes Oporinus: Ein Basler Buchdrucker um die Mitte des 16. Jahrhunderts.* Basel: Helbing und Lichtenhahn.

Stevens, Kevin. 2005. Purchasing a jurist's private library: Girolamo Bordone, Omobono Redenaschi, and the commercial book trade in early seventeenth-century Milan. In *Biblioteche private in età moderna e contemporanea: Atti del convegno internazionale Udine, 18–20 ottobre 2004,* ed. Angela Nuovo, 55–68. Milan: Bonnard.

Stevenson, Enrico, ed. 1966–1969. *Inventario dei libri stampati palatino-vaticani.* Nieuwkoop: B. de Graaf.

Stintzing, Roderich von. 1880. *Geschichte der deutschen Rechtswissenschaft.* Munich: Oldenbourg.

Sturlese, Rita. 1991. Lazar Zetzner "Bibliopoloa Argentinensis." Alchimie und Lullismus in Strassburg an den Anfangen der Moderne. *Sudhoffs Archiv* 75: 140–162.

Sudhoff, Karl. 1860. *Crato von Crafftheim und Sein Freunde.* Frankfurt am Main: H. L. Bronner.

———. 1894. *Bibliographia Paracelsica.* Berlin: Reimer.

Tejero, Emilia Fernández, and Natalio Fernández Marcos. 2008. Scriptural interpretation in Renaissance Spain. In *Hebrew Bible/Old Testament: The history of its interpretation,* ed. Magne Sæbø, 213–253. Göttingen: Vandenhoeck and Ruprecht.

Teneti, Alberto. 1957. Luc'Antonio Giunti il giovane Stampatore e Mercante. In *Studi in onore di Armando Sapori*, 1023–1060. vol 2. Milan: Istituto Editoriale Cisalpino.

Teuteberg, René. 1986. *Basler Geschichte*. Basel: Christoph Merian Verlag.

Thiel, Andreas. 1991. Der Italienhandel. In *Brücke zwischen den Völkern: Zur Geschichte der Frankfurter Messe*, vol. 1, ed. Rainer Koch, 72–76. Frankfurt am Main: Historisches Museum.

Thompson, John B. 2005. *Books in the digital age*. Cambridge: Polity.

Troje, Hans Erich. 1971. *Graeca leguntur: Die Aneignung des byzantinischen Rechts und die Entstehung eines humanistischen Corpus iuris civilis in der Jurisprudenz des sechszehnten Jahhunderts*. Cologne: Bühlau.

Truman, Ronald W. 2004. Fray Juan Ponce de León and the seventeenth-century *libreros* of Madrid. *Bulletin of Spanish Studies* 81: 1091–1107.

———. 2009. La Inquisición y el Mundo de la Erudición europea en los primeros Decenios del Siglo XVII: El Caso de los Libreros madrileños. In *Autoridad y Poder en el Siglo de Oro*, ed. I. Arellano, C. Strosetzki, and Y. E. Williamson, 203–221. Madrid: Iberoamerican; Frankfurt am Main: Vervuert.

———. [forthcoming]. Un Index Librorum prohibitorum español en la Ginebra calvinista: La edición de 1619 por Jean Crespin del Index de Madrid 1612, con un prefacio de Benedetto Turretini, professor Sacrarum literarum.

Trunz, Erich. 1931. Der deutsche Späthumanismus um 1600 als Standeskultur. *Jahrbuch für Geschichte der Erziehung und des Unterrichts* 20: 17–53.

Vaccaro Sofia, Emerenziana. 1961. *Catalogo delle Edizioni romane di Antonio Blado Asolano ed Eredi (1516–93)*, fasc. iv. Rome: Libreria dello Stato.

Vallée, Jean-François. 2008. Faire bonne Impression: Etienne Dolet et Sébasatien Gryphe. In *Quid novi? Sébastien Gryphe à l'Occasion du 450e Anniversaire de sa Mort*, ed. Raphaële Mouren, 183–200. Villeurbanne: ENSIBB.

van Boxel, Piet. [forthcoming]. *Hebrew books and censorship in sixteenth-century Italy*.

van den Branden, Lode, Elly Cockx-Indestege, and Frans Sills. 1978. *Bio-bibliografie van Cornelius Kiliaan*. Nieuwkoop: B. de Graaf.

van der Haeghen, Ferdinand François. 1886. *Bibliographie lipsienne*. 2 vols. Ghent: Vyt.

Vanek, Klara. 2007. *Ars corrigendi in der frühen Neuzeit: Studien zur Geschichte der Textkritik*. Berlin: de Gruyter.

Vasquez de Prada, Valentin. 1991. Die kastilischen Messen im 16. Jahrhundert. In *Brücke zwischen den Völkern: zur Geschichte der Frankfurter Messe*, vol. 1, ed. Rainer Koch, 113–131. Frankfurt am Main: Historisches Museum.

Vervliet, Hendrik Désiré L. 1959. Une instruction plantinienne à l'intention des correcteurs. *Gutenberg-Jahrbuch* 1959: 99–103.

Visser, Arnoud S. Q. 2011. *Reading Augustine in the reformation. The flexibility of intellectual authority in Europe, 1500–1620*. Oxford: Oxford University Press.

Voet, Leon. 1969–1972. *The golden compasses: A history and evaluation of the printing and publishing activities of the Officina Plantaniana at Antwerp in two volumes*. Amsterdam: Vangendt.

Vogel, Walter. 1933. *Der Reichsvizekanzler Georg Sigismund Seld.* Leipzig: Fischer.

Vogt, George McGill. 1924. Richard Robinson's "Eupolemia" (1603). *Studies in Philology* 21: 629–648.

Völkel, Markus. 2001. Das Verhältnis von *religio, patriae, confessio,* et *eruditio* bei Marx Welser. In *Die europäische Gelehrtenrepublik im Zeitalter des Konfessionalismus,* ed. Herbert Jaumann, 127–140. Wiesbaden: Harrassowitz.

von der Linde, Antonius. 1882. *Die Nassauer Drucke der Köglichen Landesbibliothek in Wiesbaden,* vol 1. Wiesbaden: Feller und Gecks.

Wackernagel, Rudolf, ed. 1881. *Rechnungsbuch der Froben und Episcopius, Buckdrucker und Buchhändler zu Basel, 1557–1564.* Basel: Benno Schwabe.

Wadle, Elmar. 2007. *Privilegia Impressoria* vor dem Reichshofrat. In *Höchstgerichte in Europa: Bausteine frühneuzeitlicher Rechtsordnungen,* ed. Leopold Auer, Werner Ogris and Eva Ortlieb, 201–213. Cologne: Böhlau Verlag.

Wagner, Klaus. 1996. Les Libraires espagnols au XVIe Siècle. In *L'Europe et le livre: réseaux et pratiques du négoce de librairie XVIe–XIXe siècles,* ed. Frédéric Barbier, Sabine Juratic, and Dominique Varry, 31–42. Paris: Klincksieck.

Walter, Axel E. 2004. *Späthumanismus und Konfessionspolitik: Die Europäische Gelehrtenpolitik um 1600 im Spiegel der Korrespondenzen Georg Michael Lingelsheims.* Tübingen: Max Niemeyer Verlag.

Waters, Lindsay. 2004. *Enemies of promise: Publishing, perishing and the eclipse of scholarship.* Chicago: Prickly Paradigm Press.

Watson, Timothy D. 1999. The Lyons City Council, c. 1525–75: Politics, culture, religion. D.Phil. diss., Oxford University, Oxford.

Wear, Andrew. 2000. *Knowledge and practice in English medicine, 1550–1680.* Cambridge: Cambridge University Press.

Weidhaas, Peter. 2003. *Zur Geschichte der Frankfurter Buchmesse.* Frankfurt am Main: Suhrkamp.

Wellisch, Hans. 1975. Conrad Gessner: A bio-bibliography. *Journal of the Society for the Bibliography of Natural History* 7: 151–247.

Welti, Manfred. 1985. *Die Bibliothek des Giovanni Bernardino Bonifacio, Marchese d'Oria, 1517–1597.* Bern: Peter Lang.

———. 1988. La genèse de la Bibliothèque de Gdansk (1596). In *Le Livre dans l'Europe de la Renaissance,* ed. Pierre Aquilon, Henri-Jean Martin, and François Dupuigrenet-Desroussilles, 460–466. Paris: Promodis.

Wendland, Henning. 1985. Martin Luther: Seine Buchdrucker und Verleger. In *Beiträge zur Geschichte des Buchwesens im konfessionellen Zeitalter,* ed. Herbert G. Göpfert, Peter Vodosek, Erdmann Weyrauch, and Reinhard Wittmann, 11–36. Wiesbaden: Harrassowitz.

Wendt, Bernhard. 1973. Von Buchhändlern, Buchdruckern und Buchführern: Ein kritischer Beitrag des Johann Friedrich Coelestin aus dem 16. Jahrhundert. *Archiv für Geschichte des Buchwesens* 13: 1587–1624.

Weyrauch, Erdmann. 1985. Leges librorum: Kirchen- und profanrechtliche Reglementierungen des Buchhandels in Europa. In *Beiträge zur Geschichte des Buchwesens im konfessionellen Zeitalter,* ed. Herbert G. Göpfert, Peter

Vodosek, Erdmann Weyrauch, and Reinhard Wittmann, 315–325. Wiesbaden: Harrassowitz.

Whaley, Joachim. [forthcoming]. A German nation? National and confessional identities before the Thirty Years War. In *The Holy Roman Empire, 1495–1806*, ed. R. J. W. Evans, Michael Schaich, and Peter H. Wilson. Oxford: Oxford University Press.

Widmann, Hans. 1966. Nachwort. In *Bibliotheca Universalis [1545, 1555]*, Konrad Gessner, ed., unpaginated. Osnabrück: Otto Zeller Verlagsbuchhandlung.

———. 1967–1969. Autorennöten eines Gelehrten im 16. Jahrhundert. *Archiv für Geschichte des Buchwesens* 9: 1530–1551.

Wijffels, Alain. 1992. *Late sixteenth-century lists of law books at Merton College*. Cambridge: LP Publications.

Wilding, Nick. [forthcoming]. *Printing the* Sidereus Nuntius.

Wilson, Adrian. 1976. *The making of the Nuremberg Chronicle*. Amsterdam: Israel.

Witcombe, Christopher L. C. E. 1991. Christopher Plantin's papal privileges: Documents in the Vatican Archives. *De Gulden Passer* 69: 133–143.

———. 2004. *Copyright in the Renaissance: Prints and the privilegio in sixteenth-century Venice and Rome*. Leiden: Brill.

Wittmann, Reinhard. 1985. *Bücherkataloge als buchgeschichtliche Quellen in der frühen Neuzeit*. Wiesbaden: Harrassowitz.

———. 1999. *Geschichte des deutschen Buchhandels*. Munich: Beck.

Woodfield, Denis B. 1973. *Surreptitious printing in England, 1550–1640*. New York: Bibliographical Society of America.

Woodward, David. 1996. *Maps as prints in the Italian Renaissance: Makers, distributors and consumers*. London: British Library.

———. 2007. *The history of cartography*, vol. 3: *Cartography in the European Renaissance*. Chicago: University of Chicago Press.

Worth, Valerie. [forthcoming]. *Simultaneous publication in Latin and French of medical books*.

Wygant, Amy. 2002. D'Aubignac demonologist II: St. Anthony and the Satyr. *Seventeenth-Century French Studies* 24: 71–85.

Zanden, Jan Luiten van. 2001. Early modern economic growth: A survey of the European economy, 1500–1800. In *Early modern capitalism*, ed. Maarten Prak, 69–87. London: Routledge.

Zanier, Giancarlo. 1991. *Ricerche sulla diffusione e fortuna del* De incantationibus *di Pomponazzi*. Florence: la Nuova Italia.

Zedelmaier, Helmut. 1992. *Bibliotheca universalis und Bibliotheca selecta: Das Problem der Ornung des gelehrten Wissens in der frühen Neuzeit*. Cologne: Böhlau.

Zeeberg, Peter. 2004. *Heinrich Rantzau: A bibliography*. Copenhagen: Society for Danish Language and Literature, C. A. Reitzel.

Zuber, Roger. 1980. Libertinage et humanisme: Une rencontre difficile. *Aspects et contours du libertinage, XVIIe siècle*, 127: 163–177.

Index

Wechel, André, 77, 80, 100, 102, 114, 125, 132–133, 140, 148, 169, 172, 181, 189, 198, 220, 290n32; Chrétien, 80, 133; Presses, 2, 12, 24–25, 37, 54, 60, 69–70, 101, 112–113, 117, 123, 133, 180, 228, 230, 237, 293n69. *See also* Aubry; Marne

Wechel, Johann, 73, 78, 102, 115, 129, 195, 200–201, 257n58, 280nn108, 114, 299n138

Wegelin, Johann, 256n52

Wehner, Paulus Matthias, 44

Weindrich, Martin, 282n147

Welser, Marcus, 20, 25, 48, 54, 103, 140

Wesenbeck, Matthäus, 51, 74

Whitaker, William, 185

Willer, booksellers, 21, 150, 187, 189, 212, 216, 318n74

Willer, Georg, 179, 192, 205

Wimpheling, Jakob, 300n156

Wolf, Johann Huldrich, 20, 40

Wolfe, John, 168, 200

Würrtemberg, Christoph, Duke of, 305n43

Würzburg, Julius Echter von Mespelbrunn, Prince Bishop of, 79, 302n180

Xenophon, 224

Zabarella, Franciscus, 67

Zabarella, Jacopo, 117, 120

Zanchi, Girolamo, 51, 81, 141–145, 150, 166, 195

Zasius, Huldrych, 81

Zenaro, house, 194

Zetzner, Eberhard, 327n41

Zetzner, Lazarus, 43, 102, 110, 118, 132, 184, 228, 296n104, 306n50

Ziletti, Francesco, 66, 117, 279n100

Zinoviev, Aleksandr, 47–48

Zoanetti, Francesco, 150

Zwinger, Theodor, 74, 122, 299n138

Zwingli, Huldrych, 284n177